# Because of Race

# Because of Race

## HOW AMERICANS DEBATE HARM AND OPPORTUNITY IN OUR SCHOOLS

*Mica Pollock*

PRINCETON UNIVERSITY PRESS

PRINCETON AND OXFORD

Second printing, and first paperback printing, 2011
Paperback ISBN: 978-0-691-14809-0

The Library of Congress has cataloged the cloth edition of this book as follows

Pollock, Mica, 1971–
Because of race : how Americans debate harm and opportunity in our schools /
Mica Pollock.
    p.   cm.
Includes bibliographical references and index.
ISBN: 978-0-691-12535-0 (cloth : alk. paper)
1. Discrimination in education—United States. 2. Race discrimination—United States.
3. United States—Race relations. I. Title.
LC212.2.P65   2008
371.82900973—dc22      2008002200

British Library Cataloging-in-Publication Data is available

This book has been composed in Palatino Typeface

Printed on acid-free paper. ∞

Printed in the United States of America

10  9  8  7  6  5  4  3  2

*For Elea, Jonah, and Joe*

# Contents

# Preface

FROM 1999 to 2001, I worked in a carpet-covered cubicle at a regional office of the U.S. Department of Education's Office for Civil Rights (OCR). I worked first as an unpaid intern and then as a paid Equal Opportunity Specialist (EOS) assigned to investigate and resolve complaints of educational discrimination filed by parents, guardians, advocates, teachers, and occasionally students themselves. I was to investigate and address complaints of discrimination in public schools, whether based on race, sex, disability, or language. OCR's mandate is to enforce federal laws prohibiting discrimination in federally funded educational programs against students who belong to these legally "protected classes."

For two years I listened to hundreds of parents, advocates, school- and district-based educators and administrators, and federal employees debate the daily educational treatment of children and youth in specific schools and districts in our region of the country. On paper, over the phone, and face to face, we debated how children in both segregated and desegregated schools were spoken to, disciplined, and ignored; we debated how in their everyday school lives, children were afforded or denied basic resources and opportunities to learn. In race cases, these debates were telling versions of American[1] disputes over what racial inequality of opportunity now looks like in education and what, if anything, we should do about it, both as a nation and in local communities.

The work I saw within OCR circa 2000 debated "everyday" versions of opportunity denial to students of color. While high-ranking lawyers at OCR dealt with issues of desegregation policy, most of us regular employees debated, with local educators, parents, and our own colleagues, which other policies and practices inside schools and districts denied necessary opportunities to students of color "because of race" in their ongoing everyday lives. These arguments over the daily treatment of students evidenced far broader American tensions over determining which harms and opportunity denials experienced by students of color inside schools and districts now "count" as harm worth remedying.

Our arguments over whether the everyday treatment of students of color inside schools and districts constituted racial "discrimination" became particularly heated debates over the definition and existence of "race-based" harm and the very structure of contemporary racial inequality of opportunity. Unlike in OCR's early days in the 1960s, we were no longer discussing policies designed explicitly to segregate the races or to disadvantage racial minorities. Rather, we discussed whether to permit the denials of academic and social opportunity that children and families of color experienced inside schools and districts—denials not ordered explicitly by law, but effected and condoned through law, policy, and practice, and produced, in part, at the hands of ordinary school and district educators over years or on single school days.

Protracted conflicts over how to prove, discuss, and remediate the educational harms that students and families of color experience in their everyday lives in schools and districts today can destroy relations between parents, teachers, and administrators; they can also compromise students' careers and throw entire districts into crisis. At OCR, the highest-level agency in the nation that routinely analyzes the everyday distribution of educational opportunity to children, our own regularly surfacing reticence to call any particular harm to students of color "discrimination" or to forcefully demand remedy for that harm evinced broader shared conflicts over defining and addressing racial inequality of opportunity in education today. I originally went to work at OCR because I was interested in promoting equal opportunity in education rather than merely analyzing and debating it as an academic. Ironically, at OCR I discovered that civil rights work in education is itself a continual exercise in analyzing and debating what policies and practices impermissibly deny opportunity to students from protected classes. I also learned that in our schools as well as within our government, many Americans have a habit of arguing that opportunity denials experienced by children and families of color in schools and districts do not exist, do not hurt, or are perfectly permissible. This book became a chronicle of those habits of argument and a quest to understand their logic and their implications for children.

This book is my second project focusing on discussions and debates about race in education.[2] My first book, *Colormute: Race Talk Dilemmas in an American School*, analyzed the fraught issues involved in the everyday race talk and "colormuteness"—the active avoidance of race labels such as "white," "black," "Latino," and "Asian"—that I observed in a California high school and district. I analyzed these struggles over "race talk" as central struggles over how to handle racial disparities and racialized identities in an already racialized and racially unequal nation. This book focuses on more explicit debates over racial inequality in education.[3] In this book, I explore the ways in which a host of Americans in and around an agency designed originally to advance racial equity in education debated what, if anything, should be done to remedy and prevent the forms of harm experienced in schools and districts by children and youth of color and their parents.

Roughly half of the OCR employees working in the agency's twelve regional offices are trained lawyers. The others, who are called EOSs or "investigators," have college degrees. Some of my colleagues, particularly some attorneys, were in their late twenties and early thirties, like me. Far more were in their forties and older; a handful had worked at OCR for decades, implementing the laws and regulations developed in the 1960s and after. We were white, black, Asian, and Latino, in that descending order of demographic proportion. Many of us cared deeply about equalizing opportunity for children. We spent our days alone in our cubicles and offices writing letters, reading documents, and making phone calls, and together, in pairs and threes, we discussed ways to investigate and resolve complaints. We told personal stories in hallways and inside offices; we went out to lunch; some of us became good friends. We also went "on site" occasionally, together or alone in cars or on planes, to investigate complaints in person. I traveled for investigation five or six times in my two years at OCR, including one trip to the Washington, D.C., headquarters to discuss a special project.

I lacked legal training but had just finished a Ph.D. in the anthropology of education with a focus on analyzing issues of race. Accordingly, I was hired in my regional office in part to help spearhead a special policy project that was one of the most forward-looking efforts I would see at OCR: we were to consider whether the denial of key early learning opportunities to students of color in the years from kindergarten through third grade could become a new domain of racial civil rights work. Along with my responsibilities for this project, my daily job at OCR involved performing the more local functions of an EOS. In my cubicle amid the phone conversations of my fellow investigators, and through frequent visits to the offices of attorney colleagues, I assessed incoming complaints from our region to determine whether the office would accept them for investigation under its definitions of actionable discrimination. I investigated and determined whether the alleged incidents had occurred and, if so, whether they were discriminatory in legal terms. I also discussed legally and bureaucratically prohibited and permissible behaviors with schools and districts. If warranted, I then worked by phone and letter to negotiate a resolution with the school district that would dismantle the effects of the alleged harm, satisfy some demands of the complainants, and prevent similar harmful acts from occurring in the future. Each morning I got on the train with my coffee, flashed my plastic badge upon arrival in the lobby of the city's federal building, and spent eight hours talking and writing to educators, parents, and my colleagues about discrimination, while attempting to find some scraps of the government's apparently most limited resource—natural light.

I hope readers will experience this book not as a story about OCR but rather as an analysis of contemporary debates over defining and achieving racial equality of opportunity in American education. I show that in both segregated and desegregated schools, students and families continually desired a particular form of opportunity analysis that both describes and exceeds the analysis we offered at OCR: they wanted analysis of precisely what concrete policies and practices, and by whom, offer or deny essential opportunities in children's everyday lives inside schools and districts. I also show that in response, both educators and OCR employees repeatedly expressed skepticism that the harms experienced by students and families of color in schools and districts should or could actually be remedied.

At OCR, people sometimes pursued analysis of everyday educational opportunity with energy and purpose, using the admittedly blunt instruments of law. Besides our work responding to complaints, many lawyers and investigators spent years developing new ways of analyzing and addressing the contemporary civil rights implications of standardized testing, unwarranted Special Education placement, and the unequal distribution of resources within districts. Others spent countless hours working with local educators devising plans to provide English-language learners access to curriculum as the law required, to avoid racial bias in discipline policies and procedures, and to prevent harassment based on race or national origin. Colleagues and I negotiated with districts a range of remedies that included professional development for educators serving diverse student populations, new plans for equitable discipline in both predominantly white and predominantly of-color schools, and efforts to improve racially hostile climates inside schools and districts.

When I worked at OCR, then, my colleagues and I often worked with school and district staff to consider how their policies and practices had ongoing consequences for children's everyday experiences of schooling. This book proposes that attending to such "everyday" aspects of opportunity provision is one crucial strategy in American education today. But as this book shows, much resistance prevents such attention: even we at OCR, just like local educators, often implied, or said explicitly, that it was not really necessary to provide additional opportunity to children of color. Some educators made clear that this . verdict was exactly what they, too, wanted to hear.

A word, then, about the material used in this book. Throughout my two years at OCR, I took personal notes about the ongoing arguments over discrimination that occurred during the workday, not because I intended to write a book about them but because these were the most explicit and fascinating debates over race and fairness I had ever heard. I treated the job as an apprenticeship in analyzing, debating, and pursuing equal opportunity in education. I soaked up ideas from lawyers, managers, and other investigators about the definitions, requirements, and logic of civil rights law in education, and I reflected on this process in my private notes. On my own time, I thought about my work with an analytic mind attuned to the deep arguments over racial fairness raging in the lives of the hundreds of Americans I met in and through my work at OCR.

My graduate training in anthropology prepared—and, perhaps, compelled—me to notice the scripted patterns of argument I was engaging in and learning to replicate. Because I was spending my evenings working on *Colormute*, I listened with extra-sensitive ears to my conversations about racial discrimination with complaining parents and protesting principals and superintendents, as well as to my conversations with other investigators and attorneys struggling to analyze allegations of discrimination and discuss antidiscrimination initiatives within the agency.

In retrospect, I think I scribbled down my personal reflections on these arguments because I knew that most people committed to racial equality in education never have such full access to such explicit debates over racial fairness. Working at OCR allowed me to hear the viewpoints of all parties to debates. This position offered me a multi-faceted perspective on arguments about equal opportunity that few students, parents, educators, school administrators, policymakers, or concerned citizens have the opportunity to acquire. People who participate in local conflicts have no way of knowing what the other players argue privately, and they typically have no idea what happens in arguments over fairness at higher levels of government. Federal employees get to see the crystalline structures of these debates from all sides, but they are usually deterred from speaking out about them.

While appreciating the importance and rarity of what I was learning, I sensed that government managers would not want a public servant to analyze her own civil rights work, much less the arguments percolating through her agency. So, before leaving OCR, I checked with the government ethics office about what I could and could not do with my private notes. No general regulations restrict the basic right of former employees to write about their experiences. The OCR ethics officer also assured me in writing that "There are no limitations on your use of knowledge or ideas you have gained through your work with the government once you have left."

After leaving OCR, and before writing this book, I consulted with a lawyer at the American Bar Association. He confirmed that the most important ethical imperative was protecting the anonymity of the individuals who appear in these pages. At Harvard University, where I teach, the Human Subjects office agreed that analyzing my personal notes without using names is ethically acceptable. As an anthropologist interested in American culture, I have no interest in identifying individuals or judging their actions as individuals; the dynamics of the arguments I describe are significant precisely because these patterns occurred in diverse settings across numerous schools and districts and across diverse locations within OCR. I have used pseudonyms for all persons and masked identifying information on cases so that complainants, educators, schools, and OCR employees are at no risk of personal exposure. In order to obtain formal records of the cases I discuss in retrospect here, I requested the official case file documents through the Freedom of Information Act, and the documents arrived with the names already removed. I have changed district names and some extraneous details to conceal the school districts in which these cases arose.

Although I am confident that I have the right to write this book about my work at OCR, I am occasionally afraid of the consequences. My fear is informative, because it reminds me that when I worked at OCR—and long before, according to earlier insider accounts[4]—the civil rights wing of the Department of Education bred an atmosphere of anxious apprehension that affected the employees who cared most about the equal opportunity mission, particularly the office's original charge of pursuing racial equality of opportunity. Many OCR employees I know continue to fear that their words and actions in analyzing and addressing discrimination in education, and their public comments about how OCR defines and seeks equal opportunity, will lead higher-ups or outside critics to shut down the work they are doing to assist children. This institutional fear easily translates into a more personal anxiety that talking about measures to equalize opportunity in education will lead powerful authorities to retaliate. This anxiety typically leads civil rights workers to avoid discussing publicly any aspect of OCR work that is conceivably or even remotely controversial.

Writing a book about my work experience is an antidote to such avoidance. Throughout this project, I have been guided by the ethical maxim that anthropologists share with physicians: "do no harm." Fieldwork is typically conducted with subjects who are considerably less powerful than the anthropologist herself. Although this book examines an ostensibly powerful entity—an enforcement agency of the U.S. government—the civil servants I worked with, the people who came to OCR looking for assistance, and the educators they accused of discrimination are all people I wish to protect. In writing this book, I seek not only to avoid doing harm to people who educate, care for, and monitor the well-being of children and youth but also to support them in efforts to actually provide equal educational opportunity for the nation's young people.

Many activists and advocates for students of color have given up on OCR altogether, considering it a "toothless tiger" that generates plenty of bureaucratic paperwork but does not act decisively to equalize educational opportunity for the nation's students of color. While this book is really about improving national debates over providing equal opportunity rather than about improving OCR per se, improving OCR's effectiveness by reflecting critically on its practices is obviously in the agency's own interest. Yet, in writing this book, I am still nagged by fear. Even in a democracy, federal agencies are opaque "black boxes" rarely made transparent to citizens. As I write, analyzing the government seems particularly taboo. But our government, like our public school system, does not belong to someone else; it belongs to every American. We pay for it; we staff it; it is supposed to serve us and our children. In that spirit, I offer my reflections on what I learned as a civil servant who worked with a wide range of people inside and outside the government to debate and address fundamental questions of equal educational opportunity for young people of color in our schools. These issues are too important to leave unexamined in the archives and cubicles of a government bureaucracy.

*Cambridge, Massachusetts*
*Summer 2007*

# Acknowledgments

THIS BOOK EMERGED, every day, over several years, often in the wee hours while I was raising one infant-toddler and then a second. Most important to this book's production was a Bunting Fellowship from the Radcliffe Institute for Advanced Study in 2004–5. The fellowship gave me the time and the sense of purpose to make the first dent in my notes and thoughts from OCR. At Radcliffe, I met Jenny Mansbridge, whose discussions of what she calls "everyday feminism" clarified the everyday struggles against racial inequality that I now call efforts at "everyday justice." I am grateful to Jenny for helping me clarify this thread running through my own work. Michèle Lamont, whom I also came to know that year, energized my efforts as we each pursued our own work on "everyday antiracism." Other Radcliffe Fellows, particularly Linda Krieger from the law school at U.C. Berkeley, helped me think about my work that year; many more helped me enjoy the process.

Many other people contributed to this book along the way. My former colleagues at OCR taught me what they knew about opportunity equalization, both explicitly and by example. Their friendship is crucial to me, and I deeply admire their persistence in the federal bureaucracy. Jenn Hsieh and Quang Tran, my research interns while I was at Radcliffe, found data and articles on OCR and helped me start building my arguments while I asked them questions over hot chocolate in the mornings. Jasleen Kohli researched key discrimination articles to get me started, with the help of a Mark DeWolfe Howe Fund grant from the Harvard Law School. Early conversations with Lani Guinier and Philomena Essed sharpened my arguments about how racial equality is and is not pursued. A February 2005 conference at Ohio State University titled "Meeting the Challenge of *Grutter*," convened by john a. powell, forced me to present these ideas before I was ready, helping me clarify some key arguments early on in writing this book, as did talks in spring 2006 at U.C. Santa Barbara, invited by Howie Winant, and at Stanford. Fred Appel, anthropology editor at Princeton University Press (PUP), gave early support to the project. Grey Osterud and Helen Snively suggested trimming some fat from various drafts. Anonymous reviewers at PUP, one of whom turned out to be Mitchell Stevens, gave me the gift of unusually clear, provocative feedback for final revisions. I also owe sincere thanks to people who gave so generously of their time and attention in reading chunks of the manuscript: Debbie Askwith, Prudence Carter, Christine Cooper, Jim Crawford, Frank Dobbin, Dan Losen, john powell, Michael Rebell, Alicia Redemske, the unbelievably generous Estera Milman and Alan Schoenfeld, and the students in my 2005 and 2007 American Dilemmas courses at Harvard's Graduate School of Education.

Along the way, Joe Castiglione prodded me to clarify the argument in several key ways that improved the book immeasurably. He also made me countless dinners and helped me weather the emotional difficulties of childrearing while working. Our wonderful daughter, Elea, now four, helped me realize how much every day matters to a parent; I only hope that this book is worth the hours away from her. In this book's final year, our smiling son, Jonah, helped me realize just how important every child really is.

> Power concedes nothing without a demand. It never did
> and never will.
>
> —*Frederick Douglass, 1857*

FOR THIS BOOK, I have analyzed hundreds of arguments over racial discrimination in public schools that I encountered while working at the U.S. Department of Education's Office for Civil Rights (OCR) from 1999 to 2001. I participated in most of these arguments, as I investigated cases and talked on the phone to local educators, parents, and advocates, or discussed office policies and practices with my colleagues. I overheard a few arguments in a fluorescent-lit office hallway or over the wall of my cubicle; I encountered others on the pages of circulating government documents. All centered on a longstanding, still-raging debate within American education:[1] *Which opportunity denials experienced by students of color should be remedied?*

It is not suprising that the debate raged at OCR. Like other OCR employees, I was paid to determine which harms to children in their daily lives in public schools "count" in federal legal terms as harms demanding remedy. What surprised me at OCR, and during data analysis post facto, was to find just how often both educators and OCR people argued that fewer harms experienced by students of color should be remedied, rather than more.[2] I wrote this book to examine this response empirically, and to examine how debates over serving students of color exposed conflicting American analyses of opportunity denial and harm worth remedying.

OCR was created originally in 1967 to enforce Title VI of the 1964 Civil Rights Act, which outlawed discrimination "on the ground of race, color, or national origin" in federally funded programs, including K–12 and postsecondary schools. Title VI, designed to counter legally enforced segregation, stated simply that "discrimination" meant denying people opportunities because of race: "No person in the United States shall, on the ground of race, color, or national origin, be excluded from participation in, be denied the benefits of, or be subjected to discrimination under any program or activity receiving Federal financial assistance."[3] Yet applying Title VI in education was anything but simple; it got more complex as time went on.[4] By 2000, actually determining which policies, actions, and situations inside schools and districts "denied benefits" or "excluded" participants "on the ground of race," or "discriminated" against students of color in any other way, sparked fierce debate between local communities, local educators, OCR employees, and OCR administrators. These debates revealed the same key national tension soon to be debated in the Supreme Court: determining harm "because of race" to students in the nation's schools and districts.

In June 2007, the Supreme Court decided by the narrowest of margins that two districts' race-conscious voluntary desegregation policies denied white students opportunities to enroll in their schools of choice.[5] Citing the Equal Protection Clause of the Fourteenth Amendment and *Brown v. Board of Education*, four of the justices turned the focus of analysis away from whether segregated schools still harmed students of color "because of race." Instead, their plurality opinion held that these districts' voluntary efforts to desegregate harmed white students "because of race."[6] The Court's ruling capped off several decades of legal decisions restricting even voluntary efforts to increase opportunities for students of color in the nation's school districts via desegregation.[7] This time, while one justice's concurring opinion left the door open for some forms of "race-conscious" desegregation, four of the justices held more bluntly than usual that such methods of increasing opportunity should no longer be allowed.[8]

In the work I participated in at OCR, we typically debated which policies and practices denied opportunities "because of race" to students of color, not white students; allegations of harms to students of color made up the majority of race complaints brought to the agency. Along with other employees in my region, I also typically debated the ongoing provision of opportunity to students inside schools and districts, rather than their one-time assignment to particular schools. Yet we, too, often spent our days embroiled in the same American arguments central to the Supreme Court case. We debated which opportunity denials experienced by students of color actually now demanded remedy, and which remedies for harm would now actually be pursued.

At the time of Title VI's inception, civil rights law clearly contained at its core a concern to remedy the denial of opportunity to "subordinate groups": people of color.[9] The core form of racial discrimination that lawmakers conceptualized at the time was districts intentionally segregating black students from white students. Over time, Title VI was extended to cover more opportunity denials "on the ground of race" within and between schools. "Programs" came to mean any of the activities of schools, districts, or universities, or state or local agencies, that were receiving any federal financial assistance.[10] Around 2000, OCR's Web site informed the public that Title VI covers "aids, benefits, or services" in education that included "admissions, recruitment, financial aid, academic programs, student treatment and services, counseling and guidance, discipline, classroom assignment, grading, vocational education, recreation, physical education, athletics, housing, and employment."[11] The Department of Education's Title VI regulations, as printed in 1980 in the thick *Code of Federal Regulations* book on my desk when I was at OCR,[12] decreed that recipients of federal financial assistance in education could not, "directly or through contractual or other arrangements, on ground of race, color, or national origin,"

> "deny" students services, financial aid, or benefits provided to others under the program;
>
> "provide" services, aid, or benefits that are "different" from those provided to others, or that are provided "in a different manner";
>
> "subject" students to "segregation or separate treatment" in the program;
>
> "restrict" students in the "enjoyment of any advantage or privilege enjoyed by others" in the program;
>
> "treat" students "differently" in determining admission or eligibility for benefits, aid, and services in the program;
>
> "deny" a student "an opportunity to participate in the program . . . or afford him an opportunity to do so which is different from that afforded others under the program."[13]

Our Title VI regulations also stated directly that people in schools, districts, and universities, and people running federally funded educational programs, could not take actions regarding students that had indirectly discriminatory effects.[14] OCR also interpreted "racially hostile environments" in schools and districts that were "created, encouraged, accepted, tolerated, or left uncorrected" by federal funding recipients to violate Title VI.

Title VI thus covered both policies and practices in the nation's schools and districts, whether those settings were segregated or desegregated. It covered not just student assignment but also the daily provision of resources and opportunities to learn in schools and districts, and social interactions between educators and the children and families they served. As this book shows, however, applying Title VI in real schools and districts prompted and revealed heated American debates over what it actually looks like today to deny opportunity "because of race" to students of color in the nation's schools—and who, if anyone, will or should step forward to remedy such denials. These debates raged daily within OCR, too, as colleagues confronted one another over investigations of complaints or over office policy. Much OCR work also revealed that educators, parents, and advocates in schools and districts had been debating these same contemporary questions of harm and opportunity regarding students of color long before OCR became involved.

With twelve regional offices across the country and headquarters in Washington, D.C., OCR circa 2000 primarily investigated complaints of educational discrimination filed by ordinary Americans and advocacy organizations. Starting in the 1970s, OCR's mission expanded as civil rights laws outlawed discrimination in federally funded public schools and educational programs on the bases of sex, disability, and language,[15] so we investigated complaints about discrimination on all these grounds as well as race. At the national level in 2000, OCR also provided some policy guidance to the nation's educational institutions, telling them how the agency currently interpreted civil rights law. OCR could also undertake uninvited "compliance reviews"[16] of entire districts and universities to assess their adherence to civil rights laws, though it was rarely doing so by the time I worked at OCR. Those higher up, as I will show here, often called such work too "proactive." Still, as administrators allowed, OCR employees could also propose and even develop new policy projects to improve the analysis or remediation of particular forms of discrimination in children's educational lives. I worked on one such project, the Early Learning Project, which envisioned examining how schools and districts provided key learning opportunities to children in kindergarten through third grade. In our days in our cubicles and offices, however, we spent most of our time investigating discrimination complaints we received from ordinary Americans regarding students' and families' experiences of injustice inside schools and districts with various demographics.

All this work had very important implications. It focused attention on one crucial, hotly debated aspect of opportunity in contemporary America: opportunity provided daily to students inside schools and districts. Complaints, like some policy projects within the agency, prompted explicit arguments over which acts toward students inside schools and districts, and which educational situations, should now be called *discrimination*. In legal terms, such harm "on the ground of" group membership could then be deemed impermissible, and could be remedied.[17] By requesting OCR's judgments as to which acts and situations in educational settings constituted racial "discrimination,"[18] complainants and employees alike would find themselves shackled by OCR's politicized, legal definitions of the concept. Like the Supreme Court, we were more likely to deem as beyond remedy the harms experienced by students of color than we were to actively try to remedy those harms. But Americans bringing Title VI complaints to OCR, and OCR employees responding actively to complaints or developing office policy regarding Title VI, provocatively insisted that American equality logic still required analyzing equal opportunity for students of color. More provocatively, many demanded a version of opportunity analysis crucial for our time: they demanded discussion of how racial inequality of opportunity and outcome in education are produced, in part, through the accretion of everyday experiences of opportunity denial to students of color inside schools and districts.

These analyses did not propose that policies or activities outside schools and districts were irrelevant to opportunity. Rather, they named the everyday provision of opportunity inside schools and districts as another crucial opportunity domain, and analyzed concretely how specific opportunities were provided or denied students of color. Other observers examining the cumulative denial of life opportunities to children of color today importantly urge analysis of "cumulative racial disadvantage" across policy domains, like health and housing as well as education, and even across generations.[19] In forcing debate on everyday opportunity provision inside schools and districts, complainants to OCR and proactive employees within the agency focused their analysis on a third crucial form of contemporary harm: the accretion of unequal opportunity over children's lifetimes through the aggregation of events within schools and districts themselves.[20]

To those who filed K–12 complaints at OCR and to many OCR employees, the everyday experiences of children in schools and districts were crucial moments that provided or denied essential opportunity. They argued that when José was repeatedly searched, suspended, and ejected from school as punishment for "defiance," it marred his chances of academic success, and that when a school's black students were harassed and the school and district adults failed to act, those students were excluded from full participation in the school community. They also argued that if security guards gave the names of Latino hall wanderers to the police as potential "gang members," this mattered for their educational and life trajectories, and that if the academic needs of entire districts' populations of English-language learners went unassessed and unaddressed, this denied them equal access to the common curriculum and decreased their chances of school success. Similarly, the Early Learning Project contended that when schools or districts denied students of color early opportunities to learn to read or compute, those were essential moments of denying educational "benefits" that had fundamental consequences for the children's futures.

Whether they were describing opportunities denied to individual children of color or examining the treatment of many children at once, all these analyses proposed that children be offered a form of what I call *everyday justice*: they demanded detailed attention to the moment-to-moment provision of opportunity in children's daily educational lives. They contended that specific opportunities provided on a daily basis by people in schools and districts would help constitute fair treatment; they argued that children of color should be offered everyday opportunities to learn and thrive that were equal to white children's opportunities. Particular complainants went even beyond the legal logic of Title VI in demanding everyday justice. They argued that children of color should be offered opportunities that would be ideal for any child, and that if children *experienced* denials of opportunity to learn and thrive in their everyday lives inside schools and districts, this denial deserved some remedy, even if no one intended this denial or the denial could not be proved legally to have occurred "because of race."

Most important, all these efforts focused on describing, in detail, specific opportunities that students of color needed daily from schools and districts in order to have an equal opportunity to succeed inside educational settings. Analysts examining the provision of opportunities by superintendents or teachers or security guards noted specific ways that these specific actors distributed opportunity unequally and insufficiently to children of color, or accepted harm to students of color in school settings of various demographics as normal and unproblematic. They argued that these particular acts by particular actors inside schools and districts contributed to unequal opportunity for students of color and unequal outcomes.

This book is about these specific demands for equal opportunity in everyday educational life and the resistance they encountered. For as I show here, both local educators and colleagues at OCR—and sometimes, I, too—routinely rebutted external or internal proposals for everyday justice with arguments that the everyday opportunity denials experienced by students and families of color did not "count" as impermissible harms, that additional opportunities for children of color were not required, or that harms could not be remedied using OCR's politicized legal tools. Hearing claims for everyday justice, both educators and OCR employees often contended that perhaps the denials claimed had not actually occurred "because of race," that such denials were not substantial enough to constitute unequal opportunity, or that local people should not be pressed to equalize opportunity for students of color in specific ways. Our work thus exposed an ongoing American battle between two opposing contemporary arguments:

specified demands for equal opportunity for students of color in schools and districts, and pervasive resistance to these very demands.

This book exclusively examines OCR's work with K–12 schools and districts, which formed three-quarters of the agency's work,[21] the bulk of my own assigned cases, and the focus of the one policy effort I was involved in within the agency. The K–12 districts I encountered while at OCR were of varying size, diversity, and bureaucratic complexity, ranging from a one-school district in a rural area serving predominantly Latino and white students to an urban district with 700,000 students of color. Most of the complaints I saw regarding these districts were filed by parents and, in Title VI cases, by parents of color. A few were filed by advocacy organizations.

The Early Learning Project envisioned examining the distribution of learning opportunities both within entire districts and within individual schools. Complainants' demands described the needs of both individual students and many students across entire districts. Some OCR complaints were large-scale "class complaints" (similar to class action suits) asserting that entire protected categories of children in a school district—typically students of color, English-language learners, girls, or students with disabilities—were treated unequally or denied opportunities by district or school actions. Parents and advocates alleged, for example, that black students were being disproportionately placed in Special Education or expelled without sufficient cause. They argued that Latino students across a district lacked necessary educational resources, like computers, or specific learning opportunities, like the opportunity to take advanced science. They pointed out that English-language learners sitting confused in English-only math classrooms were missing out, daily, on crucial content instruction. Complainants often also demanded analysis of opportunity for individual students: many of the complaints I encountered at OCR suggested that the treatment of an individual child or a few children exemplified barriers against these kinds of children in the school and district. These complaints often turned on specific acts against particular children, for example, a Latino student disciplined for a disputed infraction, a deaf student denied a promised interpreter, or several girls barred from a sports team. Complainants even zoomed in on how even a single everyday interaction between adults and children contributes to cumulative patterns of educational harm. For example, parents asked local educators and then OCR employees to evaluate the immediate academic consequences for a Latino student when a dean suspended him for three days and white classmates went unpunished for similar "defiance." Parents were concerned about the lingering academic consequences, for a black student, of a teacher's rough hand on his shoulder on one particular day.

Regardless of whether they were describing harm to many children or harm to individuals, the demands for everyday justice I encountered at OCR were demands that people inside schools and districts improve specific daily educational experiences of children. Even complainants denouncing aggregated achievement outcomes by many students of color, both in segregated districts and inside desegregated ones, often focused attention on specific opportunity denials by real people in schools and districts that contributed to such patterns inside the educational domain.[22] Rather than speaking abstractly about unequal opportunity, many pinpointed the practices of teachers or administrators that contributed to grade retention or to students' dropping out; they critiqued the evaluation process through which counselors and teachers referred students for Special Education or Advanced Placement classes. Their analyses prompted us, within OCR, to question the teacher actions contributing to racially biased enrollment in Special Ed or the administrative decisions leading to the unavailability of college preparatory courses to students of color.

Complainants also demanded both short-term and long-term remedies. They asked people in schools and districts not just to do their part once to provide basic learning opportunities like up-to-date books, but also to do their part regularly to offer "high-standards" curricula, to provide English-language learners with ongoing adequate access to academics, and to make ongoing efforts to improve racially hostile relations between students, parents, and educators. Within OCR, we activated such everyday justice analysis ourselves whenever we suggested how we, as an agency, might investigate the past or ongoing distribution of specific opportunities in the everyday activities of districts and schools. At those moments, we made clear that while local educators would be the ones actually providing everyday opportunity, it was a federal responsibility under Title VI to help facilitate that provision and to ensure that such provision occurred equitably in the daily practices of the nation's schools and districts.

Advocates demanding everyday justice inside schools and districts, and OCR employees attempting to evaluate the provision or denial of everyday justice in local schools and districts, were identifying local educators as crucial daily providers of opportunity and proposing ways to equalize and improve the distribution of specific opportunities inside districts and schools, not blaming local educators in isolation for racial inequality in American education or American life. Fewer complainants approached OCR to allege that states were denying resources, and OCR almost never took on state actors directly;

such complaints have typically been the subject of state lawsuits.[23] But Title VI complainants or proactive OCR colleagues circa 2000 did not ignore the need for outside policymakers to provide dollars, or for the nation's universities to produce qualified teachers, or for students and parents themselves to make ongoing efforts toward student success. Nor did their analyses argue that issues of health or housing were irrelevant to students' well-being. Rather, they framed opportunity as something that *also* had to be provided daily, through actions and interactions, by specific people whose acts inside schools and districts directly affected children's everyday educational experiences. They therefore focused attention on the ongoing provision of opportunity in locations up close to children themselves, and on educators as particular opportunity providers, calling such locations crucial but not isolated sites of opportunity provision.

I contend here that when describing in detail some everyday experiences of harm and opportunity denial inside schools and districts, analysts both outside and inside OCR provided a component of opportunity analysis that is desperately needed today, one that has the potential to reverberate beyond specific locales and even beyond schools and districts alone. They suggested not just that children had to experience *specific forms* of equal opportunity daily, but also that *specific people* had to help provide these opportunities. Such analysis proposed specific opportunities for young people to learn and thrive and specific actors who would supply such opportunities to children, rather than simply demanding equal opportunity in general, denouncing opportunity generally as "racially" unfair, or calling abstractly for opportunities from "society" or "structures." This book proposes that, more broadly, this type of concrete, specific opportunity analysis holds much promise for pinpointing some essential ways of equalizing opportunity in an era when racial patterns like "achievement gaps" are produced by countless interactions across multiple domains and racial inequality is more often allowed than ordered and applauded explicitly by laws and policies. Everyday justice analysis provides one necessary ingredient for opportunity analysis today: detailed consideration of the provision of named opportunities by specific actors within complex systems.

This book also shows that in complex systems, anyone demanding particular opportunities from particular opportunity providers is likely to prompt resistance. In OCR work, everyday justice analysis typically prompted resistance from the very people in local school districts or inside the agency who were asked to help provide additional opportunities to children of color. This occurred because demands for everyday justice suddenly requested articulated opportunities rather than abstract or general opportunity; because they contended that

ordinary people in various locations participated in cumulative processes of opportunity denial; and because they proposed that daily opportunity denials experienced by students of color in schools and districts should actually be remedied. In essence, resistance to "forcing"
educators to provide more opportunity to students of color evinced
broader disputes over pinpointing, proving, and remedying the various activity that contributes to racial inequality today.

In OCR Title VI complaints, local educators hearing allegations of
everyday injustice often resisted blame for any role in the negative educational experiences of students of color. Even before OCR's intervention, educators expressed doubts that specific opportunities had been
racially unequal, that specific people had denied opportunities, that
specific harms had occurred "because of race," or even that students
of color had been harmed or disadvantaged in their educational lives
at all. They often dismissed the harms experienced by students and
families of color—suspensions, denial of information on "gifted" programs, or harassment, for example—as too "small" to really deny opportunity.[24] In fact, OCR staff often exhibited the same habits of resistance when we were asked to determine whether specific people had
denied specific opportunities to students of color, or when we contemplated calling forcefully in a given policy or complaint resolution for
actions to equalize specific opportunities for students of color in local
settings. We, too, often rebutted claims that children of color had been
denied necessary opportunities in given educational settings "because
of race"; we, too, often refused to press anyone in particular to provide
particular educational opportunities to children of color.

That both educators and OCR employees often refused to help offer
these additional opportunities to children of color, even when they
were specifically requested, revealed a reality about contemporary
America that others have evaluated generally via surveys and interviews. While almost all Americans now agree with equal opportunity
in principle, many of us—particularly those of us who are white—resist
some opportunity provision to people of color in practice.[25] By examining such resistance arising in real-time, multiplayer interactions regarding children, I show the specific forms and human consequences of
such resistance in the educational domain. In the debates I witnessed,
few in the chain of those hearing demands for opportunity for students
of color, whether educators or civil rights administrators, set forth matter-of-factly to provide students of color with additional opportunities
when their advocates demanded them. Rather, we routinely rebutted
these demands, saying that remedying specific harms experienced by
children of color in their daily school lives was not required.

In the next four chapters, I explore four shared *rebuttals* to demands for everyday justice for students of color that I found pervasive among both local educators and federal employees in my work at OCR and have since found pervasive in contemporary debates about American education.[26] Each rebuttal resisted claims that particular acts or situations inside schools or districts harmed children of color impermissibly or intolerably. Each was offered even by people employed *to* offer children opportunity.

> Rebuttal 1: Harms to Children of Color Cannot Be Proved
> Rebuttal 2: Harms to Children of Color Should Not Be Discussed
> Rebuttal 3: Harms to Children of Color Cannot Be Remedied
> Rebuttal 4: Harms to Children of Color Are Too "Small" to Fix

In each chapter, I demonstrate that in debates over the harm experienced by students of color in schools and districts, the rebuttals typically won out: they stalled and even halted efforts to provide these students with additional opportunities to learn and thrive in the nation's schools.

Both everyday justice demands and the rebuttals that greet them are central to what I call the *new civil rights era*. This is an era characterized both by a "fragmented" system of racially unequal opportunity that complicates opportunity analysis and also by key forms of resistance to efforts to equalize specific opportunities for actual people of color.

## THE NEW CIVIL RIGHTS ERA

Sociologist Charles Payne argues that in comparison to the system of coordinated, purposeful racial inequality that characterized American schools decades ago, today's system of racial inequality in education is "fragmented."[27] That is, today's racially unequal educational opportunity is a result of the ordinary acts of many people in many places, over time, rather than ordered explicitly from on high. Today, racial inequality of opportunity and outcome in education is still the result of past generations of explicit policy decreeing that "white" children were to have better schools than non-"white" children,[28] of the subsequent exacerbation of poverty along racial lines, of the nation's failure to actively desegregate,[29] and of the intersections between opportunity denials in health and housing as well as education.[30] But racially unequal educational opportunity and outcome today also result from ordinary actions and inaction by well-intentioned people—in part, within schools and districts themselves. In this "fragmented" system, however, as this book shows, many Americans debating education rebut claims that particular opportunities for students of color have been racially unequal or should be equalized. They often make this rebuttal even while stating their belief in the importance of racially equal opportunity.

Most researchers studying our national debates using surveys and interviews agree that explicit resistance to opportunity for non-white people today has been replaced by stated general commitments to racially equal opportunity as a basic American value. But researchers also agree that when the rubber hits the road, such generic commitments are often trumped by opposition to concrete efforts to equalize particular opportunities for people of color, either because people (particularly white people) contend that opportunities have not been racially unequal or because they believe that opportunity equalization to people of color as such is problematic.[31] Many researchers have found persisting opposition to "racially conscious" equal opportunity policies like desegregation or affirmative action;[32] a subset have examined real-time opposition to programs and practices within school settings that purposefully set out to equalize opportunities for young people of color as such.[33] While examining the test scores of children of color is now national policy,[34] research shows that many Americans, particularly white Americans, contend that analyzing educational opportunity with a "race lens," or equalizing educational opportunity in racial terms, is itself racist.[35] Yet little research has shown, as I do, hundreds of Americans offering specific forms of such resistant "rhetoric" (Lamont 2000a) in real-time debates over education, without the prompts of surveys or interviews.

While most observers call our current climate the "post–civil rights era,"[36] I prefer the phrase *new civil rights era* to describe a "fragmented," debate-ridden moment when many Americans, particularly white Americans (but also some Americans of color), resist or rebut demands for specific additional opportunities for people of color even while they support the idea of racially equal opportunity in general.[37] First and foremost, as Lakoff (2004) argues, simply using language means accepting its premises.[38] This book's data suggest that speaking of a post–civil rights era falsely accepts the premise that the basic struggle for racial equality of opportunity has ended.

Second, I call this a *new* civil rights era because both demands for racial equality and rebuttals to those demands now come in new forms. First, as OCR complainants showed, demands for racial equality of opportunity in education are no longer limited to demands for equal opportunity policies but also include increasingly detailed demands for equal opportunity practices in everyday educational life.[39] In an era when racial inequality is no longer ordered by explicit law or applauded explicitly by most Americans, however, responses to all such equal opportunity demands are more complicated, too. In past civil rights struggles, Americans seeking policies to redress unequal opportunities to people of color encountered many white Americans who argued bluntly that people of color did not deserve more opportunity. In the new civil rights era, the response to demands for specific equal opportunities in everyday life as well as policy is often not "no" but a qualified "yes, but. . . . "[40] Today, in debates over education, even well-meaning people rebut demands for additional opportunities for children of color by saying that while racially equal opportunity is indeed desirable, neither impermissible nor "racial" opportunity denials can now be proved to exist in any given situation, and particular opportunities accordingly cannot be demanded from particular opportunity providers. During my two years at OCR, I heard this central rebuttal to everyday justice claims countless times; each chapter in this book is a version of it.

Some readers might contend that these rebuttals simply countered OCR's federal, legal interventions, and that educators and OCR people were not resisting opportunity provision itself. Indeed, OCR's project of "enforcing" opportunity provision locally using legal tools raised particularly explicit rebuttals against pressing people to give children of color more educational opportunity. Yet educators had offered these rebuttals to complainants before OCR's involvement, and I have heard these same debates many times since leaving OCR. I suggest that both we at OCR and local educators routinely rebutted demands for everyday justice for several pervasive contemporary reasons far bigger than OCR, and bigger even than schools alone: out of skepticism that opportunities were actually denied "because of race" (chapter 1); out of defensiveness about requiring others, or being required, to offer specific opportunities to children of color (chapter 2); out of resignation, or the sense that additional opportunities could not be provided to students of color at this historical juncture (chapter 3); and out of confusion over the scale and shape of racial inequality in educational opportunity today (chapter 4). Since our rebuttals often thwarted opportunity provision to children, I conclude by suggesting how Americans might better engage one another in analysis of harm and opportunity in contemporary schools. Indeed, the debates I saw at OCR taught some valuable, more general lessons about arguing toward opportunity for students of color in education today.

A book examining such fraught American debates will likely prompt more debates, so let me clarify a few key positions of my own. First, I am not arguing, in this book, that every claim of racial "discrimination" filed at OCR was to be immediately believed and that the accused perpetrators had to remedy each situation exactly to complainants' satisfaction. However, I am arguing that the claims of harm indicated real experiences of suffering and opportunity denial in schools and districts. I am also suggesting that in a K–12 educational context, it is essential to address, rather than dismiss, students and families of color's experiences of educational opportunity denial. In the Title VI complaints filed at OCR, some everyday experiences of injustice (like a lack of books or advanced classes) were easy to measure as harmful, while other everyday experiences, such as stigmatizing or humiliating interactions, could not be proved easily in legal terms to be illegal harms "because of race." Still, psychological research has shown that people experience injustice not only when they are denied concrete, "measurable" opportunities but also when they feel disrespected in interpersonal interactions, and when they are not listened to when they assert that injustice has occurred.[41] Research also shows that untreated experiences of everyday injustice can reduce student performance and decrease people's allegiance to "the relationship in which the injustice occurred."[42] In the demands for everyday justice filed at OCR, complainants described students and families of color experiencing injustice in all the forms debated in the fifty-year evolution of antidiscrimination law:[43] being excluded from activities, being treated as outsiders, feeling relegated to "second-class status," being ignored when complaining of unequal treatment, and being denied basic or advanced learning opportunities that other children received or that any child deserves. To complainants, all of these harms aggregated to denials of opportunity to succeed educationally. Accordingly, in this book, I often interchange the words "harm" and "opportunity denial" in describing the debates they prompted over the treatment of children. Further, all of the harms appeared to complainants to be "because of race." That is, it seemed that children of color were harmed in schools and districts, and that this harm was allowed, because the children were not white—and often because the people in charge of their children's education were.[44] This accusation prompted listeners to dismiss the very *experience* of harm: among educators, particularly white educators, and at times among OCR employees, there was a pervasive reticence to acknowledge or remedy either form of the harm that students and parents of color experienced in their everyday lives inside schools and districts. Particularly in debating endlessly whether opportunities had been denied or harm perpetrated "because of" the race of the children, we all often failed to help improve schools' and districts' actual opportunity provision to students and to improve educators' relationships with the communities they served. This is why I contend, in the book's conclusion, that providing everyday justice requires both using and transcending legal analysis, which still forces our thinking into dead-end debates over harm's causation rather than its effects on children.[45]

Second, while I am arguing that school and district employees provide crucial opportunity daily to the nation's children, I am not arguing here that such local educators are the only people involved in providing or denying children daily opportunities to succeed in school. (Or, more broadly, that educational opportunities are the only opportunities children need.) Outside actors, like judges who evaluate school assignment policies or state- or federal-level policymakers who make decisions about the distribution of dollars or the assessment of children, fundamentally enable or disable local educators' provision of opportunities to learn. A daily opportunity to learn chemistry is enabled by state legislators who provide the dollars schools use for chemistry labs. A daily opportunity to learn music is made less likely by federal legislators who pressure local educators to focus on test preparation.[46] The policy effort described in chapter 3 made clear that we inside OCR knew that the federal government could play a role in enabling the provision of equal opportunities to learn. Parents approaching OCR made it clear that their own actions affected children's educational fates. OCR complaints always demonstrated that students were reacting to educator actions on an ongoing basis. I am arguing, however, that as we detail which actors in complex systems need to provide which opportunities to children, focusing attention *also* on the daily provision of specific opportunities by actors inside schools and districts is essential today. Throughout this book, readers wondering whether the daily, often face-to-face injustices alleged here were really worth worrying about, or whether the local actors accused of injustice were fully those at fault for students' educational experiences, or whether federal actors were really supposed to be remedying the local details of daily opportunity provision are engaging and demonstrating the very new civil rights era debates that are central to this material.

Finally, in suggesting the importance of analyzing "everyday justice" in the nation's schools, I am not arguing for remedy for individuals as opposed to systemic remedy for many. Rather, I am literally arguing that equal opportunity analysis today must consider whether specific opportunities are provided or denied during children's actual school days. In my analysis, a district looking at the details of its language service for many English-language learners at once, or equalizing the availability of Advanced Placement courses to the district's students of color, would be pursuing "everyday justice," as would a school analyzing the day-to-day adequacy of its K–3 learning opportunities or educators' everyday practices of implementing a discipline policy.

This book, then, has two main purposes. The first is to examine the importance of also analyzing daily opportunity provision inside schools and districts in an era when racial inequality of opportunity and outcome in American society are created and condoned through many acts by many well-meaning actors at all levels of systems rather than simply ordered explicitly from on high. The second is to understand some contemporary processes through which such claims for everyday justice are resisted, so that we might see this resistance more clearly and so that in education, advocates and educators might generally seek opportunity for children more successfully. In the book's conclusion, I propose that advocates for students of color today can make demands for everyday justice more commonplace. Opportunity analysis in education can move to pinpointing, regularly, all the acts by all the players inside and outside schools that contribute cumulatively to educational success or harm for children. Such analysis would then move beyond seemingly blaming "bad people" for isolated mistakes or appearing as unwarranted "advocacy" or externally imposed "prescription" to routinely ensuring the provision of necessary opportunities to children.

Instructively, our work at OCR to provide everyday justice to another population of children was far less controversial. Within the office, our efforts to provide specific necessary opportunities to white children with disabilities were relatively uninhibited by the four "rebuttals" that plagued race cases. I end the introduction with this contrast to get the reader ready to engage the core debates over harm "because of race" that plagued our work at OCR.

## Everyday Justice Effort at OCR circa 2000

When the Office for Civil Rights was created in 1967, its primary mission was to secure equal opportunities for black students via desegregation. By the time I joined OCR, the office was primarily using civil rights tools to secure everyday justice for white students with disabilities. Within hours after I arrived on my first day, my desk was piled with brown legal folders documenting alleged harms against such children. Since the 1980s, in fact, complaints filed by predominantly white parents demanding specific services for children with disabilities have made up over half of OCR's caseload, while racial discrimination cases have comprised less than a fifth. When I worked at OCR, disability cases still averaged about 54 percent of the agency's caseload, while race cases averaged 20 percent.[47]

Several factors explain OCR's shift toward efforts to provide everyday justice to white students with "disabilities."[48] Each exposes something about educators' and OCR's own regular habits of rebutting claims of harm to children of color in particular.

First, OCR provides comparatively little outreach to inform people of color of continuing civil rights protections for their children, demonstrating a habit of passivity in the Title VI arena that I demonstrate throughout this book. In contrast, disability law includes explicit prescriptions to inform parents of their disability-related civil rights. The Individuals with Disabilities Education Act (IDEA) provides for parent training and information centers that assist families requesting disability services. Nothing comparable has ever existed to educate American families about employing Title VI. Over time, white parents with more money and connections increasingly availed themselves of OCR's tools for demanding civil rights to specific academic opportunities for students with disabilities, and districts got used to receiving disability service demands. Large disability advocacy organizations informed these parents of OCR's legal tools for securing disability services. As OCR colleagues told me often, each success in providing disability services brought more such parents to the office to demand them. One day at OCR, I wrote in my notes that disability complaints about individual white children seemed to "DRIVE THE AGENDA." One of my coworkers' predominant concerns was the huge number of white parents demanding services for students diagnosed with attention deficit disorder (ADD); one colleague described the ADD cases glutting the office as "like a new industry."[49] White parents filing disability complaints at OCR circa 2000 routinely told me that some established advocacy group had sent them to the agency for help obtaining assessments and services, or even helped them fill out complaint forms. Some such parents e-mailed OCR with early questions that helped them formulate their complaints. In contrast, some parents of color who filed typewritten or handwritten Title VI complaints at OCR told me that they accidentally found OCR through the Yellow Pages. In my experience, relatively few individuals who were filing complaints of racial discrimination had formal assistance from private lawyers or even from formal advocacy groups.[50] The few parents and advocates who did file Title VI complaints often spoke of local parents who shared their concerns but did not file. Their stories suggested that the few Title VI complaints that reached the federal legal bureaucracy circa 2000 were just the "tip of the iceberg" of controversy about providing everyday justice to students of color in the nation's public schools.[51] Title VI complaints, thus, always struck local educators as aberrations; educators receiving Title VI complaints in districts often expressed surprise that OCR even existed to do such work or that civil rights law even extended to "cover" students of color's everyday experiences inside schools. And by waiting for Americans to file complaints while not informing the public of its Title VI services, OCR demonstrated that it was unlikely to proactively tackle opportunity provision to students of color in the nation's schools.

There is a second reason, also important to understand for this book's purposes, why OCR circa 2000 disproportionately and successfully offered everyday justice to white children labeled "disabled" while often failing to do so for children of color generally. Disability rights law and regulation identified procedures for analyzing the effective provision of particular educational opportunities in children's everyday lives.[52] Title VI did not include these precise tools but rather told people not to "discriminate" "on the ground of race" in educational programs. This ambiguity exacerbated the endless American debates explored in this book. In comparison to the bureaucratic clarity of disability work, geared toward providing needed opportunities to children, federal law and regulation in the race realm made both proving and remedying harm to students of color nebulous and contentious.[53] Title VI work, which raised questions about the racial causation of harm to group members rather than relying on medicalized assessments of harm to individuals, always prompted the four key rebuttals I analyze here. When I worked at OCR in 1999–2001, cases involving racial discrimination were frequently subject to fundamental arguments *within* the agency over proving that children of color had been denied opportunities in ways the law disallowed.

This brings us to a final, most fundamental reason why OCR shifted away from efforts to improve everyday educational experiences for students of color and toward efforts to improve those of white students with disabilities. OCR employees were particularly unlikely to label as "discrimination" the opportunity denials experienced by children and families of color, either as individuals or as large groups. Instead, both in complaint investigation and when considering agencywide policy, OCR administrators, managers, and lower-level employees often rebutted Title VI proposals for everyday justice for students of color by asserting that we could not or would not find impermissible harm. Circa 2000, civil rights lawyers outside the agency told me that they advised potential Title VI complainants that OCR was unlikely to assist much with claims of racial discrimination. One such lawyer argued to me bluntly that he had to wonder whether OCR was "on our side or in our way."[54]

It is ironic, but also understandable, that rebuttals to everyday justice demands for students of color pervaded not just local schools and districts but also an agency like OCR circa 2000. Within OCR, these rebuttals were rooted both in contemporary legal thinking about what now constitutes permissible harm to people of color and in a long-standing but pervasive federal unwillingness to force local people to offer equal opportunity to people of color. Regarding the first issue, this book is in part about the limitations of legal definitions of harm in an era when the denial of educational opportunities is not explicitly mandated or applauded as it was in the Jim Crow era when civil rights tools were first developed.[55] Chapter 1 (*Rebuttal 1: Harms to Children of Color Cannot Be Proved*) shows that when investigating racial discrimination complaints at OCR, we engaged in raw, irresolvable analytic battles with educators and our colleagues over an American dilemma central to civil rights law: "proving" whether everyday acts in classrooms, schools, and districts hurt children of color impermissibly *because* they were children of color or, at times, whether these acts even hurt them at all. Working at OCR, I learned that civil rights laws leave harms to people of color unaddressed if no one can find particular forms of "evidence" of harm "because of race." Indeed, it is because such evidence (especially of intentional harm) is now so hard to find in legal terms that some call the current moment the post–civil rights era.[56] I also realized that many educators who dismissed local demands to assist students of color were already arguing to local parents and advocates that harm "because of race" could not be proved. This rebuttal, they demonstrated, is deeply rooted in contemporary American life.[57]

In chapters 2 and 3, I further explore contemporary debates over limiting both federal and local efforts to improve the educational experiences of children of color in the nation's local schools. Chapter 2 (*Rebuttal 2: Harms to Children of Color Should Not Be Discussed*) explores local and federal resistance to OCR's "prescribing" assistance to children of color in complaint resolution. Chapter 3 (*Rebuttal 3: Harms to Children of Color Cannot Be Remedied*) explores internal debates over the Early Learning Project, which attempted to analyze, at the federal level, daily opportunity provision to students of color in local schools and districts. In these two chapters, I explore how both OCR employees and local educators limited potential efforts to help provide everyday justice to these students by arguing that opportunity provision should not be too vigorous or too specific.

To some extent, OCR employees have always worried that if they make proactive and specific suggestions for equalizing opportunity for students of color, they risk appearing to Congress or local critics as "feds" being too muscular or opinionated in "prescribing" changes for local districts, rather than leaving local decisions in local hands.[58] More broadly, federal intervention to proactively provide educational opportunities in localities has historically been limited in the United States, with states and localities expected to fund and regulate the bulk of opportunity provision. Having refused to press for desegregation after OCR's earliest years, the federal government stepped into heavy regulation of localities only recently by imposing standardized testing.[59] Yet since the mid-twentieth century, federal civil rights laws and regulations have positioned the federal government to ensure that opportunities in schools and districts are not unfairly denied students "because of" protected group status.[60] In OCR work, both local and federal resistance to OCR's actually using federal power to examine and enable local opportunity provision for students of color revealed as much about shared unwillingness to press for opportunities for students of color as it did about resistance to federal power generally. Though educators and administrators receiving disability complaints via OCR often resisted these claims initially,[61] many eventually acquiesced to OCR's confident federal demands to assess and assist children daily in specific ways as diagnosed.[62] In contrast, both educators and even the most committed OCR employees routinely argued that we "feds" were out of order if we suggested too vigorously or specifically that equal opportunity be provided to children of color. Chapter 2 shows that as we "feds" resisted pressing in detail for equal opportunity during complaint resolution and as local educators resisted being so pressed, the result was that we all refused many chances to improve daily schooling experiences for children of color. In chapter 3, I show the force of such self-limitation within OCR by demonstrating how I myself, having arrived at OCR full of optimism about equalizing opportunity, learned to employ a "rhetoric of [negative] reaction" about the impropriety or impossibility of OCR policy pressing for any particular form of educational opportunity for K–3 children of color.[63]

Finally, this book illustrates how today, in the new civil rights era, even people pressing openly *for* racial equality of opportunity argue against everyday justice remedies, often out of pessimism or confusion about the contemporary structure of opportunity denial. Chapter 4 (*Rebuttal 4: Harms to Children of Color Are Too "Small" to Fix*) examines how people inside and outside OCR, including some complainants themselves, dismissed even our successful efforts to provide everyday justice to children of color by arguing that such efforts to provide named opportunities in children's and families' everyday lives inside schools were too "small" to actually assist much. Observers of OCR work often dismissed the importance of everyday opportunity provision, either to individuals or to entire districts' populations of students of color, by arguing either that everyday harms to students of color inside schools and districts were negligible or that providing daily opportunities inside schools would do little to counter structural or systemic inequality.

Working at OCR, I saw Americans of all political leanings offer rebuttals to demands for everyday justice for students of color by suggesting either angrily or pessimistically that providing specific opportunities for children of color in their daily educational lives was not warranted, possible, or important. Such arguments have consequences for the nation's children and for our schools.[64] During the two years I spent at OCR, we federal employees and many educators we encountered concluded, again and again, that in particular instances real people should not, could not, or would not be pushed to offer children of color the educational opportunities that they and their families desperately desired. Let us begin examining this American debate.

# Harms to Children of Color Cannot Be Proved

> Indication of harm, not proof of harm, is our call to action.
> —*Mural, Church St., Cambridge, MA, 2007*

> OCR did not find that the District discriminated against
> the students because of their race. . . . OCR did raise
> procedural concerns. . . . These concerns did not rise to
> the level of a violation.
> —*OCR resolution letter, circa 2000*

EVERY COMPLAINT alleging racial discrimination that I investigated while working at OCR was filed by a person of color (often a parent) who felt she or he had hit a wall in trying to explain to white educators that a student or students of color were experiencing harm along racial lines.[1] In each case, complainants contended that local educators seemed unwilling to believe that the students had experienced harm that could be termed "racial." The complainants were right: educators would soon make the same argument to OCR.

In most of the Title VI complaints I investigated, parents had already met with teachers, principals, administrators, and superintendents to argue that their children were being harmed *as* children of color and *because* they were children of color. When so accused, educators sometimes argued that children of color were no worse off than white children; most often, they argued explicitly that they did no harm to students *because* of their race. OCR people took many such complaints seriously enough to investigate them, but after analyzing everyday life in schools and districts using legal lenses, we often came to the same conclusion about "the facts." Our shared dismissals of claims of harm "because of race" exhibited a classic pattern of debate in the new civil rights era. Today, in response to Americans claiming harm along racial lines, other Americans routinely contend that harms experienced by people of color in everyday life cannot be proved to be "because of race" and thus should not "count" as intolerable harm. As this chapter demonstrates, the argument contending that harm to children of color is not *caused* by "race" is a key form of contemporary rebuttal to equal opportunity claims in education; it often works to gut the presumed validity of claims that students of color have been harmed at all.

Complainants saw race-based harm in everyday life. Most Title VI complaints I investigated and heard about at OCR suggested that discrimination involved a variety of personnel and extended from classroom interactions through administrators' application of school and district policies. Most discrimination complaints coupled academic inequities and social mistreatment the complainants saw as based on race. For example, an African American parent whose child attended what the assigned investigator called an "approximately 40 percent minority (black and Hispanic)" school "across from a big-bucks horse ranch" complained about racially unfair grading and racially segregated seating in the classrooms and about students of color on sports teams being "denied playing time" and "shunted to JV." Most complainants intertwined social and academic harm in a single argument condemning everyday actions that educators (predominantly white educators, and occasionally educators of color) took toward students of color in classrooms, hallways, and offices. They argued that a Latino student, suspended for a gesture his white dean falsely considered a "gang sign" because the student was Latino, was missing weeks of class and being sent to a continuation school. A Latina student who was harassed on the bus and playground by a white student and humiliated by a Latina security guard wanted to transfer out of her white-run school. The students of color at Quail High School, subjected to verbal harassment by their white peers in classrooms and on buses and degraded by their white teachers and administrators, were excluded simultaneously from the school's academic and social communities.

Many complainants also alleged that social exclusion or harm toward themselves as parents of color had academic ramifications for their children. A Latino mother was suddenly asked to sign in and wear a name tag when visiting her children's classrooms; she alleged that this practice labeled the entire family as a "problem" in the white-run school. A black grandmother who felt dismissed by both the white principal and the white superintendent when she complained about the racial harassment of her grandson contended that he was unsafe in the school setting precisely because no one took her complaints seriously. Some other examples of Title VI complaints for which I was responsible included those brought by a Latina mother who argued that her middle-school son was under excessive surveillance by the school's white disciplinary authorities, and a Native American mother who argued that her deaf son, a high school student, had not received a necessary interpreter in his predominantly white district because he was Native American.

In each case, white administrators rebutted that the incidents in question were not "because of race," or even "racial." They asserted both that the educators in question meant well and that the experiences of the children in question were not really harmful in comparison to other children's experiences. At times, in dismissing the claim of harm "because of race," they argued that the children in question were not harmed seriously at all. Thwarted in their attempts to convince principals and district administrators of the need to remedy these harms experienced by their children, parents had approached OCR to request that it intervene using the tools of civil rights law. Some filed complaints simultaneously with their state Department of Education.

At least at the outset of their OCR experience, complainants seemed to believe strongly in the potential power of the civil rights bureaucracy to validate their sense of harm to their children and legally entitle their children to better treatment.[2] Similar cases are filed every year at OCR offices across the country, most often by individual parents and sometimes by local or national advocacy organizations of various kinds (such as parent and community organizations or the NAACP). Some cases pertain to individual schools, others to entire districts. Complaints filed at various regional offices of OCR during the years I worked at the agency alleged that a district's administrators had failed to provide resources in schools serving black children, that black students in a middle school had been harassed by their principal, that parents and teachers used racial epithets in talking about black students at their high school, and that Latino students were excluded from their school's social environment. Others alleged that a host of white students had physically abused a black student, that Native American students were disciplined more harshly and more often than white students, and that schools and districts meted out harsher punishment to black students than to whites and suspended them more often. Still others alleged that black children were excluded from gifted programs, or never tested for them at all; that Latino English-language learners were placed in Special Education classes not because they had disabilities but because they could not speak fluent English; and that school personnel failed to involve their parents in school community councils or to tell them about gifted programs for their children. Still others alleged that cheerleading tryouts disadvantaged black girls, that too few "minorities" were in an entire district's advanced courses, that black students were overrepresented in Special Education for reasons other than actual disabilities, and that black and Latino students lacked course options in comparison to white students in their school district or were encouraged to leave school rather than graduate. Whether these complaints alleged single harmful interactions or aggregated patterns, and whether they condemned acts by individuals or educators' applications of districtwide policies, they always argued that the actions adults or peers took toward students of color were "racial"—that they occurred because the students were not white, and often also (though they typically stated this over the phone rather than in writing) because the educators predominantly were.[3] Complainants suggested simultaneously that they expected educational institutions to treat their children equally and that educational institutions, particularly white-controlled institutions, would rarely fully welcome or adequately serve children of color.[4] And they always argued that everyday acts taken toward children of color inside schools and districts counted—that they contributed fundamentally to racial inequality of opportunity to succeed in school.

By questioning the fairness of specific educator acts toward students or groups of children of color in schools and districts, and even when denouncing aggregated racial disparities like dropout rates, complainants always suggested that everyday actions and decisions in schools and districts piled up to help produce racially unequal educational opportunities and outcomes. Sociologists, economists, anthropologists, and other social theorists agree that everyday acts in schools and districts contribute to patterns of school achievement.[5] Yet in schools and districts, it was precisely the claim that educator acts denied opportunity to students of color, or that consequential and above all *race-based* or *racial* harm could be found in the ordinary acts and decisions of educators, that the officials and educators confronted with discrimination complaints resisted most heatedly and determinedly.

School and district staff used many names to characterize complainants as people whose claims of racial discrimination rang hollow to them: they were "kooks," "argumentative," "always coming up here," "always in my office," "high maintenance," a "loony tune." One principal sighed that she was "*always* involved with the child because of his parents' concerns." Another district representative concluded, "We tried to do what his parents wanted, but they're *difficult*." In conversations with OCR employees, school- and district-level educators and administrators routinely framed complainants as people who not only blew harms to their children out of proportion but also could not communicate without offending educators personally. Many educators receiving OCR Title VI complaints explicitly framed parent complainants as outsiders to the educational community, people who would be welcomed if friendly but who were a polluting element when arguing combatively.[6] They perceived OCR staff, too, as outsiders whose legalistic, bureaucratic ways of defining harm to children intruded into local relationships. From the recipients' perspectives, OCR's legal apparatus seemed to intrude on the informal, even " 'lawless everyday world"[7] of schools, which operated fairly without external assistance and should resolve disputes without resorting to higher authorities. Educators expressed such antilegal sentiments in disability cases, too, framing parents who complained to OCR as combative and overly litigious. Yet in race cases, educators found complainants' attempts to wield the law particularly unwarranted, unnecessary, and socially divisive.

As the designated civil rights enforcement office of the U.S. Department of Education, OCR is the highest-level federal agency in which complaints about the impermissible and intolerable unfairness of concrete, ordinary acts in educational settings are routinely taken seriously. OCR does deem allegations of everyday harms to children of color to be consequential enough to warrant federal investigation, but it often disappoints complainants' hopes that it will actually determine these everyday harms to be impermissible. What complainants did not expect from these debates was that OCR, too, would so often decide it was unable to "find" "evidence" of impermissible harm "because of race" to children of color in the everyday activity inside educational institutions. Like skeptics inside school districts, employees inside the agency, wielding legal tools, were more likely to rebut than to accept claims of harm to children and parents of color.

The first case I was assigned as an OCR employee vividly demonstrates a particular consequence of striving to prove or disprove the existence of discrimination "because of race." In endless debates over harm's racial causation, exacerbated by OCR's legal framing, parents and educators could actually keep themselves from collaborating to analyze and remedy the *experience* of harm, and the experience of harm *as racial*, by parents and students of color. In debating harm's racial causation and educators' motivations rather than analyzing actions' effects on children of color, they could strain beyond repair the very relationships central to serving children successfully.

## A Representative Case

> The existence of a racially hostile environment that is created, encouraged, accepted, tolerated, or left uncorrected by a recipient constitutes different treatment on the basis of race in violation of Title VI and the implementing regulations cited above. When

investigating such issues, OCR examines whether a
recipient has created or is responsible for a hostile
environment that is sufficiently severe, pervasive, or
persistent so as to interfere with or limit an individual's
ability to participate in or benefit from the recipient's
programs or activities.
　　　　　　　　*—Typical language for OCR Title VI letter, circa 2000*

My first case at OCR concerned a rural/suburban school district, which I will rename Longview Unified, whose students were predominantly white but included some Latinos and a few African Americans. The complaint was filed by Keisha Stedley, a black woman whose two grandchildren were among the handful of black students at their elementary school in Longview. Stedley said they were typically the only black children in their classes. "Complainant said she counted five black children in the entire K–8 school," I wrote in my interview notes, adding that Stedley said she had "met parents who used to have children at [the school] but who pulled their kids out because they felt the school was racist." The district was embroiled in a number of local disputes over whether students and parents were being harmed "because of race." I came to call the Stedley complaint Longview I, because two other parents would file Title VI complaints at OCR within a few months.

In a long, handwritten and typewritten complaint form filed in the late fall, Stedley argued that since the beginning of the school year, numerous adults in the school and district—all of whom, it turned out, were white, though she did not state this in her complaint—had discriminated against her third-grade grandson, LaRon, his fifth-grade sister, Sharmaine, and Stedley herself. "My grandchildren are Black," she wrote matter-of- factly, checking off the "Race/Color" box on the OCR form for "BASIS (Check one or more and specify for each item checked). Grounds on which you feel you were discriminated against." She also checked "Disability," writing that both children "are in Special Ed. class." Still, her attached list of incidents, and her interactions in the district, focused exclusively on her allegations of racial discrimination.

In a typed list, Stedley alleged that over several weeks at the beginning of the school year, LaRon had experienced repeated racial slurs from peers that had gone unpunished. LaRon's teachers had treated him unequally, she said, disciplining him for infractions while allowing his non-black peers to break the same rules and bother LaRon without suffering any consequences. LaRon had ended up in the nurse's office with a bleeding lip after yet another fight with a peer. Stedley said the nurse did little to help LaRon and no one had called to inform Stedley of the injury. Mentioning another occasion when an injured white student had been cared for immediately, she deemed her grandson's experience an incident of racialized neglect. LaRon's sister, Sharmaine, had also been mistreated; a teacher had humiliated her in a discussion about a class assignment. The family had already switched that fall from another elementary school in the district because of Stedley's discomfort with LaRon's treatment. In the previous school, Stedley said, LaRon's teacher had roughly grabbed his shoulder to get his attention when he did not make eye contact with her, an action that frightened him deeply.

Stedley alleged that administrators at her grandson's current elementary school and in the district office had downplayed her complaints about these incidents. It was the school staff she held primarily responsible as "negligent," she said in our interview: the district had at least removed her children from the school as requested. Still, regarding the issues of racial harassment and unfair discipline, district officials had dismissively sent her back to the school principal, who had suggested that racial slurs were not very different from being called "four-eyes." The vice principal had asked in a meeting whether Stedley herself had ever been called a "nigger," implying to Stedley that a few slurs directed at LaRon did not constitute a climate of racial hostility. Maybe school people should have put up a sign saying "no black kids allowed," Stedley told me over the phone, because then at least she "would've known where they stood."

Stedley alleged that the various acts harmful to her grandson had occurred because of the family's race and, by implication, because of the race of school and district personnel. Had LaRon not been black, she asserted, he would not have been treated harshly and neglectfully; he certainly would not have been called racist names by his peers. Had Longview educators not been white, she implied, they would not have dismissed her claims about his treatment and harassment. She had already written a letter to the district superintendent stating that her "children have been hurt physically and mentally." She continued, "With all of these incidents (enclosed) at [the school], I feel my children don't stand a chance to get a decent education. . . . My children are being called niggers by the students, because the children of [the school] are getting away with this. I feel [teacher] makes a difference because my children are black. . . . I will not tolerate this discrimination from your staff. It's not supposed to hurt to be a child or because of your color. We're all the same, even if our color is different," she explained. On her OCR complaint form, in response to the question "When and in what way did you first become aware that the treatment, act, or decision was discriminatory?" Stedley wrote that it was the accumulation of incidents and the district's inadequate response that convinced her to file: "When all these different incidents kept happening and nothing was done about it by the school district." In her list of incidents that fall, she wrote that "a child called Sharmaine a nigger. She did not say anything because the school doesn't do anything anyway."

In countering these allegations, Longview district and school representatives asserted that none of their actions toward LaRon had been "racially motivated" or "racist" and that most of the alleged interactions, except for the peer harassment, were not "racial" at all. Significantly, the school and district authorities framed "race" as injected into interactions only by Stedley and her grandchildren, rather than acknowledging that school personnel were themselves "racial" actors in their daily interactions over racial fairness in the district. This construction attributed "racial" behavior to non-white persons alone, and in this case framed Stedley as causing "racial problems." Rebutting claims about the "racial motivation" of their acts, Longview educators at times denied outright LaRon's and Sharmaine's experience of racial harm. As I noted later in the investigation, the Longview report responding to OCR's investigative queries said bluntly that "the kids *experienced nothing* that was 'racially motivated.'" WHAT

The Longview Unified school district chose Anne Hardy, a white district administrator for Special Education, to be their liaison to OCR in this complaint. Hardy had already been in contact with the family because LaRon received Special Education services. Over the course of the investigation, Hardy spoke repeatedly of LaRon's emotional "problems" and the contribution to them made by his "angry parent" as primary causes of the family's negative experiences in school. She set out to prove that Stedley's allegations were "statistically" false. The first time I talked on the phone with Hardy, she told me promptly that she had already spent several hours "doing some statistics" showing that at two schools black students had not been disproportionately suspended "to prove there isn't some big horrible discrimination going on in our district." In successive phone calls, Hardy described Stedley to me more bluntly as "a high-maintenance grandma" and a "kook." Stedley was always calling the school, Hardy said; Stedley was disorganized in the ways she presented her concerns to administrators; and she kept urging LaRon and Sharmaine to report incidents to her and to school administrators as if they were racially discriminatory when they were not.

Hardy insisted that she had responded promptly to each of Stedley's calls and had called Stedley on her own to resolve various incidents. Hardy had attended meetings about LaRon, moved the children to the new school at Stedley's request, urged Stedley to gather specific information to support her claims, and explained to Stedley that these incidents were "normal children things, not racially motivated." Hardy's personal goal, she protested, was to have the district listen to Stedley and respond to her concerns. "But she must understand that the things that happened were not based on race," Hardy reiterated; "they were with *children*—with human beings." ~~Now they are Human~~ ...

Sandwiched between Stedley's pointed allegations of racial discrimination and the district's blunt denials that race was relevant, and navigating Hardy's more pointed assertions that the Stedley family was imposing a "race" analysis on events that were simply "human," meaning non-"racial," I handled the Longview case for several months. I investigated each incident Stedley alleged to determine whether it had actually occurred and, if so, whether it was discriminatory under OCR's definitions of harm "on the ground of race." In zooming in to scrutinize these interactions frame by frame, we took Stedley's allegations seriously. But we did not treat Stedley's claims of harm to herself, LaRon, and Sharmaine as inherently valid from the family's perspective. Skepticism about harm's "racial" causation was built into every step of our legal search for "proof." Within our legalistic terms, we decided in the end that many of Stedley's allegations of harm did not amount to harms that OCR had to do anything about; unable to prove harm's "racial" causation legalistically, we concluded that the harms had not been sufficiently intolerable to demand remedy by educators, either. Our own definition of a "hostile environment" suggested that environments "left uncorrected" by educators were harmful "on the basis of race," but when wielding our legal tools, we often concluded that many aspects of harm to children were not "racial" enough in legal terms to demand formal correction.

To ascertain whether harm occurred "on the ground of race" in mixed-race schools, OCR investigators typically compared the experiences of students of color with those of white students (technically, to "students or individuals who are similarly situated") to see whether whites had been treated better, and compared the treatment of students and parents of color to standard practice to see whether some deviation from the standard had occurred. We then asked educators whether they could convincingly explain any inferior treatment or deviation from standard practice as a result of any reason *other* than race, or whether any disparate racial patterns were somehow "educationally" "justified." These "because of race" questions, which invited denials that race was relevant to harm, are central to legal analysis of discrimination. In cases like Stedley's that alleged the different treatment of students of color, investigators were supposed to ask whether the reasons school and district people gave for any differential treatment were mere "pretexts" for the "real"—that is, potentially racial—reason for their action.[8] By definition, then, the goal of the accused became to pro-

duce evidence justifying their own actions as "legitimate and nondiscriminatory": administrators wanted to raise doubts about there being
any "racial" reason behind the treatment of the child. In asking about
the causation of the harm experienced by students and parents of color,
investigators essentially invited school personnel to offer defensive ra-
tionalizations and prompted them to gather comparative data to disprove any patterns of racial harm.

After I had read Stedley's evidence, interviewed Stedley on the
phone, studied the large binder of data Hardy compiled, and visited
Longview to interview educators, it seemed clear to me and the attorney assigned to the case that while Longview educators had not totally ignored Stedley's claims of harm, they had continually dismissed the "racial" nature of those harms. After Stedley had complained of the peer harassment, the school and district had handled
those incidents according to their standard procedures for parental
complaints about conflicts among children: they asked routine questions of some students who had participated in or witnessed the
fights and slurs;[9] they had disciplined each harasser in some way,
though often for terms shorter than the school handbook required;
they had had a few conversations with the children about friendly
interactions; and they told LaRon he could come in for counseling if
he wanted to. Individual teachers had also tried to discuss the disputed disciplinary incidents with the Stedley children themselves,
but failed to discuss these issues successfully with Stedley. Further,
school officials had done little to investigate a potential pattern of accumulating harassment incidents experienced by LaRon and Sharmaine, nothing in particular to prevent or assess the repetition of racial harassment in the future, and very little to communicate to
Stedley herself about their investigations or assessments of the harassment or the disputed teacher-student interactions.

Instead, Hardy's own notes indicated, Longview staff just kept offering to Stedley "their explanation of the events" as having nothing to
do with race at all. The principal wrote a memo to Hardy that described how in his meetings with Stedley, "I also tried to differentiate
between comments or actions that could be directly considered racist,
and those which, although unpleasant, were just an unfortunate part
of life. Stedley did not seem to agree with this concept." Regarding the
disputed interactions between LaRon, Sharmaine, and their teachers,
the principal said, "I pointed out that neither of the incidents related
by Stedley involved a racial slur or any overt connotation of prejudice.
Her statement was that . . . the issue wasn't dealt with correctly because her grandchildren are black. I disputed that concept because she
had made the assumption —without speaking to the teacher about ei-

ther of these incidents—that the teacher treated children differently because of skin color." Hardy herself explained to OCR that after the time when LaRon sat in the nurse's office, Stedley "became angry and left with the children before [the principal] could talk with LaRon or her. She expressed her belief that the situation was racially motivated and that he had been sitting for hours in the office. Both [the principal] and I spoke with Stedley about what had actually happened, but she would not accept our explanation."

Hardy eventually interviewed each of the educators Stedley had accused so that each could explain to OCR how and why his or her actions were not "racial." In one of our phone conversations, Hardy even argued that the peer harassment of LaRon was not "a racial issue." I recorded in my notes: "Hardy emphasized that . . . Stedley 'has a lens colored by race.' " Hardy had said that Stedley couldn't "sort out normal children's squabble things—she thinks it's all race." According to Hardy, I wrote, "a 'small conflict between kids' was 'all racist' in Stedley's eyes."

Hardy asserted that Stedley falsely interpreted Longview educators' interactions with Stedley and LaRon as racially hostile. Hardy instead attributed racial hostility to Stedley herself: "She hasn't learned to work with us. She comes with a two-by-four ready to fight." Hardy admitted that the vice principal had made mistakes, including failing to call LaRon's doctor when he was injured in a fight, but she explained this error as a result of the vice principal's inexperience. She said she regretted that the principal had compared racial slurs directed at LaRon and other children of color to students teasing peers who wear glasses, but insisted that his intent was "not racial." When LaRon's teacher put her arm on the boy's shoulder, Hardy explained, she was simply trying to get his attention; this was not a "choking incident," as Stedley had alleged, and it had certainly not occurred "because of race."

For my part, I too was finding it difficult to "prove" race's causal role in the series of incidents using legal tools. Regarding Stedley's claims about racially unequal discipline, the available records did not show different treatment of white children in the same or exactly analogous incidents. In investigating separately each of LaRon's disciplinary interactions with teachers, I found few comparable recorded incidents involving white students. It thus remained unclear in legal terms whether, in each incident, LaRon's teachers had treated him unfavorably as a black child in comparison to non-black students. Assessing each incident separately for its "racial" nature made it difficult to assess the incidents' cumulative nature or cumulative effect on LaRon. As I wrote in my notes while analyzing the discipline incidents, "(too isolated for allegation of disparity?)." In one sense, the absence of such incidents involving white students indicated a problematic "racial" climate in the district, but this very absence made it more difficult to assess the overall climate. For several incidents in the Stedley case, the legal analysis also seemed complicated by the fact that the harassers or other students involved were "Hispanic," or "Hispanic/white." I wrote in my data analysis, "Black students definitely seem to be overrepresented in suspension rates at [the school] (1–2 percent of population, 8–11 percent of suspensions). Yet since many of the students involved in these disciplinary incidents were indeed Hispanic, how would disparate discipline be measured?"

The legal determination of discrimination hinged on why educators had taken the actions that LaRon and Stedley considered harmful. In my notes, I remarked that this "because of race" question posed the core analytic dilemma of my job. Complainants and educators always fought over how to interpret educators' actions toward students of color, and OCR, too, entered this battle over interpreting race's causal relevance. I wrote in my notes, "Danger of INTERPRETATION of actions is *huge* when looking at discrimination cases. Issue of INTENTIONS key, and most difficult—two totally different read[ing]s of same actions!! (As well as different histories of them)." The key task for me as an OCR investigator was to determine whether the problematic behavior that was racially harmful "because of race" from Stedley's perspective crossed the line into "discriminatory" behavior that was impermissibly harmful "because of race" in the eyes of the law. As a colleague, Donald, put it in discussing a complaint that accused one school of not teaching students of color effectively, the core question was, "At what point do we say that practices are not just *bad*, but racially discriminatory?"[10] Thinking about how the school district had failed to respond with urgency to Stedley regarding the incidents of racial harassment and discipline that were "harmful to Stedley, LaRon," I wrote in my notes, "Fuzzy, then: How discriminatory were they in legal terms? What's a 'violation'? . . . When is a non-response *discriminatory* and requiring of action by a district?"

Our search to prove the absolute presence or absence of illegal "discrimination" "because of race" was doing little to improve relations in Longview. Locally, Stedley was demanding continued inquiry into educator "racism," and this framing of harm's causation also prompted few educators to accept the family's experiences of harm. Both she and the vice principal described an interaction between them in which Stedley suggested "racism" was the district's problem. "The conversation . . . seemed to be directed toward me," the vice principal related. "Stedley then said I was racist. I told Stedley what I was hearing sounded like slander."

In the end, OCR's power to determine the legality of Longview educators' actions did afford us the chance to help remedy the situation that most closely approached our definition of illegal discrimination: the racial harassment of a black child by non-black children and the district's incoherent response to that harassment. Using a tactic that was routine during my time at OCR (see chapter 2), the lawyer assigned to the case, the manager overseeing our work, and I actually convinced the district to address the harassment by saying that we would *refrain* from publicly "finding" in our resolution letter that the "problems" we had found constituted "discrimination." We instead wrote a letter describing the district's insufficient attempts to both investigate and communicate with Stedley about the accumulating incidents of harassment ("District staff acknowledged that the District and School did not do a sufficient job of tracking racial harassment incidents, and that it was thus very difficult to investigate whether a racially hostile environment might exist."). Since Longview Unified had no official policy regarding racial harassment (its internal Uniform Complaint Procedures, the process for parent complaints, had not even mentioned "race" discrimination as a possible event), we worked with the district to devise and install a policy and procedures so problems could be handled more systematically in the future. We convinced them to keep records so they could monitor incidents of harassment and assess whether these incidents exhibited racial patterns. We persuaded the district to designate school and district administrators who would be responsible for investigating claims of harassment, and we suggested that the district create a new ombudsperson position to mediate all conflicts with parents.

While these changes carried some promise, the other teacher-student interactions that Stedley had complained about as harmful to LaRon were essentially washed away as not "rising to the level" of a legal violation; accordingly, we suggested no further discussion of how the district's families perceived discipline or other educator actions. Further, months of battles over the absolute presence or absence of "discrimination" in Longview removed some of the potency from even the harassment remedies we did negotiate. Implementing a racial harassment policy in Longview, much less changing the climate so that white students did not call black students "nigger" in the first place, would require educators to work proactively with children and colleagues to prevent harassment and to take seriously any claims that students of color had been harmed. Longview educators and administrators never appeared convinced that any of Stedley's claims were valid or that the insults and injuries to LaRon carried any serious weight. An early version of the new harassment policy included this statement: "The principal or designee may take disciplinary measures against any person who is found to have made a complaint of harassment/discrimination that he/she knew was not true." Disputes over proving the racial causation of educators' actions and inaction toward the Stedley family drowned out the deeper educational question of understanding how the racial harassment had arisen and how its causes could be remedied. It also drowned out more general considerations of how to make the Longview climate, including interactions among Longview educators, students, and parents, feel more welcoming to families of color.

Moreover, battles over proving harm's "racial" causation continued to rage in Longview. Stedley disagreed with OCR's solution, arguing that OCR was leaving the fox in charge of the henhouse. She said repeatedly that "Longview Unified lied" about the full litany of disciplinary incidents involving her grandchildren; she wanted "polygraph reports" because there was "no truth in it at all." She said she was having a very hard time sleeping, that her "children were hurt" both mentally and physically by the incidents, and that she planned to "take it as high as it needs to go," filing next with the state. This series of events had left scars on her grandchildren, she reiterated, and she would not let the district "get away with this." As I wrote in my notes, after months of OCR investigation, Stedley still fundamentally distrusted the district's motivations: "Grandma Stedley called to say the report she got from the district was 'all lies.' . . . I told her she'd see in our report that she raised awareness in the district and had really been able to make some changes, e.g., tracking harassment better, adding a racial harassment policy, appointing a district point person and school site responsibility person. . . . She then asked me point-blank if we had 'found discrimination.' . . . And I said, 'Yes, in terms of your children having been called racial slurs.' But I left out that her disparate discipline claims washed away."

Social relations in Longview were strained even further by successive articles in local newspapers documenting the battle over proving or disproving racial discrimination in Longview. One article on the "feds' " investigation of "racism" quoted Ms. Stedley as saying, "These children didn't know anything about racism until they attended this elementary school. . . . They were learning discrimination. I will not tolerate it. It's against the law." Controversy intensified after complaint resolution when an OCR media liaison in the national office misstated to a Longview journalist that OCR had formally "found" "discrimination" in the school district's disciplinary practices. The article in the local newspaper began, "A three-month federal investigation has concluded that the Longview Unified School District discriminated against two African-American students," and stated incorrectly that "officials with the U.S. Department of Education's Office of Civil Rights closed their investigation of the district Thursday, agreeing with Keisha Stedley, who alleged her two grandchildren were punished more harshly than white students involving several incidents at school." The newspaper reporter quoted the OCR spokesperson as stating summatively that "they (the district) weren't communicating with parents and had no idea how to handle" discrimination.

The journalist later admitted to misquoting the D.C. spokesperson, who had been reading from our closure letter delicately stating our "concerns" about harassment. Anne Hardy had expected simply to receive this closure letter detailing the district's proactive efforts to create procedures for dealing with racial harassment in the absence of formal "findings"; she was enraged by these public misstatements of OCR's conclusions and criticisms of the district's ideas and practices. The Longview administration and school board demanded a written explanation from OCR. At the request of my managers, I wrote a public retraction stating that OCR had some "concerns" about the incidents of harassment in Longview but had not found any "discrimination" in discipline. The newspaper's apologetic follow-up article, "No Discrimination Found in Longview Case but Policy on Complaints Coming," retracted its previous story but went too far in the other direction. The article began, "U.S. Department of Education officials announced Monday that the Longview Unified School District did not discriminate against two African-American students, but the department's three-month probe found fault with the district's handling of such complaints." The article quoted the "spokesman for the Civil Rights office" as now saying summatively, "we found no discrimination." "Argh!" I scribbled agitatedly on the article. "Annoying overstated reaction and seeming denial of any slurs!"

As declarations that the district "had" or "had not" "discriminated" and had or had not been "found" to have discriminated ping-ponged back and forth through the local papers, the disturbing reality I had discovered in Longview—that the school district had responded dismissively to repeated racial slurs directed against a black third grader and had refused to take seriously the racially hostile climate experienced by his family—was buried under claims about the absolute presence or absence of discrimination in specific incidents and inflammatory assertions about educators' motivations and beliefs. The controversy in the local newspapers was a replay, in an exaggerated, oversimplified, and speeded-up form, of the dispute over harm's causation that had played out within the OCR investigation.

Hardy complained to me on the phone that OCR had become a "federal bully." The problem with the newspaper reporting OCR's findings, she began calmly, was that even having such official findings in a letter "implied" that educators in Longview were not "well-meaning." "It might not be big to you, but it is to us," she said. The teachers had been misrepresented. "We haven't got any teachers discriminating against . . . we have well-meaning teachers that I can't protect," she lamented. The press coverage "made every kook in the community realize that there's someone out there to listen to them." Now, she protested, "everybody has the impression that horrible things are going on in Longview."

Beginning to cry, Hardy said that OCR's "approach with us in this fiasco has discouraged me personally enough that I'm leaving the district." She charged that "fundamentally very conscious people" had been "maligned intentionally by your agency." OCR should be "calling inappropriate complaints inappropriate and not investigating empty claims." Hardy was convinced OCR had come "looking for systemic discrimination"; in that process, "wacko parents got heard." She had done nothing but work on this case for months, she added in frustration. Appealing to me personally, she said she hoped that someone at OCR could relate to the national office in D.C. "what an incredibly destructive thing" the OCR spokesperson's comments had been to the Longview community. "Everyone is saying, 'How could Anne have been so wrong in representing our district?' " she said. "They blamed Anne Hardy. . . . I can't work where people don't trust me."

Hardy reiterated to me that Stedley had misinterpreted educators' actions through a racial lens, misconstrued their intentions as racial, and misrepresented their views as racist. "I'm not black, she is—she doesn't get it that I care about her children—I don't see color," Hardy sighed. Having contended once again that she did not "see color" in her relationships with children, Hardy acknowledged in the same utterance that the conflicts between her and Stedley were grounded in racially different interpretations of events: "I'm not black, she is." In Hardy's own analysis, these different lenses on race's relevance stemmed from the "race" of the viewer. In Hardy's eyes, the problem was Stedley's false view—which she held because she was a black woman—that race mattered to white educators in Longview. Still battling to disprove race's relevance, Hardy was also still dismissing Stedley's experience of harm.

In the weeks following Stedley's first letter to OCR, two additional racial discrimination complaints had arrived from parents in the school district. I had been assigned to investigate them because of my current dealings with the district, and the district had assigned Anne Hardy to work with me on these before she decided to leave the district alto-gether. Both complaints described harms that families experienced as racial; in response to both, district educators spring to action to dis-prove race's relevance. One complaint (Longview II) started as a disability discrimination case about the suspensions and continua-tion-school placement of a Latino high school student with partially diagnosed learning and behavior disabilities. The father soon lodged an additional racial discrimination complaint alleging that his son was being framed by school and district staff as a likely "gang mem-ber" because he was Latino. The father contended that this un-founded assumption led to his son's being unfairly suspended for small offenses and exiled to the continuation school, an institution designed to house students deemed unable to attend the district's regular programs. In a rare example of a district representative dis-puting a student's racial identification, the beleaguered Anne Hardy, sending me a pile of documents we had asked the district to gather regarding this boy's disciplinary history, flagged copies of enrollment forms she had found on which the boy's ethnicity was recorded as "white" (over the phone, the father explained that his son was "half Spanish, half Mexican"). From Hardy's perspective, this evidence re-futed the complainant's allegation that his son was experiencing race-based treatment, despite the fact that she herself had been talking about the student as "Latin" before uncovering these enrollment doc-uments. In the end, the fact that the boy was typically described and treated as Latino in the district trumped the racial assignment re-corded on his form. Ironically, even Hardy's own insistence that the boy's being "Latin" had nothing to do with how they treated him was proof of his Latino identity in the district.

The other complaint (Longview III) began with a phone message from a Latina parent I will name Laura Cachon, who said her daughter had just been hospitalized after being beaten up by a white student in an elementary school in Longview. Her message said that she was using Stedley's phone and was "organizing parents in Longview." Ca-chon eventually filed a formal Title VI complaint with OCR. She al-leged numerous instances of racial discrimination: she and her Latino husband were subjected to restrictive parking and visitation proce-dures that white parents did not have to follow; her children were har-assed by white students, white parents, and white and Latina school security guards; and school nurses denied her son prescribed allergy medication, which Cachon considered a form of racialized neglect. Dis-trict and school administrators had denied any "racial" aspect to these incidents. Cachon brought Stedley with her to several meetings with district administrators, shocking and infuriating them. Hardy told me agitatedly in our last phone conversation that the Cachon family had a sheet billowing outside their home emblazoned with the red-painted words, "Longview discriminates, contact OCR."

By enlisting the services of OCR to improve students' everyday schooling experiences, complainants were simultaneously striving to wield legal power themselves and giving a legal-political bureaucracy the power to publicly determine the acceptability of educators' actions toward their children. As OCR staff investigated complaints to find the presence or absence of "discrimination" "because of race," our important analyses of people's everyday experiences of harm were both enabled and shackled by the logic of the law. Routinely, legal logic reduced the set of children's experiences that required further attention. In investigating allegations that students of color were treated unfavorably, we typically pursued analysis down two core analytic and social dead ends: First, did anyone intend this harm? Second, was the action in question really harmful in comparison to the treatment of other races, particularly whites? Both questions fundamentally limited the harm to children that would be deemed problematic. The rest of this chapter describes, in turn, exactly how these arguments over analyzing racial intent and comparing race-group harm often distracted everyone from the educational question of whether children and parents had experienced harm in the everyday activity of schooling, and, if so, how to address this experience and prevent it from happening again. Indeed, the constraints of our typical legalistic analysis often prevented us from engaging the even broader educational goal of getting white adults to pursue positive interactions with parents and children of color. I explore, first, the problems of the general task of proving harm to be "because of race." I then move to exploring each of the dead ends in turn.

## The General Problem of Proving Harm to Be "On the Ground of Race"

OCR constrains findings of racial harm by employing legal arguments about what counts as racial discrimination. The agency's quest to rule on whether "racial discrimination" had occurred prompted irresolvable disputes over an often unanswerable question inherent in Title VI. Sure, children and parents of color felt they had been harmed and denied opportunity by the acts in question, but could they prove those acts had occurred because of race?

The text of Title VI simultaneously names and constricts the types of acts that are defined as racially discriminatory: "No person in the United States shall, on the ground of race, color, or national origin, be excluded from participation in, be denied the benefits of, or be subjected to discrimination under any program or activity receiving Federal financial assistance."[11] This language could be interpreted expansively as outlawing harm along the lines of race, prompting official concern about any harm that disproportionately affects members of particular racial groups (Latino students disproportionately represented on suspension lists, for example, with no apparent "educational" "justification"). OCR occasionally pursued this sort of analysis, which we called "disparate impact" analysis. But this text can also be interpreted restrictively, as justifying official concern only with harms intentionally inflicted on members of racial groups for "racial" reasons (Latino students suspended because of educators' stance toward them as Latinos). This second form of analysis, which we called "disparate treatment" analysis, is the most common analysis in civil rights law, and the analysis we typically used at OCR. Further, even when we investigated the racially "disparate impact" of seemingly neutral policies or practices on many children of color, we had to show such harm to have occurred to some extent "because of" the "race" of the children.

Responding to all Title VI investigations into harm "because of race," educators typically argued that harms to students of color were OCR's business only if "race," or more precisely educators' personal racism, could be proved to be the cause of the harm. Similarly, OCR managers in charge of monitoring complaint investigations often decided that complainants' sense of harm because of race could simply not be proved in legalistic terms. OCR investigators and attorneys repeatedly told one another that although children and parents had surely experienced harm as racial group members, we could not propose a remedy because we could not prove "race" to be at the root of that harm. In arguing that harm "because of race" could not be proved, we all proffered a "yes, but" rebuttal to demands for everyday justice that is pervasive in the new civil rights era: yes, opportunities should be racially equal, but opportunities were not racially unequal in this particular instance.

The "because of race" question prompted by the prevailing interpretation of Title VI was, in many cases, both interpersonally inflammatory and impossible to answer conclusively. Both outcomes limited assistance to children. To investigate "discrimination," we had to assess whether everyday acts taken toward LaRon, Sharmaine, or Ms. Stedley were "race-based," which often translated locally into a perceived quest to determine acts to be "racially motivated" or even "racist." Lay habits of claiming harm "because of race" also helped produce local resistance. As conversation analysts observe, every statement rebuts a question that is either asked openly or heard silently.[12] Parents' claims of harm "because of race" often either explicitly accused educators of "racism" or insinuated that educators had deliberately harmed children of color. Indeed, the very word "discrimination" is packed with such implications of intent.[1] Whether explicit or implicit, the presumption of willful harm immediately prompted educators to defend against the claim rather than acknowledge the harm. Our analytic requirement of looking for the superior treatment of children of other "races," white children in particular, also prompted educators to insist that students had not been treated with race in mind or treated differently along racial lines. Complainants' local accusations that white children were treated preferably had the same effect. In sum, when educators and administrators were asked to explain whether their actions toward children of color were taken because of race, they typically insisted that children had not been harmed because of race, either because no one intended to harm them in racial terms or because the children had not experienced egregious harm in comparison to children of other races. All, thus, essentially refused to remedy the harm experienced or to assist children of color in the ways requested.

We "feds" joined the debate over determining impermissible harm "because of race" the minute a complainant filed at OCR. Even filing a Title VI complaint at OCR forced a decision about harm's causal "basis" and narrowed the set of everyday acts toward children of color OCR would and would not even investigate as potentially "discriminatory." Complainants had to check a box on the official OCR complaint form indicating whether children were discriminated against on the basis of race, color, or national origin (including discrimination against English-language learners); sex; or disability. (Some complainants alleged a combination of these grounds, and OCR evaluated these multiple charges separately.) Each complainant was asked to describe how the student or group of students experienced unequal treatment because of their membership in that protected category: they were to fill in a series of blank lines or attach a narrative of events as evidence.

As I wrote somewhat ironically in my notes soon after arriving at OCR, the most important thing for aggrieved parents to do was fit their description of everyday injustice into the categories of harm prohibited by civil rights law: "Must squeeze complaints into three civil rights categories (race, sex, disability) in order to have complaint taken. It can't just be 'unfair.' " I saw no complaints alleging discrimination against low-income children as such, and had such complaints been filed, they would not have been accepted. Children living in poverty have never been recognized as a class whose right to equal educational opportunities should be protected by federal law. Even egregious instances of educational discrimination against poor children, such as policies for school financing that provide substantially fewer resources to schools in impoverished communities than in affluent ones, have been deemed at the federal level not to be "discrimination."[14] Similarly, gay and lesbian students are not protected by federal civil rights law from discrimination based on their sexual orientation. Civil rights law is also concerned only with protecting members of specific disadvantaged groups as such, not with ensuring fair or kind treatment of children as individuals. Civil rights analysis necessarily involves analyzing whether students' individual circumstances trump the possibility that harm to them was "because of race."

Discrimination in education is sometimes defined as unnecessarily or harmfully making something of a student's membership in a group—for example, suspending José because he is Latino—and sometimes defined as harmfully ignoring a student's membership in a group.[15] For example, English-language learners can be harmed by teaching designed for children who speak English fluently; dyslexic children can be harmed by being assigned tasks designed for children without dyslexia. If José's first language is Spanish, or if he has been diagnosed with a language-based information processing disorder, those differences between him and other children require positive recognition under the law.

In OCR complaints of everyday discrimination based on race (and sex), unlike analyses of discrimination against English-language learners or students with disabilities, children were generally said to be harmed when they were treated differently than the "norm." Stedley described Sharmaine's final school placement in the Longview district approvingly: "They treat her just like everybody else—that's all I ask." Only rarely did complainants in K–12 race and gender cases argue explicitly that without being recognized as "different," students of color or girls could not be treated equally.[16] These arguments abound in school and district debates over cultural differences, but they were not typically made primary in discrimination complaints. (One case I handled for OCR encompassed both forms of racial discrimination. While arguing that white students and adults in her mountain community were harassing students of color because they were "different," the complainant also argued that educators harmed immigrant students and students of color by failing to recognize their "cultures" in school programming. Complaints calling for diversity training similarly suggested that educators disserved students of color because they knew too little about them.)

Figuring out when noticing or ignoring "difference"—a student's racial identity, language needs, "disability," or sex—is discriminatory or harmful confuses many educators. Helping educators navigate through these complexities is central to my own current work.[17] At OCR, however, while Section 504 cases often hinged on disputes over whether it was discriminatory or essential to classify children as "disabled,"[18] Title VI cases typically concerned not disputes over how to classify students racially (that is, whether Juan, as a Puerto Rican, was Latino or black) but rather over how racial group membership was connected to the everyday treatment of students (that is, whether Juan was suspended "because" of his race). But typically, the notion that "race-based" treatment of any kind was "racist" had those accused of "discrimination" just arguing that they had *not* treated students "racially."[19]

OCR complaint investigation procedures further narrowed the experiences of harm that would even be considered. Filing an OCR Title VI complaint required not just framing harm as occurring "because of race" but also presenting enough initial evidence of such harm to satisfy the legal bureaucracy. Some complaints were rejected without investigation because of bureaucratic factors; these could seem particularly burdensome to people seeking redress for cumulative discrimination based on race. For example, complaints would only be accepted for investigation if the incidents they alleged had occurred less than 180 days prior to filing, regardless of the severity of the incidents. If Jermaine's white classmates scrawled racial slurs on his desk every day in September, and his parents met with school and district administrators but only pursued the matter more formally when it had become clear that the students involved would not be disciplined, OCR would not accept a complaint about his experiences that was filed in June.[20]

In a few instances, OCR rejected complaints because it could not be demonstrated that the adults who were allegedly at fault for harm to children of color actually received federal funds. This legal requirement meant that only people employed by or "significantly assisted" by the school and district could be held responsible for harming students. For example, OCR sometimes rejected claims of discrimination against adults who ran privately funded extracurricular programs. In one case I handled, a Latino advocacy lawyer charged that a school district's security guards were taking pictures of Latino students wandering the halls and passing that information to the city police force for potential inclusion in a "mug book" of gang members. It was deemed appropriate for OCR investigation because the guards were employed by the district. Other cases I investigated foundered on this question of federal funding. One district insisted it did not pay a police officer who served as an antidrug and truancy officer at the school when a mother accused him of targeting her Latino son for excessive surveillance both in and out of school. Technically, they reasoned, his behavior was not their problem, even though he had arrested the boy's father during a school-sanctioned home visit about the student's truancy. My notes on the district indicated, "They say it's not school-related (??) and that he's employed by the sheriff's department."[21]

Complaints filed under Title VI also had to include enough explicit evidence of harm "on the ground of race" in everyday life to persuade OCR staff to investigate. OCR's complaint resolution manual, as updated in June 2004 and available to the public online, declares emphatically (as it did when I worked at OCR) that "in order for OCR to proceed, the complainant must provide sufficient factual information to state a claim that, if true, would constitute a potential violation of a statute that OCR enforces."[22] Critics routinely accuse OCR of being a sympathetic mouthpiece for angry advocates and of "looking for" discrimination,[23] but the agency actually has built analytic skepticism into its bureaucratic procedures. If a complaint alleged simply that a student's teachers did not like her because she was black, for example, the complaint would be rejected outright for insufficient evidence—typically, after a phone call in which an investigator asked whether the complainant could provide "evidence" of specific incidents and practices in which this dislike "because of race" became evident.[24]

The definition of "sufficient factual information" changes under different administrations, making the analysis of "sufficient" "proof" of everyday injustice a political one. Gerald Reynolds, who headed OCR temporarily during the George W. Bush administration, made it clear that complaints offering statistical evidence demonstrating harm to students *along the lines of race* (like disproportionate suspensions) would not be investigated unless complainants could list specific examples of educators disciplining students of color without warrant and "because of race." When I worked at OCR before Reynolds, an internal team evaluating our regional office's response to Title VI complaints found that we were especially likely to dole out initial rejections to complaints about racially unfair discipline; this happened because such cases included statistics regarding suspensions or expulsions of students of color but seldom had comparative evidence regarding students from other groups who were not disciplined. To some staff members, our routine conclusion of "inconclusive" evidence of racial harm indicated that OCR was particularly skeptical about evidence of racial discrimination. Betsy, an investigator, suggested to me, "We shouldn't impose a higher standard for evidence on Title VI complaints than on Title IX or 504 complaints. We run out and investigate gender and Special Ed complaints without asking for more evidence."

In the new civil rights era, as I describe next, both lay and typical legal debates over proving harm to be "on the ground of race" set up two analytic dead ends that reduce efforts to improve children's everyday educational experiences. The first dead end is the quest to prove whether people, particularly white people, *intend* to harm people of color for race-related reasons; the second dead end is the quest to prove and measure harm to people of color only by asking whether specific incidents of harm did not happen to white people. As OCR employees translated complainants' allegations into legal terminology and sent letters announcing the investigation of possible misconduct "on the ground of race," school and district employees, proclaiming their innocence and good intentions, collected data to prove they had not discriminated "because of race" and thus were not "racist." Administrators spent countless hours interviewing employees, gathering statistics, and compiling large binders of documents containing narratives, numbers, and informal and official records to send to OCR as proof that race was irrelevant to the alleged harm. While Title VI's preoccupation with causation sometimes prompted valuable scrutiny of what had caused the various incidents that complainants deemed harmful to students of color, more typically it spurred school administrators to frame all their practices as being beyond reproach.

## THE DEAD END OF ANALYZING RACIST INTENTIONS

When complainants alleged that their children or they themselves had been treated unfairly "because of race," most educators responded explicitly that they had taken their actions for other reasons. For example, when Mrs. Hernandez alleged that her son was disciplined especially harshly for swearing on the playground because he was Latino, the principal argued that he was disciplined as the handbook allowed for breaking school rules. When the Native American complainant argued that her deaf son was denied a promised interpreter because he was Native American, district representatives argued that they could not find an appropriate credentialed professional. When asked directly why a black student had been suspended, the typical principal would say that the student's misbehavior merited the punishment and that any other suspended student, whether he "happened to be black, green, or purple," also merited the punishment. School and district administrators said they found both Ms. Stedley and Mrs. Cachon to be particularly difficult women, regardless of the fact that one was black and the other Latina. All these rebuttals argued explicitly or implicitly that harms were not because of race and did not constitute discrimination, so the educators in question did not deserve reprimand and the harms in question did not deserve remedy.

Over the four decades of Title VI's operation, racial discrimination (like gender discrimination) has most often been framed as individual or institutional acts of intended harm toward people of color, rather than as acts through which ordinary people, practices, and policies harm people *as* racial group members, even unintentionally or unconsiously.[25] "Particularly in the context of race and national origin" law, Krieger (1995) sums up with regret, "discrimination is represented as resulting from the decisionmaker's discriminatory animus toward members of the plaintiff's racial or ethnic group."[26] In courts, this legal framing of racial discrimination sets up an often impossible quest for proof: lawyers need to "find" conscious ill will toward people of color within individuals or institutional actors.

Legal analysis at OCR often had us seeking intent indirectly by asking educators whether they could explain harm to students of color as caused by anything other than "race." Yet even this less direct analysis put educators on the defensive about their intentions and the role of race in their actions. It also set up a reductive, zero sum game of determining whether race was the motivating factor behind actions or was no factor at all.

The "because of race" issue, while rooted in law, is now central to lay American analysis as well. In one case I saw, a "Chinese-American" complainant who was trying to understand a district administrator's treatment of her disabled child and herself stated unusually explicitly that she herself was having trouble determining whether the administrator had acted as she had "because of" the family's "race." In my notes, I mused, "A letter from a 'Chinese American' alleging discrimination against her autistic child—left behind on field trips, bus. Mentions repeatedly getting no response from district Special Ed coordinator. 'I don't know if this is just her way of doing business or if I was discriminated [against] because of my race.' " If the child's diagnosed autism precluded him from participating in school activities and the educators in charge did nothing to try to include him, OCR could easily deem this harm as occurring "because of disability." In contrast, determining neglect "because of race" seemingly required entering the coordinator's head to determine her intentions.

To educators, accusations of racial discrimination inevitably implied "racist" hearts and minds,[27] and indeed, complainants often framed the issue this way. After the closure of one Title VI case, a complainant tellingly requested "psychological evaluations of administrators since they are making decisions that directly affect our children." In contrast, one colleague noted to me, accusations of disability discrimination typically prompted disputes over the technicalities of following rules: even if complainants and recipients accused one another of "lying," as we saw in some complaints, they were not as often accusing one another of inner cruelty. "You're 'bad' if you've harmed kids of color," she noted. "If you've harmed disabled kids, you just learn more technical information about disability procedures." One case I saw at OCR exemplified how, in Title VI cases, recipients routinely attempted to defend themselves with statements that their "intentions" were being falsely "interpreted."[28] A mother had confronted her daughter's principal about possible "racism," and the principal had responded by defending his intentions. While the complaint did not specify the "race" of either the principal or the complainant and her child, the phrase "people like you" and the complainants' enraged response to it indicated that the two parties belonged to different racialized groups. I worte in my notes,

> A case with a girl (unknown race!)—mother saying racism—AP class, points deducted, makeup test longer than regular . . . the incidents seem at first glance quite small, but Mom seems very angry. Doesn't mention their race. . . .
>
> Letter from principal says "there was never any intention to refer to race"—comments about "people like you" was referring to *honors* students but could easily be interpreted as "racially prejudicial."

Both complainants and school and district administrators often argued that these differences in the interpretation of whether incidents were "racist" or even racial were caused by racial differences between educators and complainants.[29] Complainants of color and white educators arguing over race's relevance were both intertwined in a "racial" dispute; in a sense, both were suggesting that race was relevant to their everyday interactions. Still, white school and district officials responding to allegations of racial discrimination routinely declared that "race" was totally irrelevant to their own actions.[30]

It seemed to me during the Longview II case that given this resistance, legal proof of discrimination hinged in part on an impossible analytic task: getting inside people's heads to see if they saw children through a "race lens." This was the case in which a father alleged that when his Latino son made a gesture to a friend, the dean had interpreted it as a gang signal solely because the son was Latino. The son insisted that he had been giving his friend the peace sign, not using a gang sign. The dean's disciplinary referral form simply recorded the gang sign he had witnessed. The father felt that Anglo adults were unfairly viewing his son through a racial lens; guffawing, he said that several of his son's so-called gang clothes, such as an earring he wore to school one day, were not red (as district staff claimed of his supposed "gang member" gear) but pink. School district personnel, in turn, felt that the father was imposing a race lens onto their own actions by falsely reading their actions as racially hostile toward the son rather than as matter-of-fact discipline according to school rules about gang-like behavior. Since OCR had no way to see the dean's interpretive lens, we seemed to accept the school official's word rather than that of the student and his parent, while explaining this as an acceptance of school adults' necessary "authority" to make disciplinary decisions. I remarked in my notes: "Truth and Evidence: if the Dean says X and the kid says Y, we trust the Dean, since OCR's not in the business of eroding adult authority."

Corey, the manager overseeing my work on the case, had tried to end the interpretive stalemate by asking "whether the people at the school actually said they wanted to get rid of 'Mexican' gang members, or if they just disciplined the kid for throwing what they said was 'gang signs' in a possibly racial way." I wrote in my notes that "the use of race words makes discrimination claims easier!!" but Longview school personnel had said nothing so explicitly racial.[31] Still, the father maintained that racial assumptions were implicit in educators' actions: "The father reported that school folks said they wanted to get rid of 'gang kids,' but they were talking about the kid and his friends who just *were* Mexican." I considered the possibility of unintentional and even unconscious bias, musing in my notes, "The Dean saw a gang symbol and punished accordingly. . . . But what if Latinos giving peace signs are *more likely seen* as giving gang signs?" While such interpretive lenses seemed a crucial aspect of the incident, they also seemed impossible to prove.[32]

Given the impossibility of determining motivations, OCR investigators and attorneys typically tried to determine the racial nature of harm to the student through comparisons both to other groups' experiences—were white students gesturing to friends also suspended for "gang" signaling?—and to the normal application of the rules—was the Latino boy's suspension carried out according to the school discipline handbook? We would then set forth to see if any existing differences in treatment could be explained by any reason other than race. Yet our legal imperative was still to determine and infer indirectly, through such comparisons, whether "race" was the cause of harmful actions.

This search for causation could not avoid sparking disputes over educators' intentions.[33] As my attorney colleague Fiona, a woman of color, explained to me, no matter what our technical analysis, Title VI investigations seemed to always imply a presumption that OCR was looking for "racists."[34] Some OCR employees were wary of taking on Title VI cases because they anticipated difficult interactions over this implicit accusation. To avoid this sort of controversy, many staffers assigned to Title VI cases investigated them tepidly or tried to close complaints as quickly as possible. I reflected: "Fiona on Title VI: 'Whether cases get shut down or lead to systemic remedies depends on the individuals who get them, and how much work they want to do. People are afraid of race issues and so they don't want to get into Title VI cases—because it seems to involve calling people racists— and people don't like being called racists. But it's not personal racism, it's about a system that treats kids differently, and we need to figure out where the problem is.' "[35] Still, OCR's attempts to figure out "where the problem" *was*—the actual people and actions "treat[ing] kids differently"—always made educators defensive of their "personal" motivations and intentions.

In 1978, Alan Freeman, a critical legal scholar whose work became central to Critical Race Theory, noted that civil rights law was fixated on analyzing "personal racism" rather than the unintentionally "different treatment" of people of color by various actors within biased "systems." Rarely, he argued, did people deem discriminatory the full set of unequal conditions that victims of color experienced; rather, the law named as discrimination only the relatively few acts through which perpetrators intentionally produced those conditions. This framing routinely made it impossible to deem acts racially discriminatory at all. As Freeman argued, a "perpetrator" perspective in U.S. civil rights law—the perspective that the perpetrator is guilty of discrimination only if proven to have intended to harm "victims"—downplays and often dismisses the harm experienced by the victim, or the "victim perspective."[36] Crenshaw et al. describe how this works: the law's "construction of 'racism' from what Freeman terms the 'perpetrator perspective' restrictedly conceived racism as an intentional, albeit irrational, deviation by a conscious wrongdoer from otherwise neutral, rational, and just ways of distributing jobs, power, prestige, and wealth." They continue, "The adoption of this perspective allowed a broad cultural mainstream both explicitly to acknowledge the fact of racism and, simultaneously, to insist on its irregular occurrence and limited significance."[37] In OCR work, educators who felt personally accused of deliberately harming children resisted any move toward accepting the "victims'" perspective on racial inequality in the school system. What most complainants wanted, however, was not so much an admission of individual guilt in particular incidents as the recognition and remedy of the real educational problem: an institutional climate and cumulative series of interactions with educators that students and parents of color experienced as racially hostile, unfair, and deeply consequential for children's educational trajectories.

OCR's evidentiary standards for proof of racial discrimination in schools and districts differed significantly from those it used to determine discrimination against students with disabilities. My colleague Reba, a white lawyer, remarked that while disability cases often concluded with OCR finding violations of civil rights law, administrators often found that racial discrimination cases lacked sufficient proof of discrimination to warrant any further assistance to children. During the Reagan administration, she explained, "Republicans boosted up disability regulations [and] procedures.... Disability cases ... are so clear-cut that if the district doesn't hand the complainant the correct packet of information, it's made a violation." In contrast, she pointed out, "every time you run a Title VI case up the pole" it got turned away as "not conclusive enough." Importantly, disability complaints to OCR typically hinged on whether educators' actions or inaction harmed students *as* disabled students. In complaints demanding disability services, questions of educators' intentions were often basically irrelevant: complaints alleged some denial of required services to a disabled student, matter-of-factly deemed this harm to be "because of" disability, and set forth to get students those services.[38] In contrast, the need to determine whether harm occurred "on the ground" of race always involved dead-end debate over proving harm's racial causation rather than treating its harmful effects.

In determining whether educators' actions constituted racial discrimination, attorneys at OCR had to follow at least one of three analytic tracks established by case law.[39] Two tracks require finding intent, and were often dead ends; only one focuses more usefully on harmful outcomes affecting children. In *disparate treatment analysis*, lawyers examine whether people intentionally treated specific members of racial groups less favorably than members of other racial groups. If educators could explain their action toward children as motivated by some reason other than race, then discrimination was presumed not to exist.[40] For example, a principal could argue to OCR that Juan was suspended for a week not because he was Latino but because he broke a school rule by screaming swear words for the fourth time on the playground, while the white student next to him did not get suspended because he was screaming swear words for the first time. If no evidence suggested that the white student had prior swearing offenses (or that the principal harbored racial animus toward Juan), discrimination could not be found to exist and Juan's suspension would be deemed appropriate.

In *systemic disparate treatment analysis*, lawyers examine whether in the aggregate, through the unequal application of institutional policies and practices, members of racial groups were intentionally treated less favorably than members of other racial groups because of race. OCR complaints often alleged that group-level patterns revealed discriminatory treatment. For example, a complainant could argue, "There are no Latino kids in AP, and the school is half Latino and half white! There's discrimination involved!" Or, "the Special Education classrooms are all black, but the district is only 30 percent black! There's discrimination involved!" These complainants were essentially requesting systemic disparate treatment analysis. Intent still mattered in such cases: if educators could offer a "legitimate educational justification" other than racial group membership for the fact that Latino students were absent from AP classes or African American students were disproportionately placed in Special Education (SPED), then OCR would not find discrimination and the disparity would remain unaddressed.

In systemic disparate treatment complaints, complainants could also allege that rules that seemed neutral, such as "all students who are defiant will be suspended," were being applied in a discriminatory way with visibly unequal consequences. In the Granley school district, for example, students of color were more often deemed "defiant" using the "don't defy" rule in the school disciplinary handbook. The bags and lockers belonging to students of color were searched more frequently than those of white students, using the common rule allowing searches of "suspicious" property. Administrators used the obvious rebuttal that the specific students in question were not searched or deemed "defiant" "because of race": they simply challenged authority figures and invited searches more often than other students did.

The third analytic track available to OCR lawyers, *disparate impact analysis*, did not require any evidence of intent to harm. In disparate impact analysis, lawyers examine whether some ostensibly neutral rule or practice in a school district, such as a test or a disciplinary process, disproportionately affects and harms students belonging to a racial group. Disparate impact analysis of disproportionately black Special Education enrollment, for example, might posit that the tests and procedures used to place students in Special Education disadvantage black students whether or not the adults involved are intentionally biased. Disparate impact analysis offered tools for analyzing harm to large groups of children as race-group members, regardless of whether this harm was intended because of race. As I wrote in my notes after talking to my colleague Reba on another day, disparate impact analysis "was a test developed (in more liberal times) to let discrimination be proven without finding . . . intentional harm. Statistics can themselves *show* disparate [impact]." More precisely, they could trigger an investigation into whether ostensibly race-neutral rules and procedures inadvertently had discriminatory results. Yet disparate impact analysis could only be used to analyze patterns in the aggregate rather than harm to individuals; moreover, we were discouraged from using this analytic tool.

Disparate impact analysis has always been under fire, both in U.S. courts and within OCR. In recent years, its application to racial discrimination cases in courts has been severely restricted, thus limiting the harms to people of color that can be addressed through court lawsuits. Supporters of disparate impact analysis argue that a focus on outcomes rather than intentions is essential for addressing racial inequality today. For example, Charles Lawrence asks, "Does the black child in a segregated school experience less stigma and humiliation because the local school board did not consciously set out to harm her? Are blacks less prisoners of the ghetto because the decision that excludes them from an all-white neighborhood was made with property values and not race in mind?" As Lawrence articulates this view, advocates of disparate impact analysis contend that "the 'facts of racial inequality are the real problem.' They urge that racially disproportionate harm should trigger heightened judicial scrutiny without consideration of motive."[41] Norma Cantu, assistant secretary of OCR during the Clinton administration, stated that although endpoint statistics were not in themselves sufficient evidence of discrimination, they could serve as prompts for important conversations about how discrimination may have occurred.

In contrast, Cantu's successor, Gerald Reynolds, whom Bush appointed to head OCR and then the U.S. Commission on Civil Rights, repeatedly asserted that "statistics" about children, such as racial disparities in academic achievement or racially disproportionate Special Education placement, should not in and of themselves require investigation into potential racial discrimination against those children. Under Reynolds, the sense that employees would not be allowed to pursue disparate impact analysis in evaluating educational opportunity quickly percolated through the ranks of OCR. Employees passed the word that higher-ups would "shut down" statistics-based race complaints if they tried to open them. Several people across the agency told me that even this informally circulating internal perception chilled investigations of harm to children. By 2005, in Bush's second term, the Reynolds argument for avoiding investigating statistically based complaints was formally entered into an updated *Case Resolution and Investigation Manual* guiding OCR employees' work.[42] Thus, OCR administrators discouraged even potential disparate impact cases.

The trend toward restricting the legal tools available to find harm to people of color has been more explicit in the nation's courts. In the

2001 Supreme Court case *Alexander v. Sandoval*, the majority opinion held that individuals could use Title VI only to sue people for clearly "intentional" acts of discrimination. According to the Leadership Conference on Civil Rights Education Fund (2004), this shift made it "easier for publicly funded service programs to discriminate" against people of color through less direct practices by making it harder for individuals to challenge such discrimination through the courts.[43] As a result of *Sandoval*, OCR became one of the last avenues where it was still technically possible to pursue claims of harm to students based on disparate impact and not just on intent—as long as the agency's appointed administrators allowed disparate impact analysis.[44]

In the new civil rights era, in sum, many Americans, supported by legal logic, refuse to accept claims of harm to children of color unless someone can prove that these harms were racially motivated or somehow "caused" by "race." This direct or implied search for intent simply prompts people to defend their intentions.[45] Americans debating opportunity denial often go down a second analytic dead end: determining whether actions and events that children of color experience as harmful are "actually" harmful "because of race" only by comparing those experiences to the experiences of children of other racial groups and, particularly, of white children. Like the search for intent, trying to determine whether children of color were harmed "because of race" in comparison to white children in specific incidents often led to dead-end debates over "proving" how racially inequitable each isolated act was, rather than to analysis of cumulative harm; it, too, prompted educators to resist the claim that students of color had been harmed at all.

## Dead-End Disputes over Comparing the Treatment of Racial Groups

In education, proving that harm is "racial" typically seems to require proving that children of one group have been treated notably worse in specific incidents than children of other racial groups. Our "data request" letter stating the allegations in the Longview II case was a good example: "The District discriminated against the Student by suspending him in September and October 1999 for offenses for which similarly situated non-Latino students were either not suspended or were suspended for shorter terms." In schools enrolling predominantly students of color, students from different groups sometimes compare their treatment by school authorities; for example, African American, Latino, and Filipino students might compare notes on how they were disciplined for similar behavior.[46] In the cases from mixed-race schools that I saw at OCR, black and Latino parents typically compared their children's treatment to the treatment of white children at the same school, who provided a close-up barometer for standard or humane treatment. Sometimes, complainants compared the treatment of students in mostly-of-color schools to the treatment of white students clustered at other district schools. Less frequently, in cases regarding districts enrolling predominantly students of color, complainants compared the treatment of students of color either to the treatment of white students in other districts (a comparison, as described below, that OCR did not pursue) or to humane treatment—implicitly, to how white educators would treat their own children.

In OCR work, formal comparisons to white students' treatment were particularly vexed, even as racial discrimination often did become visible primarily in the differential treatment of children of color and white children. While information on resource disparities between schools or classrooms serving white students and those serving students of color was easily available,[47] often little information was available from which we could make formal comparisons of everyday treatment. Sometimes this was true because the daily treatment white students received was regarded as "standard" and therefore left unrecorded. Sometimes white students did not engage in exactly the same sorts of interactions with white educators as students of color did, making formal comparisons difficult. Sometimes fewer white students became involved in an escalating series of conflicts that triggered parental complaints. And sometimes no white students were around for comparison. None of these reasons for the lack of comparable information was evidence that no harm had occurred to children of color. But, under OCR rules for investigating complaints and determining discrimination, the lack of comparable information on white students often prevented the agency from finding that students of color had suffered from discrimination in their everyday interactions with educators, or even from investigating the situation at all.[48]

In the OCR cases I saw, the experiences of students of color were almost always compared to white students' experiences to ascertain whether, as their parents alleged, they had suffered racial harm. As I noted to myself, "If you want to show *discrimination*, must find the white kids." In one data summary on the Stedley case, I wrote, "Two incidents suggest [isolated?] unfair treatment, and not necessarily b/c of race, since the other children involved were often Hispanic (??)." I first realized what was problematic about this standard procedure when I read a newly filed racial discrimination complaint from the Granley school district about a series of searches of a Latino student's backpack and person. My managers first suggested that the complaint provided too little comparative evidence to be accepted for investigation.

I pondered this question in my notes: "Unclear whether basis is ethnicity. We can't take it unless upon basis of race . . . disability, etc. Need
more evidence. . . . We can't do privacy rights, but can do 'they
searched him because he was Hispanic.' Must prove that *race matters*!
Can't just have 'it happened so it must be discriminatory.' Need comparisons, too, often to whites. Norms that are deviated from because
of your race."

To investigate the complaint about these searches, which included
an allegation that the student, José, was suspended unfairly for written profanity found in his backpack, I had to investigate not just
whether white students' property had ever been suddenly searched at
the school but also whether José's written use of profanity was disciplined more harshly than white students' written use of profanity.
All the searches had involved students of color, raising enough suspicion for us to keep investigating. Yet comparing the various things
that had happened to José with the school's written discipline code
(its "normal" or customary practices) and with the treatment of white
students in precisely analogous situations required extremely detailed
race-group comparisons regarding individual incidents. For example,
the Granley case involved an allegation that José was suspended for
coming to school with a safety pin in his eyebrow. When I visited the
district, an administrator describing the pin gestured with his hands
to indicate a pin nearly six inches long. When I met José, he showed
me a standard-sized safety pin. His mother said the suspension was
an egregious use of discipline for a negligible offense. The district said
that the pin caused social disruption, as students were fascinated by
it, and that it was an example of "defiance," since José had already
been told not to wear it to school. To investigate whether this suspension was "on the ground of race," I found myself comparing the
number of days José had been suspended for wearing the pin to the
number of days white students received for their own "defiance" suspensions, none of which was exactly analogous. I scoured piles of referral forms to see whether white students were disciplined under the
"reprimand" section of the district's disciplinary handbook rather
than under the "suspension" section. I sought data on whether Latino
students were more likely to be sent home while white students received in-school suspensions for similar offenses. While seeking formal "white" comparisons for each type of incident in José's experience, I wrote in my notes that such "COMPARISONS GET VERY DETAILED,
almost silly." What was the utility of having to find racially unequal
treatment in each isolated incident in order to prove harm to José?
Complainants were arguing that racial harm was experienced through
the piling up of moments of differentially harsh treatment, but this

allegation prompted frame-by-frame comparisons to whites that made proving harm more difficult.

The problem of relying analytically on finding comparative data lay not in the "detail" of the incidents but in the routine lack of the comparative data we required to formally prove each incident "racial." In the Granley case, I could not make the comparisons required by legal logic because no one had kept records on the white students whom José's mother said had also been swearing on the playground but had not been suspended. José's mother had said that one of the searches in the office racially discriminated against her son, but I had trouble verifying that it had occurred, since no school official had recorded it. In an endless analytic tailspin, I noted that we needed evidence of "concrete disparities, preferably written down," in order to prove "*Because of race*: discrimination has to be *proven racial*."

The schools I encountered often kept detailed records on conflicts with "problem" students and parents, but they rarely kept records on the treatment of students or parents who were not deemed to cause "problems"—the very records we needed to ascertain whether the treatment of the "problem" students was fair. Parents, too, lacked access to information about other people's children. In the everyday world of school record-keeping, the lack of data on "normal" practice—often, as some would predict, data on the treatment of white students[49]—meant that often the comparisons essential for civil rights analysis did not materialize, and harm to children of color could not be proved. In some cases, school and district treatment of parents and children of color could be compared with policy statements or school handbooks as well as with the treatment of white parents and children, but without data demonstrating the preferable treatment of white people, we often just accepted educators' "educational justifications" of the treatment in question. Comparative analysis of the experiences of white students and students of color was often even more difficult because a substantial and rising proportion of public schools and districts across the country enroll only a few white students.[50] Many urban public school districts serve predominantly or exclusively students of color, although they are diverse in ethnic and racial identification and national origin. In today's segregated urban schools, proving harm or opportunity denial can be deemed impossible in legal terms because the white students necessary for comparison live in other districts. Since the 1970s, courts have restricted lawyers from using civil rights laws to make many interdistrict comparisons of harm,[51] and while I was at OCR, OCR higher-ups who argued that Title VI only "covered" intradistrict comparisons even resisted attempts by some agency lawyers to apply Title VI to interdistrict comparisons of basic resources and opportunities to learn.

Finally, a legalistic habit of scrutinizing one incident after another, taking each in isolation, was often unable to assess the cumulative nature of harm these students and parents experienced.[52] Defensively examining each incident comparatively themselves, school and district staff contended that complainants were "making mountains out of molehills"; they were unwilling to concede that the accumulation of experiences of harm could be harmful.[53]

In defending against every comparative claim of racial harm, educators often overlooked a core educational task: making sure that students and parents of color, as students and parents, feel well treated by educational institutions.[54] Parents and educators became absorbed by the task of "proving" harm to be or not be "racial" and rarely found "effective strategies for real . . . participation of parents and teachers in a collaborative task."[55]

Alternately enabled, infuriated, and prompted further by OCR's intervention, both complainants and recipients struggled even more to prove that children had or had not been harmed because of race. Often, rather than getting down to the educational business of ensuring that students and families, as members of racial groups and as individuals, felt that they would be treated fairly and compassionately, both recipients and complainants were compelled to prove or disprove something that was next to impossible to demonstrate according to OCR's standards.

## The Difficulty of "Proving" Harm "Because of Race" If Harm "Because of Race" Is Denied

The one time I shamefully squirmed out of jury duty in Massachusetts, I did so by telling the judge, who had asked if any of us had experience with the law, that I had worked in a federal agency in which I had learned that all legal "facts" were really matters for dispute. Annoyed, the judge asked me if as a jury member I would be unable to make a clear decision on "facts." "What's a 'fact'?" I asked him. Blustering, he ordered me away from the bench, and I was dismissed.

My comments about the construction of "facts" irritated the judge, but in OCR cases, everyone was aware of disputes over the interpretation of actions and interactions regarding children.[56] Children and families experienced harm; as a discrimination analyst at OCR employed to analyze schooling through a legalistic lens, my job was to evaluate the "facts" of past acts toward students and parents and to determine, with the guidance of an OCR attorney, whether such treatment was on the ground of race. OCR works hard to avoid taking the perspective of either the complainant or the recipient, but the agency's analytic tactics in effect adopt what Freeman has called the "perpetrator perspective." From the beginning of an investigation through its determination, OCR is profoundly skeptical about the complainant's subjective claim of racial harm and will allow as usable evidence only the analysis of students' observable treatment in comparison to that of other groups. To both lawyers and recipients of complaints, the complainants' experience of harm remained just an inner "interpretation" that was often neither objectively documented nor "provable."

A final example illustrates how some white educators and administrators could dismiss complaints even of repeated and egregious acts of explicitly race-based harm toward students and teachers of color. In the rural Quail district, Leyla, a Latina mother who worked as a bilingual teacher at the district's main high school, complained that the predominantly white school and district environment was racially hostile to students of color, most of whose families had arrived in the area relatively recently. She provided a long list of examples of everyday interactions that she considered incontrovertible evidence of this hostility. She described how one black student, in line for an athletics physical, had heard a white student in line taunt, "All niggers go to the back of the line." The white coach and deans had accepted the white students' explanation that they used this word only to tease one another, and the student who had made the comment had not been disciplined according to the school's code on harassment; Leyla noted with aggravation that he had even been able to go to the prom.

Leyla listed other examples of racial harm she had been collecting at the school, including a Korean student called "chink," a Chinese American girl who found "fuck China" printed inside her world history book, Latino students routinely called racial slurs during gym class, and her own discovery of a swastika and racial slurs written on the girls' bathroom walls and doors, including the unusually explicit "we hate Elizabeth because she is Japanese." She alleged that history teachers at the high school had made "racial comments" and "racial remarks toward Mexicans." Even the principal had made "racial remarks" in the teachers' lounge; once he had said he would not "refuse to shoot" were he "holding a gun to a black man's head." She also wrote that "our entire bilingual population is [subjected] to remarks by some of the teaching staff. Some would rather not have Mexicans in their classes." She offered as evidence a math teacher's statement that if immigrant students were "going to be here, they should learn to speak English before coming."

Despite Leyla's long catalogue of evidence of explicitly racial harms to students of color, the principal and many teachers, all of them white, argued to her and later to me that she and her husband, a white man who also worked in the district, were "making a mountain out of a molehill." Just one district administrator, a white man who told me Leyla was a respected teacher whose allegations he had to believe, set out with an unusual lack of skepticism to investigate and sanction any such adult or student "racism" in his district. He left the district for another job shortly after we resolved the case with a compromise of some faculty diversity trainings. My notes, taken after a conversation with Leyla, demonstrated the more typical dismissals she and her husband had received within the district in response to their complaints of everyday racial harm.

> Complainant's husband had confrontation with teacher (who had "Jap" cartoon on bulletin board)—teacher said he made a mountain out of a molehill.
>
> Principal has made numerous comments about ethnicity—has been asked to apologize by husband, who also teaches at the school (principal joked to husband that blacks only good for athletes).
>
> French teacher (Latino)—presented letter (without principal's name) about this to the school board. This was interpreted as white bashing. Classified staff told him, "Why are you upset? We hired another Mexican."
>
> (Staff of color uncomfortable/harassed.)
>
> (White) vice principal told complainant: diversity training won't work—would just waste time. Did nothing about it. Said it wasn't some inner city.
>
> Slurs in the gym line: kids didn't mean it. . . .
>
> Nazi sign in bathroom—student videotaped it. Other employees can't talk about harassment—how the district does this.
>
> Harassment by teachers: using "Jap" in class. She went to history department head. Mr. Lambert, history teacher. He was offended—he said that they *did* have a grasp of racism.

Would the educators and administrators who denied that such acts were harmful to students and teachers of color benefit much from the "diversity training" they finally agreed to? Clearly, their dealings with OCR had not convinced them that the district had any "race" problem that called for a solution. Like many white educators I met who were confronted by claims that various everyday interactions were harmful to people of color as such, they continued to argue that necessary "proof" of harm to students of color "because of race" was lacking.[57]

When the moment came for OCR to determine the existence or nonexistence of discrimination, the legal bureaucracy often argued essentially the same thing. Although the agency did set forth to remedy many "problems" uncovered in districts after promising them that we would not formally "find" discrimination, in the end, OCR was most likely to determine formally that no demonstrable "racial discrimination" had occurred at all. In the Longview I case, the newspaper article misreporting OCR's "findings," which I described as a "PR nightmare" for both OCR and the district, revealed accurately just how unusual an official finding of discrimination was: "Office of Civil Rights officials said they investigated more than 5,000 complaints in 1998 and found only six districts at fault, as they did with Longview Unified."

Districts spent their energy trying to disprove legally impermissible harm; instead, they could have been working cooperatively with complainants to analyze how students and parents of color experienced practices and policies as harmful and how such practices and policies could be improved to avoid this experience of harm in the future. Just as a teacher confronted with a student's or parent's charge of "racism" in her classroom typically spends her energy denying the accusation rather than engaging the more difficult and nuanced question of how to improve teacher-student or teacher-parent relationships,[58] local arguments typically kept raging over the summative question of whether illegal racial discrimination had occurred at all.[59]

Such debates over harm "because of race" are ubiquitous in many American schools, though they often take a less explicitly legalistic form. In settings where students of different "racial groups" attend school together, or where students and educators of different racial groups work together, students and adults routinely debate which acts and interactions are "racist,"[60] and important discussions of harm too often turn into unresolvable battles over "proof." In the districts I saw at OCR, educators' defensive insistence that they had treated students of color "fairly," or "the same" as they did or would treat white students, met the abstract, rhetorical standards of equality that complainants shared. But parents and school district personnel held very different opinions about what specific acts should be deemed harmful "on the ground of race." The clash of perspectives we navigated in OCR investigations was not a clash between "legal" and "local" ways of thinking but between divergent views of harm to children.[61] Arguments over truth and fault are really arguments over the interpretation of events,[62] and different actors in the same scene often saw the "facts" through very different lenses.

When describing how school and district staffers dismissed their claims of harm to children of color, complainants of color typically analyzed the dynamic of poor communication itself as racial. Several parents of color spoke of communities that were "99 percent white" or of being the first Latino or black families in the "mostly Caucasian" school district. The mother in the Granley district case wrote, "I would like to state that there has never been another expulsion in the history of [this] elementary school, which is predominantly Caucasian, Anglo-Saxon, Aryan, etc. This would also include all but one of the staff members. That in itself would seem a little suspicious according to ethnic balancing. " The Quail complainant, Leyla, said to me that in the "predominantly Anglo" town where she lived, people knew almost nothing about "diversity" and thought that being different was "about having orange hair." Having one's complaints dismissed in a "90 percent Anglo" context seemed like being framed as "difficult" because one was different.[63] Even in districts filled with students of color, OCR complainants all said their children were treated as implicitly less worthy than the children and parents elsewhere who were privileged to be perceived and treated as "normal."

On both sides, an undercurrent of depression and disappointment, as well as anger, pervaded these disputes about failed communication and collaboration. Through their anger, both educators and parents expressed wishes that they had better relationships. In describing thwarted attempts to communicate with educators, most parents framed themselves as unhappy "outsiders" in the local educational community. Ms. Stedley, talking of her unsuccessful attempts to talk to school and district educators about her grandson's experiences, described her feelings of separation from "that school" and "this district," not "our school" or "my district." One parent filing a complaint of racial discrimination, according to the investigator handling the case, seemed to "like to go to the press" with her accusations and had received a letter from the district saying she was "unwelcome on campus." OCR was "trying to mediate," but the parent-educator relationship had already soured beyond repair.

Colleagues told me about some cases in which people of color accused other people of color of discrimination; one common example was Latino parents arguing that black administrators neglected Latino English-language learners. Complainants of color filed some complaints against districts run by administrators of color, even, sometimes, with black complainants accusing black administrators of treating black children less well than white children or less well than they would treat white children in other districts. Most of the Title VI complaints I investigated, however, were filed by black and Latino parents in white-run schools and districts.[64] Some of these educational settings enrolled predominantly white students; in some, students of color were the majority. Asian American children were often included in OCR complaints regarding English-language learners and in some complaints of peer harassment or racially hostile climate, but Asian Americans did not so regularly file individual K–12 complaints at

OCR, though one survey of community leaders in our region made clear they, too, had many concerns.[65] By far, the majority of Title VI complaints I encountered and heard about at OCR alleged everyday injustice toward black and/or Latino children in districts run by white educators. Most argued that white educators both committed and condoned everyday harms, and everyday denials of opportunities to learn and thrive, that would do lasting harm to the academic and personal futures of the children.

The more loudly such parents or advocates expressed their grievances about what happened in schools and districts, the more white educators regarded them as "kooks" who saw animus against children of color where there was none, who saw race-based inequality where none existed, and who saw purposeful harm in the mundane everyday acts that busy teachers and administrators took toward all children—in short, who unfairly imposed a "race lens" on everyday life. Complainants arguing that children were experiencing inequitable treatment "because of race" seemed to many school and district staff to be whining about nonexistent insults and dredging up non-racial wrongs.

By the end of their interactions with OCR, few complainants or recipients invoked civil rights law as an impartial force that would "decide" their disputes objectively or fairly. Both parents of color and white educators and administrators came to see OCR as a collection of biased analysts wielding a quixotic set of legal tools. They had engaged in endless disputes over "proof," clustered around two core analytic and social problems of the "fragmented" new civil rights era: the problem of proving that harm is "caused" and "motivated" by "race," and the problem of finding sufficient evidence to prove that, in specific, isolated incidents in everyday life, people of color are harmed in comparison to white people treated preferentially in similar incidents. Throughout, the educators and administrators against whom complaints were lodged had responded to claims of harm to children with massive denial of race's relevance, which in the end enabled them to avoid starting to truly confront the events and patterns at all.

At OCR, where we were required to use legalistic tools to analyze and determine discrimination, it could take months, even years, to investigate and resolve complaints of harm "because of race." Students' parents and guardians, as well as their principals and superintendents, called OCR repeatedly to mention new altercations that had erupted between the adults involved: a complainant angrily denounced the school system to the newspapers; a father and his son's principal had a screaming match outside the principal's office; a district representative confronted a teacher advocate in a threatening way after school. As I heard about and mediated these arguments by phone from my government cubicle and, at times, in person, I stopped to scribble in my notes to myself a question that a newly arrived Martian might ask of American education: If everyone here apparently agreed that adults should not harm students of color, why were we arguing so much over whether they had actually harmed them "because of race"? The arguing itself seemed on its face to hurt the children in question more by damaging the adult relationships surrounding the child. Why, I wondered, didn't we stop arguing and get down to the business of figuring out specific ways to improve the schooling experiences of students of color? As I discuss in chapter 2, in debates over opportunity, OCR often tried to improve relationships between the parties through another habit of rebuttal that backfired on children: refusing to name harms or opportunity denials at all. While OCR thinks about racial harm with a lawyer's brain, it talks about racial harm with a politician's tongue.

# Harms to Children of Color Should Not Be Discussed

> You win more bees with honey than with vinegar.
> —*White educator, after OCR employees helped her district plan to provide learning opportunities to English-language learners*

Arriving with my coffee at our regional OCR office each day, I often set to work typing letters reminding educators that the law ultimately enabled OCR to tell them how to equalize opportunity. OCR began and concluded all investigations by sending letters to districts announcing its authority to enforce civil rights laws on all districts that receive federal funds. In this sense, in Title VI cases we positioned ourselves publicly as an agency ready to enforce everyday justice. Yet during my day, I would spend much of my time talking to managers, colleagues, and educators themselves about what not to write in these letters, so as not to be too forceful as we wielded federal power to call for specific opportunities for students of color. Though we employees were positioned in debates with educators to describe past harms and potential efforts toward everyday justice, we often told ourselves to avoid discussing these harms too clearly or directly, or in too much detail. More often than not, to please both managers and local educators, we spent our time deleting specific descriptions of the acts that harmed children of color and the acts that might help them. In this chapter, I explore this new civil rights era response to demands for everyday justice for these students and the potential consequences of talking about opportunity vaguely and hesitantly rather than specifically and in full.

At OCR, we often gave one particularly self-conscious reason why we should not discuss everyday harms to local children, or remedies for them, in detail: we wanted to avoid being perceived as micromanaging local educators' behavior, pushing what external and internal critics called the unwarranted federal "prescription" of change.[1] We were particularly concerned that critics would see us as overstepping the federal role regarding children of color. External critics routinely lambasted OCR for asking districts to provide particular opportunities to children of color without a formal finding of discriminatory intent to harm children "because of race." OCR was also particularly criticized in the papers and even to Congress for making too specific suggestions to local educators on how to provide opportunity to children of color in their everyday lives. We employees and our managers often responded to these pressures from higher-ups, educators, and external critics by purposefully deleting from our written remedies the very details regarding opportunity provision that complainants had demanded we analyze.

To be fair, we also deleted these controversial details from our resolution documents because educators would agree to assist children if we did so. Educators often told OCR that they would pursue Title VI remedies only if particular alleged harms to children, or particular requirements for serving them, were deleted from the public documents we created to "close" complaints.[2] We knew, too, that wrangling over the details of resolution documents could risk an angry stalemate between educators and OCR—and would help the children less than a collaborative relationship would. If our recommendations were too forceful, educators would resent the children and families even as they seemingly agreed to comply:[3] educators working in schools and districts, we knew, controlled both how resources were used[4] and how children were treated in everyday interactions. Thus, my colleagues reserved forceful and punitive discourse in resolution letters for what they called "bad faith" districts. From my first days at OCR, I was advised to steer case resolution as often as possible to an arbitrated compromise. Yet in this process of reducing our "force" in debates over opportunity, we OCR employees often purposefully failed to pinpoint, verbally or in writing, specific harmful acts in students' everyday educational lives and specific remedies for providing everyday justice. In this, we were especially purposeful when we were discussing harm to children of color.

As my colleagues noted, if educators wanted to improve opportunity provision proactively, we could support them in creative efforts to do so by writing minimal resolution documents, giving them maximum flexibility in spearheading local plans to respond to complaints. But this strategy of naming as few harms and remedies as possible only worked when the educators were clear on the nature of past harm and committed to preventing its future occurrence. In the quest to avoid "prescription" in the more resistant districts, we often toned down our suggestions so much that we barely mentioned the harm being remedied or the need for a specific remedy, or described only the few remedial actions that would not cause controversy with educators or with our own anxious higher-ups. Acquiescing to the common new civil rights era rebuttal that these everyday harms should not be discussed, we sometimes failed to clarify why and how everyday justice could be pursued. In doing so, we ducked one of OCR's unarguable federal responsibilities: naming opportunity denials.[5]

A colleague once described the paradox to me: OCR's work to help ensure equal opportunity in the nation's schools required using federal force and adversarial legal tools to convince educators to comply "voluntarily" with the law.[6] Yet the main reason we focused on gentle rather than forceful convincing, and deleted controversial details to foster such "collaboration," was that today, OCR rarely makes formal findings of illegal discrimination and even more rarely revokes federal funding if it does.[7] By 2000, OCR's reticence to levy the "punitive" consequences possible under Title VI had us deleting those detailed descriptions, but the agency's basic desire to avoid "prescription" of opportunity for students of color has deep roots. Understanding OCR's behavior in opportunity debates today requires stepping back for a moment into history, to the time when OCR was first charged with enforcing the most basic of daily educational opportunities for students of color: a school not segregated by law. For OCR, almost from its inception, demanding specific opportunities for students of color was a project to be avoided.

## OCR's History of "Toning Down" Communications about Harm to Students of Color

Only in its first few years of actively enforcing Title VI did OCR actively "terminate" funding to school districts that refused to desegregate schools in compliance with federal law.[8] President Nixon vowed not to let OCR cut off funding to defiantly segregated districts, gutting the threat of force underlying OCR's Title VI efforts in the South and forcing OCR away from enforcing desegregation altogether.[9] OCR quickly switched from pursuing hundreds of fund-termination proceedings to initiating none of them.[10] At the same time, OCR's annual reports to Congress regarding Title VI enforcement began to include explicit statements about an agency preference for "negotiation" rather than punitive communications with districts.[11]

This stance continued through the Nixon and Ford administrations. As a report of the Commission on Civil Rights argued in 1975 about the previous year's work at "communicating" and "negotiation," OCR's resistance to invoking punitive "sanctions"[12] for segregation was now gutting Title VI's ability to actually assist "minority children" via desegregation. OCR talking gently, the report implied, would not help children if the agency's goal was to make assistance to them seem unnecessary: its "reluctance in recent years to utilize the administrative sanction in [cases] where school districts are known to be in noncompliance has [created] irreparable damage to the strength of the Title VI program and to the minority children in those districts."[13]

Even an integration-minded OCR chief appointed during the Carter administration did not pursue any fund terminations.[14] In the Reagan era, as OCR did little proactive work of any kind to examine or equalize opportunities for students of color,[15] representatives argued explicitly in annual reports to Congress that a "conciliatory" stance achieved the best results for children[16] and that OCR's "spirit of conciliation" prompted a strategy of "negotiating" in "good faith" and working "cooperatively."[17]

Although the National Education Association called Bill Clinton's OCR assistant secretary, Norma Cantu, "the Enforcer"[18] (Cantu did spearhead new Title VI initiatives on issues like college admissions and "minorities" in special education), working at OCR under Cantu still meant avoiding both punitive discourse and punitive action. Cantu promoted to Congress OCR's important stance of "working with" and "partnering" with the "education community,"[19] but such "collaboration" was typically posed in direct contrast to "force": Cantu's pragmatic statements of a desire to work more effectively with educators typically also suggested plans for less enforcement rather than more. OCR's 1995 annual report to Congress stated that "OCR knows that problems that are addressed immediately can often be resolved more amicably and less intrusively. Thus, OCR staff are on the telephone or on-site as quickly as possible, working with parents and schools to identify and remedy problems of legal discrimination. In cases where agency intervention is not appropriate, or where the facts provide an insufficient basis to find that there is illegal discrimination, OCR can also end its involvement more quickly."[20] In my region, managers clearly communicated an agencywide preference for "collaboration," posing such efforts in direct contrast to more "punitive" and "proactive" efforts like the "compliance review": showing up to investigate a district unannounced and uninvited by a complainant. As our office director put it to us in an address to our investigation team, "Compliance reviews put people/the state on notice that OCR is a force to be reckoned with," but OCR was doing little "proactive work."

Our drive to "collaborate" *rather* than appear to be "a force to be reckoned with" had a direct effect on the language we used with districts: in Title VI cases, we often went out of our way to downplay our own potential use of "force" and to position ourselves as an agency that would not press too hard for everyday justice no matter what we found in our investigation. After my first conversation with district representative Anne Hardy in Longview, I kicked myself for not sand-wiching my punitive-sounding accusation of harm to LaRon within gentle reassurances of OCR's desire to "help" Longview. My task, I reminded myself, was to convey clearly that OCR wanted to assist the district rather than punish it with "negative consequences."

> I don't think I gave her enough of an impression that OCR can help, wants to work on things, etc. . . . I should have said more that we want to work with them to document whether the response was adequate and if not, that we can help it be so. I think I came off as saying if it wasn't adequate, there would be some negative consequences. . . . Oh well.

Of course, just showing up as a federal agency with the power to inves-tigate potential "discrimination" could still prod some educators to im-prove their treatment of the children in question. As a colleague put it to me after we both left the agency, "Ninety percent of the work of OCR was done in picking up the phone and saying, 'Hi, I'm OCR.' " Sometimes, a complainant simply filing an OCR complaint of racial discrimination could prompt some assistance to children as districts moved quickly to avoid public embarrassment.[21] For example, months after she had filed the complaint discussed later in this chapter, one parent reported to OCR that this action alone seemed to make school staff avoid unnecessarily disciplining her son.

> Things have changed more recently. Now José is being treated with more respect, in the past six weeks. Fewer adults are watching him. He is now being treated "how my son should have been treated as the beginning." The OCR request for documents may have served the purpose, may be turning the school around.

Still, though educators were treating José more carefully as the investi-gation progressed, they would remain fundamentally skeptical about the validity of her complaints of harm. In the end, the district's represen-tatives would agree to take a few actions included in a resolution letter, but they confessed privately to me that even that much felt unnecessary.

Hearing such skeptical confessions all the time from the educators we got to know over the phone, OCR colleagues urged one another to avoid blatantly "punitive" language in describing necessary efforts for opportunity provision: we knew we could not change their everyday acts toward students simply by issuing forceful decrees.[22] We at OCR ostensibly had control over federal dollars, but we rarely, if ever, invoked that power; where we had most control was over districts'

public reputations. "OCR 'policy' can come across to districts as punitive," I jotted after one dinner conversation with a D.C. colleague.
"Collaborative work in resolutions is much better for kids."

"Collaboration" in the Title VI arena seemed particularly important
to some: at a conference I organized at OCR, Gloria Ladson-Billings,
later the president of the American Educational Research Association,
told the audience that racial equality would likely be achieved not
through federal imposition but only when, through collaboration, educators came to want to work continually toward racially equal opportunity even when "there are no rules." Educators in attendance agreed
that any remedy, such as the "diversity training" that OCR routinely
ordered for educators, "won't work" if it was "seen as a punishment
or order." As I wrote dutifully in my notes after a conversation with
educators at the conference, "What *incentives* can be offered for districts to do a better job?"

So, in our desire to avoid "punishment," we instead tried to offer
districts "incentives" to avoid federal sanction and to inquire locally
into methods for offering equal opportunity. But this resulted in a fundamental murkiness about OCR's ultimate power to name harms or
to tell educators to do anything. This murkiness was particularly embedded in the ways we described the past and future treatment of children of color. As the Longview I case was ending, Hardy broke down
in tears after the newspaper fiasco about OCR's "bullying" and Stedley
reported to the papers that OCR's judgment wasn't "harsh enough"—
and I sat at my desk worrying about the ambiguous power of OCR's
language. As I wrote in my notes, we had made no specific statements
of "findings" about past harms in our letters to Longview and never
mentioned OCR's power to enforce the remedies we had proposed:
"Paper comes out saying we made formal findings of discrimination.
We didn't *really* . . . we hedged and wheedled our way. Saying we had
*concerns*, to a resolution where they agreed/'volunteered' to do stuff."

We at OCR often marched into investigations with strength, confident in our warrant to collect data on the treatment of children of
color, but we particularly "hedged and wheedled" our way to case
closure by toning down our language about harm and about OCR's
power to "force" educators to provide opportunity or remedy harm
in any particular way.[23] As I show in the next section, we toned down
the language of accusation, our descriptions of our investigation, and
our suggestions for remedy, at each stage promising educators that
we would delete from public documents any language that was too
forceful or specific about providing equal opportunity to students of
color. In doing so, we often failed to focus attention on crucial aspects
of students' educational experiences.

## EXAMPLES OF TONING DOWN OCR COMMUNICATIONS CIRCA 2000

### Toning Down the Language of Accusation

One day I left a message with a district representative to "set up a time to discuss" a case that was nearing completion. I recorded in my notes my persistent worry that accusing the district of actual "problems," and accordingly "pressuring" the representative to provide the students in question with opportunity in any particular way, would make her resist the agreement even more stridently. My "fear," I wrote, was "that she will feel pressured, annoyed, will get angry . . . [but] what can you do? We want to close cases. If we're saying that there is a *problem*, this leads to controversy regardless."[24]

During investigations, we often responded to the potential for educators feeling "pressured"—and becoming stubborn, which we sensed might delay the closing of cases—by softening our own language of accusation about potential "problems" in their treatment of children. Some such softening occurred from the outset of any case to help educators weather what one of them called the "shock to the system" of receiving an OCR letter with racial discrimination allegations. We would typically call the district, ask for the representative who would be assigned to an OCR case, and verbally alert him or her to the coming letter, offering assurances that the investigation would help pinpoint what "everyone wanted"— fair treatment for students. We also toned down the language of accusation when heading toward complaint resolution. Before I called one district to resolve a case, one manager told me that we should "prime [the district] to know we have 'concerns' so they're not shocked by the letter." Another colleague described her phone tactics this way: "I try to take the argument of 'well, neither of us wants unequal treatment, I'm sure . . . let's see if it's unequal . . . oh, wow, it is!' You need to practice a surprised look."

At any point in the complaint process, it was sometimes crucial to soften the letters' inherently accusatory text about "discrimination" allegations by carefully minding our language over the phone. But this did not always work: some administrators simply insisted repeatedly that they had not "discriminated" and turned the analysis immediately and repeatedly on students or their parents instead. After OCR first requested data regarding the allegedly discriminatory discipline of one Latino student, one superintendent responded that the school district had simply "provided the student the same respect, courtesy, and guidance that are afforded to all students that attend the school. Each student is treated with dignity and respect regardless of nationality or ethnicity. All students are expected to abide by the rules of the school."

Because we knew that most recipients of complaints would respond by denying their own culpability like this, when we called districts about an impending letter, we often offered them the chance to resolve the complaint immediately through a negotiated settlement with the complainant. We called this practice "early resolution," mediating a negotiated settlement in lieu of conducting an investigation.[25] At times, we accomplished an early resolution without ever sending a formal letter relaying the complainant's accusations. This tactic saved time when both parties were amenable, but at times it also allowed us to avoid investigating allegations. As I wrote in my notes on one case,

> I find myself saying that it might be best to head off a full-on investigation, since OCR has strict standards for what it considers evidence of "discrimination." . . . I say this because she has *so many complaints*, I think, and I got baffled by the idea of investigating *each incident*.

In disability cases in particular, administrators often accepted the early resolution offer and closed the complaint with a few remedial actions suggested by the complainant. Districts could simply give children the Special Education evaluation or service their parents had demanded. In many disability cases, a colleague said, the players had already scheduled Individualized Education Program (IEP) meetings to resolve the issue. On the other hand, in many race cases, educators were either ignoring complainants' demands or complainants sought more systemic remedies, making early resolution impossible or unadvisable. In the Quail district, I suggested early resolution to resolve a complaint of a racially hostile environment, but the parent said she had already told district administrators that she wanted "a change of attitude" districtwide. She also wanted "the district to admit that they have a problem," a classic request of complainants seeking Title VI remedy via OCR. She also wanted the district to form conversation groups between students and faculty, and to hold diversity training by "professional people."[26] She also thought that Quail "needed to be monitored" by OCR. Later in the case, she described a local mediation meeting with "all the people she complained about" and confessed her worry that while some administrators appeared "willing to negotiate," she would get only "lip service" or would "be attacked by all of them at once."

Within OCR, we also feared "attack" for proposing ways of offering opportunity to students of color. My colleagues sometimes pursued early resolution in Title VI cases because they were deeply anxious that external and internal critics might "shut down" any particularly active complaint investigation and resolution. Our fear of seeming too "proactive" was particularly strong when children of color were being assisted. My colleagues particularly feared being seen as "prescribing" services for English-language learners (ELLs), who were predominantly Latino and Asian American students. Politicians and public figures critical of bilingual education for Latino students had complained directly to OCR's chief D.C. administrators that OCR employees told districts that bilingual education was one of many legal ways to serve students learning English as a second language. (In fact, research evidence showed it was one of several effective ways that districts could offer equal academic opportunity to ELLs as the law required.) In some regions, the agency's fear of antagonizing these critics resulted in OCR employees asking districts to "volunteer" a "plan" to offer services to English-language learners before OCR conducted any investigation of them. A colleague described how staff in another regional office would "usually go to a district with a few hundred LEP [limited English proficient] kids and say, 'We won't investigate you if you demonstrate a program'" on paper, without ever examining whether the students were being assisted to access academic content as the law mandated.

Later, under the George W. Bush administration, OCR employees were encouraged to "mediate" resolutions between complainants and recipients before investigating at all; as one colleague put it, this tactic broadcast to the public that "we [OCR] don't know what you've done or what you need to do, but if you can agree on this we'll go away." These many refusals to investigate meant that local educators were never engaged in specific discussions of how they might serve students of color equitably on a daily basis.

According to some educators, OCR's most effective efforts circa 2000 utilized a mix of gentle and forceful communications but always geared those tactics toward explaining specifically to educators how and why particular acts denied students opportunity in civil rights terms or might be helpful in achieving equal opportunity. One day over lunch at the office, for example, I met satisfied visiting representatives from Greenville, a district where a colleague had worked to help develop a detailed plan for offering ELLs adequate opportunities to access the common academic curriculum as the law required. Before OCR became involved, the district had not been offering any purposeful "ELD" (English language development) for English-language learners (whom the district here called LEP, or "limited English proficient," students), violating federal law.

As I paraphrased in my notes, the Greenville district educators first suggested that OCR had accomplished much of its work—of equalizing opportunity provision to ELLs—through the basic threat of consequences. The educators laughed, over lunch, about a pre-OCR "briefing" where district administrators had instructed them to tell OCR investigators things like "multicultural education is infused throughout all aspects of our program" so they could avoid OCR intervention. The educators joked about having a "set" of bilingual materials in the district that they could show visitors but was never used. "OCR involvement, making ELD a compliance/accountability issue," had "made top administrators *care* about getting compliance." OCR employees' "personal presence" had "promoted" in the district both "knowledge of LEP programming" and concern "for LEP kids' education at all."

Still, while OCR could "spark a focus" on learning opportunity for ELLs simply by its forceful evaluative presence, "commitment" to serving such children well had to "be built internally" through collaboration. According to the district's LEP coordinator, it did help that "people doing LEP work within the district knew that OCR would be the hammer as needed," but OCR would always "win more bees with honey than with vinegar."

Thus in Greenville, OCR's more collaborative work had prompted educators to pinpoint their own specific ways of assisting students. Their district, like many, had relatively few people who adamantly resisted providing any services for English-language learners, for whom OCR had to be the "hammer" to "force" "compliance." It also included "people/advocates who want reform and are afraid to lose their jobs" at the hand of hostile district administrators, and who appreciated the chance to brainstorm about serving ELLs more successfully and in accordance with the law.[27] In this context, they said, OCR had accomplished the most by "investing" in "homegrown expertise" on LEP issues, so that local educators could suggest concrete steps forward to one another. Those in charge of LEP services in Greenville had previously been "pretty good . . . at ascertaining how well students know English, but not anything else," these educators reported. OCR had helped the district equip itself to serve LEP students by connecting district leaders with local and state educators who did have ELD knowledge and by facilitating connections between Greenville and other districts so they could "help" one another.

Still, the "power of law," as I paraphrased one Greenville educator, was to raise the stakes beyond such "collaboration" and "help" to also push "compliance."[28] OCR's presence meant that "evaluations may depend on" actually providing ELLs with daily opportunities to access the curriculum as the law required. Many educators in Greenville were less "worried about the community uproar of being charged discriminatory" than "about having to make real changes."

Exchanges like this suggested that OCR seemed to prompt the most everyday justice for children when assuming a stance of collaboration backed up by potential confrontation, while talking very specifically with districts and schools about how they could pursue equal opportunity. This stance was a difficult balancing act in an agency whose core tools prompted confrontation but whose central method of avoiding confrontation was to avoid discussing harms to children in any detail. More typically in the ELL realm, this same pressure to resist talking "prescriptively" induced managers and lower-down employees to delete from resolution documents any language describing specific academic opportunity denials to ELLs and specific suggestions for ways districts might equalize their opportunities to learn English. One colleague described how she finally closed a longstanding complaint by hinting minimally at OCR's "concerns" about inadequately assisting English-language learners. District representatives told her later that given the plan's vagueness regarding serving ELLs, "we never knew what to do. And anyway, you just said you had 'concerns,' and never found a violation!"

Under the administration of George W. Bush, OCR employees investigating Title VI cases were expected to make a formal finding of discrimination before guiding schools and districts toward any more equitable policies and practices. As a colleague (no longer at the agency) put it to me, the Bush-era requirement on the one hand reframed OCR as a federal agency with "teeth": district administrators might feel that "OCR people do real investigations, and we're scared of them." When OCR went "right to resolution" in the middle of an investigation, my colleague said, "people agree to create a bunch of paper, 'don't investigate us if we do blah blah,' and the case is *closed* but change isn't necessarily *achieved*. OCR also looks easily avoided." Yet since OCR was likely to not prove racial discrimination, it had little chance to talk about assisting children of color. As one OCR employee told me in 2005, the agency was providing far more guidance on how not to analyze and find racial discrimination than internal direction on how to do so. In a search through OCR's current internal Web repository of "policy guidance" regarding investigating and determining Title VI discrimination, he had found no published guidance on investigating language discrimination against ELLs, racial harassment, or the disparate distribution of educational resources by race.

When I worked at OCR during the Clinton-Bush transition, we often downplayed the need to undertake specific acts of opportunity equalization *after* investigation, during the resolution stage. We did so when we replaced the language of formal "findings" with the gentle language of "concerns." This tactic usefully allowed districts to make changes and save face, but it also removed the pressure to talk about helping students.

## Toning Down the Language of Complaint Resolution

Under Cantu, if any of the data we gathered suggested a potential civil rights problem, we were allowed to mention these problems as OCR "concerns" to districts and to ask districts to consider how to remedy them. In a restrictive legal context where we were far more likely to not formally find racial discrimination than to find it, OCR's discourse of "concerns" was often the only way we could get educators to act to protect children of color from harm that they and their families experienced.

This language of "concerns" was technically weak on legal grounds, but in some cases it was quite powerful socially, if our concerns were discussed sufficiently. Whatever OCR puts in writing in the analytic section of a resolution letter, either as formal "findings" or as "concerns," becomes public record. Both recipients and complainants get copies; the media may publish letters of findings, along with the Voluntary Resolution Plans (VRPs) we negotiated to close complaints, if complainants release them; and all OCR documents can be requested through the Freedom of Information Act.

Knowing the potential public visibility of every OCR document, many district representatives agreed to pursue remedies as soon as OCR said it might write a letter specifically stating that OCR had found no "discrimination" but had some "concerns." After a final conversation with a complainant who had read a closure letter describing OCR's "concerns," I wrote in my notes that "she wanted me to say they'd discriminated," but "the district wanted to not admit discrimination. They made all these proactive changes but wouldn't admit racial discrimination of any kind." Indeed, some districts expended substantial energy coming up with voluntary agreements to resolve "concerns" as a specific way to keep the word "discrimination" from being used in OCR's final assessment. As I wrote in reaction to one complaint, sometimes this energy seemed focused less on helping children than on deleting the public language of "discrimination."

> I realized last night that I was confused about why districts wouldn't just make these changes immediately. If *they* are so worried about *not* discriminating, why would we have to argue with them at all? Why couldn't we just suggest changes and implement them?
>
> It's because what they're *really* afraid of is being *accused* of *having* discriminated—the public nightmare of the accusation of "racism" itself. Discriminating *itself* is not so troublesome.

While some districts pursued substantive remedies for children in exchange for the "concerns" language, other district representatives made clear that the "concerns" language did not prompt them to want to discuss assistance to children with any detail or real seriousness. During the remedy stage, some districts seemed most committed to keeping the remedies described in closure documents as minimal as possible. For example, in the Longview III case, Laura Cachon had alleged in part that her children were harassed by peers and security guards, and that extra visiting and parking rules had been imposed on her and her husband as one of the school's few Latino families. In her case, we wrote a draft closure letter and VRP noting our "concerns" about these incidents and describing how the district would largely resolve these concerns by implementing the anti-harassment policy developed recently to close the Longview I (Stedley) case. Still, the administrators and their attorney made clear that they resented even this written implication of their fault, and in doing so they revealed that their voluntary efforts in response to our "concerns" in the Stedley case did not seem necessary either. An administrator from Longview had called me to explain his colleagues' negative reaction to our draft documents stating OCR's "concerns" about the experiences of children and parents in the district. As I wrote in my notes, their own "basic concern," he said, was that the very existence of a VRP in the Longview III case implied that "discrimination" had in fact occurred as Laura Cachon had alleged. Understandably, given the recent media fiasco in the Stedley case (see chapter 1), his colleague had "a concern about 'this family' [the Cachons] taking the VRP and turning it into 'yes, the school did discriminate' and then 'taking it to the media.' " I paraphrased the administrator's worries in my notes: "*doing* these things in the VRP is no problem, but they're afraid of what the family will *make* of it." The district said it preferred that OCR write no resolution plan at all but rather produce a "letter saying what they were actually doing per their existing [anti-harassment] policy" created in the first Longview case. There was just one bit of language the district did want included in the closure documents: the "critical thing," the Longview lawyer repeated from the other end of the line, was for OCR to state explicitly that there was "no violation." The lawyer then added revealingly that in the first (Stedley) case, too, "There was no violation, though." The district was "not saying there were never errors—an error did happen," he added quickly. Yet the "error" was "honest, nondiscriminatory."

I wrote in my notes after this conference call that the key issue being contested here was "BLAME," and, accordingly, which acts of assistance to students of color were actually required. This intricate communicative dance, I noted, was itself a result of the communicative "nebulousness of requiring 'voluntary' resolutions to 'concerns' about 'nonviolating.' " Amid this nebulousness, OCR itself was in effect agreeing to delete any discussions of harm in the Longview III case and to just "write a letter saying what they're already doing, rather than 'OCR told them to do it under duress because they discriminated.' " Before talking with Longview district representatives about the wording of these resolution documents, my manager, Corey, had urged that we tell them explicitly that we would be deleting "discrimination" language from the documents. "We should reassure them that we're making no formal findings of discrimination—it's all procedural," he said. I reminded him: "But we do have some serious concerns about [the district's] response to harassment" and about their "application of policy" unequally to parents. For example, as our draft closure letter noted, "OCR did not find that the School responded to all the reports or complaints of harassment brought to its attention." Cachon had written to school officials that a white student was "continuously harassing, intimidating and even physically hurting minority children," and that he "constantly called the children wetbacks and the black children niggers along with his threats." Yet, our own letter noted, "the parents and Students were still expected to take additional steps to follow up on the complaint before any District action was taken. For example . . . parents of the Student Class were told to contact the transportation department regarding the bus driver supposedly ignoring slurs made by the white child."

In our meeting, however, Corey still reminded the Longview district administrators and their attorney once again via speakerphone that "our letter will clearly state that we are not finding a violation—we had concerns and raised them with the district." I scribbled afterward that in the final letter discussing such "concerns," we risked actually deleting the discussion of harm itself: I shouldn't "downplay it *so* much ('you didn't do *anything*!') that they are misled!! This again is going to come down to the wording of blame."

The Cachon parents, for their part, were soon writing to OCR to contest our vague descriptions of harm and remedy in the closure documents. Our claims of "insufficient evidence" of racial discrimination were a surprise, they wrote; they were "sadly disappointed" by the letter describing the "status on our case," they said, and were attaching a list of "suggestions" for remedy that were not in the complaint resolution document either. These were ideas "to help end discrimination in this district, at least a step toward that," that the family had compiled after speaking "with numerous parents and community members." This list included various specifics they felt we had not discussed. The community desired "accountability by removal/demotions of personnel discriminating, allowing discrimination, or not addressing discrimination problems," and wanted complaint forms in school offices, in various languages, for parents and students. They suggested a "large and visual harassment policy" posted in multiple languages; the hiring of "minority administrators" and staff at the school site and district levels; detailed processes for responding to complaints ("this way complaints are not 'hidden under the rug,' or never addressed," they wrote); an independent "Ohms Budman"; and "diversity training in addition to the above suggestions."

To Cachon, OCR had failed to provide a remedy that was specific enough to get the district to actually improve a climate that felt hostile to many students and parents of color. Our resolution letter was indeed vague in its framing of the extent of harm and remedy. For example, it stated, rather convolutedly, that "OCR had several concerns regarding the effectiveness of the School's complaint investigation process and the actions taken to address harassment issues and to ensure that any harassment that was found to exist did not recur." We wrote, "Rather than responding to these complaints [of harassment] by conducting thorough inquiries or investigations into a determination of whether racial harassment existed, other school actions were taken." While our resolution letter described some of these "concerns" in relative detail, we had taken pains to state in each case that no "violation" had been found. We stated that as far as we were concerned, the district's promises to implement the "actions already taken" for the Longview I case "resolved" the issues. To complainants, speaking gently of OCR's "concerns" like this often seemed to allow the district to simply "get away with" its harmful actions, to avoid apologizing to either students or parents, and even to avoid ever speaking again about the specific harms. Psychological research suggests that people responding to experiences of injustice and disrespect often seek to "educate" the offender about which acts were unjust and disrespectful, and seek "to educate the perpetrator about the more general unacceptability of his or her behavior, not merely its unacceptability vis-à-vis the victim." They also want evidence that the offender understands.[29] Complainants often indicated that they wanted to "educate" educators about harm to students, so they expressed their concerns when the wording of resolutions was so nebulous that educators were not likely to clearly understand the harm and potential remedy.

My OCR colleagues and I were quite conscious of our own reluctance to tell educators they had to do anything in particular to assist children of color. A veteran colleague from another region in the agency once described her theory of "four civil rights scenarios for driving change" in districts in Title VI work, and I jotted them down.

Only the first one, the rare case with clear-cut evidence of illegal discrimination, indicated OCR's efforts to "force" districts to "do something they don't want to do."

1. Need ironclad case to force them to do something they don't want to do
   at all.
2. Less strong case—they give you stuff for nuisance value if you will go away.
   (We'll change policies/procedures, do training—we'll broker agreements
   but with potentially little outcome!)
3. Case not strong—but recipient wants to drive change anyway and publicly
   blame OCR for it.
4. Not very strong case, and we go away. (This would happen in minorities in
   Special Ed cases.[30] One district asked OCR to prove IQ tests were racially
   biased—OCR couldn't. The district said "go away.")

In an era when evidence could so rarely support an "ironclad case"
of discrimination "because of race" (see chapter 1), OCR "forced" educators to "change" far less often than educators and outside critics of
federal "prescription" thought we did. Instead, we at OCR typically
spent much energy dancing around the agency's basic reluctance to
"force" educators to do anything to assist children of color. Educators
"wise" to OCR's likely refusals to "enforce," as one manager put it,
could obstruct OCR's efforts entirely: like the Wizard of Oz behind his
curtain, OCR relied on a public view of its omnipotence even as it attempted to broker agreements with districts gently rather than "enforce" them. Still, outside critics called even OCR's humble negotiations too heavy-handed. "To outsiders this looks a lot more like
'intimidation,' " one critic wrote in 1987.[31] At one monitoring visit,
three of us OCR employees were simply examining whether a school
offered its English-language learners services to access academic content, but the principal said that our questions "seemed more like an
inquisition" than an attempt to "help."

After about nine months at OCR, I made some notes under the heading, "Things I don't get about OCR." The first was "POWER." I mused
about the questionable "power of having 'concerns' ": "How we get
districts to do stuff even when we don't 'find a violation.'" I was also
particularly confused about the reticence with which we often "*word*
statements/descriptions of blame," as well as our habit of negotiating
with districts to undertake a minimum of written efforts to satisfy our
"concerns" regarding children of color. Our minimal written discussion of necessary actions supported some educators who wanted to
devise local plans to proactively equalize opportunities for students of
color, but my colleagues noted that when educators were hostile to
claims of harm, these minimal written discussions could allow educa-

tors to argue later to local parents and advocates that "we won't do it if it's not in the plan."

In the disability cases where OCR could not definitively state that "violations" had occurred, interactions with districts sometimes exhibited the same power battles over naming and remedying harm as did typical race cases. Describing a colleague's troubles with a district that had "stalled infinite times" on meetings about "a disabled kid" but technically still was complying with the law by scheduling those meetings, I noted that internal managers were still telling this colleague that OCR couldn't, on paper, "say they 'violated' yet." If districts were never told they "violated" the law in a disability case, too, I wondered, what could they simply "refuse to do"? One OCR colleague, Bobbie, spent more than a year trying to get a lawyer for a district to allow pediatric evaluators into a young student's classroom to evaluate his disability services. As I paraphrased in my notes, "Bobbie thinks lawyers for districts make negotiations much more difficult—they're paid a lot and refuse to compromise; everything must be filtered through them, etc." Another colleague explained that one district had actually "started cooperatively," but then its attorney got involved in "obstructing" by demanding legal findings of violations before the district would agree to pay for any disability services: "Christie wants a violation letter sent out. Districts themselves often respond well to a little investigation and then 'we have a concern . . . can you change this?' Attorneys often are far more obstructionist."

District representatives could be similarly "obstructionist" in demanding formal "findings" before setting out to assist children. In a complaint from the King district, a huge urban district in our region, I became embroiled in disputes with Christie McCormack, the disability services coordinator, over OCR's warrant to suggest specific actions to assist Latino children. The issue was compensating a number of Latino students with learning disabilities who had missed out on academic instruction for several months when they had no regular teacher, but were monitored in the basement by a shifting crew of teachers on their free periods. The educational problem was that the students had learned almost nothing for several months; the legal problem was that these teachers had not officially examined and addressed the students' IEPs. Still, I described in my notes an uncomfortable call in which McCormack kept arguing that our "concerns" about the months of missed instruction exceeded "the regulations." The students were now being served by a permanent teacher trained in disability services, the "RSP [Resource Specialist Program] teacher," who, she argued, was meeting the students' needs retroactively. OCR's "concerns" that the students had languished without appropriate services for several months had no enforceable basis, she contended. She classically demanded to know if we had "found discrimination." My notes indicated that I felt McCormack, not OCR, had the ultimate power to decide whether to offer the children assistance.

> The first thing I say is, "We're ready to close the complaint, but we have some concerns. So we're sending down a voluntary resolution plan." She asks, "Did you find discrimination?" My heart sinks. "Uh . . . yes, in that we're concerned about the provision of services according to the students' IEPs for the time until a full-time RSP teacher was implemented in November." She says the compensation has already been given. I ask how it happened so quickly. She turns to asking me how our regulations include the issue of *timely* provision of services . . . [she also said we were] discounting the services provided by credentialed teachers. I say we're concerned with whether their IEPs were consulted . . . she says [the IEPs] said "math" and "English" and they put math and English teachers in there.
>
> I say we are concerned with compensation, and that the VRP details how we want to make sure it's determined. So if they can demonstrate they've already done it, fine. She says they will look at the VRP but probably won't sign it. I ask why. She says there's "nothing in the regulations" about timeliness. She finally calms down when I say we are concerned with whether the students' IEPs or individual educational needs were even discussed until November.

Hanging up the phone in frustration, I wrote in my notes that as in typical race cases, "the nebulousness of OCR's (non-)power" in the absence of formal "findings" of "violations" of "regulations" led to "controversy at every level" over offering children of color opportunities to learn.

> How to answer the question "Did you find discrimination"? Corey says that she's wise to the fact that OCR isn't making many formal findings. . . . But, as Bobbie said at lunch, the "not-formal-findings-we-have-concerns" strategy works [only] if you have a district that is ready to work with you. If not, they know OCR won't go to enforcement, won't follow through . . . and D.C. probably won't either.

Disability-related cases typically offered the chance for concrete, seemingly simple remedies to make OCR go away. After months in which McCormack and other district administrators denied the need to give remedial assistance to the students, McCormack finally did agree by phone (though I could hear her sighing) to sign a VRP promising summer school and tutoring to compensate the students for the many hours of class instruction the district had failed to provide them. Somewhat satisfied by this remedy, I still wondered what services the district would actually provide to these students once the case was closed, even if it assured us that these hours of these children's lives had been spent as promised.

As Gloria Ladson-Billings mentioned at our conference, securing "compliance" might mean securing something like a precise "time in program" for students, but the true "practice/spirit of the law" would be found or lost in "what happens in the classroom." In the King resolution letter, our written description of necessary remedy stated that "the compensatory education itself will be administered by an RSP teacher or other appropriately certified special education staff knowledgeable about accelerating math and reading instruction." We added, "The District has agreed to provide OCR with a report on the compensation determined for each individual student, including documentation of how that compensation was measured, the qualifications of those involved in measuring the compensation, the qualifications of those involved in providing the compensation, and when this compensatory education will be administered." Though this still did not ensure that the "compensatory education" would be of high quality, the children's legal right to IEP implementation at least allowed us to ask about it somewhat specifically.

In race cases, our remedies often displayed a far more egregious lack of detail: specific potential ways of assisting children were routinely deleted from the analysis altogether. Over and over, as OCR revealed itself to be an agency that would not formally "find" racial discrimination, we negotiated over stating, on paper, the minimal amount of district effort necessary to respond to non-findings. In our final efforts to produce documents resolving race complaints, we often tried so self-consciously to make the district's efforts to assist children sound "voluntary" rather than prescribed that we completely failed to describe necessary actions. These failures were particularly consequential in the race arena, since complainants often requested multiple actions to remedy complex, cumulative educational situations or climates.

*Toning Down "Prescriptive" Language in Resolution Documents*

In writing case resolution documents, we often worked hardest to avoid the implication that OCR had forced districts to do anything in particular, so we replaced "enforcement" language with overt comments about educators' stated willingness to assist students "voluntarily" rather than under duress.[32] In districts where educators were reluctant to suggest any ways to provide additional opportunities for children of color, we often suggested ideas for change and then, if the district agreed, wrote documents saying it had "volunteered" these changes. Just as districts preferred the "concerns" language to "discrimination" language, they preferred the "volunteered" language over appearing coerced by OCR. But this language of "voluntarism" often led us to avoid suggesting any specific changes in students' educational experiences. As I wrote in my notes, as one colleague wrote a report on a race-related discipline case for a weekly agency memo describing key cases in each region, she told me that much of her writing efforts involved "trying to take out anything that could be a 'red flag' to higher-ups that OCR employees were being too pushy or too prescriptive with districts." She mimicked her own attempts at reassuring higher-ups, which involved deleting her own discourse about harm while padding that discourse with caveats: "Disproportionate discipline isn't *itself* a problem . . . pre-suspension conferences won't *make* them keep difficult kids around," she said sarcastically. "I spend my life worrying about this," she added ruefully.

Circa 2000, "race/affirmative action" was called a "sensitive" area in one e-mail from an office director, along with Title IX athletics, sexual harassment, and charter schools. So OCR particularly had to avoid "prescribing" specific changes in such "red flag" areas. With "race" itself generally "red flagged" at OCR, managers often forced employees to draft letters again and again to delete specific language about how to treat students of color more equitably. One colleague told me about such a resolution letter that had been through more than twenty drafts.[33]

Whenever it discussed ways to assist students of color, OCR seemingly could not avoid critiques that it was abusing federal power. Some critics suggested that by *deleting* its discussions of specific remedial acts for students of color, OCR was exercising excessive "control." In a widely read 1998 report, *Federal Control out of Control*, former OCR employee Jim Littlejohn, a vocal opponent of bilingual education, critiqued the agency's habits of deleting specifics while suggesting unwritten improvements to educators.

> OCR pursues its own agenda and oversteps its Congressional mandate. Instead of providing leadership for educational institutions through clear enunciation of national policy and forthright findings of fact, OCR officials practice double-speak to justify unwarranted interference in local educational decision-making. This secret sub-regulation, pursuant to un-promulgated policies should be of concern to all.[34]

In 1997, one critic, a former OCR employee under Reagan, angrily called OCR's current communicative habit of deleting specific discussion of Title VI remedies "subtle activism." Its indirect strategy "enable[d] OCR to get results through informal conciliation that would never be possible—or legally supportable—were OCR to have to decide these questions on the basis of a single nationwide standard."

> As it turns out . . . a low profile approach to civil rights hasn't stopped officials bent on pursuing an activist civil rights agenda. Often, by making civil rights nonadversarial and noncontroversial, bureaucrats have been able to obtain results that would have been inconceivable in an earlier era. Indeed, at a time when the country as a whole appears to be backing away from affirmative action and other race-conscious remedies to racial inequalities, federal civil rights agencies are advancing an agenda in some ways more radical than ever before.[35]

I found exactly the opposite: in deleting language from documents to avoid sounding prescriptive, OCR typically pressed for far less assistance for students of color rather than more. Cases regarding English-language learners were a prime example. Linda Chavez, head of the conservative Center for Equal Opportunity, was an "English-only" advocate who routinely approached higher-ups in Congress and at OCR to complain—inaccurately—that OCR employees forced bilingual education on districts in their work to assist English-language learners. Colleagues told me that Jim Littlejohn had "sent a survey to all districts asking if OCR had ever directly or 'indirectly' pushed bilingual education," and in response, all ELL cases were now "going up to DC to be 'vetted.' "[36] A neighboring region was asked to read all our region's resolution letters about necessary assistance to English-language learners and to recommend deleting any material that it found overly "prescriptive." Resolution documents describing potential methods for serving English-language learners in any detail were to be gutted. One colleague told me that the neighboring region "wanted us to rewrite a fourteen-page agreement to say [the district] wrote it, volunteered it," even though "the district never felt the complaint was even valid." Another colleague agreed: "Until we sat down and said 'we found violations of federal law,' they weren't interested in even talking to us." In doing the "rewrite," they were supposed to delete much of the letter's specific discussion about serving English-language learners, while putting each newly shortened VRP on the district's letterhead rather than OCR's "so it looks like they decided to do it."

Lost in such "rewrites" was detailed discussion on how these children could be offered equal opportunities. One colleague told me that before this, our region's resolution and monitoring agreements about necessary services for ELLs had "become more detailed over time, because OCR has learned what districts need" when considering various ways of serving ELLs in compliance with law. Our region had tended to give districts many suggestions to consider because "people who know program design for ELLs often don't *exist* in districts." Detailed suggestions could assist both the willing and the unwilling. Some districts were glad to work with OCR to figure out "detailed steps to identify and assess ELLs" in their own districts, but in less willing districts, to get any language services in place for ELL students as required by law, OCR had to apply pressure and offer detailed suggestions for change. Our region had previously brought in experts from state departments of education to help districts generate research-based ideas for improving language instruction. Now, as a colleague put it, feds were to delete all terms that were "state" turf: "Even terms like SDAIE [Specially Designed Academic Instruction in English] and 'ELD,' " pedagogical methods of assisting English-language learners, were "critiqued" by internal readers "as 'State' words" that had to be deleted as if they were inherently "prescriptive." The monitoring region's managers questioned all references to instruction practices and asked of each item in a resolution letter, "Where is this in Title VI?!"[37]

In this context, where some saw federal assistance to children of color as so unwarranted, some colleagues attempted to aid the interested districts by commenting on their programs "under the radar," meaning over the phone rather than on paper. I did the same when verbally discussing with districts some possible, tested tactics that had worked in other districts dealing with racial harassment, faxing them sheets from a book produced by the nation's attorney generals. One colleague suggested that such "extra suggestions can be very useful—and used." Some educators I worked with wrote to thank me personally for sharing potential tactics. Over the years, OCR employees have offered such "technical assistance" to districts at the end of an investigation as a way of helping them assist students. One colleague suggested, however, that since "under the radar" assistance never showed up as requirements on paper, hostile districts could always argue that acts to assist children of color were "not in the plan." When OCR showed up to advise more hostile districts without some legalistic "hook" warranting their suggestions, it often would "run into" the response, "Who the hell are you?!"

I wrote in my notes to myself that given this hostility to federal civil rights intervention, one of my "fears" was that educators would respond to specifically worded closure letters by contesting each item: "If you show them too much of the closure letter [before sending it], they could resist it, too, though those are 'the facts.' " Yet I also feared that if closure documents simply gave districts the solutions to implement without explaining in detail the logic behind them, resistant educators would dismiss these demands for change. "Why *wouldn't* they rise up in confrontation" against OCR's unexplained demands? I asked myself. I worried that while OCR held the ultimate power to put descriptions of harm and remedy into formal text on government letterhead, OCR routinely relinquished that power by allowing resistant districts and higher-ups to veto certain pieces of text.[38]

An office meeting with the neighboring OCR region's director confirmed this fear: vague resolution letters and VRPs often did fail to communicate concrete ways to serve children. As a colleague put it, this regional office was known for resolving cases informally rather than after serious investigation, with district promises of vague "plans to plan" for assisting English-language learners. As I paraphrased the group conversation in my notes, the director argued to us that only with "bad guys" did OCR have to negotiate "full," detailed "policy." With most districts, the region purposefully put as little as possible on paper stating directly what districts had done "wrong." A colleague described this region's strategy of early resolution as an "under the radar" approach that "leave[s] almost no paper trail," which both districts and the region appreciated. Yet the director himself noted somewhat regretfully to us that while the strategy of informal, verbal resolution definitely closed cases more quickly, it also indicated OCR's resistance to civil rights enforcement itself. Nationally, he suggested, OCR often made verbal agreements on the "sidebar" rather than stating in writing that districts had done anything in particular wrong or might do anything in particular right. And such off-the-record resolutions, he concluded, were basically unenforceable.

Nader (2002) uses the phrase "harmony model" for a legal model that favors conflict resolution over open confrontation or harsh punishment. She argues that it allows the most powerful actors to retain ultimate control over the language and terms of compromise.[39] In OCR's attempts to collaborate, those ultimately in charge of many final descriptions of harm and necessary assistance to children were those who wanted the least stated: OCR higher-ups afraid of "prescribing" unwarranted assistance to children of color, and local educators who would agree only to a minimal number of uncontroversial remedies.

As I describe next, in a representative case I handled in the Granley school district, an OCR attorney and I "toned down" OCR language as both educators and OCR higher-ups demanded in the interests of "harmony": we included only uncontroversial details in the case resolution documents, deleting statements of prior harm and necessary remedy that had elicited objections. As our investigation in Granley uncovered a host of specific incidents when a young Latino student had potentially been targeted for excessive disciplinary surveillance, disputes hinged on the question of whether OCR had the authority to suggest improving the district's disciplinary practices in any particular way. In this case, our unwillingness to name particularly controversial harms backfired on our effort to "collaborate" with educators to analyze opportunity provision. As we secured a written agreement to the few uncontroversial instances of harm we were all willing to specify, it became clear that Granley educators had not been convinced to rethink or discuss the many ways they had heaped disciplinary consequences on this young man.

A Representative Case

Early in the spring of 2000, Lisa Rodriguez filed a complaint with OCR alleging that her son José, an eighth grader, had been discriminated against on the basis of race in the Granley school district through a long list of disciplinary incidents and searches of his clothes, backpack, and home. Granley was a suburban elementary district so small that the superintendent shared the same building with the principal and K–8 students. "We're Hispanic in a predominantly white area," Rodriguez explained, estimating that the school was "85 percent white." According to the state Department of Education's Web site, the district's student body was 73 percent white and 18 percent Hispanic; 93 percent of the teachers were white.

Communication between the Rodriguez family and the school district had been poor, such that some specific harms experienced by José and his family had not yet been discussed by particular players. The superintendent told me and the lawyer conducting the interviews that he had had no interaction with the Rodriguez parents regarding the searches until he received the letter from OCR regarding alleged "discrimination." The family had articulated various other specific concerns about José, however: several other administrators described numerous uncomfortable phone calls and meetings with José's parents. The superintendent insisted that José's teacher had "tried to clear the slate with José over and over," but "there was no improvement, [and] no cooperation from the home to get him" to school, much less to behave properly there. On the other hand, Mrs. Rodriguez was convinced that the district's educators and a school-based drug and truancy officer had targeted her son in a host of incidents because the school associated Hispanics with "gangs and drugs." She said the disciplinary treatment of José was more extreme than that of other Hispanic families she knew, but those families also felt that the treatment of Hispanics was not quite right in the Granley district. Perhaps her son's disability made him slightly more defiant, she argued; part of her original complaint, which was handled by the state Department of Education, involved the school's tardy implementation of his IEP. But, as I wrote in my notes, she was more convinced that "it's because of race, because of the way he looks." At 5′ 5″ José weighed 200 pounds. She alleged that the school had "singled him out" throughout the semester "as connected to gangs and drugs. If he had been Caucasian, they wouldn't have felt the need to search his home and person." I paraphrased Mrs. Rodriguez's summative assessment of the school and district: "they take discipline too far with her son." Mrs. Rodriguez told me that, above all, she wanted an apology for excessive disciplinary targeting of José.

Our investigation soon showed that in the fall semester, José had been disciplined almost every day he was in school by his white teachers, his white principal and superintendent, and the white drug and truancy officer based at the school. Granley educators acknowledged in frustration that José had been subject to an unusual amount of disciplinary attention. He had been disciplined for dozens of infractions, including "defiance of authority," "inappropriate behavior/comments," "inappropriate bodily contact," and "disobedience, profanity, defiance." As I wrote in my notes, it was clear to me from the beginning that in Granley educators' eyes, José was generally "seen as 'oppositional'/defiant." This framing of José clearly played a role in his becoming so defiant.[40] As José's teachers and administrators described various incidents, it appeared that they interpreted much of his behavior as "defiance" and then searched for particular rules in the school's handbook and policies to justify disciplining him. In one suspension José received for showing up at school wearing a safety pin through his eyebrow, he and his mother reported to me that the principal leafed through the discipline book in front of José while deciding what rule to use to suspend him. Such seemingly cavalier discipline made José even more resistant to their disciplinary attempts. José said he had told school administrators that "if they came at him with respect, he'd come back at them with respect."

While José was occasionally sent to a "support room" for specific offenses such as "profanity," he was often suspended from school.[41] He was then disciplined for truancy at the suspension's end when he failed to come back to school. By the time we received the complaint, educators and the school's drug and truancy officer had referred him to the county truancy board, which carried possible police consequences. Lisa Rodriguez told me that she had been threatened with prosecution for her son's absence record.

As we put it in our data request letter to the district, the first of three allegations made by Lisa Rodriguez that fit into OCR's rubric of potential "discrimination" under Title VI was that "the District discriminated against the Student by targeting him for three racially motivated searches without probable cause." In the first semester of the year, Rodriguez said, José had been searched in the office several times. On one occasion, the principal and the school's drug and truancy officer, Officer Yardley, had searched José's backpack after he had refused to give up a note he was passing around in a class, which the superintendent called "contraband." These searches, which his mother at one point called "a racially motivated search for drugs," became key incidents in our investigation. As we investigated each incident, we found that a number of these incidents had not been officially recorded; several educators presented contradictory facts about why the searches had occurred and even, in one case, whether the search had occurred at all. As we wrote in our final resolution letter, "In discussing this incident, School site staff and administrators provided varying reports to OCR of whether and why the alleged search occurred, and who was present at the incident." The district eventually agreed to expunge one of these searches from José's record, but wrote pointedly in a revision to the VRP that "the District expresses its concern about threats of violence made by students."

This issue of "threats of violence" stemmed from a search involving Officer Yardley and a school administrator searching through José's backpack, which he accidentally left overnight in the school office. They had searched a notebook they had found in the backpack, ostensibly to ascertain the identity of the backpack's owner; they had then suspended José for rap lyrics they found in the notebook, which they categorized as "obscene, racist, and threatening language." I wrote in my notes that these lyrics, which I saw in photocopied evidence the district sent to OCR, "do include some profanity, 'nigga,' mention of drugs, automatic weapons," as was common in many rap lyrics at the time. The officer and principal had interpreted them as gang-related threats and suspended José on that basis. In the end, examining "policy," we concluded that the search itself was not unwarranted, though its consequences seemed extreme and the only other two students who had been searched that year were also students of color. We wrote in our resolution letter conciliatorily that "OCR concluded that the district had a legitimate nondiscriminatory rationale for searching the backpack, namely, identifying the owner of abandoned property, and that there was insufficient evidence to establish that the search was overly extensive."

An even more contentious incident involved a search of José's home by Officer Yardley, the school-based police officer who did antidrug counseling and monitored truancy. José had repeatedly missed school because of his suspensions; he refused to show up for numerous detentions; and he failed to turn in assignments during his days at school. To deal with his truancy and discipline problems, school administrators had referred him to Officer Yardley. After a few counseling conversations that José described as useful and one successful visit to José's house earlier in the year that got him back to school, Officer Yardley went to José's house later in the semester. There he ran a warrant check on José's father and searched the house (including several small bags, another search that José's parents interpreted as an unwarranted search for drugs). He then arrested José's father, who was out of jail on parole, in front of José.

The issue we discovered as we investigated this search, and the one with the most obvious potential consequences for José's life trajectory, was the ambiguous role of Officer Yardley. In discussing the incident, Officer Yardley himself noted some ways in which his school and police roles were indistinguishably intertwined. For example, José made some comments to him in a counseling context about what Yardley called some "gang issues" in José's family—an allegation the family denied; these had Yardley "looking into the family" in his police records and ultimately arresting the father in his police capacity. Few people at the school discussing the incident seemed to be able to distinguish between Yardley's police and school-based roles, or to think that their intertwining could potentially be harmful to young people by linking students with school discipline or attendance problems to the criminal justice system. As the superintendent put it to me in an interview, the "community liaison" and antidrug roles were "kind of separate," but both fell under the umbrella of the "police officer being on our campus." Still, the attorney and I were repeatedly told by Granley administrators that the school district did not actually pay for the officer with federal funds, making his activities off-limits to OCR. "So the school district *pays for* the officer, but it doesn't 'employ' him," I wrote in confused frustration in my notes.

Investigating a list of other incidents, we found that Officer Yardley had repeatedly been pulled in to discipline or counsel José in routine school-related incidents as well as in incidents regarding his truancy problems, and the involvement of a police officer in these examples of regular discipline raised the possibility that José was unfairly targeted. José was repeatedly referred to Officer Yardley instead of school administrators. According to the school's referral forms, Yardley was involved in many of José's suspensions for "causing campus disruption and defiance." "Why *police* involvement?" I wrote in my notes after the backpack search.

Granley educators described the involvement of a police officer in a student's everyday life as a result of an informal invitation and nothing that risked potential harm to children. The criterion for sending the officer to a home, the superintendent said matter-of-factly, was "conversations." As I wrote in my notes after our interview, the principal said that "whoever is there to say, 'Hey Officer Yardley, go out there' [to a house], does it." No school official tracked the officer's behavior regarding any specific student or family. They did, however, hear a lot about students' families from Yardley. In José's case, we learned, Yardley had passed on to school administrators hints about his father's prison experiences and his older brothers' encounters with the law. Officer Yardley explained to me that José's "attire and room" had suggested to him "indications of gang membership"; José's mention to Yardley in a counseling context of some "homies" in a community where the Rodriguez family had lived previously "indicated gang affiliation" to Yardley. As the principal put it to me, Yardley "shared that information" about José's family, "but I don't know in what context—in a meeting." José mentioned skeptically that the confiscated note that had led to one search of his backpack had contained the word "homie," a typical word in rap lyrics that the principal and his teacher had falsely interpreted as "gang related."

Our investigation demonstrated that over time, circulating such information on José contributed to framing him as connected to illicit or illegal activity. The superintendent noted, for example, that he had received two phone calls from parents about problems they were having with José in the community, alleging that he used drugs and alcohol and was threatening other students. He had not only told these parents that he would keep an eye on José as a potential school "safety" hazard but had also circulated this information to other school officials. "I said but if he threatens kids on campus, or if we have any suspicion of drugs, guns, or knives, we'll take any action to make their students feel safe on the campus," he recalled. The principal told us she had heard the same information circulating around the school and had dismissed it as "hearsay," but the superintendent made clear that he had circulated it on purpose. "I probably talked to a couple of staff members who had José," he responded, "to let them be aware of the allegations of his drug involvement." As I wrote in my notes during our visit to the Granley campus, "the transfer of information is troubling," as "the vague circulation of suspicions and allegations" about José played a clear role in increasing the disciplinary consequences Granley educators meted out to him.

Describing our investigation of these events in our eventual resolution letter, we said nothing about this troubling practice of circulating damaging information—or misinformation—about José. We commented solely on a different "concern" that the district agreed to remedy: "the lack of any standard process for conducting searches or initiating school-related referrals to the officer." In the VRP, the district agreed to "take measures to adopt a more formal procedure before requesting that the Officer make a home visit," including keeping a log of the home visits he made. They also agreed "to take measures to improve the consistency of how it documents and conducts searches of a student's person or property." In a monitoring call I made six months later, the principal indicated just how uncontroversial this agreement had been: she reported to me that they had "constructed the home visit log after the VRP knowing it would get little use," simply to satisfy OCR. Officer Yardley had made no home visits that year; his ongoing interactions with students remained unmonitored. Teachers had "been informed about the policy for involving the Officer," which now required administrator approval, but this information was not yet in the staff handbook.

The written agreements we negotiated in our VRP regarding the school's habits of disciplining José failed to discuss the more controversial situation in the district: that educators had treated even mundane acts by this Latino student as a severe disciplinary threat and even potentially criminal threat to the mostly white school community.

The Granley educators staunchly defended one act of allegedly disparate discipline: they had suspended José for "defiance" for coming to school with a safety pin through his eyebrow. Rodriguez and José both said José had been told he could wear such a piercing as long as it was a "closed loop" and not a straight pin. He had come to school once before with a sewing needle in his eyebrow, and a teacher had sent him to the superintendent, since two children apparently fainted at the sight. School administrators said they had warned José not to wear any pin and that his returning to school with it after a suspension was an egregious act of "defiance" of the school handbook's rule not to wear objects that would cause "disruption." One administrator said that crowds had gathered to look at the still-bleeding piercing; in an unwittingly telling statement about who in the Granley district was considered to be "our children," another argued that "our children don't see that very often."

José's father said that the principal summarized the piercing to him as "not culturally acceptable," a framing the father considered "racism." The father reported to me that the principal had also explained to him that "José is culturally different." The father had agreed that

José was "culturally different" from most students at Granley, but he had argued that there were "no criteria forbidding wearing earrings." He told me afterward that he was "shocked" at José's suspension for the safety pin as "not culturally acceptable." To him that meant being treated as "an inferior race, not my kind." He said he had told the principal, "It's not important what kind of shoes he has on—it matters if he's learning. You've stopped trying to reach him. You just try to harass him." Still, the father reported, he and the principal had "come to an agreement" that if José's piercings seemed dangerous, the father himself would outlaw them. Yet the deeper problem embedded in these interactions remained unsolved, the father reported: José now "feels the lack of trust, feels like he's seen as a thug." José was coming home these days and reporting all sorts of unfairness: "a white substitute teacher has her tongue pierced in front of all the kids, but a little Mexican guy can't have his eyebrow pierced." His son now had the sense that he and his family were "targeted." As I paraphrased in my notes, José himself argued when I met him at the family's home that he repeatedly saw the school "attack his family."

As we wrote in our resolution letter regarding the safety pin incident, we found at least one white student "who had committed a second dress code offense or who had defied the instructions of school staff by wearing an inappropriate item" but was "simply cited for dress code violations" rather than for "defiance." On the basis of this single comparative fact, the district skeptically agreed to expunge the piercing suspension, while asking us to write in the documents that "in agreeing to the VRP, it is specifically understood that the District is not admitting or conceding any violation of State or Federal law." As we headed toward case closure, Granley personnel continued to justify each of their acts as appropriate under disciplinary policy. Officer Yardley argued that "under the penal code," he was "entitled" to search abandoned objects to determine their ownership. The principal made clear in our interview that although the "mother expresses dissatisfaction with every suspension, as 'unfair' (albeit in a 'respectful tone')," she had tried to show Rodriguez that she "was following policy, that it was important to her to be consistent according to policy."

Still, as Granley teachers and administrators discussed specific disciplinary incidents, they indicated that their rationales for invoking any given policy to discipline José were far from clear. While the principal could not remember which previous offenses had piled up to make the safety pin incident worthy of suspension for continued "defiance," she stated simply that "because of his defiance, he needed to go home for the day."[42]

Over time, specific decisions to discipline José for various "policy"-linked reasons had added up to José's being disciplined all the time, and harshly so, simply because he was becoming the type of student educators were supposed to discipline. The superintendent said that it was not typical for him to become involved in discipline at Granley but that he had been involved in a number of José's suspensions for "defiance" because of José's "record" and because the disciplinary incidents "reoccurred." The principal explained, equally circularly, why the rap lyrics found in José's backpack had resulted in his suspension: such harsh consequences "would be typical for a kid with discipline issues." While she couldn't remember the "thought process" that led her to determine that this was José's "third profanity offense" and thus worthy of suspension, "it might have been that by this time, anything was [a three-day suspension] because of all the other incidents." By this point, she said, she wouldn't even have had to look up his files; she would have just suspended him as a statement of the need to "obey the rules."

One of José's teachers stated that while his own "personal policy" was to try to just give "warnings" and trips to the support room and that he even at times had "wiped [José's] academic slate clean" in order to "motivate" him, "extreme behavior problems" could lead to instant suspensions under the school's rules, and José was just the type of "extreme" student who "doesn't respond" to more minor consequences. One administrator defined "defiance" to me as "not cooperating, not going to where they are told, not following teacher rules," a definition that could be stretched to cover any of José's behaviors at any given moment and could result in the involvement of a police officer as easily as a trip to the school's "support room." In our final resolution letter, we restated our private worries about excessive discipline meted out to José as a general "concern" with "the possibility of arbitrary discretion in the use of disciplinary sanctions."

Our written resolution did not call for what would really help José: concrete conversations among Granley educators and the Rodriguez family about why educators were seeing José as likely involved in criminal activity, about whether their disciplinary measures, particularly the suspensions, were actually working to engage José and reduce his "defiance,"[43] and about how and why educators had circulated rumors that he was involved with gangs and drugs. Rather, we negotiated with the district toward less controversial remedial actions to which both our higher-ups and the district would agree.

Shortly before we were to send our closure letter to the Granley district, managers in our office decided they wanted to read it. In the original draft, I proposed including specific discussion of the problematically blurred roles of Officer Yardley. My draft also included specific descriptions of our findings and concerns regarding the murky standards for suspending students for "defiance." I wrote in my notes how a number of managers in our region responded to the draft of the Granley letter.

> Corey comes over to say there's a problem with the Granley letter. Roger thinks it comes down too hard on the district (which was cooperative) and that it appears to be criticizing them for every little thing they're doing. In Roger and Danny's office, I ask if detail itself seems critical or if it's the *way* we said it. Roger and Danny say it's detail itself, really—these things could have been *talked about* in the negotiation process, but the VRP itself stands for all this evidence/findings, so there's no need to put it all in the written public document. OCR used to do investigations more like litigation—all findings went into letter, all evidence, and then OCR *demanded* remedial action. Since then, with the complaint resolution manual [*which prioritized early resolution and mediation*], higher-ups wanted a more collaborative relationship with districts—to resolve as you go along. The complainant doesn't have to know the details, just the outcome. You can talk to the complainant over the phone about it if they want to know.
>
> Corey suggests putting the information into an investigative report in the file. Roger says he's not sure if he would even suggest that (though he won't disallow it), since the police stuff looks like we're getting into law enforcement's jurisdiction and into every decision they made about an individual student in keeping their campus safe. Even though the officer sounds like a jerk . . . in the hands of a Rush Limbaugh, [the VRP] sets OCR up for critique of overstepping government's bounds.
>
> In here I say the point of the detail was to teach, or explain to, a bewildered district. Roger says we should have just *talked* to them for this explanation, and I say we did that.
>
> They want a short, three-page summary. OCR used to routinely write fifteen-page letters.

After talking to the attorney on the case, I wrote to myself,

> are we trying to get civil rights done well, or *not to offend*? If details = accusations → defensiveness → anti–civil rights attitude, that's bad. But if details → understanding → good civil rights attitude, that's good!

Once again, to avoid setting "OCR up for critique of overstepping government's bounds," the attorney and I reluctantly began the typical process of deleting controversial "details." For their part, the Granley administration was willing to sign on to the VRP as soon as it allayed *their* "specific concerns." In a conference call to discuss a draft version of the VRP with the Granley administrative team, the lawyer for the district said that the district had "no problem with general concepts"; rather, they had "some specific concerns to go over," and then we could "come to an agreement." The lawyer requested that we "somehow tinker with the language" regarding the "formal procedure for arranging home visits" by the officer. They would agree to write procedures for which situations "necessitated the services" of Officer Yardley and to train teachers and administrators on these procedures, yet they stressed that they needed to afford Yardley and other administrators the ability to pursue "criminal" activity. While the district next agreed to expunge the body piercing suspension, they said they "objected" to expunging the suspension for the "threatening" graffiti found in José's backpack, "because some recent violence in the U.S. can be traced back to written violence." Left unaddressed in the eventual VRP was the central controversy in these specific incidents: was it unnecessarily harmful for a Latino student's rap lyrics to be deemed "criminal," for his crumpled note to be deemed "contraband," his behavior deemed worthy of police involvement?

OCR's final resolution letter, after our deletions, was more conciliatory. It stated, "Based on the concerns raised by the different accounts regarding the searches of the Student,"

> the District has agreed to take measures to improve the consistency of how it documents and conducts searches of a student's person or property. In addition, to address concerns raised by the School's process of sending the Officer to homes for School-related business, the District has also agreed to take measures to adopt a more formal procedure before requesting that the Officer make a home visit.

Regarding the disputed suspensions, our letter urged weakly that the district "modify its discipline policies to reflect its disciplinary practices of working to keep students in school as much as possible for lesser offenses that do not result in undue disruption or otherwise compromise the safety of the District's schools."

Several important yet similarly convoluted sentences included in the VRP suggested vaguely that the district should develop "policies" to ensure against *potential* "discriminatory enforcement of discipline," but these sentences were so murky as to be practically worthless: "The District will develop policies designed to more fully ensure that its discipline policies are implemented in a consistent and nondiscriminatory manner with regards to repeat occurrences of less serious offenses." The "policies" went largely undescribed. A description of a planned "training" on discipline and defiance was to "include a discussion of the District's definition of the offense of 'defiance' and will offer administrators and staff possible strategies for working with students who are repeatedly deemed as defiant." Ruefully, I wrote in my notes, "Maybe the *discussion* of what dress code violations are/defiance is will serve the purpose, rather than racking up a huge list of criteria." Yet in "monitoring" correspondence after we resolved the case, I learned that in the absence of written "criteria" requiring discussion among staff about avoiding specific harms in discipline—avoiding unfairly circulating rumors about "drug" and "gang" involvement, for example, or presumptively deeming student language literally "criminal," or defining countless minor behaviors as "defiance" worthy of extensive discipline—the principal herself conducted the workshop on "how to 'creatively' defuse defiant behavior." "Defiant as in refusing to do what is asked," she explained to me over the phone.[44]

Near the end of the case, I had called the Granley superintendent to say the VRP was coming and that the complaint would be resolved when we got it back signed. As he continued to talk about protecting the "whole campus" from "gang" affiliates like José, the superintendent still did not seem to see any validity in the Rodriguez family's claims of disciplinary unfairness to José.

> He asks what "resolved" means. I say they'll get a letter detailing the facts about which we had concerns, and then what the district volunteered to do to address these concerns. I say the VRP specifically says that there's no admission to violation of law. We'll then monitor just to make sure the changes actually are implemented. He is quiet. "So what did you think of the process?" I ask. He says, "Well ... in twenty-eight years I've never had this happen. It's a shock to the system ... as a former teacher, you know ... we really try our hardest for these kids. ... I'm supportive of the process—you and Chester did a great job, working with us—but it's just a shock to the whole system. The student was new this year, he came from Trudell, a gang area and all ... and we did what we had to do for the whole campus. ... It's a shock to then have a parent file such a complaint.

At OCR, we had a particular tool to wield in discussions of harm to children: "detailing," on paper, specific past acts that had harmed children and alternative acts that might ensure against specific harms in the future. Yet the details we chose to retain in closure documents were typically just those on which educators and higher-ups would agree. My attorney partner on the Granley case, Chester, told me that district representatives who had fiercely resisted allegations of discrimination sometimes softened when reading a VRP drafted by OCR that suggested only specific uncontroversial remedies. As educators grudgingly accepted these changes to placate OCR, their skepticism about the complaint's overarching validity was assuaged through a simple bureaucratic task of what one recipient called "dotting i's and crossing t's" to counter or erase a few agreed-upon incidents.

At the agencywide level, finally, higher-ups at OCR have often deleted necessary written specifics describing harm to, and remedy for, students of color in favor of no documents at all. For example, OCR administrations of various political leanings have prevented the public circulation of "technical assistance" documents designed to inform educators and the public of OCR's specific definitions of racial discrimination, either through negligence or through outright refusal.[45] Upon entering office, the George W. Bush administration immediately removed from circulation all printed documents designed to inform educators and district officials on how to comply with Title VI and put those documents under administrative "review." OCR employees were discouraged from handing out many explanatory materials OCR had been giving districts for years as "technical assistance" to explain Title VI and other civil rights laws. A former colleague checking the OCR intranet site in spring 2005 found that even the internal guidelines for OCR employees investigating English-language learners' civil rights were no longer available. Also missing were the guidelines for investigating racial harassment cases that had been available when I worked at OCR. I had given a copy of this booklet to both the Longview and Quail district administrators so that they could see the specific components of a "racially hostile environment"—a concept they had found too overarching to address. Now the entire concept had been deleted.

## THE CONSEQUENCES OF NOT DISCUSSING HARMS TO CHILDREN OF COLOR

One academic I met in my work at OCR argued that in national equity debates, OCR had to "be the conversation starter, so other equity advocates can follow up." Yet OCR often pursued conversations about equity in the Title VI arena vaguely to avoid antagonizing critics. OCR's habit of deleting specific discussions of harm to children of color was one version of what I call colormuteness in contemporary American education: the active refusal to talk in racial terms about patterns, policies, practices, and disparities.[46] Our effort often seemed to be focused on deleting talk about past harms and future remedies in order to avoid criticism for getting too specific.

Many of my OCR colleagues grumbled quietly that we had to provide clear and specific expectations during both investigations and resolutions in order to prompt positive changes in districts and schools. As one colleague put it, "Talking about the past is useful if people learn from it—if people don't know why what they did was wrong, they don't successfully plan for the future." Only "if they're already convinced of wrongdoing," she said, "they can successfully *not* debate the past." We also knew from our disability work that requirements in writing would particularly hold educators "accountable" for their remedies: as I wrote in my notes, I saw "incredibly detailed IEPs with parents wanting written specifics that people will be held accountable for."[47] Verbal conversations left remedy reliant upon the specific individuals who had been on the phone with OCR. As one colleague put it, "OCR should be very clear about what it is looking for, for the school's purposes, because OCR forces reforms." When cases closed with convoluted or vague descriptions of OCR's "concerns," educators skeptical or unclear about which acts actually harmed students were often being asked, as I have written elsewhere, "to fix a machine without discussing where it was broken."[48]

In race cases, OCR was often quite specific in its *investigation* of harm, sending "data request" letters to districts demanding detailed information on specific incidents alleged by complainants and asking detailed questions of both complainants and recipients during the investigations. Complainants, too, often sent OCR painstaking documentation of their specific allegations of everyday injustice: binders of photocopied suspension referrals, report cards, and permission slips, and handwritten logs documenting conversations with teachers and principals. As investigations proceeded, administrators, too, took notes documenting everything the complainants said in interactions, and sent faxes and letters and reports analyzing the allegations. I cringed whenever we received a giant binder of data from a complainant or recipient, anticipating just how many hours of my life would be consumed in reviewing it.[49] But examining such details was central to figuring out how to treat students equitably. When we deleted such details at the remedy stage, we often left unsettled the question of which moves actually denied students opportunity.

As I show in the next chapter, it was not just in debates with school districts that OCR employees resisted suggesting particular opportunities for students of color. Ironically, an OCR manager once suggested to me that getting school districts to agree to offer these children opportunities to learn was easier than getting OCR higher-ups to do so: it was hard "to legally get into some educational issues without someone else shutting it down." After a dinner conversation with another colleague in the D.C. agency headquarters regarding an office initiative to examine early elementary opportunity, I paraphrased his advice: "It's better perhaps to do things in collaboration with districts at the office level rather than try to make 'policy,' because 'policy' attempts can get shut down by political needs to silence." As the next chapter shows, within OCR we often proffered a standard contemporary rebuttal to our *own* efforts to actively ensure, as an agency, that students of color in the nation's schools would be provided equal opportunities to learn. We claimed that unfortunately, some harms to students of color simply could not be remedied.

# Harms to Children of Color Cannot Be Remedied

> The work of the Algebra Project takes the form of an "if,
> then" sentence: If we can do it, then we should.
> —*Bob Moses, educational civil rights activist, 2001*

> People only say what you can't do.
> —*OCR colleague, 2000*

WHEN Title VI was passed in 1964, just ten years after *Brown v. Board of Education*, the core form of educational discrimination lawmakers conceptualized was intentional segregation. From 1967 through the early 1970s, OCR muscularly threatened recalcitrant districts, primarily in the South, with the loss of federal funding if they continued to run purposely segregated schools.[1] Title VI also made it possible to analyze a much broader set of educational policies and practices, declaring that any "exclusion from participation," "denial" of "benefits," or "discrimination" "on the ground of race, color, or national origin" was illegal in "any program or activity that receives federal funds." As a colleague once put it, Title VI in the educational realm basically ordered that federal funding recipients "be fair to kids of color." Its call for justice was both deeply powerful and dangerously vague.

Nearly forty years later, during the first years of George W. Bush's administration, OCR began to define policies and practices designed to promote racial integration in education as being a form of race-based discrimination. At the time, the Supreme Court was actually determining that higher education affirmative action policies intended to diversify student bodies could consider race as one of many factors when admitting individuals;[2] a conflict over the constitutionality of voluntary integration policies in the nation's school districts was heading toward the Court.[3] In 2004, OCR produced a report providing "guidance" on "race-neutral" approaches to programming, school assignment, and admissions for school districts and universities. The booklet insinuated generally to educators and administrators that to comply with Title VI's prohibition of harmful, different treatment "on the ground of race," they should avoid any use of racial categories in policies and practices designed to equalize opportunity. The booklet implied to nervous superintendents and admissions offices that civil rights law now defined "discrimination" as any programmatic treatment of students as members of racial groups.[4] This cautionary advice was actually not correct; federal courts still permitted narrowly tailored race-conscious admissions procedures and desegregation policies. A few years later, the Supreme Court would actually leave open the potential for some race-conscious desegregation efforts.[5] But in seemingly defining as discrimination the very sorts of remedies it had been created to enforce, OCR demonstrated that what will be said to count as racial harm in education is a political question that depends on who is in charge.

OCR's definitions of impermissible harm to students of color have shifted somewhat with each administration, but the general trend in OCR's definition of racial discrimination between *Brown* and Bush demonstrates how the nation has so often reinterpreted civil rights law to constrain and rebuff claims of educational harm to young people of color. Today, rather than defining discrimination generally as race-conscious policies designed to *deny* opportunities to students of color, many now redefine discrimination generally as race-conscious policies designed to *provide* opportunities to students of color.[6] While Bush would initiate No Child Left Behind, federally requiring race-conscious attention to students' test score outcomes, his administration would still denounce race consciousness in evaluating educational opportunity. In the national context, the very attempt to proactively equalize academic opportunity for students of color was coming to seem suspect; in response, around 2000, many employees within OCR were ceasing to argue optimistically for an expanded reach of civil rights strategies to assist children of color in particular ways. Rather, in internal debates, they were arguing pessimistically that proactive efforts to provide these students equal opportunities to learn might no longer be allowed at all by those in charge.

Circa 2000, hundreds of people were employed at OCR to use civil rights tools to ensure, among other things, that students of color were not denied educational opportunities because of their race. But few of us believed wholeheartedly—before or after the transition to the Bush administration—that powerful people in control of OCR work from above, or critics from outside, would actually let us use civil rights tools "proactively" to equalize these students' daily opportunities to learn in the nation's schools. We even worried at times that we would be told we had no warrant at all to enforce racially equal opportunities to learn using our civil rights tools.

As the first chapter demonstrated, legal definitions of harm "because of race" do set real constraints on OCR's abilities to name as "discrimination" various harms toward children of color; so do administrations' own habits of defining "race-based" harm. As the second chapter demonstrated, American habits of critiquing federal "prescription" also reduce OCR people's sense that they can tell local educators which opportunities to provide. Yet out of fear, we at OCR often anticipated critique and limited our own assistance to children. This chapter demonstrates how, in the new civil rights era, people more generally constrain the potential power of equal opportunity effort by arguing repeatedly, in resignation, that someone powerful will disallow attempts to equalize opportunities for children of color in particular ways.[7] Today, anxious "rhetorics of intransigence"[8] that imagine the limited potential of efforts to equalize such opportunities permeate the arguments even of those who advocate for equal opportunity efforts. This chapter shows how at OCR, such pessimism and learned defeatism about the possible uses of civil rights tools within our politicized bureaucracy led us to sabotage our own attempts to help equalize even the most basic of the daily academic opportunities denied to children of color. Daily, debating ourselves, we echoed a more general contemporary rebuttal to claims for racial opportunity equalization: "yes, opportunities should be racially equal—but we are not allowed to equalize them this way."

OCR work offered a salient example of such learned defeatism. Having completed my Ph.D. examining issues of race and equal opportunity in education, I had been hired to help spearhead the Early Learning Project at our regional office, which considered whether and how OCR might examine inequalities in K–3 educational opportunities available at schools serving students of color. In this project, we would directly tackle a national problem: the everyday denial, to many students of color, of core educational resources and early opportunities to learn. As the project proceeded, we began to imagine pressing for access to specific academic resources and opportunities that experts seemed to agree were necessary for all students. Then, even the small subset of people who originally conceived of the project started worrying that it would probably be impossible to use civil rights law proactively to evaluate or remedy the differential academic opportunities routinely offered to racial groups in U.S. classrooms, schools, and districts. While some colleagues expressed doubts about whether the legal tool of Title VI could technically allow us to proactively equalize specific learning opportunities and others worried that looking at specific opportunities would seem too "prescriptive," most colleagues had a more fundamental fear: that powerful higher-ups within the agency and external critics across the country would probably not allow us to wield the law openly and forcefully to afford early learning opportunities to children of color at all.

The Early Learning Project's abstract argument for equalizing academic opportunity encountered no internal resistance. Few people up and down the chain of command denied the reality that many children of color lack fundamental opportunities to learn during their first years of school. We convened a conference to discuss the great body of research evidence proving that students of color often receive substandard curriculum, fewer facilities, less qualified teachers, and substandard teaching and learning opportunities in comparison to their white peers in other schools and districts, and even in classrooms within desegregated schools.[9] OCR staff, both regional and national, accepted this evidence. Everyone I talked to at OCR agreed that racially unequal early elementary opportunities routinely contributed to racially unequal academic trajectories; in particular, students of color are tracked into lower "ability" levels that ultimately fail to prepare them for college. Everyone seemed to agree generally that K–3 academic opportunities in the nation should be racially equal and, where not racially equal, equalized.

The issue that was in dispute was the concrete project of getting OCR involved in analyzing, evaluating, and remedying the specific academic opportunities denied to these children in real classrooms, schools, and districts. As our work on the project proceeded, an argument about its limited potential took shape through a rather bizarre contention: that "education" and "civil rights" were two distinct realms that could not be intertwined. OCR exists precisely in order to link civil rights and education; it is the Department of Education's civil rights wing. But my colleagues asked themselves whether OCR really could or would help ensure that these students were provided the specific academic opportunities to learn experts deemed necessary for young children. And in response, many colleagues started fretting generally that examining "educational" opportunities to learn for students of color might not be civil rights turf at all.

These worries were largely confined to our work on behalf of students of color. Circa 2000, OCR people routinely framed contemporary civil rights work for children with disabilities as *about* providing access to concrete academic opportunities, and we confidently analyzed in detail whether such students received the everyday learning opportunities experts asserted they needed. But when it came to racially equalizing specific academic opportunities for students of color, even basic opportunities deemed essential by research, many people at OCR anxiously and sweepingly argued that "civil rights" people could neither analyze nor equalize "education."

This argument was fueled by both cynicism and fear. Many of my colleagues expected that higher-ups would shut down any activity using civil rights law to analyze racial groups' academic opportunities in any detail. We feared that "proactive" efforts to wield Title VI would put at risk even our most basic Title VI work.[10] We worried that we would be "shut down" both figuratively and literally by powerful critics inside and outside the agency if we attempted to enforce access to any specific opportunity to learn. Yet those powerful critics were often straw men we ourselves foresaw sabotaging our own efforts. In a process of institutional self-regulation,[11] we in OCR came to mimic the critics' arguments that OCR could not wield Title VI to help equalize specific educational opportunities in the nation's schools. Repeating these arguments, we argued anxiously and with resignation that we could not pursue such everyday justice—that the entire realm of everyday academic harm to children of color was off-limits.

This chapter demonstrates first that our pessimism about OCR's limited reach was not simply paranoid but based in some reality. Over the decades since OCR's creation, powerful people had argued that OCR should not name as discrimination various academic harms to students of color. Critics have long resisted any active federal enforcement of equal academic opportunity to learn for these students at the local level. Circa 2000, OCR staff wishing to do so argued—to some extent correctly—that powerful actors might deem even acknowledged academic harms to be beyond OCR's reach.

But this pessimism about the law's limited potential to assist children of color had infiltrated even those most committed to creative efforts to use the law, so that we came to sabotage our own efforts as being somehow out of order. In this chapter, I examine my own apprenticeship[12] in OCR's rhetorical habits. My growing pessimism about using civil rights tools to equalize opportunities to learn through the project demonstrates the strength of this pervasive rebuttal that pursuing specific academic opportunities would never be allowed. Other OCR employees—who had also entered the agency committed to using legal tools to pursue equality—told me of their own apprenticeship, over time, in the agency's habit of arguing that "civil rights" workers were unwarranted to examine the "educational" treatment of students of color. At this moment of designing an agency policy initiative, OCR staff argued defeatedly that not just the details of children's everyday academic lives but even their most basic academic opportunities were totally off-limits to "civil rights" analysis. In doing so, we framed as impossible the basic task for which the agency was originally created: employing civil rights law to analyze whether educational opportunities were being unfairly denied to children of color.

## OCR's History of Constraining the Definition of Racial Discrimination in Academic Opportunity

Crenshaw et al. call for "the use of critical historical method to show that the contemporary structure of civil rights rhetoric is not the natural or inevitable meaning of racial justice but, instead, a collection of strategies and discourses born of and deployed in particular political, cultural, and institutional conflicts and negotiations" (1995, xvi). Today's definitions of racial discrimination in education have evolved through ongoing argument over what educational opportunities young people of color are entitled to. Disputes over defining the reach of Title VI in education have always been, in essence, disputes over which opportunity denials to students of color would be deemed significant and worth remedying.

More broadly, regarding academic opportunities, a child's "right" to education has itself long been up for debate. Students of law and education in the United States are often shocked to learn that the Constitution does not guarantee any child an education as a "fundamental right" protected by federal law. Many state constitutions declare that the state has a responsibility to educate its youth,[13] but that does not automatically entitle children either; people have had to sue states to actually provide adequate educational resources.[14] Most Americans believe in a universal right to public education, and this lay notion is fundamental to demands that this "right" be extended to all children regardless of race, gender, or disability.[15] Still, Americans have long struggled over how to offer educational opportunities fairly and in ways that do not violate the Constitution.

American history has a long list of such violations, even though courts have only recognized them as unconstitutional since the mid-twentieth century. Law was long used to deny academic opportunities to children of color rather than to provide them. When laws excluded these children entirely from public institutions, communities of color often funded their own schools. When provided a publicly funded education, most children of color studied in segregated and underresourced settings apart from white children, either in separate buildings or in separate classrooms within schools. Chinese students in the West,[16] Hispanic students in the West and Southwest,[17] and African American students throughout the nation were taught in segregated settings. Native American students were often educated in white-controlled settings designed to erase the influence of their parents' culture.[18] When children of color did attend schools and classrooms with white children and teachers, they were often denigrated intellectually and socially by their teachers and classmates.[19] In the early twentieth century, for example, Mexican American families had to fight for equitable opportunities within white-controlled, racially mixed schools that segregated their children into "low-ability" classes, deemed them mentally retarded, and punished them for using their native language.[20]

Throughout American history, various racial/ethnic groups struggled for equal access to academic opportunity because they had been excluded on the basis of race. While their struggles are not as well documented as those of African Americans, Hispanic and Asian American parents, organized first by national origin (such as "Mexicans" and "Chinese"), tried to utilize legal channels to ensure that schooling was available to their children at all and to resist local orders of segregation.[21] Parents also pushed for seats in restricted, resourced white public schools and finally for equal treatment within them.[22]

After the 1964 Civil Rights Act's Title VI expanded the federal civil rights toolkit to protect people from discrimination "on the ground of race, color, or national origin" in federally funded programs, including schools, various groups of parents began formally to press the federal courts and Congress for various equal educational opportunities for their children. In the 1970s, these groups succeeded in forcing Congress to include subsections in legislation that would protect students in schools from discrimination based on sex (Title IX of the Education Amendments of 1972) and disability (Section 504 of the Rehabilitation Act of 1973). Legal pressure from advocates for the children of immigrants succeeded in 1974 in getting the Supreme Court to apply Title VI's prohibitions on "national origin" discrimination specifically to linguistic discrimination in schools against students learning the English-language.[23]

Expanding the legal definition of "discrimination" past segregation alone, the civil rights movement pursued both academic opportunities and social opportunities in education through the law and started pushing to analyze various aspects of everyday justice in student experience. Title IX, for example, covered both equal admissions to programs and colleges and equal opportunities to compete in athletics. Disability and language-minority laws and regulations were even more explicitly academic. For example, in *Lau v. Nichols*, a case regarding Chinese-speaking students in San Francisco, the Supreme Court argued that English-language learners placed in English-only classes experienced discrimination under Title VI if no language instruction were provided. A "sink or swim" policy, the court decreed, discriminated impermissibly against these children on the basis of national origin by denying them access to the common curriculum. Even before *Lau*, a famous May 25, 1970, OCR memorandum argued similarly that Title VI should apply to equalizing the academic opportunities of English-language learners.[24]

For each population of children protected by civil rights law, OCR has had substantial power to define discrimination in education as the denial of specific academic opportunities in children's everyday lives inside schools and districts, beyond the basic rules laid down by legislation and Supreme Court rulings. Federal enforcement agencies such as the Department of Health, Education, and Welfare (later the Department of Education) developed federal regulations, each approved by Congress, designed to "effectuate" the enforcement of federal civil rights laws. Since "Congress, whether by design or inaction, often fails to define intelligible standards or governing principles to guide subordinate agencies in their work," agencies such as OCR have real power to expand or narrow the equal opportunity logic of prior laws and legislation.[25] While Congress and courts repeatedly limited OCR's power to enforce discrimination remedies, particularly desegregation, Title VI gave OCR the opportunity to define racial discrimination as broadly or as narrowly as administrations and administrators desired.[26] In the end, OCR's "implementing regulations" for Title VI would contain few specifics about assessing the denial of academic opportunity: as an OCR colleague put it, OCR's definitions of racial discrimination remained the vaguest because they were the most hotly disputed. The regulations gave few specifics about what acts or situations constituted "discriminatory" denial of access to educational "benefits" and "services." And compared to the regulations regarding sex-based, disability-based, and language-based discrimination, OCR's Title VI regulations offered few specific and detailed rules regulating the ways schools and districts should equitably provide *academic* opportunities to learn.

Title VI's open definitions of racial discrimination as the "denial" of "benefits" and "services" meant that in principle a wide range of harms could be found discriminatory, but in practice, the range of impermissible opportunity denials to students of color has actively been reduced, particularly regarding academic opportunities. Even those running OCR, whether bowing to external critics or determined to restrict the power of civil rights tools, have used this open definition to argue explicitly that OCR should not name as "discrimination" specific academic harms experienced by students of color.

*OCR's History of Constraining the Academic Reach
    of Title VI from Within*

Throughout OCR's history, someone, either within or outside OCR, has resisted every call to assist students of color academically, whether that call has emerged from an outside advocate or an employee within the agency. Often, they have argued that Title VI itself does not, should not, or cannot frame a particular form of academic opportunity denial as illegal. This rebuttal has served to halt many proactive efforts to equalize academic opportunities.

OCR's first and most famous such effort—desegregating districts across the South—sparked so much political resistance that it was quickly quashed. Through the 1970s, a Congress hostile to Southern desegregation worked actively to hinder OCR's work,[27] while the Supreme Court, confronting de facto segregation in the North and West, started to gradually restrict national desegregation efforts as well, especially through rulings that excluded suburbs from metropolitan desegregation.[28] Nixon campaigned against HEW's desegregation efforts in the South; once elected, he fired OCR's desegregation-oriented director and then threatened to fire OCR employees who advocated busing as a method to equalize black students' opportunities to learn.[29]

As the primary agency responsible for imposing fiscal consequences on districts refusing to desegregate, OCR helped stall systemic desegregation nationwide. Soon, the NAACP challenged OCR's inactivity in both K–12 and higher education. In *Adams v. Richardson* (1973),[30] the NAACP Legal Defense Fund charged OCR and HEW with failing to enforce Title VI on Southern and border-state colleges and universities that OCR had already found to be illegally segregated.[31] The D.C. federal district court judge agreed and ordered OCR to start resolving its enforcement activity in a timely manner. Ironically, this order to speed up desegregation work pushed OCR to close desegregation cases rather than open them.[32]

Nixon encouraged OCR to investigate the distribution of resources between schools and various forms of discrimination within schools, such as tracking, discipline, and testing, as a way of turning the agency's attention away from desegregation in the South, thus pushing analysis toward some aspects of everyday justice in schools and districts and away from others.[33] Employees attempting to investigate academic opportunity undertook some labor—intensive compliance reviews of entire "great city" districts, addressing racially inequitable teacher hiring and unequal resource distribution to de facto segregated schools whenever it could convince districts to deal with these issues "without a prior finding of intentional segregation of students."[34] External and internal observers labeled OCR's new work an active campaign to accept "separate but equal" segregated education rather than pursue desegregation across the nation as originally charged: "As one OCR official candidly put it, 'It really was a return to *Plessy*—if blacks could get equal services in their separate location, that would be fine.' "[35] Still, these efforts were far more comprehensive than any pursued at OCR when I worked there. By then, the entire project of proactively pressing for opportunities to learn for children of color had been deemed suspect.

OCR responded to the *Adams*-enforced pressure to close Title VI cases with a new reluctance to undertake time-consuming compliance reviews and instead began waiting for Americans to approach it with complaints. This trend toward passivity persisted over the next several decades under various administrations.[36] Circa 2000, our office director explained in a staff meeting that OCR's work was no longer "proactive." I wrote in my notes afterward, "OCR did proactive work originally" but "became complaint-oriented potentially to slow the agency down in the 1970s, around busing, etc."

OCR's shift toward waiting for Title VI complaints, rather than acting "proactively," played a role in shifting its caseload away from race cases altogether and toward disability cases, which were typically filed on behalf of individual children, could be most easily closed through federal pressure on educators to follow clear procedures, and were filed in growing numbers through the 1970s, 1980s, and 1990s.[37] Under President Carter, though the *Adams* court found OCR to be no longer "guilty of deliberate nonenforcement" of Title VI, the agency was now permitting a huge backlog of "hundreds of unresolved complaints." [38] The *Adams* pressure to close complaints continued to escalate, and OCR came to focus on closing complaint investigations rather than opening uninvited reviews of districts. As OCR moved to focus on gender, language-minority, and disability rights as well as Title VI, the complaint-based workload began to overwhelm the agency. Through the 1970s, advocacy organizations such as the NAACP's Legal Defense Fund—joined by groups like MALDEF (the Mexican American Legal Defense and Educational Fund), the Women's Equity Action League, and the National Federation of the Blind—continued to appeal to courts to force OCR to resolve complaints more efficiently and effectively: "Too much was expected of OCR. . . . Pressed by so many claims for relief, from so many different groups, in such varied forms, the Office became almost paralyzed."[39]

Through the 1980s and 1990s, complaints about disabled students dominated OCR's workload. In 1989, one observer noted that "the complaint orientation forced OCR to address most of its resources to those constituencies which were most prolific with complaints," so "the handicapped" were "claiming" over half of OCR's "enforcement efforts."[40] By 1993, other observers noted, "Although created under the Civil Rights Act of 1964, OCR spends most of its time addressing the rights of the handicapped. . . . OCR's enforcement priorities were determined . . . by the civil rights community's most sophisticated and vocal members—the parents of handicapped children."[41]

In a book on the "ironic legacy" of Title VI, Halpern (1995) notes that OCR's original focus on race-related civil rights activity became gradually eclipsed as Title VI's civil rights logic was extended to other communities, especially women and people with disabilities. This basic demographic fact played out at OCR, particularly regarding disability. But more important, as Halpern argues, OCR's own administration has consistently hindered its work to protect students of color from discrimination. They have done so, in part, by refusing to define many harms to students of color, particularly academic opportunity denials, as a "civil rights" problem and a government priority.[42]

OCR's chief administrator, an assistant secretary for civil rights in the Department of Education, is appointed anew by each incoming administration and always shapes the agency's analytic and policy trajectory regarding Title VI, through both subtle bureaucratic moves and outright top-down changes in civil rights policy. Ideological considerations about how the assistant secretary will weigh in on OCR's definitions of racial discrimination (and, secondarily, sex discrimination) in educational opportunity have always been an important factor in his or her appointment, more important than whether the person has any "civil rights" experience.[43] Clarence Thomas, with a background in corporate regulation, was Reagan's assistant secretary of OCR for a brief ten months before he left to head the EEOC; Thomas later became a key voice on the Supreme Court against "race-conscious" policies for equalizing academic opportunity. President George H. W. Bush nominated Michael L. Williams, a former Justice Department lawyer "without substantial ties to traditional civil rights groups,"[44] to be his assistant secretary of OCR; Williams led a campaign against race-specific scholarships while in office.[45]

Under the Reagan administration, OCR frequently and openly opposed civil rights remedies for students of color, and also stopped collecting race-based data on academic opportunities and outcomes.[46] Clarence Thomas instituted a "first come, first served" policy of casework at OCR; according to Norma Cantu, whom I interviewed in 2005, this policy stalled even large-scale race complaints about unequal academic opportunity in entire districts.[47] As Cantu put it to me in the interview, Thomas's policy not only encouraged complainants to approach OCR with non-race-related issues that could be more quickly resolved. The policy also pressured OCR employees to tell advocates that bureaucracy itself made it impossible to investigate claims of even egregious racial inequalities in academic opportunity.

Clarence Thomas ... [had] a very mechanistic approach to handling the cases where it was first in, first out, without assigning any kind of priority to the handling or any kind of flexibility to the investigators for the handling of race cases. Say you had filed a race case saying that no African American *ever* had been allowed into a gifted and talented program in the entire state of Georgia. You requested all the names, all the "gifted and talented" students, and you saw zero, zero, zero, zero, zero for however many counties there are in Georgia. You filed a complaint in the OCR saying, "This prompts a need for further questioning. I'm not saying it's a quota, but I'm saying we can ask some more questions because we see too many zeros here." Clarence Thomas put that complaint in the queue. So if there are 4,000 other complaints in front of you, most of them individual, they're going to get dealt with in the order that they arrive in the office. No matter how urgent, how pervasive, how severe. And the investigator says, "Oh, we're told we have no discretion." And so that, I think, makes the statement about race. When it's not any more pernicious than a parent complaining that due process [to get disability services] took twenty days instead of ten.

Under Cantu, OCR opened some compliance reviews of potential racial discrimination in entire districts regarding high-stakes testing practices, "minority" (student of color) overrepresentation in Special Education, racial harassment, and racial tracking of students of color into low-"ability" groups in high schools. OCR also increased its work on sexual harassment, athletic opportunities for girls and women, and language-minority services. Contrasting her to those who had held her position in previous administrations, a 1994 article from the NEA newsletter termed Cantu "the Enforcer,"[48] while critics argued that now "those attempting to expand the boundaries of . . . discrimination have an eager friend and ally in OCR."[49]

When I was hired near the end of the Clinton era, however, OCR's internal apparatus was still doing relatively little work on racial discrimination in educational opportunity. Between 1995 and 2003, according to OCR's annual reports, disability complaints were roughly 50 percent of the complaints received nationally at OCR; race cases (including ELL work) were roughly 20 percent of the cases received, while sex cases were about 7 percent.[50] Regionally, these demographics were heavily weighted toward getting disability services for white students. At one staff meeting, we were told that of the total cases coming into our region, 48 percent were K–12 complaints about disabled student services, typically charging that this lack of services denied the student a "free and appropriate public education" (we called these "FAPE cases"). Almost three-quarters (72 percent) of the 27 FAPE cases currently open in the office involved white students, while just five of the cases were about Latino students and just three cases involved African Americans. The statistics caused Reba, my lawyer colleague, to suggest at this meeting that the office should look into "who it is that finds their way to OCR" and "take some affirmative steps" to reach other communities. Still, as one office director put it to me privately, the demographic of predominantly white and middle-class complainants characterized the agency's overall pattern nationally. He felt, as I paraphrased in my notes, that OCR's current attempts to provide online complaint forms would only increase racial disparities in access to the office.

> Those who don't know about OCR are people of color/poor. OCR is putting its complaint system online, and this may well exacerbate the problem because white people/women (especially those pursuing Title IX athletics) have computer access. "Isn't this itself a civil rights issue?" I ask. He agrees, laughs, says the administration is publicly very quiet on many issues.

Top administrators at OCR have actively created the perception that the agency's Title VI tools are not available to assist people in pursuing educational opportunities for children of color. In 1988, a congressional committee examining OCR's work noted that lower-level staffers themselves perceived many race discrimination issues, both social and academic, as "off-limits" even to investigation: "There was a clear perception among the regional office staff that certain issues were 'off limits' and could not be investigated. Most of the issues involved race discrimination. Among such issues were discrimination involving disciplinary actions and the placement of black students in special education programs." [51] Through e-mails and conversations with higher-ups and colleagues under Cantu, we were told that many Title VI issues were "sensitive" or "red flag" issues that would invite external criticism and had to be handled with great care; the next administration would explicitly name some civil rights tools as off-limits.

George W. Bush's nominee for assistant secretary of OCR was Gerald A. Reynolds, a utilities lawyer. Bush appointed him in 2001 during a congressional recess. Reynolds argued openly before his appointment that he did not believe in certain core methods of analyzing racial discrimination in education, particularly "disparate impact" analysis, which was developed in the 1970s as a way to open and investigate civil rights complaints based on racially disproportionate statistics. For example, Reynolds did not favor opening cases triggered by statistics showing that suspiciously high proportions of a district's or school's black students were placed in Special Education. Reynolds enacted no formal policy prohibiting disparate impact analysis, but after his appointment, as Losen (2004) describes, top OCR administrators distributed internal memos instructing employees to avoid investigating cases in which complainants requested that racialized or gendered statistics trigger investigations of potential discriminatory opportunity denial in students' everyday school lives. This web of statements against disparate impact analysis, eventually accepted by lower-level employees who handled incoming complaints, constricted the sense of what educational acts and patterns would be allowed to count as potential civil rights concerns within OCR.

After Bush appointed Reynolds to run the U.S. Commission on Civil Rights in 2004, Reynolds argued on NPR that "statistics" showing racial achievement gaps or racially disproportionate Special Education placements should not in and of themselves raise suspicions of, or require investigation into, potential racial "discrimination."[52] Though Reynolds was no longer working at OCR, this mind-set soon became broadcast as OCR policy. In 2004, the National Women's Law Center (NWLC) said, OCR responded to growing complaints of the underrepresentation of women and people of color in faculty positions in math, science, and engineering by issuing a generic letter stating that "statistical disparities, standing alone, do not constitute discrimination." This response, the NWLC argued, "flies in the face of long-standing principles of anti-discrimination law, which view disparities of this magnitude as a red flag for unlawful employment practices and should, at the very minimum, trigger a serious investigation."[53] Several years after I worked at OCR, the caution against disparate impact analysis was entered into the agency's publicly available complaint investigation procedure, via a caution against starting cases with racial "statistics."[54]

Reynolds had resigned in October 2003, after awaiting final Senate confirmation that failed "amid Democratic concerns about his opposition to affirmative action."[55] After that, the Bush administration resisted appointing anyone to direct the agency,[56] though OCR's substitute assistant secretary, Kenneth L. Marcus (Reynolds's former assistant), presided informally. During this nebulous period, according to the NAACP, some staff working at the agency's headquarters were affiliated with anti-affirmative action groups that were busy filing OCR complaints against universities considering race when admitting applicants.[57] Under Marcus, office resources went into producing the "Race-Neutral Alternatives" document suggesting prematurely to districts and universities that Title VI required them to avoid race-conscious student assistance or assignment altogether. An article on the document in *Education Week*, the country's primary venue for education news, was titled "Bush Has Own View of Promoting Civil Rights."[58]

Indeed, OCR was actively positioning itself as an agency that would use its legal powers to ensure that fewer polices in schools and districts, not more, set forth directly to assist students of color as such or in particular ways. In George W. Bush's first term, according to colleagues, OCR undertook almost no proactive Title VI compliance reviews. In Bush's second term, the employees I talked to knew of no proactive reviews of racial patterns in "gifted and talented" course placement, minority Special Education placement, or services for English-language learners. "OCR develops policy while working on these issues proactively," one employee said. "So without doing reviews we can't develop policy." While passively avoiding or actively steering employees away from Title VI work on behalf of students of color, the Bush administration steered OCR toward altogether new definitions of "discrimination." OCR's Web site soon invited the public to learn about OCR's newest antidiscrimination work: protecting the Boy Scouts and other "patriotic" "youth groups" from "discrimination," which meant allowing these organizations to meet in public facilities even if the organizations excluded gay youth.[59]

The new administration quickly reshaped OCR's definitions of discrimination both publicly and internally by tabling some key Title VI efforts in progress. For example, when I worked at OCR during the Clinton administration, senior OCR lawyers produced two guides designed to wield Title VI to protect students of color from everyday denials of academic opportunity. One guide, a research-based manual for districts and universities, explained how to avoid increasing racial disparities through many widespread high-stakes testing practices. *The Use of Tests as Part of High Stakes Decision Making for Students: A Resource Guide for Educators and Policymakers* was "The Testing Guide" to people within OCR. The other was a resource comparability manual designed to help OCR investigators assess whether academic resources (books and teachers) and facilities (classrooms and science labs) were denied to students of color within school districts. The manual's authors told those of us working on the Early Learning Project that they also wanted to prompt analysis of interdistrict resource inequity, such as disparities between cities and suburbs, but higher-ups had said that this was impossible. The Testing Guide received public criticism for suggesting that racial disparities on standardized tests could trigger discrimination analysis.[60] The "Resource Comp" project was critiqued internally as too "proactive." When the Bush administration came to power shortly before I left OCR, we were told that such policy documents would be put on indefinite hold for "administrative review." The Testing Guide, which had a brief public release in 2000, was "archived" under Bush; it was available only under Archived Documents on the OCR Web site with the caveat, "retained for historical purposes."[61] The resource comparability guide was released for internal office use, but no proactive work on the subject continued. On OCR's public Web site as of late 2004, a "Topics A to Z" information section contained an old, and non-functioning, link to Tests and Testing. No link existed for resource comparability.[62] OCR's Web site instead offered readers the 2004 downloadable report on "race-neutral" approaches to programming and admissions, explaining that "The Office for Civil Rights seeks to provide educational institutions with information about the 'race-neutral' options available to them."

By the time I worked at OCR, just before the change from Clinton to Bush, employees had learned to shut down their own efforts to use Title VI to protect students of color, both in specific complaints and in efforts to suggest new policy directions. If they did not shut down their efforts themselves, they reasoned, nervous supervisors would do it for them. The eight-year Clinton era, in which Cantu permitted some new work on issues of racial discrimination in academic matters (such as the development of the testing and resource comparability guides), was drawing to a close, and regardless of whether Al Gore or George W. Bush were elected president, somebody new would soon be in charge of defining discrimination for the office. Cantu told me in our later interview that during these years "everybody seemed to be watching" OCR. "People were in a high state of anxiety at that time," she said, and the public searchlight made every move and statement seem weighty and dangerous. Whatever one put in the "script" as official OCR "policy" in those last days, she said, would be used or misused by whoever took power. Every OCR employee seemed on notice that any public move of OCR in the Title VI realm, even by the lowest-ranking staffer, could harm the office—and by extension, we felt, the nation's children—if it fell into hostile hands. Doing civil rights work from within OCR in the new civil rights era was often largely about anticipating that internal or external critics would "shut down" efforts to equalize specified opportunities for students of color—and, accordingly, about anticipating critics and shutting down such civil rights work ourselves.

While I was at OCR, the employees seeking to pursue the Early Learning Project routinely doubted that we could use civil rights laws to afford children of color the specific academic opportunities that experts said all children need. While we reminded ourselves dutifully that OCR employees should beware of forcing any particular academic approach on districts, we learned to parrot a far more general defeatist argument circulating around the agency: that for students of color, "education" and "civil rights" were altogether separate domains.

## Diminishing the Reach of Civil Rights Tools by Distinguishing between "Education" and "Civil Rights"

Some years before working at OCR, I was a high school teacher. In both jobs, I observed starkly underresourced and crumbling schools of the "apartheid" variety described by Kozol (2005). In schools that served students of color almost exclusively, teachers like myself with emergency credentials taught underskilled students in underresourced classes. Elsewhere in these districts white students attended resource-rich schools with seasoned teachers, advanced coursework, and a multitude of electives. In the districts that managed to get white students and children of color into the same schools, white students were still typically clustered in "gifted" or "advanced" classrooms, where they received enriching curriculum and experienced teachers unavailable to students of color in the next classroom.[63]

Nationwide, children experienced such racially unequal academic opportunities daily. And activists were making straightforward demands to remedy them. For example, they were bringing finance equity cases at the state level, rooted in state constitutions' language about providing "all" state residents with adequate opportunities in schools. The Campaign for Fiscal Equity filed a case in New York arguing that the state's school finance system denied children of color in New York City fundamental resources enjoyed by white students in suburbs. The ACLU filed a lawsuit against the State of California alleging that the state's unequal and inadequate distribution of classroom space, school facilities, qualified teachers, AP courses, and other academic resources to students of color violated its responsibility to provide adequate education to students. These arguments about financial inequalities and inequities in basic resources were straightforward. They suggested extending analyses of educational equity to include the terrain that educators take for granted: everyday opportunities to learn. They framed educational opportunity as a question both of money and of what learning opportunities money was used to buy. They took into account the opportunities to learn that students of various groups were actually being offered or denied on an everyday basis.[64]

I brought this way of thinking about educational opportunity to my work at OCR, focusing on opportunity provision within districts and schools. The regional Early Learning Project was exactly what I had imagined "civil rights work" in education to be: it envisioned evaluating specific opportunities that experts deemed necessary for all students to learn and thrive and considering whether those opportunities were unfairly denied to students of color in their classrooms, schools, and districts.

The project stemmed from a previous Clinton-era OCR initiative to investigate and reduce racially biased high school "tracking," the routine placement of supposedly more able students, typically white students, into advanced courses and supposedly less able students, typically students of color, into remedial courses. Research demonstrates that nationwide, such tracking regularly produces racially skewed classroom sequences or "tracks" as early as elementary school. While such early tracking is ostensibly an educator response to incoming racial differences in student skill sets (itself often due to inequities in preschool access and quality),[65] tracking practices often incorrectly assess students' actual ability, while producing unequally skilled students during the schooling years. Jeannie Oakes, a national expert on tracking who briefly served as an outside adviser on the Early Learning Project, argued to us at a symposium that the racial tracking of students starts in elementary school through three mechanisms. Within classrooms, students of color are placed into low-level, fixed "ability groups," particularly regarding reading, and a watered-down curriculum retards their learning opportunities. Students of color are separated into Special Education classrooms and rarely placed in "gifted" classrooms. Finally, disproportionate numbers of students of color are asked to repeat a grade.[66] OCR's work to investigate and remedy high-school level tracking had revealed that too few high-track or AP courses were available to students of color, but it had also raised deeper questions about the much earlier process of slotting students into ability groups.[67] The Early Learning Project aimed to look in detail at the earliest provision of opportunities to learn, to see if and how the K–3 opportunities offered to students of color measured up either within desegregated schools where students of color were quickly tracked to low-level groupings or for all students in schools serving students of color exclusively.

A 1998 internal report written by a small group of OCR employees in my region proposed the Early Learning Project as a "divisionwide early intervention activity" in the Title VI arena. The report argued that through its small number of Clinton-era compliance reviews, OCR had found "statistical disparities in minority and majority enrollment patterns" and "tracking and ability grouping practices" in many districts at the high school level. "The bases for these disparities" appeared "to include" a host of practices creating unequal opportunities to learn, such as a "lack of staff development and training in working with underrepresented students; insufficient training and numbers of counselors; inconsistent application of placement criteria; low expectations of minority students by school staff; insufficient data collection to assess student progress and retention; inappropriate tracking; insufficient primary language support for LEP students; and unequal distribution of resources (e.g., access to technology)." OCR and district master plans "designed to address these concerns" at the high school level had spurred local attempts at change. However, "despite OCR's efforts in this arena, the effectiveness of these efforts have been mixed at best," the report argued, because the efforts did not address the early practices of tracking and early opportunity denials. "It has become clear," the report continued, "that the equal access to quality curriculum and teaching which Title VI mandates must be enforced from the earliest grades if all students are to have truly equal opportunity to succeed." The report proposed "an ambitious study project to learn more about the causes for minority students' lagging achievement in the early years and to develop a Title VI approach to address the challenges faced by districts in meeting the academic needs of young minority students. We see this 'early failure' issue as one of the most critical facing minority students."

From these hopeful beginnings, the Early Learning Project's framers, who were primarily my regional colleagues, inserted tellingly defensive language that from the outset constrained OCR's imagined efforts on this "critical" issue. The report acknowledged OCR's lack of information about the causes of early elementary tracking and "failure" by students of color: it argued that "OCR has traditionally had difficulty identifying and addressing the inequalities in standards and instruction in elementary education that contribute to unequal success in secondary school." To justify the project, it argued that "to date, OCR has yet to develop an effective enforcement strategy to assess equal access to education in the early years which would afford traditionally underrepresented students the opportunity for greater success later in their educational careers." While the report suggested correctly that OCR employees were not yet practiced at investigating concrete early opportunities to learn and indicated that providing learning opportunities on a daily basis was the local educator's job, the report set up the rhetorical habit that contributed to the project's demise: distinguishing OCR's "civil rights" efforts from "educational" efforts regarding "instruction," "success," "failure," and "achievement." The report cautiously assured readers—agency higher-ups and, potentially, public foes who might hear of the initiative—that OCR would not get itself involved too deeply in the educational domain of learning opportunities. "The purpose of this effort is not for OCR staff to become experts in the areas of curriculum design or pedagogical theory," the report stated with a pointed caveat. "Rather, the purpose is to provide OCR staff the background information needed to develop sound legal approaches under Title VI to ensure equal educational opportunities from the earliest years."

The report proposed inviting experts in education to advise OCR lawyers and investigators in a concerted collaborative effort "to learn of best practices and to formulate compliance activities to ensure equal access for students at the earliest grade levels." Once it had learned about educational "best practices" from outside experts, the document proposed, OCR would devise a legal strategy for enforcing equal access to the early educational opportunities deemed necessary for all. The office would disseminate information to the public on this newly expanding arena of Title VI work, so educators could start analyzing opportunity proactively in their own schools and districts and parents could start demanding specific opportunities. The office proposed distributing "information regarding the Title VI requirements for providing equal access to the core curriculum." OCR would pursue its ongoing legal work on "access," while sharing the academic and educator-derived "best district practices to customers and stakeholders to ensure such access." OCR would facilitate continuing partnerships with colleges and universities and "form partnerships with parents and advocacy groups to empower them to pursue issues of equal educational access." With bureaucratically inflected optimism, the report stated OCR's final plans for enforcing early learning opportunity, adding a dash of government-style plans for massive change. "It is anticipated that effective compliance reviews and technical activities beginning in Fiscal Year 2000 will have the potential for positively affecting thousands of minority students currently being denied access to high quality curriculum and services," the document concluded.

When I reread this document after leaving OCR, I was shocked by these strongly stated expectations that we could formulate a new arena of Title VI work to ensure equal early access to academic opportunity nationwide. When I started planning the Early Learning symposium as a volunteer intern early in 1999, I shared this sense of optimism and possibility. Yet, during the symposium and in the months of follow-up work I did to synthesize our recommendations and propose a strategy for analyzing K–3 opportunities to learn, something changed: conversations with colleagues inside and outside OCR slowly hammered my optimism into a pervasive anxiety and pessimism about the likelihood of getting OCR to focus its attention on securing these specific equal academic opportunities. The very colleagues who had put the project in motion now worried incessantly that moving forward with it would incur the wrath of internal and external critics who would argue that it was not OCR's place to do "educational" analysis.

As the project moved beyond its original planning documents, it became clear to me that OCR could make powerful generic statements on its Web site about its mandate to pursue equal educational opportunity for the nation's students, and OCR employees could write proposals for the project that clarified the need for such work for students of color. But, once we began concrete efforts to help equalize concrete opportunities, many of my colleagues argued fearfully that a civil rights agency would not even be allowed to take up these issues. As I noted wonderingly, colleagues repeatedly articulated an argument from higher-ups that they had learned over time to argue themselves: "a sense of quality of education issues being outside OCR's purview."

At first I proceeded without recognizing this perceived constraint on the project. In February 2000, OCR convened an Early Learning symposium for education researchers, elementary school practitioners, and OCR lawyers and investigators titled "Isolating Key Spheres of Elementary Equity: Defining Equal Access to Early Learning Opportunities." The point of the symposium, as I stated in my introductory remarks to the assembled guests, was to consider broadening the definition of racial discrimination in education by examining how and whether the racially equitable provision of opportunities to learn in the K–3 years was a civil right under Title VI. At the symposium, OCR lawyers and managers from across the country came into contact with educational researchers, advocates, principals, teachers, and superintendents from across the country. The researchers presented overwhelming evidence that K–3 students of color routinely did not have equal opportunities to learn within and between schools. Teachers of students of color had low rates of certification and retention. Curricula for students of color were often unavailable or inadequate, and the students often lacked necessary resources to learn anything but basic literacy and math. At times, students of color lacked even classrooms, or seats. Confronted with this data, conference participants agreed that this early denial set the students up for disproportionate failure and that OCR should work to help equalize their early opportunities to learn as a form of basic civil rights work. One academic explained bluntly why OCR should intervene in districts and schools: "States are holding schools accountable for test scores, but not for teaching children—no one is holding them accountable for providing opportunities to learn." One D.C. lawyer, similarly frustrated, said, "OCR is allowing districts to deny students access to the core curriculum"; she then said that "marrying civil rights with educational practice" was "hard, but necessary." Still, we faced the task of questioning whether denials of adequate academic "access" and preparation could be deemed discriminatory by OCR. This would involve negotiation with the OCR lawyers and government managers in attendance over whether OCR should and could be involved in analyzing and equalizing opportunities for learning.

While all agreed that the denial of K–3 resources and facilities was a clear violation of the nation's equal opportunity logic,[68] only a small subset of the conference attendees, including researchers and educators, thought it was actually possible for OCR employees to evaluate and help remedy the opportunities to learn that were or were not available to students of color. The problem, as framed, was not just OCR's lack of "educational" expertise but also the ability of OCR to judge the presence or absence of specific opportunities. I had expected this critique, and in preparation for this debate at the symposium itself, I had asked each of our academic and educator speakers to prepare checklists outlining the concrete opportunities their research and expertise suggested were key in early elementary school. I had asked each of them a basic question: "If you were an OCR observer walking into a school or district, what would you look for in order to see whether students were being offered an equitable early elementary education?" At the symposium, I asked OCR staff and the assembled educators to discuss these checklists in small groups, asking themselves, "Are there any items" on the checklists "you find particularly difficult or problematic for OCR to see or measure in schools, or particularly difficult to implement in schools?" During these discussions, I reflected in my notes on the arguments that ensued. OCR lawyers, who routinely perused the minute details of Special Education plans for disabled students, worried about monitoring the academic opportunities available in classrooms serving students of color: not only would this require excessive educational expertise, but OCR had no legal warrant for the task. Lawyers who routinely argued that legal texts and regulations for English-language learners did allow us to analyze "well-prepared teachers" and teachers' "knowledge of subject matter" and "instruction" were now arguing that such analysis typically did not characterize Title VI efforts for "regular" students of color. In my notes, I recorded some typical anxieties about overstepping the federal role in education. People were arguing that "instruction . . . seems like a district decision"; one colleague answered the question of "instructional practice—can OCR deal with it?" with a resounding "no." I also reported the age-old anxiety about seeming too "prescriptive" as a federal agency: "Access to knowledge: we can't do yes or no on any *brand*-name, or fall into traps on the reading wars." Other anxieties were less about a federal agency entering local debates on "instruction" and more about whether OCR could even appropriately ask questions about the "quality" of educational resources, such as about teachers' qualifications. "OCR hasn't typically asked whether the teacher is certified," I scribbled.

During the symposium, even while the academics repeatedly argued that the "true spirit of educational equity law" required engaging "what happens in the classroom," participants argued that OCR employees should stay out of examining the details of opportunities to learn altogether. When a professor spoke on his research center's synthesis of research on equitable teaching strategies, one lawyer responded by saying bluntly that issues of teaching were "touchy-feely stuff" off-limits to lawyers. One lawyer from D.C. headquarters argued that "traditional compliance issues" and "comfortable OCR areas" did include comparing the provision of "qualified teachers," and she agreed with one academic who put succinctly the obvious more qualitative requirement that to be "qualified," "teachers must understand learning and understand how to teach." Still, she argued that analyzing teacher preparation in any detail was an "educational" issue, not a "civil rights" issue.

During the conference, OCR colleagues offered various subarguments explaining the legal, political, and bureaucratic constraints on the Early Learning Project. Some anticipated particular legal difficulties in using Title VI to demand that students of color have equal access to opportunities to learn. Lawyers worried that since the children of color who were denied educational opportunities were disproportionately poor, this intertwining of race and class would confound available legal logic, which prohibits only racial discrimination. As one lawyer put it bluntly, "You need the *racial* hook—cases lose because you can't link it to race."[69] Other OCR lawyers noted that since Title VI covered only the actions of actors who received federal funds directly, OCR might not be able to deal with unequal learning opportunities that were a result of parents' socioeconomic position rather than district policy. As I noted, one lawyer argued that "parent-teacher organizations might create disparities via contributions. Is the source of the disparity within the district's control?" Some people stated as particularly worrisome the thought that OCR might be seen publicly as attempting to regulate racially equal academic "outcomes." As one lawyer put it bluntly, "An achievement gap is not necessarily a Title VI violation. Title VI is about equal inputs and opportunities; it doesn't guarantee equal results."

Others expressed more specific worries about federal employees looking at opportunities to learn in schools. The teachers and principals feared that lawyers would encroach on the sacrosanct turf of teaching and learning; the lawyers, in turn, worried that they and OCR investigators were not equipped to examine actual school- and class-room-level opportunities to learn. For her part, a professor worried that OCR's focus on "compliance" would squash the "spirit" of equity among teachers. At the conference, I repeatedly noted that people from both within and outside OCR stated their reticence to engage federal OCR employees in the very "nitty-gritty," "academic" work all in attendance deemed essential for solving "educational problems." While all agreed in principle that educational opportunity was a civil rights issue and that helping to provide and enable it was a federal responsibility, in conversations about OCR actually embarking upon this work, most attendees argued that civil rights lawyers could not easily enter the academic realm. Despite the project's basic premise of linking civil rights and "education" and despite the obvious fact that OCR itself, as the civil rights wing of the U.S. Department of Education, existed to effectuate this linkage, the "key tension at the symposium," I scribbled in my notes in bewilderment, was a stated tension between "education" work and "civil rights" work.

Neither at the conference nor afterward did I hear anyone argue that educational matters were the domain of other parts of the U.S. Department of Education, OCR's institutional home. Rather, the problem was a vaguely framed distinction between civil rights and academics. Both OCR employees and educators at the conference did offer the century-old argument that the "feds" should avoid intervening in "local" educational issues, even the availability of basic opportunities to learn; more argued that "civil rights" lawyers simply did not understand "education" and could not assess educational opportunity at the school or classroom level. But OCR people argued most vehemently that higher federal and political powers would not *allow* our "civil rights" agency to analyze and enforce the presence of concrete academic opportunities for students of color. One regional director framed the political problem of OCR pursuing "educational" issues using "legal" tools. To him, it was a matter of "doing it without recognition. Surfacing the issue might do more harm than good—because it could get squashed. OCR's a lightning rod. How to legally get into some educational issues without someone else shutting it down." He feared that this anticipated "shutdown" would come from higher-ups within the agency who were trying to avoid anything remotely controversial in an election year. "My worry," I would write similarly in my own notes some months later, was that even when talking about the project to people within the agency, I would find "that *saying* we're looking at academics will get it shut *down* so we *can't* look at academics."

After the symposium, in summaries and review papers, I tried to demonstrate the experts' consensus about "academic" opportunities essential for any K–3 classroom so that we could have a research-based benchmark against which to evaluate when students had access to equitable opportunities to learn. As my numerous scribbled-on versions of these documents demonstrated, colleagues helping me edit them were teaching me core forms of anxiety about and resistance to the "academic" nature of the project within the agency. As they read my drafts, colleagues repeatedly argued that while in theory, Title VI enabled OCR to analyze whether K–3 opportunities to learn were racially equitable, current law and politics made this analysis too dangerous. One OCR colleague circled the word "quality" throughout a paragraph of my early learning analysis, in a section arguing that we had to analyze "the quality of" classroom instruction and curriculum, assessment practices, and professional development. She did scribble in the margin an important question ("How does OCR measure?"). But, after talking to her, I wrote in the margin a more general reminder to "get rid of 'quality' altogether. . . . 'Quality' is one of those words that triggers bureaucrats. She's been told over and over that 'we are not to judge quality—we do legal.' " I was also repeatedly warned to avoid language that sounded "prescriptive" and to refrain entirely from using "the word *discriminatory* to describe unequal opportunity legally—it's a 'conclusive' word." A lawyer reminded me that to be politically astute, we should avoid calling our analysis of "opportunity to learn" a "legal analysis."

Learning quickly, I inserted many tellingly anxious caveats in Early Learning summary drafts instructing readers not to imagine OCR linking its legal work with educational work: "There is no need for OCR investigators to presume to be judges of instructional or curricular quality, or to pass judgment on any particular educational strategy." To circumvent any problems of OCR lawyers judging academic quality, we eventually proposed that OCR should simply ask teachers, principals, and district representatives to describe how and whether they knew the opportunities they themselves were providing were of a quality adequate to afford students the opportunity to reach common standards. But OCR colleagues' anxious rhetorical moves to decouple the terms "academic" or "education" from "legal" or "civil rights" were often forceful and explicit, demonstrating a deep fear about appearing to help equalize opportunities to learn in any specific way. During one project meeting, colleagues told me to delete from my report on the conference the most basic goal ("number 3") I'd written down, of "creating a Title VI argument" that OCR could use to tackle K–3 academic cases.

REBA: Maybe take off number 3, people will go right to that and be afraid of this.

OTHERS: Make clear that it's a draft. Don't call it a policy.

REBA: Don't make it something in writing that looks like an indicator of where the department is going—be very "personal"—your own personal diary.

ROGER: Ask people *not* to share it widely—there's always someone looking for a reason to embarrass the department.

People explicitly told me to discuss the specifics of our analysis verbally within the office rather than put into writing any analysis that could be viewed publicly. Any inquiry from higher-ups about the progress of the Early Learning Project received a purposefully vague description that we were "still developing" our thinking. When one "higher-up from D.C." called the office to ask about the "follow-up on the symposium," our office director, Ruben, "just reported back that we were 'working on a divisionwide activity—nothing completed yet.' " Hearing of the call, which came just as I was completing my documents on the symposium, I scribbled in my notes, "Argh!! Argh!! Argh!!"

In some instances, my colleagues even advised me to delete altogether any specific discussions of academic opportunity denials to K–3 students of color. One morning in August 2000, I arrived at work ready to present our regional Early Learning efforts to a group of visiting higher-ups from OCR's Washington, D.C., headquarters. In hurried meetings over the previous days, my colleagues and I had deliberately deleted from the planned presentation all language we feared might be controversial. Having worried about whether to present our ideas "in the document, or orally," we deleted from both handouts and my verbal presentation "specific" and "remotely prescriptive" language on how we might define equal opportunity for K–3 students of color. "Keep everything tied very obviously to *standards*," I noted, and delete "anything that sounds opinionated . . . at all."

As I walked down the hall to the meeting, a colleague ran up and asked me anxiously to delete another piece of language from the presentation: our specific ideas about detailed data that OCR could request from schools and districts under review, such as questions about the credentials of their K–3 teachers and the efforts schools took to assist struggling K–3 students. My colleagues worried that such "data requests" should be discussed privately in our region, not in public with the higher-ups. I agreed. As the meeting began, I found myself turning my satchel around in order to hide its "Educational Equity Association" logo. As I wrote in my notes, I was anxious not to seem "too radical" or too much of an "advocate" to the OCR higher-ups. After the meeting, at lunch with a group of sympathetic regional and visiting colleagues, I remarked that I had been incredibly nervous that morning. "And then I thought, 'Wait a minute, I'm talking about how to improve civil rights work to a group of civil rights workers, so why am I so nervous?' " I laughed. One veteran lawyer responded wryly, "Welcome to OCR."

Around OCR and elsewhere in the Department of Education, even more general descriptions of plans to equalize opportunities for students of color were edited to avoid seeming too "radical." One colleague told me about a proposal written by a D.C. OCR employee for a department-wide conference on improving instruction. Planned by participants from across the Department of Education and the National Academy of Sciences, to inform superintendents and school leaders, it had gone "through twenty-six drafts" before it got "buy in" from the entire department. The very title of the conference, which would also address best practices for overcoming racial "achievement gaps," had been revised continually. My OCR colleagues sighed that even language like "achievement gap" had to be deleted, as to many it connoted "pouring resources into the bottom, ignoring the top." The term "equity" had also been deleted from the summary description of this conference, as it was "almost as negative a term as 'civil rights' now."

After nine months employed at OCR, I was exhausted. In my personal notes, I sighed, "Government is always about constraining what you can get done/controversy—CONTAINMENT." When I told two of my colleagues, Corey and Bridget, that I was "tired of spending so much energy 'spinning' the Early Learning stuff instead of just discussing its substance," Corey had replied sarcastically, "But PR is what we do! We've got to do what we know best!" Bridget had added with similar congenial sarcasm, "She's so cute. An ideals person. . . . I love it."

If OCR were to tackle early learning opportunities at all, it was impossible, given the experts' recommendations, to ignore academics in pursuing a civil rights analysis. I wrote in an Early Learning draft that "though OCR staff have traditionally seen themselves as lacking the authority to investigate very deeply into 'educational' issues, the symposium made clear that academic opportunities to learn are the crux of elementary equity." There was simply no way to think about racially equal K–3 opportunity in American schools without thinking about access to concrete "concepts" and "skills," I wrote: "The symposium pinpointed the K–3 years as the years in which a well—known set of *foundational skills* are either afforded or denied young students of color, and in which children of color are either afforded or denied equal early access to a broad range of *foundational content and concepts."* In a later draft of the same document, I obediently deleted the next sentence, which had made a colleague "cringe" in anxiety: "Denying students of color foundational early elementary opportunities to learn can thus be considered a discriminatory act."

While everyone reading or creating documents in the project had become reluctant to link words like "discrimination" and "learning," our analysis suggested that we had to apply civil rights logic in detailed analysis of the academic opportunities to learn that were offered or denied to young members of race groups. To provide equitable access to academic programs, as Title VI required, we had to look in some detail at the quality of academic opportunity: Were up-to-date books available? Did the curriculum offer skills and concepts required by common assessments? Meanwhile, we had to count, more quantitatively, the available and unavailable learning resources. Our repeated internal statements that OCR could not analyze these very aspects of educational opportunity framed our project as doomed to failure. Heading back to my cubicle after being told to delete the word "discriminatory," I planned to continue writing up my summary documents on the K–3 opportunities that all the academics and educators at our symposium deemed essential. Yet, as I wrote to myself, I marveled at the difficulty of figuring out how to get this Early Learning analysis actually circulating within OCR without getting it "shut down." "WHAT DOCS TO GIVE TO WHOM? FOR WHAT?" I wrote in confusion in my notes, echoing a colleague's recent warning that any document I wrote about potential academic opportunity work at OCR "might get out, Congress might get mad."

At first I chalked these fears up to election-year worries, but OCR had a long-standing rhetorical habit of distinguishing between education work—sometimes called work on "academics," or evaluating "educational quality"—and civil rights work—framed as the basic project of equalizing some set of opportunities to race groups. Repeatedly, over the years, both outsiders and insiders had used it to counter claims that the office should tackle specific instances of racially unequal opportunity to learn in schools and districts. As the agency's work had expanded from desegregation to include forms of discrimination within schools, the habit of arguing that federal civil rights lawyers from "above" should not intervene in local education in the South had morphed to rhetorically distinguish all federal "civil rights" work from school-based "education" work as well. For decades, those entering the agency committed to linking the "civil rights" and "education" domains in both school- and district-level work had been taught to decouple these domains rhetorically.

During the symposium in February 2000, a colleague from the agency's D.C. headquarters told me that when she began working at OCR in the 1970s, she had posed a few key questions to her colleagues about the scope and reach of educational civil rights. Examining the national demographics of Special Education placement, she had learned that many black students nationwide were placed in Special Education not because they had physiological or psychological disabilities but because no one had taught them to read. She had reasoned to her colleagues that "if not teaching kids to read leads to Special Ed referral and that leads to disproportionate representation of kids of color in Special Ed, shouldn't we be focusing on people teaching kids to read?" A lawyer colleague had replied to her question with a memorable rhetorical distinction: "That's education, that's not civil rights. We don't *do* that."

Circa 2000, OCR employees routinely taught one another this logic of splitting "education" from "civil rights." Any internal use of the classroom-connoting word "pedagogy," framed as inherently being "local" and "educational" rather than referring to "federal" and "civil rights" issues, tended to spark the rebuttal that "the feds" were to stay out of the "academic" arena altogether. Even Norma Cantu suggested to me in a 2005 interview that the project's interest in instruction perhaps veered outside of OCR's jurisdiction. The government was supposed to make "general" rules, she said, and keep its hands off of "pedagogy" as a state or more local concern. Cantu herself had tried to target issues of everyday educational opportunity while at OCR, initiating compliance reviews about "the placement of minority students in special education and low-track courses" at the high school level and about "providing nondiscriminatory access to gifted and talented and other high-ability programs and classes."[70] But actually examining K–3 opportunities to learn, even in collaboration with educators and academics, was another thing: as she put it to me, "pedagogy" was the domain of "educators," not for lawyers or federal people to "micromanage." To her, "pedagogy" was "so uniquely state-driven that I think it might be hard. Look at the struggle they're having with NCLB [No Child Left Behind].[71] It's hard to be general in areas of pedagogy. People push back."

Cantu's comments illustrated the way OCR people anticipated various forms of resistance and counseled one another to avoid various controversial efforts. Yet federal people outside OCR and even outside the Department of Education seemed much less worried about the government pursuing detailed, "academic" analyses of educational issues. On one trip to OCR headquarters in D.C., I tagged along at the invitation of a colleague—the lawyer who had been told in the 1970s that OCR did not *do* education work—to a congressional hearing about a new National Reading Panel report on literacy instruction. In a room full of mostly white people in suits, I listened as white members of Congress asked white academics pointed questions about literacy research, phonics, and data analysis. I was confused by this matter-of-fact federal-level discussion of educational matters after a year of worrying whether "the feds" could address educational issues within OCR. So, on our cab ride back to the office, I asked my colleague why OCR was so concerned about getting into early reading issues. If representatives or senators were so clearly interested in literacy, I asked, why did OCR have to worry about analyzing early academic opportunity? Leaning against the cab door, she replied, "It's a question of articulating the logic of this being a *civil rights* issue."

Slowly, I realized that the argument against linking education and civil rights was not just about federal involvement in providing opportunities to learn; it was also an argument against purposefully and actively providing *students of color* with access to any given educational opportunity. "I haven't realized this before now—why it's so hard to link achievement to civil rights," I wrote in my notes later during my D.C. trip. "It's because 'civil rights' is about adding race to the achievement conversation." A civil rights definition of "achievement" issues would mean that academic opportunities had to "be racially fair." Promoting equal access to academic services for other categories of children, particularly the "disabled," caused comparatively little anxiety within the agency: disability work was precisely about affording students equal access to opportunities to learn, and in that arena, no one decoupled the notions of "education" and "civil rights." More broadly, intervening federally to ensure equal access to educational opportunity in the local worlds of schools and districts was what OCR work was all about. An interest in pursuing "educational excellence" was explicit in the OCR mission statement.

What made our Early Learning quest a controversial linkage of civil rights and education was that we were working to frame concrete learning opportunities as opportunities to which students of color deserved equal access by law. Resistance within the agency existed not just to the "federal" project of OCR employees looking at education in detail but to the project of examining and equalizing those opportunities for students of color. And while we who were working in the civil rights wing of the Department of Education continually reminded ourselves that the federal project of equalizing opportunity racially was suspect, the rest of the department soon veered squarely in a new direction: federally demanding racially equal "outcomes" from local schools.

Federal intervention into the world of educators was clearly not anathema to the Department of Education, as long as these interventions were about testing children of color on basic skills rather than ensuring them access to concrete opportunities to learn before those tests. A year after I left OCR, George W. Bush started using the Department of Education to impose No Child Left Behind, a congressionally mandated system of high-stakes testing and penalties for schools and children that imposed the tightest federal controls on schools and districts in U.S. history and massively affected the daily pedagogical experiences of the nation's children. NCLB's federal mandates were deeply racialized: under the law, schools were to face serious penalties—including financial loss, external takeover, and closure—if they could not narrow their racial "achievement gaps" revealed in disparate outcomes on standardized tests; the mandates essentially forced local schools to focus pedagogically on test preparation.[72] NCLB was promoted as a tool for racial equity (ending the "soft bigotry of low expectations"), since it forced educators to discuss and address racialized disparities in test score outcomes. But what the Bush administration demanded was racial equality in test score outcomes, not in opportunities to learn.[73] While the administration created forceful sanctions for racialized outcomes in NCLB, it did not enforce even the one equal opportunity provision that did make it into the law, a requirement that all students have access to "qualified teachers."[74] As Norma Cantu told me in 2005, the Bush administration's lack of interest in enforcing racially equal opportunities to learn broadcast a lack of interest in civil "rights" themselves: "The two lawyers who were the architects behind NCLB wrote an article about what it means to have 'no child left behind,' and that was fun to read because they were laying it out in terms of their understanding of the legal issues—and they didn't mean rights."

This same distinction between "education" and "rights," I later realized, was sabotaging the Early Learning Project itself, and we at OCR had helped reproduce this distinction in our own arguments about the project's likely problems. OCR's Web site clearly describes its mandated purpose: to "ensure equal access to education and to promote educational excellence throughout the nation through vigorous enforcement of civil rights."[75] But we in OCR argued repeatedly, in resignation, that OCR likely could not enforce the civil rights of students of color to "academic" opportunities to learn. Thus, we OCR employees

ourselves relinquished the potential of civil rights law to equalize opportunities to learn. Meanwhile, more confident "feds" moved to use
federal power to demand better academic outcomes without more
equal academic opportunity.

Part of the issue in the Early Learning story was a basic anxiety
among lower-level employees about appearing to direct the agency's
agenda from below. On another draft after the symposium, I responded to advice from colleagues: "Make more summary," I told myself as I edited. "Take out what OCR should do." But well-established,
high-level lawyers ran into resistance as they tried to steer OCR work
toward analysis of other aspects of educational opportunity for students of color. Nervous managers argued that OCR was endangering
itself politically by even trying to expand its civil rights efforts for students of color onto academic turf. As veteran OCR employees worked
on the resource comparability project, developing a legal strategy to
measure access to basic educational facilities and resources for these
students, they struggled to establish the effort at the agency before the
upcoming election. The "resource comp" project seemed safer to these
attorneys than did the Early Learning Project, as it investigated only
what one colleague called the "basic skeleton" of academic resources
(e.g., the availability of science equipment), not the actual learning opportunities utilizing these resources (the teacher's training to teach science, or opportunities to learn science at all in K–3 classrooms). A high-
level OCR lawyer working on the resource comparability project had
argued optimistically at the Early Learning symposium that "Title VI
is one of the most powerful civil rights tools" for measuring this "basic
skeleton of educational opportunity," even as he had framed the Early
Learning Project's more detailed analytic proposals as potentially impossible. Merging the Early Learning Project with the "resource comparability" project, which was further along in its development, was
one suggestion that arose partway through the project, but this lawyer
suggested nervously that adding any of our "academic equity stuff"
to the resource comparability analysis would "make the resource comp
stuff too controversial," even more than it already was. People whis-
pered that even the resource comparability project's tackling of "basic"
racial resource inequities plaguing the nation was likely to be "shut
down." And as Bush entered office, it was: no proactive work continued on developing or training employees on the "resource comp" analysis, and the new administrators halted all ongoing projects for "review" until further notice.

Some equal opportunity efforts did sneak through before the shift
in administration: some months after the Early Learning symposium,

one D.C. OCR lawyer called to tell me in great excitement that a basic question about teacher certification had finally been added to an "Elementary and Secondary" federal survey distributed regularly to every school in the country. Certification had been a key resource measurement suggested by our experts at the conference, since the teachers in schools disproportionately serving students of color are disproportionately not certified (and thus not formally trained to teach). Her excitement about this addition reminded me once again that analyzing even basic educational opportunities, such as having a trained teacher, seemed a shocking and unlikely development around OCR. I wrote in my notes after our conversation, "TRYING TO GET OCR TO FOCUS ON "EDUCATION" OR ACADEMICS! . . . WHY A STRUGGLE?!!" I confessed to a supervisor my surprise that the survey instrument had lacked this question about teacher certification. He replied, "Doesn't surprise *me*." Returning to my desk in frustration, I scrawled in my notes, "I CAN'T WORK HERE. Excitement is SQUASHED routinely. No forward motion at *all*!" Another manager agreed with me after I expressed my frustration to him that OCR was a "political vacuum—people only say what you can't do."

The following day I added to my notes:

Things I don't get about OCR
—what issues we do/don't have detailed jurisdiction over
—why can we get into details of discipline, IEPs, but not "education"?
   What's "education" to OCR?

Defining racial discrimination in "education" within OCR in the new civil rights era seemed largely about crossing academic opportunities to learn off the list of opportunities deemed required by law and policy. My colleagues and I often framed our self-constraining as an attempt to save the agency's basic tools for assisting students of color—a hallmark of what Hirschman (1991) calls "jeopardy" rhetoric. Open discussion of active efforts to assist such students, we reasoned, could result in hostile targeting of these very tools. Just a few people within the agency were motivated by the perception that the window of opportunity was closing to wield the legal sword of Title VI openly in the battle for equal opportunity to learn. One D.C. higher-up told me privately that his goal was to try to "ram through" the resource comparability project before the election.[76] But most advocated postponing Title VI efforts until after the election, or pursuing their own work in the Title VI arena "under the radar" in anticipation of "shutdown." One supervisor told me directly that "nothing" "proactive" on Early Learning or anything else would be happening before the administration turnover. By that, he meant any Title VI work that set forth to discuss explicitly how the law could be applied.

> ROGER: Nothing will be done between now and the election—in January, we will discuss the proactive program again.
>
> ME TO ROGER: When you say "nothing," what kind of "nothing" do you mean?
>
> ROGER: Compliance reviews, pulling back on proactive activities—compliance reviews. A hunker-down period—not making waves.

We waited anxiously for a green light to pursue racially equal academic opportunity, but that authorization never arrived.

At OCR, Title VI seemed to be about saying what we could "only" do to afford students of color equality of opportunity to learn or what we could "not" do, rather than what we could do. Still, the Early Learning Project made clear to me that the law itself could allow careful attention to concrete academic opportunities provided or denied. The question was whether anyone powerful within OCR would pursue using the law for this particular purpose.

While I was at OCR, a multiracial coalition of advocacy groups outside the agency increasingly argued that equitable academic opportunities to learn should be educational civil rights in the contemporary United States.[77] Claiming an academic opportunity as a "right" asserts, once and for all, that denying that opportunity is harmful.[78] Richard Riley, Clinton's secretary of education, publicly pronounced "education" the "twenty-first-century civil right"; the comment caused a stir among us but we did not employ it further. Working deep within a civil rights agency, OCR employees who agreed with this position anticipated criticism from higher-ups and outsiders if we pursued it; we argued anxiously that calling academic opportunities to learn a civil rights issue would send the agency careening into the bayonets of its foes.

Our self-sabotaging of the Early Learning Project spoke volumes about how afraid many Americans are, in the new civil rights era, to demand that students of color actually be given the particular opportunities that are denied to them. It was clear to all of us that adequate opportunities to learn were routinely absent in schools and classrooms serving young children of color; clearly, this denial set them up for disproportionate failure. But somehow it felt out of order to call loudly to equalize such opportunities. Watching the gradual establishment of No Child Left Behind—including a large, cheery red schoolhouse set up in the D.C. office—we accepted with a sigh that the government could demand racially equal outcomes but not racially equal opportunities to learn.

Dismissals and self-defeats mark this era: Americans, in resignation, routinely deem everyday justice for students of color to be impossible. And some Americans, in confusion, deem such justice to be unimportant, as the next chapter shows. In dismissing the arena of everyday school and district life as an arena of harm appropriate for focused attention, I argue, we exhibit a key misjudgment about how opportunity structures take shape in contemporary America. The final chapter explores this last new civil rights era rebuttal: everyday harms to children of color in American schools are too "small" to fix.

# Harms to Children of Color Are Too "Small" to Fix

THIS CHAPTER explores one final way that people debating education resist demands for everyday justice for students of color today. They claim that everyday harms to children of color inside schools and districts are too "small" to fix. Some people argue that harms experienced in everyday life are too "small" to add up to racial inequality of opportunity, while others argue that "big" structures of unequal opportunity cannot be remedied through everyday activity. Some people argue that no one in particular can be seen denying opportunity; therefore, no one in particular should be pressed to provide it.

It is harder than ever to figure out how racial inequality works and what to do about it. For racial inequality is no longer ordered explicitly by laws and policies that seem to exist far above ordinary people. As sociologist Charles Payne has noted, the system of racially unequal opportunity that prevails in contemporary American society is "fragmented," in comparison to the deliberately coordinated system of inequality that prevailed in the past.[1] Rebecca Blank (2005) notes that unequal opportunity today has accumulated across generations, and that opportunity denied in one domain, like health care, affects opportunity in another, like education. Amid this complexity, Eduardo Bonilla-Silva notes, research finds the contemporary "invisibility," to many Americans, "of most mechanisms [that] reproduce racial inequality."[2] Unlike the Jim Crow era, when white supremacy was enforced both by explicit law and by vigilante violence, today's system of racial inequality of opportunity and outcome seems to "just happen" (Payne 1984), in part because it now takes shape through myriad interactions among countless Americans of various racialized groups. Some make policies that in effect condone racially patterned opportunity denial, or that exacerbate denials in particular domains. Most of us, interacting as individuals, are unaware of the role we play in the continuing production of inequality—either by failing to provide opportunities we have the power to provide, or simply by individually allowing racially unequal structures, patterns, and events to go unconfronted.

Given this fragmentation, demands to redress even the most obvious racial inequalities of opportunity in education, such as the blatantly unequal and inadequate allocation of basic learning resources to schools serving predominantly students of color,[3] or the most obvious inequalities of outcome, such as dropout rates or "achievement gaps," often prompt resistance because people are unsure where the fault lies for such inequalities. Any claim that a particular actor, act, or process generates inequality is challenged by someone locating causation elsewhere in the system. Similarly, many Americans express skepticism about assertions that *their* everyday acts in our fragmented system contribute to racial inequality in any fundamental way. Even many advocates who do see racially unequal opportunity in American society at large fail to pinpoint how, or whether, such inequalities could be dismantled in part by everyday activity by specific, local people; overwhelmed by inequality's fragmentation, they just call repeatedly for "big" change.

Still, in a "fragmented" system, we must now accept that racial inequality in education is formed not just by past generations' behavior or by dynamics outside of schools, but also in part through everyday acts, including moments when ordinary people inside educational systems distribute opportunity unequally or accept children's experiences of unequal or inadequate opportunity.[4] And if racially unequal educational outcomes are produced in part through the daily activities of ordinary people making decisions at administrative desks or interacting with children, those ordinary people can do a lot to help equalize opportunity. Pursuing racial equality of opportunity in education today requires all the people whose decisions and actions affect children ensuring, through *their* everyday activity, that students actually experience necessary academic opportunities to learn and social opportunities to thrive on a daily basis so that each student is supported continually and sufficiently toward school success. I call such opportunity as provided and experienced in everyday life *everyday justice*. Legislators and officials from afar can enable the provision of everyday justice, but in education, adults up close to children finally provide it.

The problem with pursuing everyday justice in a fragmented inequality system is that complaints of everyday *in*justice are always resisted. Since it takes multiple acts by many people at many levels of influence to produce racial inequalities of both opportunity and outcome, and since racial inequalities are also inherited from the past and produced across social domains, Americans often argue in misguided ways over the scale at which harms occur and the scale at which remedies for inequality should proceed. We argue that harms to children of color are too "small"—or too "big"—to be worth fixing through everyday activity.

For all the resistant players in OCR debates, this dismissal began as a failure of analysis: a refusal to acknowledge that local people's ordinary actions could play a role in denying students equal opportunity, or that it was essential to press specific actors to remedy everyday experiences of opportunity denial. From all of us, such dismissals often took shape in a key rebuttal of the "fragmented" new civil rights era. We contended either that remedies attempting to shift everyday practices within institutions were too detailed to pursue or, on the flip side, that everyday harms to students of color were too minimal to be worth fixing. Educators who resisted claims that their own everyday practices and interactions in schools and districts were harmful to students of color routinely dismissed students' and parents' experiences of unequal opportunity as too small to count as discrimination.[5] Outside critics claimed that OCR's proposed remedies for improving the daily provision of opportunity to students of color were too detailed and too "micromanaging" of educators' daily behavior. OCR employees who resisted the Early Learning Project were rejecting our own efforts to equalize the daily provision of opportunities inside educational settings. And while complainants' demands for everyday racial justice certainly did not frame everyday acts as "small," complainants and other advocates for students of color did complain, frequently, that OCR's remedial efforts were literally too "small" to help. While these players were often on opposing sides of debates over discrimination, at times all parties failed to acknowledge that far-reaching, "big" changes in education must include concrete, specific, and ongoing efforts to improve and equalize students' everyday academic and social experiences within educational settings. In overlooking the details of ongoing opportunity provision inside schools and districts, we overlooked the need to fully remedy racial inequality of opportunity that children and parents experienced on a daily basis.

In this chapter, I examine some explicit arguments from people both within and outside OCR that the everyday harms OCR pinpointed in its analyses were too "small" to add up to inequality or that the remedies to such harms were too "small" to be worth pursuing. I argue that these critics overlook one key scale at which contemporary racial inequality is produced and exacerbated. I suggest that the texts of civil rights laws prohibiting disability discrimination, language-service denial, and sex discrimination in education offer somewhat more successful models for precisely analyzing the daily, concrete building blocks of equal opportunity. Finally, I discuss how, in resisting demands for everyday justice in the new civil rights era, white people in particular (here, educators) resist the contention that we ourselves participate in producing racial inequality and that we should be involved in daily efforts to pursue equal opportunity. By the chapter's end, I hope to have convinced the reader that in calling such efforts unnecessary, Americans across political and even racial lines neglect one crucial analytic task of the new civil rights era: to pinpoint how specific everyday activity in specific places exacerbates racial inequality and to clarify ways specific actors might help equalize opportunity daily instead.

## THE CASE FOR EVERYDAY JUSTICE

Tellingly, since the beginning of the historic civil rights movement (and even long before), parents and educators of color have contended that policy remedies for racial inequality in education should include ongoing efforts to equalize students' everyday experiences inside schools.[6] No critic has argued that these efforts be pursued instead of policy remedies. Rather, they have advocated additional efforts to address the ways that educators and peers treated students in daily interactions and administrators made decisions in school and district offices, adding this arena of everyday activity to existing analyses of systemic harm. Martin Luther King argued at the time of *Brown* that educators had to go far beyond "desegregating" bodies to enable students to interact on an equal status basis inside schools, calling everyday efforts "integration" as distinct from desegregation.[7] During the busing wars of the 1970s, legal scholar Derrick Bell suggested that "civil rights" remedies that were limited to balancing enrollments in school districts overlooked everyday acts by teachers, administrators, and peers inside schools, and thus often simply pushed unequal opportunity into new forms.

> Remedies that fail to attack all policies of racial subordination almost guarantee that the basic evil of segregated schools will survive and flourish, even in those systems where racially balanced schools can be achieved. Low academic performance and large numbers of disciplinary and expulsion cases are only two of the predictable outcomes in integrated schools where the racial subordination of blacks is reasserted in, if anything, a more damaging form.[8]

Analysts who support desegregation as a proven policy method for equalizing basic resources and academic opportunities for many children at once have argued that achieving "true integration" within desegregated schools still requires educators to make ongoing efforts to overcome both external and school-based forms of unequal opportunity.[9] Others acknowledge that while policymakers must pursue resource equity between schools and districts, the daily distribution and use of those resources to and within schools and classrooms finally provides the equalizing opportunity.[10]

People who filed complaints at OCR circa 2000 asked not just for basic resources when their children lacked them but also for positive and supportive everyday interactions between their children, themselves, and educators. They wanted equality of educational opportunity to pervade schools' and districts' daily practices. Before our pessimism overcame us, we who spearheaded the Early Learning Project sought to work not just on the "basic skeleton" of educational resources and facilities, as our colleagues in the resource comparability project were suggesting. We also wanted to examine whether through school and district activity, young students of color were being given daily opportunities to learn the foundational skills and concepts presumed by common standards. Both complainants and our project's proponents wanted to look at the role that school and district educators played in providing or denying students these opportunities. Crucially, neither analysis imagined that educators bore sole responsibility for equal opportunity; in the Early Learning Project, for example, we recognized that external public policies shape student assignment and assessment, and control how resources are allocated to schools. But both analyses extended beyond these concerns to include the daily provision of educational opportunity inside schools and districts. Analysts examined face-to-face interactions between educators, parents, and students, the daily use and distribution of educational resources, and the more indirect interactions lodged in daily enactments of school and district policies.

Title VI focused our analysis solely on the actions of federal funding recipients, and in OCR work, we focused analysis primarily on educators at the district and school level. Most educators saw this focus as unfairly spotlighting their responsibility. As they understandably resisted an *exclusive* focus on their behavior, however, they expressed a telling resistance to *any* inclusion in analysis, though they generally spoke in favor of equal opportunity. Few educators, slogging away in schools and districts, would easily accept that their own behavior was even partially "at fault" for the problems students and parents of color were experiencing. But our analysis of the consequences of everyday behavior did not have to be heard as "blaming" educators alone for racial inequality, as some critics fear.[11] And it did not denounce, wholesale, educators' interactions with students and parents of color. Rather, our analysis focused on how some everyday actions by educators played a role in providing or denying racial equality of opportunity.

Despite OCR's numerous failings, then, some of our efforts to pursue everyday justice taught a valuable lesson for the new civil rights era. We presumed that one aspect of equalizing educational opportunity today was to ask whether specific actions inside schools and districts helped provide or deny necessary opportunities to children of color. Despite our frequent passivity and the shackles of our legal analyses, we employees sometimes did analyze, concretely and precisely, how educators helped ensure, or failed to help ensure, that students were moved closer toward equal opportunity rather than further away from it.

Still, these demands for everyday justice rankled because they implicated ordinary people in the construction of racial inequality. Most of the people we interacted with felt that OCR was misguided in examining educators' everyday behavior; they saw our attempts to equalize students' everyday experiences of opportunity as misguided as well, and thought that changing specific forms of everyday opportunity provision inside educational settings was too "small" to really be meaningful or worth doing.[12] Such rebuttals suggested that actions designed to improve and equalize students' daily opportunities were unnecessary or inadequate, or saw as misguided any analysis partially implicating school and district actors for "larger" inequalities. These rebuttals often reductively imagined the project of equalizing opportunity in the new civil rights era.

Those who critiqued OCR's efforts as too limited were right about one thing: in formulating our suggestions for resolving complaints, OCR employees ourselves routinely reduced a wide array of potential remedies to a few concrete ones. We pushed for José's suspension to be expunged and for post-harassment counseling for LaRon. When we felt that we needed to prompt changes in the everyday lives of many children at once throughout the school district, we pushed for a faculty training day on "defiance" in José's district, or a new policy statement on harassment in LaRon's district. As we wrote up our "resolutions" describing how everyday acts in school and district settings could be retooled, we typically ended up pinpointing the need for change either for a few children or in single pieces of systems at a time.

Still, our error was not in our analysis of everyday justice but in the purposeful constriction of our remedies. We failed children not when we proposed concrete improvements in everyday opportunity provision, but when we actively did less to equalize opportunity than we could. Critics asked whether analyzing and securing changes in the everyday activity of educators distracted from large-scale efforts at equality or "micromanaged" people who did not deserve such supervision. I contend that this work was one necessary component of working toward equal opportunity for students of color today.

## DISMISSING EFFORTS FOR EVERYDAY JUSTICE AS TOO "SMALL"

While working at OCR, I often critiqued the scale of my own efforts, because I was asked most often to investigate the treatment of individual children. OCR circa 2000 more often investigated the treatment of individual students, particularly those with disabilities, than the treatment of large groups of children of any kind. Observers in the mid-1990s had described this strategy bluntly as "diminished" and "limited" in "scope."[13] Indeed, the focus on individuals often felt like a diminished framing of harm. I responded in my notes one day to such a complaint, about a high school student whose parents had asked OCR to help secure some accommodations on reading assignments for his learning disability: "Ted is in the next cube fighting for Johnny's right to use Cliff Notes. Why is the civil rights establishment spending resources on this?" Was it harm worth worrying about at the federal level if one white male student was denied a special list of assignments every Friday on multiple colors of paper? Or if another was denied a laptop to use during timed writing tests? It certainly seemed to me like a misdirection of civil rights efforts.

But my critique neglected a key reality: disability law recognizes that analyzing such everyday experiences for individuals might well be core to ensuring their civil right to access the common curriculum. If children are appropriately diagnosed and served, "disabled" students' IEPs, the cornerstone of their rights, hold educators accountable for providing the specific academic assistance professionals have deemed necessary to enable each student to compete on as level a playing field as possible.[14] As I discuss in more depth later on, this framing of equal opportunity, which requires detailed attention to the quality of opportunities provided in daily life, is a core model for everyday justice efforts. In the race arena, however, educators receiving detailed complaints of everyday harms to children of color—either as individuals or in large groups—often dismissed such everyday harms as too "small" to actually add up to unequal opportunity.

Some of my most thought-provoking moments at OCR came when recipients of complaints acknowledged that some children of color had been wronged by school or district practices, but then argued defiantly that these harms were too minimal to be remedied. One particularly memorable complaint was brought by a teacher in the urban King district who sought compensatory education for a handful of Latino students with learning disabilities who were left unmonitored for months by any consistent teacher. A sympathetic teacher, hearing of her colleague's quest, responded that finding a credentialed teacher or compensating the students would not solve the larger problem. At an underresourced school full of low-income Latinos, she explained, "abled" Latino kids lacked many of the same opportunities. The district's less sympathetic disability coordinator, Christie McCormack, argued that the district as a whole lacked credentialed teachers, so providing remedial education to this handful of students would accomplish nothing and was unnecessary. Both focused on the overwhelming scale of the problem, as if the effort for this handful of students was too small to be necessary, rather than saying that credentialed teachers were necessary both for this handful and for all students throughout the school and district. A colleague at OCR called this the "equal opportunity failer" argument: districts' "defense against charges of discrimination against ELL kids" was "that they don't provide *any* of their kids (all or almost all of whom are poor kids of color) anything resembling an education." At our Early Learning conference, one OCR lawyer reported wryly what a judge had said after he examined efforts in one city: since all the city's students were students of color and were being served equally poorly, there could be no discrimination involved in poor service to any subset of them.

Pedro Noguera (2003), following educational theorist Paulo Freire, suggests relatedly that advocates for children of color often do children a disservice by simply denouncing the daunting problems of urban schools. Instead, they could analyze how partial solutions might assist subsets of students in "limit situations," while they also pursue efforts toward comprehensive change. By arguing generally that "big" changes must take place instead of, rather than alongside, pinpointed changes for smaller numbers of children or specified changes in the everyday treatment of many children, we risk failing to make any concrete change at all, as "big" problems can seem impossible to solve.[15] External critics, students' advocates, and even OCR employees all often argued depressively that our efforts to reorganize specific aspects of everyday activity in schools and districts would likely make little "dent." For one, we sometimes dismissed OCR's own analytic and remedial efforts as "nitpicking" and "counting noses."

## *"Nitpicking" and "Counting Noses"*

People frequently argued that OCR "nitpicked" or "counted noses" in analyzing equal opportunity instead of addressing opportunity systems in their full complexity or responding to harms and opportunities that "really mattered." Critics contended that like all bureaucracies, OCR scrutinized tiny details and made people follow stupid little rules.[16] Particularly famous in this regard are stories of negative reactions to OCR's enforcement of Title IX. In 1997, a critic wrote mockingly,

> Not five months after the release of [Norma Cantu's] proposed guidelines [on sexual harassment], the country was treated to a celebrated series of stories regarding efforts by elementary school officials to root out sexual harassers among five- and six-year-olds. Nervous school officials felt compelled by OCR procedures to treat every playground antic as a possible instance of sexual harassment requiring separate investigation and prompt remedial action.[17]

In Title VI cases, too, recipients of complaints routinely resisted OCR's attempts to make detailed judgments about their everyday treatment of children. Understandably, educators usually argued that they deserved to exercise their own "professional judgment" in determining how to work with children and parents.[18] As I wrote in one note to myself, "Danette is telling a district they need to have a system for tracking racial proportions in dress code violations. District sounds like it's resisting doing this 'data review' too often." But districts routinely resisted OCR's efforts to get educators to evaluate or reorganize the details of their own practices at all.

Though educators and many external critics argued that OCR micromanaged educators, advocates criticizing OCR's remedies took a different tack: they contended that OCR's framings of harm were narrow, bureaucratic reductions of real problems. During our Early Learning conference, for example, one attorney pointed out that when OCR analyzed parent-school relations, it "often reduced" the problem "to how many parent meetings do you have a year." People called such quantitative assessments "counting noses." As I paraphrased in my notes, one academic at the symposium told me privately that "when OCR just orders quantity—number of hours of professional development— schools and districts follow this lead and say the quality of professional development is irrelevant." Many of the education professors at our symposium spoke of OCR's reductive legal vision of "equality," and admitted to me that they were reluctant to follow the "reductive" assignment I had given them before the symposium: to make bullet-pointed "checklists" of necessary K–3 learning opportunities that OCR should look for in districts and schools. The academics argued repeatedly that the task inherently constrained their analysis of the problem to measuring and counting opportunities rather than analyzing the full process of educating equitably. One professor said that he was "frustrated with the constraints of law OCR works with."

Put another way, these academics were grumbling that OCR was unwilling to think beyond what one attorney called the "basic skeleton" of educational resources and engage the full range of equal teaching and learning opportunities. "Education," one academic concluded, was concerned with "effectiveness, classrooms, teaching, learning," while "civil rights" was concerned solely with "measurable resources." At the time, I myself critiqued OCR for reducing the analysis to quantitative measures. Agreeing with one academic who argued that " 'compliance' might be time-in-program, but the practice/spirit of law is what happens in the classroom," I wrote in my notes, "If OCR can't deal with this info, they will never be any good." After the conference, an OCR lawyer joked about this tendency: "When things can be quantified it helps with the race analysis. Half as likely to have an effective teacher—what's effective?—oh, well, but they're half as likely!"

The counting we did at OCR sometimes seemed silly at first glance. For example, a colleague told me about investigating a complaint alleging that parents of English-language learners were excluded from the school environment. OCR measured the participation of these parents in part by counting how many minutes they were allowed to speak at school board meetings. As it turned out, they were given the same amount of time as English-speaking parents but had to spend half that time translating their comments for the audience, so they had half as much time as other parents to state their demands. But this example of counting was not misguided: the limited opportunity that immigrant parents got to talk at school board meetings limited their ability to state their concerns about their children. Other complainants pinpointed everyday instances of inequitable treatment by counting up the number of minutes of instruction or days of suspension students received. Many complaints that had OCR "counting noses" were guided by the complainants, demonstrating that they did not see such counting of time spent or opportunities offered as analytically reductive.[19]

We at OCR often diminished our response to complainants' claims of harm not because we "counted" such unequal opportunities but because we often counted only a subset of opportunities and pinpointed just some of the many changes that it would take to provide equal experiences of schooling for students. Sometimes we refused altogether to press actors to provide additional resources for many students at once (as in the demise of the resource comparability and Early Learning projects). Conversely, when we rejected the detailed practice of counting up and pinpointing controversially unequal opportunities, we often failed to prod educators to analyze the effects of such everyday actions. The resolution documents we eventually produced often suggested that full remedies required the recipients to take *only* a few specific steps, such as simply informing students or teachers about a district's new harassment policy, rather than involving them all in activities that might help prevent harassment in the first place. And vague language describing imprecisely what had harmed children and what could help them rarely convinced educators to do anything in particular to assist children. Thus, we often failed to describe necessary efforts for everyday justice. Suggestions for sweeping, large-scale assistance sounded better, though, and some critics of OCR's pinpointed remedial efforts misleadingly assumed that these efforts would inherently serve students more effectively. One example of such a misleading critique was Keisha Stedley's final argument in Longview I: that OCR should have "replaced all the teachers" instead of writing a district harassment policy.

### Misleadingly Celebrating "Big" versus "Small" Changes

Working at OCR, I sometimes found it annoyingly bureaucratic to tweak districts' policy handbooks and rule structures. I longed for efforts that would change more aspects of many districts all at once. Like my colleagues, I also sighed that we were spending too much time remedying harms to individual complainants rather than doing proactive work for many children. Many of us interested in Title VI work liked the idea of serving many children simultaneously and were often frustrated with OCR's tendency to avoid doing so. The office's refusal to enforce even the "basic skeleton" of equal resources was particularly frustrating.

But when it came to affecting students' daily educational experiences, OCR's sweeping efforts for many were not inherently effective. We sometimes resolved complaints with VRPs suggesting broad changes in district policies, which we assumed—and, indeed, stated on official forms—would affect many children districtwide. Every case resolved at OCR ended with the investigator filling out a form denoting the number of students supposedly assisted in the district. In cases where we had prompted any changes at all at the district level, we often just recorded the number of students in the district. Filing a "closed" complaint away on the shelf, an employee could often think happily that she had done something substantial for those thousands of children by simply writing a sweeping statement on paper about what those on high would do to assist them.

But when our resolutions called for sweeping changes to serve many children, we often wondered whether we were achieving everyday justice for actual children. Efforts to monitor OCR resolutions often demonstrated that sweeping policy resolutions afforded only shallow assistance. One of the most seemingly "big" remedies I saw at OCR was constructed to close an academic complaint. A community organization in a large, majority-black district had alleged that in comparison to white students, black students did not have equal academic opportunities either within or between schools. At first glance, I wrote in my notes, OCR had accomplished an unusually "substantial" resolution to this academically oriented case. The VRP required a long list of policy actions that would be taken for all of the district's children: "Consistent criteria for placement in AP, or in different level classes (e.g., math 9, pre-algebra, algebra); uniform course offerings; academic justification for remedial classes or 'elimination of such classes'; high-level content and performance standards, consistently implemented; teacher training." But no detailed description stated how the district would actually accomplish these items. They were statements about desired policy endpoints, not a description of "implementing" equal opportunity on a regular basis. I wondered in my notes, "Was this ever monitored?? How? . . . Clearly, a plan does not equal its implementation!" I realized that the list of policy actions was actually not precise enough at describing plans for opportunity provision: while "criteria" for AP placement could possibly be standardized once and then obeyed each year, it remained unclear how or whether the district would monitor the actual "implementation" of more complex things like "high-level standards" and what exactly they would "train" teachers to do. This district, I knew, was a "huge bureaucracy . . . they can't even get it together to hire qualified teachers who applied to teach!"

At one team meeting, I heard that this district's "compliance officer," who was the contact person for OCR complaints, was "overwhelmed" with multiple tasks. She had not only "to 1) address complaints filed against the district" but also to "2) be their affirmative-action coordinator and 3) be their 504 [disability services] coordinator." When I attended a meeting with the district's representatives about implementing the agreement, the investigator repeatedly had to ask them to explain how their efforts in the district linked up with the overarching requirements of the voluntary resolution plan. That the representatives could not map each ongoing effort onto the VRP's required policy shifts did not mean that the district was doing little to assist children. But it was clear that OCR's own "big" remedy had not necessarily prompted specific activities in the district to remedy the academic inequities originally pinpointed in the complaint. For example, teachers were now being trained as promised but on a prepackaged remedial reading program, not in providing "high-level content."

Though we learned that large-scale or overarching remedies do not always result in children being given specific, daily opportunities, assistant secretaries of OCR have repeatedly stressed the generic need for large-scale effort in their annual reports to Congress. In 1991, OCR's annual report to Congress admitted that cases on behalf of individuals were overwhelmingly taking up the time and resources that could also be used for investigations for many children at once.[20] The 1993 annual report to Congress suggested muscularly that

> OCR must direct itself towards impact on students' lives. OCR will max-imize the impact of available resources on civil rights in education. OCR will consider as broad a range of input as practicable in the setting of its priorities to ensure that OCR addresses the most acute problems of dis-crimination. OCR will provide tangible assistance to the greatest number of students possible.[21]

Advocates frustrated when OCR refused to tackle the most "acute problems of discrimination" have typically demanded policy changes affecting all of a district's children at once, particularly on the issue of basic resources and opportunities to learn. Proponents of desegrega-tion policy, for example, have long framed OCR's efforts to pursue daily equality of opportunity within schools as an example of its reluc-tance to equalize more systemic unequal educational conditions for children of color.[22] In truth, under certain administrations, OCR has pursued everyday justice within schools instead of policy efforts to equalize opportunities racially between schools. Thus, it has failed to help ensure a crucial aspect of everyday justice: a well-resourced and well-cared-for school for all children. Under Nixon, for example, OCR purposefully pursued in-school opportunities for children of color in lieu of desegregation, starting with compliance reviews in the 1970s that examined tracking, classroom conditions, and discipline inside schools, as well as resource distribution to segregated schools.[23]

Yet in these efforts, OCR was less helpful to students of color because it focused on harmful everyday practices in schools instead of equaliz-ing opportunities between them via policies like desegregation. It could have done both. As the courts turned away from desegregating the sub-urbs, OCR officials also decided formally in 1974 to emphasize within-school problems *instead* of desegregation. Thus, they purposefully left intact districts' unequal opportunity structures.[24] One OCR official ar-gued tellingly that OCR had to analyze forms of racial discrimination other than segregation "because compulsory metropolitan-wide deseg-regation on a massive scale simply was 'not in the cards.' " To him, "the most OCR could do on behalf of the large numbers of minority children who lived in big cities was to focus on educationally harmful discrimi-nation within the schools."[25] Under Reagan, OCR was solidly pursuing efforts to assist children of color inside school buildings *rather* than efforts to redistribute children or opportunity between buildings. And by the time I worked at OCR, as we saw when the resource comparability project failed, the agency was now rejecting efforts to equalize resources even to segregated schools as "over the top of Title VI."

In the new civil rights era, then, the real problem arises not when people examine everyday life as a crucial arena of opportunity provision but when people refuse to enable or provide opportunities to students of color, and when they frame specific remedial acts as the only efforts necessary to solve complex problems.[26] Similarly, the problem is not investigating the treatment of individuals but refusing to make efforts that might assist large groups, or improve in specific ways the daily treatment of many students in the aggregate. As a regional director put it in a staff meeting circa 2000, another problem was that we waited to get complaints from energetic individuals instead of setting forth "proactively" to assist children with fewer advocates: OCR's resources were typically "bogged down in solving individual cases rather than proactive activities." Critiques of OCR's efforts to assist disabled students similarly misconstrue the key problem: that the agency serves the disabled while resisting service to children of color and refusing to advertise its services to their parents. Bunch and Mindle indicated in 1993 that the other real problem of OCR's focus on individual complaint investigation (rather than compliance review) was that OCR was particularly adept at *not* finding discrimination,[27] a problem Halpern (1995) makes clear was longstanding at OCR.

In her first annual report to Congress in 1993 (on 1992), Assistant Secretary for Civil Rights Norma Cantu noted that the core problem was OCR's "passivity," particularly in assisting students of color. She accused "the past administration" of adopting "a passive approach to civil rights enforcement" in the Title VI arena, arguing that OCR had stopped issuing "policy guidance" to districts and was no longer proactively "initiating" investigations into "areas of likely discrimination." She concluded that "on the whole, underserved populations, such as racial minority students and limited English proficient students, were neglected by OCR."[28] The real problem with OCR's efforts—even under the more proactive Cantu—was not that we examined daily life as a key site for providing opportunity but that we actively pursued less assistance for children of color "rather than" more.

*The Real Problem of Actively Doing Less for Children of Color*

Crenshaw et al. (1995) suggest that civil rights efforts have actively pursued minimal assistance to people of color, in part by misleadingly

saying that both "small" harms and "big" structures are beyond remedy. They point out that since the 1960s, courts have been unwilling to
call "discriminatory" most of the routine, unintentional, daily activity
that contributes to racial inequality; courts have also actively limited
the ability of law to treat wide-scale patterns of unequal opportunity
as racially discriminatory rather than the misfortunes of chance.[29]

These same dynamics of actively doing less played out within OCR.
People arguing that less assistance to students of color was possible
typically won out over those advocating for more, whether that assistance was framed as "small" or "big." At times, managers explicitly
advised their subordinates to resist constructing remedies that went
"beyond the scope" of complaints about specific incidents and to keep
our Title VI "resolutions" as minimal as possible.[30] At one team meeting with a cohort of investigators and attorneys, an office director told
us to avoid including more "problems" or more children, no matter
what patterns we uncovered. We were to address only specific problems alleged by the complainants: "Don't go beyond the scope of what
the person asked for," he summed up. He implied strongly that as we
narrowed our "scope" in the quest to close cases, our remedies would
often feel like cop-outs. As I paraphrased in my notes, he advised us
to "think resolution rather than victory."

When OCR does include more changes in its resolutions, it is often
criticized for going beyond its mandate, which scares OCR employees
into actively reducing their efforts.[31] Yet, of course, this advice to not
go "beyond the scope" of the complainants' original charges is a basic
U.S. legal axiom. It is a key principle of U.S. law that "the nature of
the violation determines the scope of the remedy": typically, the legal
goal is only "to restore the person wronged to the position he would
have occupied 'but for the commission of the wrong.' "[32] This legal
mandate can produce purposefully minimal solutions to complex
problems. As a *New York Times* reporter wrote of a community wracked
for years by disability lawsuits, people in the district had been trained
by this string of lawsuits to do the "minimum" required by law.[33]

Legal remedies for racial inequality of opportunity may be especially
at risk for "solutions" that actively do less. As Taylor (1986) notes, it
is hard to "match remedy to the scope of a violation" when complex
"conditions" of racial inequality might require many remedial actions.[34] Another problem is that people interpreting legal definitions of
racially equal treatment can sometimes knowingly set the bar low. A
supervisor cautioned during the Early Learning Project that "best practices suggested by experts" set a much higher bar than "legal requirements," while an OCR investigator said even more defeatedly in one
group discussion on the project that we perhaps had to distinguish

between "over-the-top quality" and the "minimal/necessary" quality that would count as "compliance."[35]

As my colleague's resigned suggestion indicated, OCR's problem was pinpointing harms "minimally": that is, pinpointing a few and refusing to pursue others. We often purposefully stopped conversations with educators about harm and remedy for children of color with a few remedial actions, rather than continuing to deeper conversations about the various activities in a district or school that might help equalize opportunity or improve a social climate. As our office director advised, we would "think resolution rather than victory."

As OCR employees push to close cases, various pressures prompt them to do less rather than more. Since the *Adams* case (see chapter 3), in which OCR was sued for doing too little to enforce Title VI and for having a backload of unresolved cases, OCR has been under both internal and external pressures to close cases more quickly.[36] When I worked at OCR, closure or resolution of a complaint was the basic standard for success. Cases that remained open and unresolved for months were by definition unsuccessful. Though we knew, and argued, that real civil rights work occurred through sufficient analysis of harm and thorough negotiation of remedy, our speed at closing cases seemed the key concern of higher-ups, who were constantly designing strategies for closing cases more quickly. We routinely told recipients over the phone that if they "just" agreed to a few remedial acts, we would close the case.

Timely resolution of cases is obviously in complainants' interests, though it can mean limiting the remedial acts to which recipients must acquiesce. Complainants repeatedly expressed frustration with lengthy investigation, as complaints could stay open and unresolved for several years.[37] But what complainants really wanted from OCR was assistance for children and youth, not just case closure. One day a representative from another region came to talk to our regional office about their office's efforts to close cases in a timely manner. I later wrote critically in my notes that within OCR, "writing letters" to close cases sometimes seemed to be framed as OCR's civil rights work. Echoing a dichotomy I heard muttered a lot by colleagues at OCR, I argued that "this is positioned, in that region, as about writing letters, not about helping kids—it's about closing complaints (that happen to be about civil rights)."

OCR also actively reduced its efforts to assist students of color by failing to monitor its cases over time. Overwhelmed by the task of evaluating a VRP's effects on children's everyday lives and constrained by critics' allegations that OCR forces excessive efforts on school districts, OCR employees often took for granted a district's assertions that it had implemented the agreed-upon plan. Did those actions actually assist children? That determination was not always part of OCR's vision of its monitoring role, and OCR often even failed to guarantee the everyday justice efforts that its resolution letters pinpointed and negotiated. For example, several years after I left OCR, I received a telling e-mail query from a nonprofit lawyer (who had found me on my university Web site) describing an OCR case from several years earlier. A Native American tribe had filed a complaint in another regional OCR office alleging racially discriminatory discipline and peer-on-peer harassment of Native American children. Several years after OCR signed a resolution agreement in which this school district promised to end the harassment, OCR determined that the district had complied with the VRP's requirements and officially stopped monitoring the case. The tribe was now arguing to the lawyer's organization that the district had simply told OCR it was implementing the VRP, even though the original problems were still rampant. The lawyer wondered whether the tribe should bother approaching OCR again.

> Based on our review of documents from OCR and the school district in question, it seems fairly clear that the regional office did not meaningfully oversee the district's efforts to comply with the prior Resolution Agreement. OCR made no site visits after the initial compliance review hearings. It relied on letters from the district to determine compliance. Although the district submitted its letters in a timely manner, OCR took more than 9 months to respond to each one. The district's submissions were frequently unresponsive and/or evasive. OCR rarely challenged the district on what appear to be obvious insufficiencies. Given this history, are we being overly optimistic in thinking that we can get more effective relief from OCR the second time around?

I do not know if this lawyer and the tribe pursued their case. Other civil rights lawyers have told me explicitly, however, that some advocates for students of color specifically avoid contacting OCR on the assumption that in investigation, resolution, and monitoring, OCR will pursue less assistance to such students, rather than more.[38]

OCR efforts could inadvertently produce "minimal" change from educators as well: even when educators responding to OCR's monitoring told investigators that they had "dotted every i and crossed every t" on a VRP, the bureaucratic phrase could imply that educators assumed that these changes overcame the need for educators to pursue other, additional changes. Indeed, while educators often resisted specific enumerations of past harms to children, they sometimes responded with relief when we enumerated just a few specific ways to assist them, which sped up the process of resolving complaints and made that process seem artificially manageable. Some districts agreed to tinker with a few details in order to make OCR go away. One OCR colleague, Reba, had become convinced that the agency was in a sense designed to minimize remedial efforts: she argued that OCR slowed angry citizens' revolts against schools through the reductive remedies that emerged after the bureaucracy processed their complaints.[39] To Reba, complainants' rage could be channeled into the detail of solutions that amounted to mere tinkering. Although OCR's attention amplified the volume of complaints, she argued, as months went by, recipients and OCR together reduced complainants' racial justice demands to a few bullet points on a government document.[40]

Indeed, as recipients dotted i's and crossed t's, systemic problems could falsely seem to be solved through single remedial actions. For example, when complainants denounced the Delano district for treating its Latino hall wanderers as criminals, their energy could be channeled into a training for security guards. Did OCR reduce the problem at hand by pinpointing such a remedial action? Or did we reduce it by framing the actions we secured from educators as the only changes necessary to solve the deeper problems under the specific complaint? As we tried to resolve complaints, our precise descriptions of necessary efforts were not inherently small, but they could be minimal if we framed no other efforts as necessary.

Advocates routinely confuse pinpointed changes and minimal changes. For example, one participant at a community organizing conference in 2006 described the dangers of accepting specific changes for children from a school or district as a process of racking up "trophies" that gave the false impression that larger changes had been achieved. At every event I have attended where advocates discussed ways to equalize opportunity for students of color, people have argued that changes assisting some subset of students in their everyday lives were too small and that activists needed to overhaul entire "systems" instead. But such sweeping calls for systemic change also can miss the mark by failing to suggest precisely enough what anyone in the system, including actors who interact daily with students or parents or whose daily acts and decisions affect many students and parents simultaneously from farther away, might do differently. It is naïve optimism to believe that any strategy for everyday justice will automatically resolve racial inequality by itself, but we cannot dismiss detailed equity efforts in everyday life as "small." In doing so, we also dismiss the seriousness of academic and social harms that students experience on a daily basis, and we suggest dangerously that since no remedial act to shift everyday activity will ever be sufficient, it is fundamentally misguided to pursue this scale of remedy at all.[41]

*The Consequences of Critiquing Everyday Remedies as "Small"*

To many advocates critiquing efforts at everyday justice, the real problem is racially unequal "structures" and "systems." Social theorists
often discount "everyday acts" as too small to be "potential loci of
change and transformation."[42] Some even argue that schools themselves, concerned as they are with the everyday treatment of students
and interactions between small groups of people, are too inconsequential to serve as key sites for progress toward racial equality.[43] These
arguments leave most educational practice out of the analysis.[44]

In a nation with egregious racial disparities in wealth and educational attainment, debate over the scale of both problem and remedy
pervades public thinking on how racial inequality is produced, and on
how it can be challenged. To many social scientists, framing everyday
activity as one site producing or exacerbating racial inequality leads
to unsatisfyingly "micro" analyses of "local" inequalities, instead of
necessary "macro" descriptions of inequality in the national "aggregate."[45] To many, analyzing interactions between individuals or the
daily impact on many children of school or district policies and administrative decisions, as did complainants to OCR, misses the mark by
failing to critique systemic inequalities in society.[46] For decades, analysts discussing institutional racism have been heard as arguing that
the daily experiences of people in interaction are neither the cause of
racial inequality nor the place to look for its solution.[47] Of course, those
who denounce as "minimalist" this project of analyzing everyday interactions often do so to denounce the law's particular reliance on
proving individual actors' intentions, its insistence on evaluating incidents in isolation, and its refusal to look at many systemic conditions
of opportunity denial.[48] Still, in use, many statements about the need
to examine and change "structures," "systems," and "institutions" instead of "acts," "interactions," and "individuals" fail to pinpoint how
ordinary people contribute to producing patterns of opportunity denial. Conversely, they ignore how ordinary people might actually help
dismantle such patterns in part through their own everyday activity.[49]

Advocates calling for change in the "structural processes" affecting
schools and districts often suggest abstractly that we must engage in
"structural" or "systemic" overhaul, instead of also reorganizing per-
son-to-person interactions inside schools and districts or remedying
denials of particular opportunities to children. Students of mine have
left short talks by Jonathan Kozol[50] inspired to overturn the entire
structure of "apartheid schooling," the vicious disparities in basic resources that disadvantage urban schools relative to those in the suburbs. But many remained confused about how, exactly, to participate

in dismantling this structure, and about whether they, as educators, could help improve educational opportunity while this structure exists.[51] In calling for systemic change, some observers even argue explicitly that focusing on changing everyday life within schools and districts is a cop-out from making substantive change.[52] And, as I have shown throughout, many people minimize the harms that students of color experience through everyday interactions in educational settings, including interactions over fundamental opportunities to learn.[53]

Therefore, many advocates for children of color continue to see as inadequate the types of proposals for everyday justice that people made to and within OCR. Yet in the new civil rights era, this is itself a reductive way of thinking about the production of contemporary racial inequality and the various ways ordinary people can help equalize opportunity on a regular basis. If we dismiss everyday activity within schools and districts as a site for expanding opportunity, then we leave people in schools and districts with nothing to do. At OCR, the demands for everyday justice that I encountered specified concrete daily examples of harm to children of color and proposed concrete ways that specific people could help remedy that harm.

## Considering Demands for Everyday Justice as Concrete and Precise Demands for Particular Opportunities

As complainants analyzed how everyday school experiences could harm children, they framed unequal opportunity inside schools and districts as daily experiences of opportunity denial that accumulated over time. To complainants, interactions between students and educators, and specific decisions by administrators, denied students specific academic opportunities to learn and social opportunities to thrive; they eventually contributed to an academically limiting and socially unwelcoming environment for the children. Thus, the negative everyday experiences felt like the building blocks of educational disadvantage. What pushed each parent of color who came to OCR over the edge was a sequence of events and experiences aggregating into an environment that seemed hostile or damaging to their children as children of color, either in comparison to local white children or in comparison to the ideal treatment of children elsewhere.

In their reactions to their schools and districts and then in their complaints to OCR, they summarized a host of everyday interactions between children, educators, and themselves, everyday implementations of policies, and everyday decisions about resource distribution into systemic patterns they called racial discrimination. Their complaints made it clear that actors in educational dramas often experience larger patterns as aggregates of individual events: parents routinely added up numerous incidents and experiences in alleging a pattern of discrimination.[54] Single events, when added to others and repeated over time, stood as evidence of a racially unequal situation and showed one way that systemic inequalities were constituted inside the educational domain. And indeed, to them, the *experience* of such accreting disadvantage *was* disadvantage. They saw children coming to experience and respond to schools over time as environments where "no black kids" were "allowed," where "Mexican" kids were "targeted" or "attacked," or where advanced courses felt out of reach. They saw children refusing over time to attend those schools, shutting down while inside them, and falling further behind academically. They, like researchers, suggested that both "objective" resource denial and the very *experience* of "bias" could depress student performance,[55] as students lost faith in educators and stopped expecting academic success.

When OCR staff went to schools and districts to examine alleged opportunity denial, the resistance we encountered suggested, ironically, that educators did not view OCR's work as inconsequential "tinkering." For educators, like complainants, educational interactions with parents and children were the center of everyday life. Parents and grandparents, teachers, principals, and OCR staff argued over whether a dean had falsely assumed that a Latino student's gesture was a "gang sign," or whether school administrators too easily dismissed a white child's racial slur toward a black child, or whether an administrator could be blamed for the absence of credentialed teachers. They argued over whether the specific acts had harmed children "because of race" and whether particular events constituted "discrimination" or racial inequality of opportunity, but they rarely disputed the importance of everyday educational activity in general.

By prompting arguments over the fairness of particular educational practices, policies, policy implementation, and outcomes, complainants often prompted us to analyze the concrete ways in which today's educational disparities are produced in part inside schools and districts over time. For example, people debating the overrepresentation of black children in Special Education argued about the daily practices and policies through which a host of individual black children were evaluated, diagnosed, and placed; they went far beyond simple critiques or justifications of the disparate outcome. Similarly, MINSPED (Minorities in Special Education) policy and investigation efforts within OCR focused on daily processes of evaluation and referral. "Resource comparability" efforts examined specific resource denials. Colleagues doing *Lau* work on behalf of English-language learners in districts examined whether the educational programs were actually providing children with daily access to academic content as the law required. In other Title VI cases, claims of harm to individual children, such as Mrs. Rodriguez's complaints about the "defiance" suspensions given José in the Granley district, often prompted discussions of whether such harms were occurring beyond the child in question: people debated how similarly situated children from the same group were treated and how policy was applied to those in other groups. In debating the details of the everyday treatment of specific students, educators and parents debated broadly whether discipline in the district was being doled out in accordance with its own policies. In Title VI cases, as we tweaked the details of treatment for individual students, such as expunging José's safety pin suspension, we often prompted discussion about interactions with many children. In devising remedies, too, moves to support individual students often reverberated beyond them. Even individual complaints sometimes requested both remedies for individual group members and school- and district-wide policy changes to prevent similar incidents from happening to other children.

Thus, at first glance OCR complainants were only working to "advance or defend" specific children's personal interests,[56] but they were simultaneously arguing that "the community's everyday concerns can be transformed into broader questions of general import," and using particular instances to push for more detailed analysis of everyday opportunity provision.[57] They were often "defining problems in such a way that the harm that these problems produced reached beyond the individual": by defining their children's problems as larger community problems, they "felt authorized" ethically and morally to "mobilize the law" for this larger cause.[58] To them, everyday experiences represented a disadvantaging environment in crystallized form. Thus, both complainants and OCR staff stimulated concrete analysis of how school and district adults acted toward students on an ordinary, daily basis: how they disciplined students, assessed them, taught them, placed them in programs, assigned them resources, and talked to them and their families. In suggesting that such everyday activity could contribute to school-based racial inequality in opportunities to learn and thrive, these analysts were forcing us all to consider ongoing interactions and educator decisions alongside more typical analysis of educational opportunity as solely the provision of equal resources from on high. Equal treatment for students of color, they suggested, would mean concrete opportunities and resources provided through continuing relationships.[59] In the complaints I saw that emerged from predominantly white schools, the question did not turn on the school-wide absence of educational resources, but rather on patterns of interaction with educators that denied particular educational opportunities daily. When the complaints came from underresourced schools serving predominantly or entirely students of color, they pointed out both needs: basic resources and the ongoing provision of opportunities to learn.

Complainants also indicated that academic opportunities were provided or denied not just at explicitly "academic" moments but also in many social interactions inside schools and districts. A series of unwarranted suspensions given to a black student caused him to fail a course; slurs lobbed at Latino students eventually made them unwilling to attend school. A black father complaining that his son was harassed and disciplined unfairly contended that the situation "hindered his ability to receive public education." Thus, they argued that providing equal academic opportunity to students of color required improving social interactions among educators, students, and parents as well.

Some of our most influential educational thinkers have similarly indicated the need to examine precisely how opportunity is provided or denied in part by ordinary people, through these concrete everyday relationships, interactions, and decisions that affect students. For example, in 1938, John Dewey argued that everyday interactions between teachers and students should be educators' "immediate and direct concern."[60] Others have focused on interactions between educators and parents as key to opportunity provision.[61] More recently, scholars have argued that resources must be both allocated equitably and used well in concrete daily interactions between educators and students in schools and classrooms,[62] that any educational policy is only useful to children if administrators and teachers make it improve students' daily experiences of teaching and learning,[63] and that achieving racial equality in education requires both that policymakers distribute concrete resources to meet the needs of children and that educators inside institutions distribute a sense of human worth equally through caring and "enabling" relationships.[64]

These visions of educational justice do not discount resource provision from afar but extend beyond it to a more comprehensive and concrete analysis of how "enabling" opportunities are provided or denied in the everyday activity of multiple actors, including those in schools and districts.[65] While some critics thought OCR's ability to "enforce" such everyday opportunity provision exceeded Title VI altogether, a similarly precise approach to everyday justice is explicitly laid out in the other arenas of discrimination law that OCR enforces: disability, language services, and sex. Civil rights laws and regulations in these

realms have been particularly precise at suggesting that specific opportunities must be provided equitably and daily.

### Other Legal Road Maps for Everyday Justice

I realized early on at OCR that the more detail the text of civil rights
regulation offered to define what practices constituted educational discrimination, the easier it was to find and remedy denials of educational
opportunity.[66] As I wrote in my notes one day, textual specificity could
lead to clear thinking about how to "protect" students.

> OCR has a very good record with disability rights, much better than its record
> with Title VI rights, because they have such clear-cut regulations to work
> with! CLARITY = protection against discrimination. RULES = protection against
> discrimination. LABELS/DIAGNOSES = protection against discrimination.[67]

Specific definitions of harm authorized parents, advocates, and OCR
alike to demand specific assistance for children. At OCR, we felt totally free to investigate the professional qualifications of teachers and
instructional assistants for disabled students; we investigated in detail, without worrying, the classroom placement of such students, required by law to be "least restrictive" and appropriate to their assessed needs. We investigated specific academic services for
individual students with disabilities, comparing them to the services
local professionals had deemed optimal for them. In short, we pursued everyday justice for (predominantly white) disabled students
with confidence, openness, and success. After investigating yet another disability case brought by white parents who were monitoring
every detail of their child's education, I noted that white parents really knew how to use civil rights law. Students of color kept ending
up in Special Education situations with some "vague remedy" for
their academic needs, but white students received "specific" aid "targeted at remediating specific skills."[68]

When allowed to proceed unhindered, my colleagues' work to secure academic opportunities for English-language learners could be
similarly successful at pursuing everyday justice because the text of
case law, related regulations, and OCR policy memos unmistakably
allow agency employees to ask whether the academic practices offered
to English-language learners in their daily educational experiences are
effective, research-based, and having a positive impact. The political
controversy constraining *Lau* efforts within OCR was over how specific
federal suggestions for local academic assistance could be, but such
arguments against "prescribing" certain kinds of language services

rarely maintained that the law did not *allow* any analysis of necessary daily academic opportunity for "ELLs," as OCR people discussing the Early Learning Project would argue regarding other students of color. To enforce Title VI for English-language learners using the specific prohibitions of *Lau*, my colleagues were able to investigate whether teachers were properly credentialed, whether the assessments that administrators used could adequately pinpoint students' language proficiency and academic needs, whether teachers had been trained in strategies for teaching ELLs, and what academic opportunities were actually being provided to a specific group of ELLs pulled out of their classroom for an hour each day.[69]

Like disability law, *Lau* explicitly allowed us to define everyday denials of access to the core curriculum as "discrimination"; what constrained us in this effort was agency reticence, not the law, and we could far more easily remedy such everyday denials for disabled students. Indeed, D.C. higher-ups rarely called OCR disability services work "prescriptive," even though law and regulation for protecting "disabled" students had OCR telling schools and districts in clear mandates to assess disabled students, hold meetings on their needs and educational goals, plan individualized programs for their education, and follow these programs to the letter. This was in part because "experts" hired by school districts or parents were clearly the ones diagnosing harm to students. OCR's role was simply to push for these diagnoses and then enforce the experts' prescriptions. But my colleague Reba explained it bluntly: "The Republicans have kids with disabilities." Because disability cut across all race groups and political communities, its political support was secured under all administrations.[70]

Another factor makes both the *Lau* and disability regulations particularly enabling of everyday justice efforts: they ask, specifically, whether the everyday treatment of children effectively offers them educational opportunity, in comparison both to "standard" students and to an ideal of "effective" education for each student. The Section 504 regulations state literally that equal treatment requires schools to provide academic experiences that give disabled students access to content as "effectively" as non-disabled students get that access. The Section 504 regulations' extended appendix states specifically that the logic of civil rights law for "the disabled" is to "afford an equal opportunity to achieve equal results." For a disabled individual, actually receiving the specific academic opportunities necessary to succeed is deemed a "civil right."[71] Similarly, *Lau* work demands that educators offer English-language learners daily opportunities that allow them to access the common curriculum as effectively as English speakers access it.

The text of Title VI provides an overarching logic outlawing the denial of opportunity "because of race" rather than a road map for providing specific or "effective" opportunities inside schools and districts.[72] It also fails to articulate the crucial logic of the need to "afford an equal opportunity to achieve equal results." While Title VI's vagueness could allow for broad interpretation and application, it often has permitted people to argue that daily access to particular effective, adequate, or even "equal" academic or social opportunities for students of color is not required. Furthermore, in disability and *Lau* work the very categories "disabled" and "English-language learner" suggest inherent "disadvantages" that require remedy by law; in Title VI work at OCR, however, arguments often centered on whether students of color were denied opportunities "because of race" and were thus "disadvantaged" in any way during their schooling experience.

Still, other arenas of OCR work afforded more precise analysis of how disadvantage happens inside educational settings. For example, the department fleshed out regulations and internal "policy guidance" to implement Title IX of the Elementary and Secondary Education Act of 1972 (which forbid discrimination on the basis of sex); these also enumerate in more detail than Title VI the academic and social opportunities that must be equitably afforded to students. For example, in the athletic realm, OCR is allowed to analyze "whether the selection of sports and levels of competition effectively accommodate the interests and abilities of members of both sexes," and schools and districts are mandated to offer such "effective accommodation."[73] Title IX regulations allow OCR employees to compare specific athletic resources being offered to the sexes, such as "the provision of equipment and supplies," "scheduling of games and practice time," "opportunity to receive coaching and academic tutoring," and the "provision of locker rooms, practice and competitive facilities."[74] The regulations governing perhaps the most controversial Title IX realm—determining equal access for girls to math and science—are far less specific than the regulations regarding equality of athletic opportunity (as one female colleague pointed out critically to me), but at least the Title IX regulations make concrete the ways that sex discrimination in education might play out in various educational realms, such as admissions, counseling, and course enrollment. While critics have argued that Title IX's requirements constitute legalistic micromanagement, they break down "sex discrimination" into many of its component parts and force some concrete analysis of the everyday acts that can add up to an inequitable experience for girls.

No such specificity governs Title VI analysis of everyday denials of academic or social opportunity in education, so our attempts to pursue everyday justice for students of color always seemed excessively "prescriptive." When we did analyze opportunity for these students in detail, we were proactively applying Title VI's basic logic, rather than doing so in ways the regulations explicitly prescribed. OCR's Title VI regulations prohibiting "separate," "different," or "segregated" treatment or the "denial" of "benefits" "on the ground of race, color, or national origin" in federally funded programs say little about actually applying this logic to educational settings. For example, unlike Title IX, the Title VI regulations say nothing about examining the "disproportionate" demographics of "particular classes," about whether counselors may direct certain groups toward low-status careers, or about how to measure the quality of academic facilities afforded to one group in comparison to another. In fact, they offer little specific guidance about ways that racial discrimination might become manifest on a daily basis in schools or districts. Some extended appendices to Title VI detail racial discrimination in vocational education, demonstrating how detailed Title VI work could be in other arenas if the regulations were as specific.[75] As the same critical colleague pointed out, it was telling that we employees had particularly specific instructions for making vocational educational opportunities equitably available to students of color, but no specific instructions for making advanced educational opportunities equitably available to them.

Again, the educational opportunities provided inside schools and districts are enabled, particularly financially, by actors and forces outside educational settings. Educators cannot provide many learning opportunities if they are not given the funds and freedom to do so. Students also enter school buildings with economic advantages and disadvantages inherited over generations and accruing across domains other than schools;[76] both students and parents obviously help construct students' fates. Yet school and district actors have control over countless aspects of daily opportunity provision. Title VI's basic logic of questioning any denial of "benefits" along racial lines, combined with the sorts of concrete and specific analysis of providing necessary and "effective" everyday opportunity prompted by disability and language service analysis, could undergird many concrete steps toward everyday justice for students of color inside American schools and districts.[77] Yet such efforts would require acknowledging that ordinary people's ordinary actions inside schools and districts sometimes deny educational opportunity to students of color—or, more basically, that they play a role in the production of racial inequality.[78]

## WHY PEOPLE—PARTICULARLY WHITE PEOPLE—RESIST APPLYING EVERYDAY JUSTICE ANALYSIS TO THEMSELVES

The school-level educators I came to know while at OCR never argued, either to parents or to OCR, that systemic resource disparities did not harm students of color. They suffered from the lack of resources along with their students, and they placed the blame on district, state, or federal actors outside the school. And district actors, like Christie McCormack in the King district, blamed funding inadequacies outside the district's control for resource disparities they also often acknowledged as harmful. But when these educators were themselves accused of harming students of color with particular acts, they typically resisted both the claims of harm and responsibility, as well as the suggestion that they be involved in the remedy.

To many observers in the new civil rights era, no one orchestrates the disadvantages children of color experience.[79] Accordingly, when confronted with concrete claims that they themselves have denied students opportunity in a given instance, most resist this claim, quite heatedly. Indeed, no one set of actors can be held solely responsible for racial inequalities of opportunity or outcome. But many Americans will not agree that they play any role at all.

Given the complexities of inequality formation today, people who do focus on any one set of actors unsurprisingly prompt those same actors to argue that something is wrong with the analysis and that their own acts should be removed from it. Analyses of responsibility often feel like analyses of sole responsibility, and OCR's legal tools did not help ease this feeling: when OCR wielded Title VI to analyze actions by federal funding recipients in education, we took the analytic lens off of actors outside of schools and districts, like people making decisions about health care or housing. Blaming educators *only* for racial inequality in education would itself be a "minimalist" analysis[80] obfuscating the social and policy contexts of both educators and families and the everyday activity of students and parents themselves. But holding educators responsible at all simply meant analyzing their participation; and even before OCR's involvement, school and district staff typically responded to complainants by denying their own responsibility altogether. Often, they contended that fault should be assigned either to "structures" beyond their control or exclusively to the child and his or her parents. Thus, at times we all faced the key question one OCR complainant asked explicitly: "Who has responsibility for the child?"

Today, racial inequality is built, allowed, and exacerbated through a complex web of ordinary policy and practice by people at various levels of systems, typically in the absence of explicitly announced intention. So any claim that children of color are denied opportunities by anyone in particular prompts resistance from those accused. Indeed, it even prompts resistance from those accused indirectly. Many Americans would agree in principle that if Johnny languishes without books in a crumbling elementary school building while Julie thumbs through newly printed novels in her gleaming school library, Johnny has a valid claim of unfairness. But what if Johnny points out that he and other black children in his mostly black school lack such resources "because of race" while Julie and other white children in her mostly white school enjoy them "because of race"? Many Americans—particularly white people, who may now feel particularly accused of enjoying accumulated advantages or of accepting resources being denied to children of color—will become skeptical and annoyed by this more causal claim. Even those ready to agree that the book disparity does harm Johnny and other students of color disproportionately may find it preposterous to think that specific actors have played any recognizable role in the disparity, rather than just the unfortunate race-class disparity in neighborhood income.

Imagine now that Johnny's claims about racially unequal opportunity become more detailed and pinpoint actual "perpetrators" in his local setting. Imagine that Johnny and his friend Jermaine, also black, are no longer arguing simply for their right to books but arguing, six years later, for their right to enroll in AP calculus. Johnny, who now attends a mostly black high school, claims that both his superintendent and his principal have unfairly denied him access to AP because his school has no AP class or AP teacher; Jermaine, who attends a more desegregated high school where an AP class is available, argues that over time, his teachers have failed to equip him to enroll in it. Such claims of injustice involve teachers who prepare or fail to prepare students and the principal or superintendent who provides AP courses and AP teachers or fails to do so. That complexity will certainly generate even more skepticism, and those included in the analysis will particularly resist analyzing these patterns as harm "because of race." Johnny's principal will likely argue simply that he scheduled no AP class because no one in his school was prepared for it. The superintendent will likely argue that AP teachers simply chose to teach in other schools. Jermaine's teachers will likely argue angrily that they tried their best to teach him. In the new civil rights era, an analytic and social hurdle appears in any attempt to analyze whether opportunities are being denied children of color along the lines of race, on account of race group membership, or sometimes even denied them at all. The hurdle is how to analyze the role of specific people in complex multiplayer interactions that contribute to racially unequal opportunities and outcomes over time.[81]

Centuries and decades ago, opportunity denial in education involved a triad of overt harms by specific actors: the writing of explicitly discriminatory law, the creation of effectively discriminatory policy, and overt incidents of interpersonal discriminatory practice, such as white principals standing at school doors and refusing black children entry. Educational opportunities denied along the lines of race became accumulated disadvantages in job preparation and community wealth;[82] the 2007 Supreme Court ruling forbidding various voluntary desegregation policies risked allowing accumulated inequalities to exist long into the future.[83] But today, a crumbling school serving children of color, a school climate stigmatizing children of color, or an AP calculus roster excluding students of color has been constructed through an aggregation of events that involves even more than court rulings, historical actions, or inequalities in "domains" outside schools and districts.[84] Everyday decisions and activity inside schools and districts also contribute to such patterns; everyday acts by even well-meaning educators disadvantage and harm children of color by failing to counteract prior opportunity denials; daily decisions by teachers and administrators can deny opportunities to students of color at particular moments and over time.

Dovidio and Gaertner (2005) argue that today, racial harm routinely involves "a failure to help, rather than an action intentionally aimed at doing harm."[85] Today, racial harm also accumulates because ordinary people fail to find children's experiences of harm troubling. Often, racial disparities in both opportunities (supplies, facilities, and AP classes) and outcomes (academic failure or the disproportionate presence of students of color on suspension lists) are taken for granted as normal inside schools and districts, and the normalization itself exacerbates racial inequality. As I described earlier, we at OCR often convinced ourselves that we could not or did not need to dismantle even obviously racial patterns or to respond thoroughly to even obviously harmful situations. But the educators I saw get accused of contributing to harmful disparities or climates often dismissed those accusations outright. Indeed, some educators even resisted claims that children experienced harm at all; few suggested readily that they would set forth to remedy that experience of harm. In dismissing the complainants' versions of their experiences, they vastly exacerbated students' and parents' experiences of racial discrimination. Each complainant I encountered at OCR argued explicitly that teachers and administrators had harmed their children in large part by dismissing families' claims that everyday harms actually hurt.[86]

Americans are not particularly good today at analyzing and discussing how everyday experiences in schools accrue to harm children over time,[87] and this failure of analysis is particularly consequential in education. Education is an ongoing process of providing opportunities to children through countless interactions of multiple actors inside opportunity structures. As I wrote in one draft document on the Early Learning Project, looking at opportunity provision moment to moment and over time inside schools was central to analyzing educational opportunity.

> Curriculum proceeds quite rapidly in a cumulative way in the early years of elementary school, quickly building upon skills acquired the previous hour, day, or year. Students who are allowed to languish early often languish forever, permanently denied access to grade-level learning opportunities; this might be considered an example of "irreparable harm."

Similarly, as we unpacked the academic and social patterns in complaints to OCR, such as the overrepresentation of a district's black children in separate Special Education classes, their absence from an entire school's Advanced Placement courses, or their dramatic overrepresentation on lists of those harshly disciplined, we found that such serious patterns were in part the outcome of a combination of everyday actions by educators in many locations over many years. Discriminatory discipline patterns involved many deans, over years in a school's or a child's life, suspending students of color for excessive lengths. Patterns of racial tracking within schools revealed, when peeled like onions, an aggregation of educators over days and years equipping some students but not others for AP calculus.[88] Even single events involving individual children of color were the outcome of many acts by many people.

As educators resisted an analysis pinpointing their partial responsibility for harm, they encountered a particular problem of determining causality in education: adults' and students' actions are intertwined over time in students' educational trajectories, as students react to adult actions and vice versa. For example, the altercations that led to José's many suspensions in the Granley district were partly his responses to previous suspensions; in part, José wore a safety pin back to school because of a host of prior interactions over it. José was not suspended solely "because he was Latino," but the causal rebuttal "we didn't suspend José because he was Latino, we suspended him because he was defiant!" has a key logical problem. If José was in fact suspended more often as a Latino student, he might actually have become more defiant in school settings when approached by disciplinary personnel. In one disciplinary file I read at OCR, through a seemingly endless string of mounting referrals over the course of years, a younger child with small offenses like chewing gum in class became an older child making angry threats to his teacher. Anyone who has read such files knows that students routinely start acting "difficult" over time through interactions with other people. Anyone who has been a teacher or a parent knows that parents, too, are intertwined in children's educational fates, and that they too can become "difficult" over time as they seek to protect their children's access to opportunity.[89]

Racially disparate academic outcomes are also built over time as adults and young people interact. Yet analyzing the longitudinal causation of racial inequalities over everyday lives in complex systems is analytically very difficult, and it prompts people to refuse even partial responsibility. Even social scientists admit the deep difficulty of trying to analyze when any given set of actors has contributed to producing unequal opportunities or outcomes over time.[90] Rarely do fights over responsibility suggest partial, unwitting responsibility in a way that might goad the accused to take responsibility. Like civil rights law, educational research on racial disparities in education is often a quixotic search to determine the primary roles of various actors in complex chains of causation. In educational research, too, every finding regarding particular players' causation of racial disparities is challenged. In a telling statement about the social ramifications of being included in such analyses, each time one author admits that social science cannot fully determine the role educators play in producing racial achievement disparities, he suggests that educators have been "absolved" from blame.[91]

Nor have social scientists consistently offered sufficiently detailed analyses of how everyday practices of providing and denying opportunities to children accrue over time. We often quickly describe who or what "caused" unequal endpoints rather than fully analyzing the process of offering opportunity to children along the way. Indeed, social scientists concerned about patterns of racial inequality in American education often portray the aggregated processes of social reproduction as a giant sorting machine slotting young people into the existing inequitable social order; they more rarely show us the roles ordinary people play in this positioning. Soon after I became a professor, a colleague summarized much social science research by writing a simple equation from educational sociology on a napkin: "race + class = achievement." As a correlational statement this equation is demographically correct—across the nation, school achievement is still predicted by race and class—but as a causal statement, it does nothing to unpack the daily activities through which children are denied opportunity along race and class lines.[92] Nor does it prompt anyone to see themselves as intertwined in these activities.

Advocates concerned with fairness for young people similarly tell stories of large populations denied opportunities along racial lines, but they often focus on unequal endpoints rather than how concrete policies in action or daily acts and decisions by actual ordinary people play a role in distributing opportunity. They tell audiences that Latino students in Tucson are segregated in inferior schools while whites are tracked to white-dominated "magnet schools," that African American students are tracked into Special Education in California or Massachusetts, and that Latin American immigrant students are dropping out of high school in Texas. Often, they characterize these patterns as the result of discriminatory denials of opportunity without analyzing how real people participated in producing these patterns in intertwined interactions with students and families: through unequal distribution of school enrollment information, unwarranted Special Ed referral processes, or the countless interactions that precede drop out.[93] People concerned with stating endpoints often fail to analyze the role of daily actions by actual people: how, as Philomena Essed (2002) puts it, "the system is continually construed in everyday life."[94] Charles Payne (1984) writes similarly that many observers stop the analysis of "opportunity structures" "before inquiring as to how those structures are created and maintained."[95] In today's "fragmented" system, Payne argues, observers often fail to see, much less describe, how "the processes sustaining inequality are shaped by chains of interaction extending across many individuals or organizational units or institutional boundaries. . . . Who can name the person responsible for 'structural unemployment'? Inequalities that were once clearly done *to* people, imposed upon them, come increasingly to seem as if they just *happen* to people." This "fragmentation" of harm and resulting analytic blind spots, Payne suggests, means in the end that "there are no longer wrongs of which we have to be aware."[96]

Determining the causal role played by any given interaction or action in a child's everyday life is indeed difficult, and it is understandable that educators resist taking responsibility for harm. As a final example, let us put aside for one moment the aggregate causal question of why so many black or Latino students are not in AP classes and attempt to understand why just one individual student, José, is not in AP. If we can find that José was academically qualified but educators actively discouraged him from AP enrollment, the pattern of classic discrimination becomes clearer. But suppose that we find that by eleventh grade, José was not in possession of the skills required for participation. To analyze his situation, we will have to consider all the details of educational practice José experienced, not just at the moment of AP enrollment but also longitudinally over the course of his educational career. The analysis of José's absence from AP begins before his birth, with the health care that legislators and social service providers did or did not make available to his Spanish-speaking immigrant mother, or the wages her employers did or did not pay her.[97] We might start by trying to compare the relative weight of various statistical factors in José's childhood, factors that are both economic and racially patterned (his mother's educational degrees at his birth, the number of books his parents have bought for his room),[98] but this analysis will be unable to analyze the actual experiences of José in K–11 classrooms.[99] We will have to consider how the language and literacy experiences José enjoys at home mimic, or do not, the language and literacy experiences he will have at school.[100] We will have to consider some subset of the key school-based moments shaping José's educational "pathway,"[101] what Johnson (2004) has called the "thousand daily interactions" shaping any child's path.

Since José is a hypothetical case, we can take some of these typical moments from the findings of researchers. We might consider as partially causal the kindergarten moment when José's Spanish-speaking father drops him off with his backpack and leaves for work without understanding the posted notices that list his opportunities to meet with José's teacher, or the first-grade moment when José's father, invited to monitor his son's nightly homework, defers to what he believes is the school's expertise.[102] We will have to consider the third-grade moment when a teacher tells José he shouldn't become a farm laborer like his grandparents,[103] or the fourth-grade moment when José mutters a critical remark about another teacher and gets suspended.[104]

We will also have to consider the details of his pedagogical experiences, examining how José's teachers monitor or neglect to monitor his progress, as a child who speaks Spanish at home and English at school, toward mastery of written English skills,[105] and how his teachers prod or do not prod him to master other core subjects, such as math.[106] We will have to consider, comparatively, any extracurricular resources enjoyed by José's white classmates, statistically more likely to have access to middle-class advantages.[107] We will have to consider the fourth-grade moment when José is placed in remedial reading, and the fifth-grade moment when his teacher tells his mother he should be in Special Education, primarily because he cannot write in academic English.[108] We will have to consider the sixth-grade moment when José is assigned to an uncredentialed teacher for the third year in a row; unqualified teachers are disproportionately found at schools serving predominantly students of color as a result of district pay structures, administrative decisions, and educator choice.[109]

We must also consider the midyear moment when this uncredentialed teacher once again unwittingly misses a chance to help José learn to read better, and a key end-of-the-year whirlwind sequence: José, still unable to understand the class text, throws over a desk in frustration and gets suspended from school as the maximum sentence for "defiance,"[110] comes back to class a week later even more lost, stops attending class, misses an excessive number of class days, fails the grade, and gets retained to spend an extra year with his uncredentialed teacher.

Finally, we will then have to consider the pull-out services José experiences in eighth grade, where he is shown a slow series of vocabulary flash cards while his classmates continue to read short stories,[111] the moment in ninth grade when the school dean sees José throwing what the dean decides is a "gang sign" to a friend and suspends him for the maximum sentence of five days, the moment in tenth grade when a security guard's questioning of José and a small group of friends in the hallway turns into a shouting match and results in the third suspension that spring and consequently, after a total of twelve missed classes, a failing grade in English 10.

That José's school and district educators would resist claims of harming José "because of race" is unsurprising. Given that all of these people connected to José over time can be argued to be in some way at fault—as is José himself, particularly as he matures—can we place blame for José's absence from AP exclusively on his eleventh-grade teachers, his principal, and his dean? Can remedy even be demanded from the school system alone? Over time, some of the adults serving José or witnessing his story will see him as a difficult individual, especially once his downward trajectory has been documented on piles of paper and has resulted in repeated altercations with teachers. Educators will always resist the accusation that José's experience is the fault of school or district people, rather than José, along with any claims of José's treatment having a "racial" component.

Rather than pinpointing the causality in isolation of any act or set of actors, getting one's conversation partners to even start analyzing shared responsibility may require what Stone, Patton, and Heen (2000) describe as an analysis of each actor's contribution to the problem being debated, rather than pinpointing the sole player responsible for it. Yet given the complexity of interactions in schools and districts, working backward from a racially disproportionate outcome to the real people and actions helping create that pattern is always a hotly disputed approach.[112] While people conducting experiments can suggest they have isolated the effects of specific actions, we cannot stop daily life to analyze causality.[113] And a basic educational question is often lost in polarized arguments over fault and causality: how might students of color, like all students, be assisted to succeed at each moment on the educational pathway?

What we end up doing in educational settings, then, is fighting to be "absolved" from blame for the harm experienced by students of color rather than getting down to the business of collectively making sure that they experience success. The rebuttals to racial discrimination complaints that I saw while working at OCR showed that in particular, white people tended to dismiss both claims about harm's daily occurrence and suggestions of how they might participate in remedying it. Those closest to the drama, the educators, did so largely because when asked to analyze their own participation in the students' negative experiences, it felt not just like a suggestion that they were personally "racist" or "prejudiced" but also an excuse for people of color who refused to take responsibility for their own problems. Parents of color and others complaining of racial injustice were received not as advocates seeking assistance for children but as hostile complainers bent on punishing predominantly white educators for racism. Educators often refused to look at their own activity as potentially and unintentionally harmful to students of color; even those who felt distressed by student failure could not see themselves "maintaining" "structures" at all. Somehow, to do so would mean admitting to being "Bad Persons," rather than helping analyze how "bad structures" could be "maintained by perfectly wonderful people."[114] OCR employees had this same problem: focused as we were on the harms caused by educators, we often failed to see how in our own daily actions we, too, maintained "bad structures" by arguing repeatedly that the educational situations families and students experienced as inequitable were not "discriminatory" situations in which we could intervene to improve. To us, as to complainants, harm "on the ground of" race in education seemed shaped over time, as one OCR lawyer put it at the Early Learning conference, in part through "the accretion of small discriminatory acts" in children's educational lives. Yet as we unpacked structures into their constitutive everyday acts, we often deemed those everyday acts, taken in isolation, insufficient in legal terms to "cause" an unequal or harmful outcome "because of race." Breaking Saturn's rings into their isolated dust pieces, we too often became unable to see the rings, much less address the dust seriously.[115] And as we resisted "forcing" opportunity provision, we often failed to prompt serious analysis of who might do what to support student success.

We at OCR shared with local educators the four rebuttals to everyday justice demands explored in this book; meanwhile, educators, as those closest to students and parents, were most angrily resistant. In schools and districts, predominantly white educators' resistance to these analyses of harm lay close to the surface. In telling me about the racially hostile climate in her district, the Quail complainant added that one first-year Latino teacher in the district had already quit his job because the principal had taken as "white-bashing" his complaints of harm to students of color. Instead, many educators argued repeatedly that they had the best intentions and that students and their parents created or imagined these unpleasant results.

To educators, each isolated incident that complainants deemed "discriminatory" often seemed too "small" to be harmful at all. For the person accused, it is often easy to dismiss a claim of everyday harm because it is quite possible to do harm without realizing it. Only after I had stopped teaching 10th grade in 1995 did I start to recognize the many moments when I had failed to provide students of color with opportunities to learn to write and read, or when I had disciplined students of color egregiously for relatively minor infractions. Had I been accused directly of such harms at the time, I may initially have resisted the allegation. Conversely, as a new educator thirsting to improve, I might have found it useful to take children's or parents' claims of harm at face value and adjust my behavior accordingly. Many more seasoned educators did not respond so sympathetically when confronted by either parents or OCR. Once educators started defending themselves from allegations of racial "discrimination," they often constrained any impulse they might have had to believe claims of everyday harm made by people of color and to believe they had played any role in that harm.

OCR, too, in the end, would dismiss many events in children's lives as insufficiently troubling to require our intervention. We regularly indicated to educators that they could leave large swaths of everyday activity unexamined. Our routine "failures to help" echoed in the nation's schools and districts; in effect, we, too, often "dismissed" much everyday activity as too "minimal" to count as harm worth remedying.

Others, however, dismiss the entire arena of everyday activity as too "small" to "count." Even people believing claims of everyday racial harm can implicitly dismiss those harms as "small": today, both laypeople and social scientists routinely suggest that in comparison to the blatant discrimination of the 1950s, discrimination has become more "subtle." The phrase is meant to suggest that discrimination is harder to see rather than to suggest it is less harmful, but in ordinary use this characterization of the forms discrimination now takes tends to diminish estimates of harm's severity and force proof of its existence.[116] Of course, not all harms toward children of color in public schools today are subtle or seem small to observers. Some harms are obvious to most who see them: for example, students of color still disproportionately attend schools that are crumbling while white students attend schools that gleam. But crucially, everyday decisions that contributed to such opportunity denials inside districts, or everyday failures to level the playing field of learning opportunity inside classrooms, or everyday conflicts between educators and students or educators and parents were not "subtly" harmful to those who brought complaints to OCR: to complainants, such decisions and interactions had serious negative consequences for children's educational lives. This was the accusation that educators resisted.

As one OCR lawyer put it, we were often investigating "the accretion of small discriminatory acts into a pattern where the minority school (or kid) is *always* at the bottom." Yet while OCR investigated "small discriminatory acts," OCR regularly failed to deem large numbers of such acts impermissibly harmful to students of color, or to investigate and address countless other acts in the complex educational system; perhaps most importantly, we often failed to convince educators that specific events and situations were harmful "because of race" or even harmful at all. From the beginning of an OCR investigation to its conclusion, the alleged "perpetrator," typically a white person, always "interpreted" incidents and situations as far less harmful than did the alleged "victim," typically a person of color. As I investigated the Longview II case's controversy over "gang member" suspensions, I noted, "Very different sense of weightiness, importance of everyday interactions—people of color find everyday interactions far more damaging than white people imagine them to be."

The Title VI complaints that I processed and heard about at OCR were indeed often angry claims from Americans of color that specific children were being treated unequally by specific people, almost always white people, in specific schools and districts through specific acts.[117] But they were also largely complaints that (typically white) superintendents and principals and teachers rejected their claims of harm rather than attempting empathetically to address their experiences as valid and worthy of remedy. By the time most complainants left their interactions with OCR, they felt the same way about the civil rights bureaucracy. OCR employees, like local educators, often failed to recognize or address the harm, and this failure of recognition and remedy actually harmed children and parents further.

OCR people did not dismiss claims of harm from the outset as too "small" to count as "discrimination," but by the end of many investigations or policy efforts, we, like all resistant players in OCR dramas, suggested that countless aspects of everyday justice would not be pursued. We, too, essentially allowed racial inequality of opportunity and experience in schools to be reproduced bit by bit. For racial inequality is also formed today as people accept children's experiences of everyday injustice, or suggest that the daily experience of unequal opportunity is unremarkable, untroubling, or irremediable. In a fragmented era, it is more necessary than ever to collaborate with others to analyze how and whether specific actions within complex systems deny children opportunities they need. Yet today, Americans often rebut this very sort of analysis. The conclusion suggests some ways out of this analytic impasse.

# Arguing toward Everyday Justice in the New Civil Rights Era

MANY OBSERVERS call this the "post–civil rights era." The phrase is meant to describe more than our temporal location, although the mass marches and legislative victories of the civil rights movement are now to many a distant memory. It is meant to characterize an era in which white Americans in particular resist specific measures to equalize opportunity for people of color, even while now stating shared beliefs in the basic premise of equal opportunity.[1] On surveys, researchers now find some people of color resisting specific policies designed to equalize opportunity racially for groups other than their own as well.[2] It is also meant to characterize an era in which people of color express profound pessimism about the possibility of ever enjoying equal opportunity using civil rights strategies;[3] in which courts have almost fully gutted such expansive efforts at equalizing opportunity as school desegregation,[4] and largely attack the "very principle of racial antidiscrimination" central to civil rights law as itself "racist" in its use of racial categories to assess and equalize opportunities in schools, workplaces, and other social institutions;[5] in which public statements of any remaining support for racial equal opportunity policies qualify such support as being both tentative and limited;[6] and in which "civil rights" tools designed to fight intentional Jim Crow segregation are inadequate to fully address contemporary structures of racial inequality.[7]

Those coming to OCR demanding everyday justice in education circa 2000 attempted, in this complex climate, to use civil rights' basic logic and OCR's civil rights leverage to demand still that real people in specific locations provide specific forms of equal opportunity to children. Title VI complainants alleging racial discrimination circa 2000 demanded equal opportunity as a still-existing American requirement. Many were more precise than ever before in describing how opportunity denial in educational settings took shape daily. They analyzed not just endpoint statistics but also the treatment of children at specific moments in their educational lives, as well as their cumulative treatment and experiences throughout their educational careers. They also focused on the need to improve the details of children's ongoing, daily experiences in schools and districts, in addition to providing basic resources and opportunities to learn. They compared the treatment of children of color not just to the treatment of white children but also to the ideal and humane treatment of any child. Above all, when confronting today's "fragmented" system of opportunity provision, many OCR complainants, and some colleagues actively investigating complaints or spearheading the Early Learning Project, did not demand opportunity vaguely or in general. Rather, they pinpointed some specific necessary opportunities that any child deserved and asked specific people to help ensure that children of color, too, could actually experience those forms of opportunity in their daily schooling experiences.

As I have shown here, all of these specific analyses prompted resistance, and all such resistance reduced the opportunities and assistance provided to children. In effect, as people resisted legal "discrimination" allegations or federal intervention, we repeatedly called for doing less rather than more to provide children of color with opportunities in schools. In doing so, we implied disturbingly that children of color were not "worth" the opportunity provision (Lamont 2000a); we even exhibited a fundamental "lack of empathy" for these children (Feagin, Vera, and Batur 2001, 230) and we implied that well-educated children of color were not in fact in the common interest (Bell 1995a). Given this, for advocates the overarching project might still be to convince listeners, and particularly white people, that it is "worth it" to educate children of color successfully in our schools. Yet my experience at OCR convinced me that some of our resistance was also particular to a "fragmented" era, in which it seems harder than ever to determine who denies which opportunities to which children. Ironically, given this very fragmentation, advocates will have no choice but to figure out ways to draw in the resistant listeners, getting them to help analyze harm and opportunity in unprecedented detail.

To demand everyday justice is to demand on the one hand that children experience specific forms of opportunity on an everyday basis in their own lives; it is also to demand that in *their* everyday lives, specific people with influence over children's everyday lives provide them with specific forms of opportunity. Helping children to experience opportunity in school required that deans, principals, and campus police officers avoid circulating vague rumors about a student's "gang" and drug activity, as in the Granley case. It required that security guards refuse to take hall wanderers' pictures to send to the police, as in the Delano case. It required that teachers read documents about student needs, as in the King case. In the Longview I and III cases, providing opportunity required that principals and superintendents follow up on complaints of racial harassment. In our fragmented system, advocates must take the abstract American demand for "equal" opportunity and supplement it with precise, routine demands that specific actors provide specific opportunities to children. Drawing in resistant listeners to participate in such detailed opportunity analysis will at the very least require avoiding the dead-end debates demonstrated here.

A general solution to refusals to analyze everyday justice inside schools and districts, this book's particular subject, is simple but counterintuitive. It is to analyze everyday justice more often, while repeatedly inviting others to join in the analysis. If it were routine for students, parents, and communities to ask educators to analyze the daily provision of necessary opportunity inside classrooms, schools, and districts, educators might cease to hear descriptions of opportunity denial to students of color as allegations of unusual acts of "racism" and might instead learn to hear them as understandable and even useful proposals to provide specific opportunities that children need. Similarly, if it were routine and commonplace for communities and educators, as well as other decision makers, to analyze together how children could be provided with concrete necessary opportunities both inside and outside schools, requests that educators provide specific opportunities would not appear to be an aberrational show of unwarranted "prescription" or "advocacy." Further, in schools and districts, opportunity provision would truly seem volunteered from inside rather than imposed from outside.

Whenever naming precisely some everyday acts that harm and some opportunities that are necessary on a daily basis inside schools and districts, advocates can take care to say explicitly that the current conversation pinpointing particular school- and district-based harms and opportunities does not imply that additional harms and opportunities are to be ignored, nor that demanding particular opportunities from actors outside schools and districts (and expecting efforts from students and parents) is somehow unnecessary.[8] Rather, the goal is a running conversation on *who* needs to provide *which* opportunities and make which efforts. Since this book has focused on disputes over opportunity provision by educators, some specific suggestions for making everyday justice analysis routine in educational settings emerge from this book's four chapters. Several of these suggestions apply more generally to improving arguments over harm and opportunity in education today.

## SPEAK OF UNINTENTIONAL HARM RATHER THAN INTENTIONAL HARM

Chapter 1 showed that arguing over harm's intentional causation is a dead end in the new civil rights era: when considering the experiences of students of color, listeners too often argue simply that harms "because of race" cannot be proved. Accusations of discrimination "because of race" prompt people to defend their intentions morally and personally, thus clouding any analysis of unintended bias or unwitting participation in harm. An educator could accept a claim of disability discrimination without losing face personally, since the question of motive was secondary to the question of harm itself. As my colleague Reba put it to me once, a harm to a child with a disability could be framed simply as a technical failure in processes and procedures of diagnosis and service, simply as "filling out the wrong form." A complaint of racial discrimination, on the other hand, always seemed a moral claim about people's bad intentions.[9] A complaint of harm to children of color was, accordingly, always resisted.

While analyzing educator bias is still essential (Pollock 2008), in the new civil rights era, arguments about specific harms to students and families of color inside schools and districts might be more productive if they focused on the unintended occurrence and consequential experience of harm and opportunity denial, rather than seeking primarily to prove the harm's intentional causation.[10] To prod educators to analyze harm, advocates might even speak of *unconscious* bias (Banaji 2001, Krieger 1995) or *unintentional* harm *along the lines* of race, emphasizing, as Lamont (2000a, 71) suggests, the "universal" nature of people's desires to pursue opportunity and feel well treated. While some advocates may find suggestions of racist intentions necessary to prod educators to analyze harm at all, my experience at OCR suggested that educators typically take the accusation personally and just resist it. Talking from the outset as if educators act in good faith and thus harm children *unwittingly* may produce more willingness to analyze harm (and even bias) than if we imply "bad" faith. So may arguments that propose that improving service to children of color is actually improving service to children, period,[11] or that explain how all Americans have a common interest in well-educated, successful children (Bell 2005a).

### INSIDE SCHOOLS, INCLUDE THE SUBJECTIVE EXPERIENCE OF HARM AS EVIDENCE OF WAYS TO IMPROVE EDUCATIONAL ENVIRONMENTS

Refusing implications of their own personal "racism," educators confronted by complainants typically refused to take seriously children's and families' stated experiences of harm as race group members. Yet experimental research finds that for students from often-stigmatized groups, even the *subjective experience* of discrimination is potent enough to depress educational trajectories: "Group members' perceptions that they are being treated unequally can reinforce objective inequalities between those groups," as students lose both trust and motivation in educational settings.[12] Advocates can restate this fact when discussing the need for students to experience opportunity and caring treatment inside educational institutions, and the need for educators to listen to students' and parents' suggestions for improving educational environments. While the legal task may be to "prove" harm incontrovertibly through comparisons to whites, the educational task—the response in children's interests—is to take seriously claims that children and parents desire more opportunity in particular settings. Educators listening seriously to suggestions for improvement will also improve relationships with students, parents, and communities, an outcome that is also in educators' interests. I paraphrased in my notes how a lawyer colleague had explained to me that while OCR had "legal" constraints, parents often really needed to hear "deep listening" in educators' responses. "We may have a legal evidentiary problem with establishing discrimination," I noted, but in interpersonal terms, acknowledging the experience of harm went a long way in improving interactions with complainants, "since they *feel* like the environment is racially hostile."[13] Some parents do become hostile and "difficult" as they assess harm to themselves and their children; some children and youth themselves become "difficult" in interactions over time as they experience opportunity denial. Listening to analyses of opportunity denial is still in educators' interests, as *not* listening will simply corrode these relationships further. Psychological research suggests that people desire to be listened to when they claim injustice and to be given a voice in naming those injustices.[14] Such research suggests that if a person accused of injustice communicates that an action or situation in question may have unintentionally been harmful, such a statement can greatly ease conflict with the "victim." Such communication, if sincere, "does more than neutralize the offense. . . . It can also convey respect for the victim and affirm his or her status."[15] Conversely, school and district climates will sour further if people feel dismissed: "people show a marked disinclination to comply with authorities when they think those authorities have treated them disrespectfully," and the untreated "perception of injustice" is "capable of producing an involuntary decrease in commitment to the relationship in which the injustice occurred."[16]

In educational settings, which are not courtrooms but environments supposed to nurture and enable children, we must ask whether it really matters whether sufficient comparative proof of harm exists if a third grader and his grandmother have come to feel that the ethos pervading the school and district is "no black kids allowed." From an educator's vantage point, any educational environment in which students and parents feel discouraged, disadvantaged, disliked, or stigmatized should be worth analyzing, not least because *not* analyzing such an environment will simply lead to more conflicts over harm. I am not suggesting that children and parents should be treated patronizingly as blameless "victims" in interactions inside schools and districts; OCR complaints made clear that students' and parents' reactions to educators help produce students' educational fates. What I am suggesting is that their claims of harm should be seriously engaged. Instead, by continually demanding "proof" that daily experiences inside schools and districts "really hurt" students of color impermissibly, unfairly, or "because of race," educators (and often OCR people as well) continually provided reasons to not remedy the harms students and parents experienced. In so dismissing experiences of harm, educators missed a chance to improve their school community in ways that would actually benefit them as well.

## Compare Opportunities to an Ideal, Not Just to Those of White Children

As chapter 1 suggested, legal analysis of even blatant opportunity denial to students of color is often shackled by the difficulty of proving that such opportunities are denied "because of race," particularly in comparison to white children. Indeed, even when examining inequalities as "objectively" measurable as a lack of a teacher or books, we at OCR also repeatedly added a "but" to our abstract " 'yes' to racial equality,"[17] arguing that we could not find incontrovertible "proof" that students of color were denied such opportunities on purpose in comparison to white students.

When analyzing the everyday provision of opportunity, rather than simply comparing the treatment of children of color to the treatment of white children, as the law prompts, advocates might consider making comparisons to ideal treatment as well. In cases involving language minorities and students with disabilities, as I described in chapter 4, the treatment of a particular child or children is often compared to ideal treatment—to an ideal of effective service provision designed to enable the child to compete on a level playing field. Ironically, in interaction with school and district educators, comparing the treatment of children of color to ideal treatment for any child may prompt fewer defensive rebuttals than comparison to whites' treatment, which seems often to prompt white listeners in particular to dismiss the entire claim of harm. Comparisons to ideal and effective service might also better help people pinpoint which opportunities students need from whom in order to have an "equal opportunity to reach equal results."

I am not suggesting that advocates cease comparisons to white students' treatment. Indeed, such comparisons remain a key way that inequality of opportunity becomes visible; for example, a claim that black students' opportunities for "gifted" education are "unequal" is far strengthened by evidence of showing exactly how white children are disproportionately encouraged to enroll,[18] and a claim that early learning opportunities in a mostly Latino district are inequitable is always strengthened by evidence of enriched opportunities provided to white children elsewhere. Rather, I suggest that arguments for educational opportunity position young people of color not just as members of federally protected groups who desire and deserve equal treatment in comparison to white young people but also as children and youth who desire and deserve to experience care and opportunity in school settings as human beings. As Guinier (2004) notes, demands to end *"demeaning"* treatment rather than simply *"differential"* treatment might serve as what Derrick Bell calls "petitions for racial justice in forms that whites will realize serve their interests as well as those of blacks."[19] All parents and children desire to feel full inclusion and opportunity in educational settings; thus, all will benefit when we routinely ask whether acts treat children ideally.

## Retain the Original Core of the Civil Rights Lens: A Concern with Equal Access to Opportunity for Members of Groups Long Underserved by Schools

Reframing the needs of students of color as human needs and their experiences of racialized harm as damaging to *children* may help convince skeptics to listen to the grievances articulated by families of color and their advocates.[20] Still, it is essential to retain the original core of the civil rights lens, which forces consideration of whether and when members of historically oppressed and excluded social groups are particularly denied care and necessary opportunity in contemporary educational settings. As Anne Hardy put it in Longview, she already saw the harassment of LaRon as an incident between "children—with human beings"; what she did not see or acknowledge was a child's painful experience as a race group member, or the potential for educators to ignore harm to students of color as such. In the new civil rights era, the most successful arguments for everyday justice for students of color may frame those students both as human beings who deserve care and equal treatment and as members of groups who have disproportionately experienced cumulative harm in schools and still disproportionately experience it.

While students' needs must be assessed on an individual basis, some student experiences of opportunity are racially patterned.[21]

## SPEAK CLEARLY ABOUT OPPORTUNITY DENIAL AND PROVISION

In chapter 2, I explored OCR employees' efforts to delete forceful or specific written language about opportunity for students of color, fueled by a fear that clear and strong analyses of harm and remedy would be resisted as unwarranted "prescription" of equal opportunity. Obscuring the analysis of harm and plans for remedy as advised, we often ended up imprecisely describing what opportunities had been denied students of color or what should or could be done to remedy those opportunity denials.

In the new civil rights era, advocates manipulating the force of language used to discuss necessary assistance to children of color inside *or* outside schools should never sacrifice the clarity of that language. People with power over the details of children's everyday lives do need to be convinced rather than simply forced to assist children; some people may require external pressure to get started at all. Yet whether people are moved by gentle or forceful communication, they must move to provide specific necessary opportunities. Research has shown that even people with strong desires to "include" or equitably serve children of color often remain confused about how actually to do so on an everyday basis.[22] While making language less precise may convince people to collaborate, it may not convince people to collaborate on anything worth doing.

Whether proceeding gently or forcefully, the important thing in the new civil rights era is to pinpoint *precisely* which policies and practices can provide necessary opportunities to children and which acts, by which actors, deny such opportunities. Advocates can hold onto general equal opportunity discourse as a general warrant for efforts providing equal opportunity to students of color; they can talk forthrightly as if opportunity denials to students of color actually must be remedied and avoided, since they contradict a shared American belief in the importance of opportunity provision. But while generic demands for "equal" opportunity must be retained, they will no longer suffice. Neither will descriptions of unequal endpoints (e.g., Latino dropout) suffice. Analysis today requires specific descriptions of actions and situations that contributed to that outcome, and specific suggestions of remedial actions that can be pursued. When examining opportunity provision by educators, for example, advocates might routinely ask of specific policies, administrative decisions, and everyday practices,[23]

Does *this act* deny students, particularly students of color, necessary access to the opportunities and benefits of education?

What *alternative* act might provide necessary opportunities and benefits?

Advocates can also come prepared with specific alternative actions that specific actors both inside and outside schools might pursue. Rather than simply denounce given opportunity denials, they can suggest specific forms of opportunity provision. In OCR work, such specific suggestions from complainants often greased the wheels of resolution and concretized ways of improving service to children.

## Cite the Basic American Vision of Equal Opportunity as Warrant for Equalizing Opportunities to Learn for Students of Color, and Analyze Opportunity Provision Unapologetically

In chapter 3, I discussed how, in the new civil rights era, pessimists often hand victory to critics by making the defeatist argument that harms to children of color cannot be remedied. Even advocates can give up on the potential for equal opportunity effort, citing constraints that jeopardize the work. In the new civil rights era, advocates can instead cite the basic American vision of equal opportunity and set forth unapologetically to analyze whether concrete fundamental opportunities to learn are available to children of color. At times, this may involve transcending the shackles of legal analysis and simply announcing that fundamental opportunities to learn actually must be provided to children. Why should Americans frame the provision of fundamental opportunities to learn as a project somehow radical or out of bounds?

Even as our civil rights tools are gutted by courts and even as they limit our thinking about how, when, and whether racial equality of opportunity can appropriately be pursued in education, education can still find power in the basic "civil rights" notion that fundamental opportunities should not be denied to children historically underserved by schools.[24] Civil rights laws do leave unaddressed harms that the laws themselves cannot recognize, and they constrain the assistance to children that is deemed imaginable. Yet the most basic premise of the U.S. civil rights movement—that fundamental life opportunities should not be denied to human beings, particularly those historically excluded along racial lines—remains not just fundamentally unfulfilled in American society but also embedded in American logic.[25] Advocates can draw upon this logic, unapologetically, whether they seek recourse legally or not.

## Pinpoint the *Many* Specific Actions That Contribute to Students' Experience of Inadequate Opportunity or Exclusion

Chapter 4 explored how analysts might make it commonplace to pinpoint the specific actions that *contribute* to students' experience of inadequate opportunity or exclusion rather than pursue the dead-end tactic of arguing over whether specific actions *alone* "cause" unequal outcomes. To analyze the various activities that accumulate to *help form* a child's educational experience, we might analyze acts that seem to contribute to exclusion or underachievement over time. Educators will be convinced more by analysis of how specific actions contribute to multiplayer processes causing racially unequal opportunity and outcome than by suggestions that they single-handedly "cause" such outcomes. Any educational outcome always involves actors outside of schools and "domains" other than education; any racial "result" in education, Rebecca Blank (2005) notes, is the result of "many causal factors," including those "within families and neighborhoods and outside of the schools."[26] Acts also pile up to disadvantage children over many years; children and youth help construct their own fates. Indeed, OCR complaints showed that children's educational fates are produced cumulatively, over time, as students and parents react to educators and vice versa. If advocates make clear that educators are not *solely* responsible for student outcomes, educators might more willingly focus on analyzing, on an ongoing basis, how their own specific actions in schools and districts *contribute* to an experience of harm or disadvantage. Advocates can bring data on how various incidents *contributed* to the troubled educational pathways of individual children, or suggest the *various* acts inside and outside an educational setting that students and parents see as contributing to aggregated patterns like "Latino dropout" or "black underachievement." Educators discussing "achievement gaps" as outcomes many people "cause," for example, might more willingly analyze the ways that specific suspensions, teaching interactions, or exchanges with parents may have contributed over time to students' achievement outcomes, and collaborate with advocates in determining how such negative experiences could be remedied or avoided.[27]

### NEVER DISMISS THE ARENA OF EVERYDAY OPPORTUNITY PROVISION AS TOO "SMALL" TO "COUNT"

To some advocates, calls for everyday justice—that is, demands that people provide specific, named opportunities to children in their everyday lives—feel too "small," like a failure to demand more "systemic" change or work toward "justice" more generally. Analyzing the daily denial of opportunities within schools and districts should indeed supplement, not supplant, other analysis: of the cumulative denial of opportunity across generations, the denial of opportunity in health and housing, the denials of opportunity by actors outside schools and districts, or analysis of new policy remedies for desegregating the nation's communities.[28] But to change children's actual experiences of schooling we must do more than issue stirring or vague calls for justice. Specific people in specific places must do specific things to provide specific opportunities. Analyzing the ordinary moves by ordinary people throughout educational systems that provide or deny named opportunities to children is never a "small" effort, and advocates should never dismiss such detailed analysis as though it is. Describing particular opportunities precisely is never a copout from "real" change. Our "fragmented" system requires not either-or analyses pitting efforts imagined as "small" against those imagined as "big," but both-and analyses pinpointing all of the acts by all the players necessary to improve the educational experiences of children.[29]

In the 1950s and 1960s,[30] confronted by a resounding "no" in response to demands for equal opportunity, the civil rights struggle was waged in part through a powerful combination of language strategies. These included moral confrontation, with memorable speeches alongside spectacular acts of nonviolent resistance; forceful confrontation, with messages held aloft in boycotts and marches as well as shouted during riots; a quest to obtain legal rights, through the opinions of court cases and the texts of legislative proposals; and discussions with other Americans in stores, in schoolyards, and in the streets.[31] Through these strategies, civil rights leaders, lawyers, and the "everyday activists"[32] who struggled on the streets and at schoolhouse doors succeeded in embedding the message of equal opportunity in American life. In the new civil rights era, abstract equality-of-opportunity talk often receives little rebuttal, but it is not sufficient to convince anyone in particular to do anything in particular differently for students of color. Today's rhetorical task is to argue explicitly and forthrightly, both to those on high and to those down the hall, that particular opportunities are essential and particular harms demand remedy.

# Notes

1. By "American" I mean involving all residents of the United States, a phrase that is too clumsy for repeated use. I use "American" as U.S. residents use it to describe themselves and their activities, despite the fact that geographically the term includes the entire hemisphere. For a comparative view, see Levinson 1996, who describes how everyday negotiations between students and teachers in Mexican schools engage "Mexican" national struggles over defining and achieving equality.

2. Nader (2002) makes a point in *The Life of the Law: Anthropological Projects* that is also central to my own work: "disputes" illuminate "what ordinary people think is important" (7). Nader also suggests that disputes over the definition of "justice" are particularly "ubiquitous" in ordinary life: "The search for justice is a fundamental part of the human trajectory, although the meaning of justice and its forms varies. Feelings of wrong and right are ubiquitous, as are feelings of injustice" (14–15).

3. My other work has examined people negotiating, among other things, the fact that racial groups are social rather than biological categories (Pollock 2004a, 2004b, forthcoming). In a legal institution such as OCR, the concept of "race" is not contested as a social construction of any kind. Rather, OCR's civil rights work takes racial categories for granted as marking groups of children to which opportunities are or are not distributed fairly. In the past, lawyers shaped and often questioned the boundaries of racial groups (see Haney Lopez, 1996), and some government agencies continue to do so today (see Cose 1997 for a discussion of the U.S. Census's debates over the category "multiracial"). OCR typically did not.

4. Former OCR chief Leon Panetta's memoir on OCR (1971) is primarily an autobiographical project rather than an analytic one.

## INTRODUCTION

1. Anthropologists have long studied processes of legalistic conflict and resolution in particular communities as a window on the wider debates in the cultures to which disputants belong. See Greenhouse 1986, 28–29. Much work in legal anthropology looks at lawmakers' worlds and/or at everyday dispute processes in communities that utilize the law, arguing that such disputes display and utilize broader cultural arguments (for a useful collection, see Falk Moore 2004); this book does both. Although few works in legal anthropology focus on educational systems or federal bureaucracies, all offer models for ana-

lyzing everyday interactions between citizens and legal structures, for theorizing how legal thinking infuses various actors' everyday definitions of equality, and for seeing "legal" struggles as larger cultural ones. See, e.g., Nader 2002; Sarat, Garth, and Kagan, 2002; Ewick and Silbey 1998; Collier and Maurer 1995; Engel 1991; Merry 1990; Yngvesson 1988.

2. Former OCR colleagues examining drafts of this book have agreed that the arguments and patterns I analyze here are representative of OCR's work on race, and of debates between OCR employees, local educators, and advocates. It is impossible to assess quantitatively how often such arguments occurred in OCR work agency-wide. Simply tallying OCR's summation of cases in case files, or aggregating the language OCR employees finally wrote in resolution letters, would not reveal the consequential debates that really mattered in our work—the debates that raged during actual participation in complaint investigation, complaint resolution, and policy development.

3. Title VI of the Civil Rights Act of 1964, 42 U.S.C.2000d et seq.

4. This book's examination of contemporary controversies over implementing Title VI fits with several trends in policy analysis. Levinson, Sutton, and Winstead (2005) argue that policy research, particularly the anthropology of policy, should seek not to merely assess implementation ("Has the policy been effectively implemented? Does it work or not work?") but rather to examine the full social process of policy formation and implementation across multiple actors and sites. Susan Wright (2005) argues that anthropologists should study both face-to-face interactions between players in the policy process and people who do not interact directly or even know one another because, she contends, policies are transformed as they flow across this larger field. See also Shore and Wright 1997. Other scholars have looked at policy implementation as a social process of negotiation rather than simple rule imposition. See Honig 2006. More specific to this book, legal scholars have demonstrated that social movements, and popular arguments over the appropriate distribution of opportunity, shape and reshape courts' interpretation, implementation, and limitation/expansion of laws' power to assist particular populations, particularly, in U.S. history, people of color. Such work demonstrates courts' response to public questions of "*what* harms, and *whose* harms" are appropriately outlawed (Siegel 2004; 1486); see also Guinier 2004, Post 2003. This book focuses not on *courts'* responses to "the constitutional convictions of the nation" (Post 2003, 111) but on those "convictions" as wrestled with by a host of Americans in OCR work. I explore how employees working within OCR, complainants, and educators encountering OCR shaped, activated, or constrained the law's power to assist students of color, and how, in doing so, they demonstrated such popular "convictions" about which harms were to be denounced or permitted.

5. *Parents Involved in Community Schools v. Seattle School District No. 1* (05–908); *Meredith v. Jefferson County Board of Education* (05–915), S. Ct. (2007).

6. Advocates for desegregation, and researchers supporting desegregation, had submitted amicus briefs to the Court describing, in part, the social harm of *segregated* schools to white students: white students in segregated schools missed out on the social and academic benefits of diversity. This framing of

segregation as harmful to white students has typically been secondary, in civil rights history, to framings of segregation as both socially and academically harmful (originally by design) to students of color. *Brown v. Board of Education* found segregation harmfully stigmatizing to students of color; research has since found that contemporary segregated schools serving students of color are typically underresourced. Such schools are also concentrations of student poverty (given the intertwining of race and class in the United States), which depresses student performance. See Civil Rights Project 2006.

7. For discussion of these earlier opinions and their role in American districts, see Orfield and Eaton 1996. For example, courts fundamentally limited city-suburb desegregation, released districts from desegregation orders despite continuing segregation, and allowed districts to resegregate.

8. The individual opinion of Justice Kennedy, who joined the plurality in outlawing the voluntary desegregation plans, left the door open for districts to consider race without directly making an individual's race the core or sole factor determining her school admission. "The plurality opinion is too dismissive of government's legitimate interest in ensuring that all people have equal opportunity regardless of their race," Justice Kennedy wrote. See *Parents Involved in Community Schools v. Seattle School District No. 1*, Slip Op. at XX (Kennedy, J., concurring). For example, Justice Kennedy suggested that districts might consider race when determining where to build schools, how to draw attendance lines, or even how to target students for particular school programs. Justice Stevens, in dissent, anticipated that the decision would prompt years of race-related litigation.

9. Siegel 2004, 1541. Siegel discusses antidiscrimination law's fifty-year evolution in defining harm. Siegel demonstrates that in the years since *Brown v. Board of Education* (347 U.S. 483 [1954]), lawyers and courts have argued continuously over defining which acts toward students of color should be deemed impermissible "discrimination." Originally, in *Brown*, legally enforced segregation on the basis of race was called the impermissible harm. Observers then started to debate whether *segregation* was the harm or the *racial classification* accompanying and undergirding the segregation was the harm. According to Siegel, courts responding to white resistance to *Brown* shifted toward the logic that *Brown* outlawed any classification of people by race. In essence, this was the argument made by the four Supreme Court justices in their 2007 opinion ruling against two desegregation policies making race the key classification determining student enrollment: they decreed that race-conscious policies of voluntary desegregation were impermissible harms "because of race" to white students. Siegel would call such reasoning a flawed interpretation of *Brown's* original logic, which was concerned with race-based harms to students of color. Siegel contends that "most Americans" now falsely frame antidiscrimination laws like *Brown* as having been arguments that "state action classifying on the basis of race" at all "is unconstitutional" (1546).

10. OCR's Web site informs the public that "these civil rights laws enforced by OCR extend to all state education agencies, elementary and secondary school systems, colleges and universities, vocational schools, proprietary schools, state vocational rehabilitation agencies, libraries, and museums that

receive federal financial assistance from ED [Department of Education]. Programs or activities that receive ED funds must provide aids, benefits, or services in a nondiscriminatory manner." http://www.ed.gov/about/offices/list/ocr/docs/howto.html (accessed June 13, 2007). "Federal financial assistance" has been held to include direct federal dollars, federal dollars in aid to students, or property from the federal government. Any "federal financial assistance" subjects the entire "program or activity" to Title VI. After battles with the Supreme Court, which tried to narrow the definition of "program" in *Grove City* (465 U.S. 555), the Civil Rights Restoration Act of 1987 allowed agencies once again to interpret "programs or activities" broadly to include all activities operated by a recipient. The Justice Department also informs the public online that "When enacted in 1964, Title VI did not include a definition of 'program or activity,' " but with the Civil Rights Restoration Act, "Congress, however, made its intentions clearly known: Title VI's prohibitions were meant to be applied institution-wide, and as broadly as necessary to eradicate discriminatory practices supported by Federal funds." http://www.usdoj.gov/crt/grants_statutes/legalman.html (accessed June 13, 2007).

11. http://www.ed.gov/about/offices/list/ocr/docs/hq43e4.html (last accessed June 13, 2007).

12. OCR's definitions of discrimination in education are most explicitly stated in the *Code of Federal Regulations* (CFR), the thick reference book I had to cite in every letter I wrote to districts and complainants as a warrant for OCR's jurisdiction over school and district staff's behavior. "100.3 34 CFR Ch. 1, 7–1-98 edition" was the basic Title VI citation I pasted in when informing school districts that OCR had the power to investigate a complaint of racial discrimination filed by someone in their district. Though I read the *Code* through once and then rarely referenced it directly, the *Code* remained on my desk throughout my employment, a testament to these regulations' nominal control over my daily activity and, in theory at least, over the daily activity of people in U.S. schools and districts.

13. 100.3 34 CFR Ch. 1, 7–1-98 edition, 303–4.

14. "Recipients" of federal funds could not "utilize criteria or methods of administration which have the effect of subjecting individuals to discrimination because of race, color, or national origin." 100.3 34 CFR Ch. 1, 7–1-98 edition, 304.

15. By law, in addition to enforcing (in education) Title VI of the 1964 Civil Rights Act, OCR is responsible for enforcing Title IX of the Education Amendments of 1972, which outlaws sex discrimination in educational programs; Section 504 of the Rehabilitation Act of 1973, which outlaws discrimination against the disabled; Title II of the Americans with Disabilities Act of 1990; and the Age Discrimination Act of 1975. Since the mid-1970s, OCR has interpreted Title VI to also prohibit discrimination against students whose native language is not English. See also the 1974 U.S. Supreme Court ruling in *Lau v. Nichols*. On this gradual extension of Title VI's equal opportunity logic to populations other than African Americans, see Halpern 1995; Skrentny 2002. OCR's Web site now announces its government-mandated purpose notably broadly: to "ensure equal access to education and to promote educational excellence

throughout the nation through vigorous enforcement of civil rights." See OCR's main Web site at http://www.ed.gov/about/offices/list/ocr/index .html.

16. The *Code of Federal Regulations* offers the following description of the OCR "compliance review": "(a) *Periodic compliance reviews*. The responsible Department official or his designee shall from time to time review the practices of recipients to determine whether they are complying with this part" (100.8, CFR Ch. 1, 7–1-98 edition, 309).

17. Focusing mostly on disputes between lawyers and judges as stated in judicial opinions, legal scholars have framed much of U.S. law as argumentation over defining discrimination: e.g., Siegel 2004; Bell 1995a; Haney Lopez 1996; Krieger 1995; Crenshaw et al. 1995; Nowak 1995; Delgado 2000; Yudof, Kirp, and Levin 1992. A handful of studies regarding disputes over defining discrimination in education policy note debates involving OCR: Rebell and Block 1985; Rabkin 1989; Setty 1999; Losen 1999; Halpern 1995; Crawford 1995. Arguments over racial discrimination have been explored primarily in studies of U.S. courts.

18. Nader and colleagues (1980) examine people without formal "access to law" who complain as best they can to whomever will hear them and mediate disputes. OCR often acts as a third party that tries to intervene legally when face-to-face contact in local school districts has not worked. OCR also functions as an alternative to individual lawsuits, which have been radically curtailed. See *Alexander v. Sandoval* (2001), in which the majority opinion held that individuals could use Title VI in courts only to sue people for clearly "intentional" acts of discrimination.

19. Rebecca Blank (2005) discusses three forms of "cumulative racial disadvantage": disadvantage that accrues over *generations*; disadvantage that accrues *across social domains* (like health care, housing, and education; see also Rothstein 2004); and disadvantage that accrues over a person's lifetime *within a single domain*, such as education. OCR complainants discussed the last.

20. Blank (2005) extends her analysis of cumulative *disadvantage* to discuss cumulative racial *discrimination*, or the specific acts and policies causing, on the ground of race, the accretion of racial disadvantage over time. The authors (including Blank) of an amicus brief submitted to the Supreme Court in favor of desegregation policies (*Parents Involved in Community Schools v. Seattle District No. 1.*, and *Meredith v. Jefferson County Board of Education*) utilized Blank's work to discuss three forms of "cumulative discrimination" affecting opportunity in education ("Brief of the Caucus for Structural Equity as *Amicus Curiae* Supporting Respondents," http://kirwaninstitute.org/publications/ki_pub _docs/Caucus_for_Structural_Equity_Brief.pdf [accessed April 30, 2007]). First, over *generations*, the accumulated affects of various discriminatory policies impact young people of color. A generation after postwar economic policies were applied preferably to whites, for example, "African Americans whose parents came of age in the 1940s and 1950s will receive less than one-tenth the inheritance of their white peers" (15). Second, discrimination *across domains* like housing and health combines to create cumulative discrimination in educational opportunity. For example, "Housing discrimination constrains

many black and Hispanic youth to attend high-poverty schools. Children in these schools are much less likely than their affluent peers to attend college, and more likely to drop out of school or complete their education in a correctional facility" (13). As adequate health services are denied segregated communities, "Health difficulties in turn undermine student academic performance" (16). The authors suggest, as a third realm of cumulative discrimination, the important accumulation of "discrete incidents" of discrimination in children's everyday lives *within a single domain*, like education ("inequality also arises from interactions within a single social domain over time. . . . A student judged precocious in elementary school is more likely to be placed in college-prep classes in high school, making her a more appealing college admissions candidate" [16]). Yet they do not discuss this accumulation of everyday "interactions" directly, indicate how it is to be analyzed, or discuss how to distinguish a "discriminatory" interaction from a non-"discriminatory" one. In alleging "discrimination," OCR complainants did precisely this: they examined how specific everyday experiences of harm and unequal opportunity inside the educational "domain" added up to unequal educational opportunity along racial lines, and called this cumulative disadvantage "discrimination" "because of race."

21. A quarter of OCR's complaint work circa 2000 pertained to postsecondary institutions.

22. Advocacy organizations such as the NAACP, the National Women's Law Center, and the Federation for the Blind sometimes (though very rarely) file complaints at OCR on behalf of populations even larger than one district (lawyers and advocates have typically filed multidistrict resource cases using state law). Even these OCR complaints say something about everyday practices inside schools and districts. In 2003, the NAACP asked OCR to investigate the opportunities denied black students throughout the state of Florida. The complaint cited opportunity denials producing racial gaps in test scores, graduation rates, and participation in gifted programs, and argued that black students suffered discriminatory consequences from standardized tests, such as unwarranted grade retention. Matthew Pinzur, "NAACP Announces Civil Rights Complaint about Florida's Education System," *Miami Herald*, Aug. 28, 2003, http://www.miami.com/mld/miamiherald/6641916.htm?1c (accessed Nov. 4, 2004).

23. Lawsuits utilizing state law have accused state actors of unfairly or inadequately distributing state monies or educational resources to local districts. See Schrag 2003. On equity and adequacy in school finance, see Ladd, Chalk, and Hansen 1999. Lawsuits have also wielded Title VI as one tool when accusing states of failing to provide resources equally to all of the state's students (e.g., *Williams v. State of California*, settled August 2004). One colleague suggested to me that given states' typical control over the distribution of state resources in education, "the pope" would have to intervene to get OCR to use Title VI to sue a state.

24. Daniel Solórzano (e.g., Solórzano, Allen, and Carroll 2002; Solórzano, Ceja, and Yosso 2000) also finds resistance to claims that everyday experiences in educational settings harm students of color. Following the work of psychia-

trist Chester Pierce, Solórzano defines a version of everyday racial harms he calls "microaggressions": that is, "subtle insults (verbal, nonverbal, and/or visual) directed toward people of color, often automatically or unconsciously" (Solórzano, Ceja, and Yosso 2000, 60). (Pierce wrote of "The subtle, cumulative miniassault" as "the substance of today's racism" in "Psychiatric Problems of the Black Minority," in S. Arieti, ed., *American Handbook of Psychiatry* [New York: Basic Books, 1974], 516. Cited in Solórzano, Ceja, and Yosso 2000.) Solórzano and colleagues argue that the repeated, "cumulative" experience of microaggressions on a college campus, including "subtle and overt daily put-downs" from both peers and professors (67), can create a climate hostile to African Americans and depress the performance of African American college students: "Racial microaggressions in both academic and social spaces have real consequences, the most obvious of which are the resulting negative racial climate and African American students' struggles with feelings of self-doubt and frustration as well as isolation" (69). Still, "Without careful documentation and analysis, racial stereotypes, the threats that they pose and the assaults they justify in the form of racial microaggressions can easily be ignored or down-played. Nonetheless, these findings demonstrate that the cumulative effects of racial microaggressions can be devastating" (72). OCR complainants contended that they experienced an even wider array of everyday opportunity denials in schools and districts and that such everyday experiences indeed had devastating consequences for student achievement and well-being.

25. See Bobo, Kluegel, and Smith 1997. Hochschild and Scovronick report that when asked to express their opinion on surveys today, "ninety percent of Americans agree that 'equal opportunity for people regardless of their race, religion, or sex' is 'absolutely essential' as an American ideal, and the same huge proportion agree that 'our society should do what is necessary to make sure that everyone has an equal opportunity to succeed'" (2003, 10). Yet while Americans overwhelmingly agree abstractly on equal opportunity principles, we disagree fundamentally on concrete ways of applying them. Hochschild describes disagreement on equal opportunity policies as occurring both among white Americans (Hochschild and Herk 1990) and between white and black Americans (Hochschild 2004). As Hochschild and Herk (1990) conclude, "white Americans increasingly accept racial equality and integration in principle, but disagree with each other, [and] with black Americans . . . on how to implement those principles" (309). Hochschild and Scovronick (2003) demonstrate that this principle also holds true in national debates on school reform; "Americans want all children to have a real chance to learn, and they want all schools to foster democracy and promote the common good, but they do not want those things enough to make them actually happen" (4). For interview and survey studies suggesting white Americans' particular simultaneous ideological agreement with racial equality logic and hostility to concrete efforts to achieve racial equality, see Bonilla-Silva 2003a; Sears, Sidanius, and Bobo 2000. The authors collected in Doane and Bonilla-Silva 2003 find in white Americans' discourse "one of the most researched puzzles in the study of race relations": "that traditional measures of prejudice suggest a growing liberalization of white racial attitudes, while whites continue to oppose public policies that

are intended to bring about greater racial equality" (Ditomaso, Parks-Yancy, and Post 2003, 189).

26. To discover these rebuttals, I asked of my data: What shape did arguments for and against particular forms of opportunity provision for students of color take? What threads wove together a particular set of opportunity claims with a particular set of responses? This tactic, I hasten to admit, illuminates one shortcoming of the evidence analyzed here. Civil rights law in education focuses far more on what adults do to children than on how children respond to what adults do. In consequence, the arguments I observed and analyzed during my work at OCR disproportionately represented adults' voices and viewpoints about young people's experiences and for the most part neglected students' comments and opinions about adults' actions. At OCR, I typically heard about young people's experiences of harm through adults' reports. Still, examining how adults interpret, judge, and then respond to young people's experiences in schools is a crucial starting point. In the dramas that determine children's educational pathways, adults speak the opening lines.

27. Payne 1984, 38.

28. See Blank 2005.

29. Orfield 1978; Orfield and Eaton 1996.

30. See, e.g, Rothstein 2004.

31. See, e.g., Bobo, Kluegel, and Smith 1997; Hochschild and Herk 1990.

32. Researchers pointing out the conflict between people's reported support for equal opportunity and their resistance to actual equal opportunity measures typically find white people professing beliefs in racial equality on surveys and in interviews, but then, on those same surveys or in response to other interview questions, admitting reservations to concrete policy measures designed to equalize opportunity. See also Sears, Sidanius, and Bobo 2000. As researchers using surveys and interviews have discovered when studying this contemporary gap between Americans' rhetoric about equality in the abstract and their resistance to concrete equality demands, surveys and interviews are imperfect methods to gather data on what Americans "actually feel" about race (see also Pollock 2004b). Surveys and interviews often record what people think they ought to say, which does not necessarily correspond to what they say at other moments, actually do, or would do in real-world instances. For similar discussion, see Bonilla-Silva 1997, 2003a. As Hochschild and Herk (1990) admit of survey-based conclusions about white Americans' racial attitudes, "Knowing how white Americans feel generally about blacks, racial equality, equal opportunity, and integration just does not tell us very much. It is only at the level of specific implementation—*how* will the schools be desegregated? *where* will the blacks moving into your neighborhood live? who will *your* son or daughter date?—that a more complete picture of racial attitudes emerges" (324). According to Steeh and Krysan (1996), more specifically worded survey research affords this more "complete picture" of responses, but whether such responses reflect actual "attitudes" is another question altogether. Interviews also prompt scripted responses to questions about race rather than necessarily reflecting "attitudes." Still, much such research shows substantial white resistance to equal opportunity measures. Some scholars

argue that unconscious prejudice now undergirds such continued resistance (Banaji 2001); others argue that white people say they believe in equal opportunity but really do not (Bonilla-Silva 2003a; Feagin, Vera, and Batur 2001). Bobo and Tuan (2006) thus sum up: "To be sure, the surface content of publicly articulated prejudice has softened from the blunt racism of the Jim Crow era, becoming ever more sophisticated and polished" (7). Bobo and Tuan conclude that "prejudice" itself explains "whites' opposition to minority group claims" (29) less than do whites' struggles to retain "group position"—that is, to avoid giving up power to non-whites.

33. On resistance to redistributing students of color from racially isolated "tracks" to classrooms throughout schools, see Oakes, Welner, and Yonezawa 1998; on resistance to increasing the presence of non-white students in Advanced Placement courses, see Mickelson and Cousins 2008. On resistance to many other forms of racial equal opportunity effort within schools, see the many research essays in Pollock 2008. For two examples of ethnographic analyses of such debates in school settings, both among white educators and among more diverse populations, see Lewis 2003a; Abu El-Haj 2006.

34. See Losen 2004 on the federal policy No Child Left Behind (NCLB), which levies heavy sanctions on schools unable to close racial "achievement gaps" in standardized test scores. As Crawford (2007) also describes, NCLB orders racially equal outcomes but not racially equal opportunity.

35. On what I call "colormuteness," or educators' refusals to describe students or school patterns in racial terms, see Pollock 2004a. See also the many essays in Pollock 2008. Much resistance to offering equal opportunity to students of color *as such* can be described as what Siegel (2004) calls an "anticlassification" logic in post-*Brown* America. By "anticlassification," Siegel refers to the argument that the Constitution (and equality effort more generally) requires that we refuse to "classify" people racially, even when that classification is in the service of equalizing opportunity for historically subordinated racial groups. Siegel calls such an argument a misreading of *Brown*'s original intent, which was to remedy the subordination (via segregation) of black people, not to refuse their "classification" as "black." On resistance to race-conscious desegregation policies in education, see Ryan 2003.

36. The phrase "post–civil rights era" appears in the work of a number of scholars, including Cashin 2004; T. Perry 2003; Bonilla-Silva 2003a, 2003b; and throughout Doane and Bonilla-Silva 2003.

37. Bobo, Kluegel, and Smith (1997) call this an era of "laissez-faire racism."

38. Lakoff (2004) argues that the use of rhetorical phrases, which he calls "frames," serves to condone the analysis embedded in those phrases. Lamont (2000a,b) shows how "everyday" "racist" and "antiracist" "rhetoric" reveals national "mental maps" for thinking about inequality.

39. The general concerns articulated by OCR complainants about the harmful daily experiences of children of color within schools (particularly those controlled by white adults) have long been held by Americans of color. For example, Carter Woodson, a celebrated African American historian, argued in 1933 in *The Mis-Education of the Negro* that each day, the black student learning a white-controlled curriculum would have his very "mind" "brought under the

control of his oppressor" and would learn primarily to "find his 'proper place' and . . . stay in it." What everyday justice claims offer today is detailed analysis of *how* such harm occurs through specific everyday acts by specific people.

40. This conclusion converges explicitly with that drawn by Hochschild and Herk (1990) in their analysis of survey data, though they attribute the "yes, but" response to white Americans only. As this book will show, I heard many "yes, but" responses to concrete equality demands from OCR employees, many of whom were white but some of whom were people of color. Hochschild and Herk write that: "most whites now say 'yes' to racial equality and integration, then add some sort of 'but . . . ' to their affirmation. It is that phalanx of 'but . . . s' that blacks see when they decry white racial hypocrisy, and it is the combination of 'yes' and 'but' that makes American racial politics so difficult to negotiate" (309).

41. Miller (2001) provides a review of decades of psychological research on the experience of injustice. Miller suggests, following Bourdieu, that "When they are denied the respect to which they believe they are entitled, people feel as unjustly treated as when they are denied the material resources to which they believe they are entitled" (533). According to this psychological research, "The most commonly reported experiences of everyday injustice involve some form of disrespectful treatment" (530). See also the work of Iris Marion Young (1990), described in more detail in chapter 4.

42. Cohen (e.g., 2008) finds experimentally that "subjective inequality," or the perception of biased treatment, can depress the performance of students of color. On research showing victims' decreased allegiance to "the relationship in which the injustice occurred," see Miller 2001, 543.

43. Siegel 2004, 1539. Lenhardt (2004), extending the work of sociologist Erving Goffman (1963) and economist Glenn Loury (2002), defines racially "stigmatizing" acts as acts that contribute to social exclusion (809). Lenhardt additionally calls racial exclusion the denial of full social "citizenship."

44. Research shows that when parents of color confront white educators in the pursuit of fairness, both parties complain that typical parent-teacher conflicts include additional dynamics of racial tension and mutual distrust. Warren 2005; Diamond and Gomez 2004; O'Connor 1997; Tatum 2008; Wyman and Kashatok 2008. As Lareau (2003) found in her study of parent-school interactions both within and across lines of race and class, educators wanted little pressure from any parents: they generally "sought an approach that was a contradictory blend in which parents were actively involved and consciously responsible for guiding their children's school experience but were still polite, compliant, and supportive of educators' programs" (219). Lareau suggests that many middle-class parents, both white parents and parents of color, push too aggressively for their children's educational opportunities to fit educators' preferred profile of the "polite" and "compliant" parent. Still, research shows that middle-class and white parents are most successful at securing opportunities for their children from the nation's predominantly white and middle-class teaching force.

45. Dean Rivkin (2002) speaks more generally of "the growing dissatisfaction with traditional models of lawyering for achieving meaningful social change and the obstacles that lawyers steeped in the traditional models of practice face when they contemplate putative transition to new forms of advocacy and practice."

46. On the opportunity consequences of federal legislation focusing on test preparation (No Child Left Behind, which I discuss more in chapter 3), see, e.g., Crawford 2007.

47. OCR has presented data on its caseload in annual reports to Congress since the 1980s. According to my analysis of these reports, during the period from 1981 through 1992, under the administrations of Ronald Reagan and George H. W. Bush, disability cases averaged 52 percent of the agency's caseload, while race cases averaged just 16 percent. From 1993 through 2003, under the administrations of Bill Clinton and George W. Bush, 54 percent of the agency's caseload was, on average, disability work, while race cases averaged 20 percent. Title VI (race) cases included complaints alleging discrimination against English-language learners. The remainder of complaints filed when I worked at OCR were complaints of discrimination based on sex (around 7 percent); complaints of age discrimination (2 percent); complaints where people alleged multiple forms of discrimination (nearly 15 percent), and complaints filed on issues over which OCR did not have jurisdiction, such as economic discrimination, fraud in schools, prisoner civil rights issues, and so forth. In 1989, Rabkin noted of OCR that "the share of resources devoted to investigating discrimination against blacks dwindled to less than 10 percent, and the share devoted to non-English-speaking minorities dwindled to barely 5 percent in the 1980s. Meanwhile, women claimed one-third of its enforcement efforts, and the handicapped more than half" (69). See also Bunch and Mindle 1993.

48. Though I will refrain from doing so throughout this book, I often put "disability" in quotation marks because basic questions of defining and diagnosing "disability" are central to claims of disability discrimination. Early law and regulation used the word "handicapped," which has been rejected because of its pejorative connotations and implicit reference to physical limitations. Still, the definition of "disability" remains in flux. Today, the "disabilities" diagnosed as affecting schooling include physical disabilities, learning disabilities diagnosed by psychological testing, and emotional difficulties. Regarding learning disabilities in particular, some parents (particularly white and middle-class parents) seek the special targeted services for which students with disabilities are eligible, while others fight against the application of this label to their children, assuming that it will stigmatize their children or place them in slower tracks (see Hehir 2005). Scholars have argued that any framings of "disability" are social classifications rather than natural facts by pointing out the mutability of "disability" diagnoses and noting that in different contexts, the same children are not seen to lack "ability" (Mehan 1996; Varenne and McDermott 1998).

49. Parents were using civil rights law in the disability realm to demand that ADD be recognized as a specific disability deserving accommodations.

50. Although the NAACP provides online directions for filing OCR complaints, I met no Title VI complainants who had used these directions, and I met very few who had worked directly with lawyers in their communities. Some groups of immigrant parents aggrieved about school districts' failure to serve English-language learners approached advocacy lawyers who urged them to file complaints at OCR. However, far more parents filing disability complaints found OCR through private or advocacy-group lawyers with close ties to extensive parent support networks. The problem of people finding OCR to file Title VI discrimination complaints has existed throughout the agency's history. For example, in 1975 the Commission on Civil Rights noted that "recent immigrant groups" were unaware of OCR and its tools, in part (ironically) because the agency failed to address language barriers in access to OCR complaint forms. Yet in some regions, the commission noted, particularly outside the South (where the agency concentrated its initial desegregation efforts), other Americans of color were also unaware of OCR. See Commission on Civil Rights 1975. When I worked at OCR, a manager agreed that outside of white middle-class parents, public ignorance of OCR was itself "a civil rights issue."

51. Scholarship on legal claims would assume 1) that only a fraction of the complaints brought to schools and districts probably end up filed at the federal level, and 2) that OCR Title VI complaints were a smaller fraction still of the conflicts that raged between students, parents, and educators but were never "claimed" formally even at the local level. In "Studying the Iceberg from Its Tip" (1990), Siegelman and Donohue observe relatedly that just a tiny fraction of complaints reaches the courts. Ewick and Silbey (1998) argue that while legalistic controversies permeate American life, only a small minority become explicitly "legal." Similarly, Felstiner, Abel, and Sarat argue that researchers should examine the practices through which "injurious experiences . . . mature into disputes" by examining how *naming* ("saying to oneself that a particular experience has been injurious") transforms into *blaming* ("when a person attributes an injury to the fault of another individual or social entity"), and then into *claiming* ("when someone with a grievance voices it to the person or entity believed to be responsible and asks for some remedy." "A claim is transformed into a dispute when it is rejected in whole or in part" 1980–81, 634–36). Since only some "experiences become grievances" and only some "grievances become disputes" more formally (632), they argue, "study of the emergence and transformation of disputes may lead to the judgment that *too little* conflict surfaces in our society, that *too few* wrongs are perceived, pursued, and remedied" (632).

52. Disability law provides that individualized assessment of students' potential disabilities be available to parents on demand, and educators are required by law to provide particular services once professionals diagnose them as necessary. Indeed, the basic tool of special education law and policy is the Individualized Education Plan, or IEP. OCR has been particularly good at prodding this matter-of-fact provision of specific services. The white middle-

class parents I met were good at securing outside diagnoses, often paying private doctors and psychologists to diagnose disabilities and then using OCR to get specific services provided.

53. In 1964, Title VI gave the government the power to cut off federal funding to districts and universities it found to be excluding students from programs or denying them services "on the ground of race," but after articulating this powerful principle, Congress left to the executive branch the tasks of concretizing what harm "because of race" looked like in education and deciding how to ensure daily compliance with its own "implementing regulations." As Halpern (1995) shows, Congress would repeatedly intervene to stem OCR's power to enforce antidiscrimination law—particularly OCR's desegregation efforts—by limiting OCR's power to cut off federal funding. But OCR's own regulations, which remained nebulous, never fully solved the problem of *clarifying* Title VI: that "from the very inception of Title VI, it was unclear what compliance with the statute required. The statute did not define discrimination based on race or national origin—it merely outlawed it" (Halpern 1995, 295). Edwards and Nordin define implementing regulations as "rules made by federal agencies pursuant to the rulemaking power delegated to them by Congress." They add that "agency case law demonstrates the *adjudicatory* power by virtue of which questions of policy are elaborated and individual disputes resolved on a case-by-case basis" (1980, 39). A definition of such "REGULA-TIONS" appears in the *Glossary of Terms Used in Legal Research*: "REGULATIONS— rules or orders issued by various governmental departments to carry out the intent of the law. Agencies issue regulations to guide the activity of their employees and to ensure uniform application of the law. Regulations are not the work of the legislature and do not have the effect of law in theory. In practice, however, because of the intricacies of judicial review of administrative action, regulations can have an important effect in determining the outcome of cases involving regulatory activity. United States government regulations appear first in the *Federal Register*, published five days a week, and are subsequently arranged by subject in the *Code of Federal Regulations*." http://lawschool .westlaw.com/shared/marketInfoDisplay.asp?code=MI&id=155&mainpage= 17#17 (accessed October 18, 2006).

54. This was law professor Derrick Bell, who suggested that "Policies of effective schooling for minority children are not likely to be a major priority for OCR. . . . Indeed, we will likely have every reason to wonder whether they are on our side or in our way." Bell maintained that what he had argued long ago about civil rights lawyers (1995a, originally published 1976) is still true: even when individual lawyers want to pursue equality of opportunity energetically, "civil rights lawyers are still paid and influenced by the organizations with which they work" (Derrick Bell, e-mail communication with the author, November 26, 2004).

55. As I discuss further in chapter 1, many other observers, particularly critical race theorists, have noted that judges and courts have long been unwilling to name as "discrimination" any acts of harm to people of color not announced by explicitly stated racial hatred. Crenshaw et al. (1995, xiv) articulate a long-

standing "deep dissatisfaction with traditional civil rights discourse," particularly its refusal to call most harms to people of color "discrimination." Analysts in the Critical Race Theory tradition suggest that lawyers and courts shifted attention away from ordinary harmful behaviors, focusing too narrowly on punishing only the most explicit, aberrational, and purposefully cruel acts perpetrated against people of color rather than also dismantling as discriminatory the full range of normalized unequal opportunities people of color were suffering on an ordinary basis. See Lenhardt 2004; Guinier 2004; Freeman 1978; Crenshaw et al. 1995; Lawrence 1987. Crenshaw et al. conclude bluntly, "In our view, the 'legislation' of the civil rights movement and its 'integration' into the mainstream commonsense assumptions in the late sixties and early seventies were premised on a tragically narrow and conservative picture of the goals of racial justice and the domains of racial power" (1995, xvi). Halpern (1995), writing on Title VI and OCR, explores the "limits of the law": those using a legal framework are forced to "frame their analysis in terms of contrived concepts, issues, questions, and remedies that the legal system recognizes and deems legitimate" (ix).

56. Even those attempting originally to shape the nation's civil rights laws suggested that as "legalist" solutions, those tools would provide inherently limited power to fully solve the nation's complex race problems. Mack (2005) argues that "As World War II began, the leaders of the African-American civil rights bar argued that the future of the civil rights movement lay in cross-racial, class-based economic alliances with whites," even "*rather* than in legalist transformation through the courts" (265) and that they planned to pursue not just "transformative litigation" like *Brown* but also "race uplift" through "the support of [black] business and local institutions" (352). Guinier (2004) argues that civil rights law reductively pushed solely for racial desegregation rather than a broader distribution of opportunity to all those who lacked it. In Guinier's analysis, this "minimalist" analysis (96) embedded in civil rights laws such as *Brown* actually prompted poor white Americans to unite with elite white Americans against black Americans, despite the fact that the economic interests of poor whites diverged from those of elite whites. Anthropologists have argued even more pessimistically that the more legal "rights" are extended, the more benefits for certain "kinds" of people actually get reduced, as they no longer seem to fit within the logic of the law. See, e.g., Collier and Maurer 1995.

57. This book examines the "official" and "unofficial" acts of OCR employees, "ordinary people" as well as "feds," in interaction with parents, advocates, and educators who were all engaging and "invok[ing] legal concepts and terminology" (Ewick and Silbey 1998, 32). "Legality also operates through social life as persons and groups deliberately interpret and invoke law's language, authority, and procedures to organize their lives and manage their relationships. In short, the commonplace operation of law in daily life makes us all legal agents insofar as we actively make law, even when no formal legal agent is involved" (20). Many legal anthropologists and scholars in the "law and society" tradition expand their definition of "legality" to include the actions of "unofficial actors as they take account of, anticipate, or imagine 'legal acts and

behaviors'" in their everyday lives (273). Ewick and Silbey note that another key figure of "law and society" scholarship, Lawrence Friedman, "rests his accounts of law and the legal system on a definition that includes both the official acts of formal legal agents and the unofficial acts of these officials" (272). Ewick and Silbey offer an argument that is central to the approach to law adopted in this book: "Rather than imagining law as existing apart from social relations (i.e., so-called natural law), or conceiving of it as produced solely by groups of powerful law 'makers' (i.e., the positive law of legislatures, and common law of appellate courts), much law and society research portrays law from the 'bottom up' as a continuing production of practical reason and action. This research provides a view of law emerging from the routine, often discretionary, encounters among professional and nonprofessional actors, involved in diverse projects, employing different legitimating discourses, material resources, and political power to achieve a wide range of goals" (19).

58. Other researchers have shown federal administrators in OCR and in the rest of the Department of Education actively refusing to equalize local opportunities for students of color, both in the halcyon days of the civil rights movement and today. See, e.g., Orfield 1978; 2000; Losen 2004; Halpern 1995. On local "control" and OCR, see Panetta and Gall 1971; Rebell and Block 1985.

59. As discussed further in chapter 3, the Education Department under George W. Bush overcame this typical reticence to involve federal actors in local educational decisions by imposing No Child Left Behind (NCLB), a set of testing and test-score requirements that was the most extensive federal educational intervention in U.S. history. NCLB did not, however, require the federal government to provide substantial resources or substantially regulate the provision of equitable opportunities to learn. Losen 2004.

60. Skrentny (2002) calls the establishment of equal opportunity logic, laws, and policy in federal bureaucracies a "minority rights revolution," fueled by both social movements and "mainstream Euro-American males and minority advocates, wearing suits, sitting at desks, firing off memos, and meeting in government buildings to discuss new policy directions" (5). Omi and Winant (1994) argue that the U.S. "state" "incorporated" and effectively dissipated the energy of the civil rights movement; Winant (2004, 23) argues accordingly that "it is dangerous to assign to the state the task of safeguarding racial justice."

61. District educators were typically resisting paying for disability services, while school-level educators were resisting the extra work of actually providing the services. Often mediated via OCR were local questions of whether specific diagnosed "disabilities" (such as ADD) did or did not entitle children for paid services under law and regulation. For example, as I wrote in my notes one day circa 2000, only recently had the failure to provide academic accommodations for students with ADD "become a box we check off as a legitimate type of discrimination."

62. Engel (1993) has found similarly that many school district representatives acquiesce to disability service demands once those are framed in the language of the law and legal enforcement.

63. On the "rhetoric of reaction," see Hirschman 1991. Hirschman's rhetorics of reaction are "arguments that are in effect contraptions specifically

designed to make dialogue and deliberation impossible" (170). Examining mostly American and European texts, Hirschman finds that three key rhetorics of reaction have been employed over the past several centuries in response to "progressive" demands for change, or more opportunities for more people. The "perversity" thesis asserts that all attempts at change will backfire; the "futility" thesis suggests that the changes demanded really will not work; and the "jeopardy" thesis suggests that the proposed moves will jeopardize past accomplishments. While Hirschman asserts that it is principally "conservatives" who have employed these rhetorics of reaction, he also notes that "radicals" (79) and even "progressives" themselves have employed them in response to "naïve progressives'" calls for change (51). I encountered Hirschman's argument after completing this book, and I found that his three core types of argumentation often aligned with the arguments I analyze here. In successive chapters, I mention these "rhetorics of reaction" where they apply.

64. Michèle Lamont's interview-based work (2000a) argues that when asked to critique and explain racial inequality, people tap into nationally available ways of thinking and talking about inequality, which she calls "repertoires" or rhetorics of explanation. My study examines such rhetorics operating in real time as people interact in public institutions and everyday relationships. This book treats everyday arguments over the treatment of children as actions with real-world effects as well as statements with predictable structures. This book's close examination of arguments as patterned social interactions with concrete consequences takes its cues from conversation analysis and interaction analysis in anthropology, sociolinguistics, and sociology. My work builds upon that of many others who have thought about how social reality is produced through the social interaction of talk. For classic analyses arguing generally that language shapes behavior and ideas *about* proper behavior, see Foucault 1979; Wieder 1974. Scholars working within the tradition of conversation analysis have long been particularly interested in words as actions that produce real-world consequences. For further discussion of this tradition, see, e.g., Duranti and Goodwin 1992; Erickson 2004. See also Mishler 1986; Varenne and McDermott 1998. Mehan (1996) argues further that a "social constructionist" tradition of research has been particularly concerned with how institutional orders are "both generated in and revealed by the language of the institution's participants" (243). "Because language *is* action," Mehan writes, "different uses of language constitute the world differently" (262, emphasis mine). On everyday race talk and its effects, see also Pollock 2004a. Many scholars who have studied rhetoric, or persuasion strategies, focus on political discourse and its effects on elections or social movements; see White 1992; Jamieson 1996; Lakoff 2004. Hirschman (1991) analyzes a much broader selection of texts. Like Lamont (2000a), I am interested in everyday argumentation strategies, including the structure and effects of arguments that ordinary people employ to make and respond to claims that equalizing educational opportunity is necessary.

REBUTTAL ONE
Harms to Children of Color Cannot be Proved

1. Much more rarely, K–12 teachers filed complaints at OCR on behalf of their students, saying their own principals and administrators had rebuffed their efforts to help students. The only such case I was assigned at OCR was technically a disability case, but concerned Latino students. While at OCR, I heard of no complaints filed by K–12 students themselves, though I heard of one such complaint in another region. A recent ACLU lawsuit in California, *Williams v. the State of California* (2005), primarily utilizing state law but also employing Title VI, was settled by instituting a complaint process that would allow students themselves, along with any other person connected to the state's public schools, to file complaints with their school, district, and the state to repair inadequate facilities or provide necessary academic resources. At this writing, the effectiveness of this process has yet to be evaluated.

2. In their analysis of everyday legal consciousness exhibited by ordinary people, Ewick and Silbey (1998) define three stances toward the law: acting "before the law," viewing the law as omnipotent and objective; acting "with the law," treating the law as a strategic tool; and acting "against the law," regarding the law as a disciplinary authority to be resisted. Complainants were exhibiting the first two stances by filing at OCR. See also the consumer complaint letter-writers studied by Nader and colleagues (1980) and the law-users studied by Merry (1990). Similarly, the Rosebud Sioux Tribal Council filed a complaint with OCR in 2002 alleging that a school district in South Dakota unfairly targeted tribal youth with disciplinary measures in comparison to white students and, at the extreme, arrests; it argued optimistically, "It is the hope of the Rosebud Tribal Council that the complaint with the U.S. Department of Education will end the targeting of Indian youth within that system" (quoted in Steinberger 2002). In another complaint in Baltimore alleging that black students received harsher punishments than white students for the same infractions, the cofounder of the local African American advocacy group filing the complaint stated optimistically that she believed the OCR investigation would reveal the "truth" about whether black students were discriminated against (Shelsby 2004). In Ewick and Silbey's terms, complainants saw "the possibility of putting the law to their own ends" (1998, 131). The third form of legal consciousness, taking a stance "against the law" and treating it as "something to be avoided" (192) or resisted, was more often adopted by the "recipients" against whom complaints were directed: the local educators, principals, and district officials, recipients of federal funding, whose actions toward students and potential failure to address complaints were subject to investigation and possible censure by OCR.

3. The tendency to perceive and complain about unfair treatment in a child's schooling is not confined to people of color. As Lareau (2003) found in her

study of parent-school relationships circa 2000, white middle-class parents were the most regular and vehement complainers about perceived harms to their children in school. The parents who came to OCR to complain about harms to their children (most often, regarding disability) were disproportionately white as well. Nader argues more broadly that Americans generally make a habit of complaining formally about their treatment in many realms: "Americans are probably the most prolific complaint-letter writers in the world" (2002, 41). Still, parents filing Title VI complaints made an additional claim about negative schooling experiences: they pinpointed everyday actions in educational settings as academically and socially harmful to children of color *as* children of color. They also often argued that educators harmed children "because" the children were not white, potentially "because" those educators harbored negative feelings toward their children on that basis, and potentially "because" the educators themselves were often white. Ninety percent of K–12 educators in U.S. public schools are white, while over 40 percent of the student body is made up of students of color. Scholars find that lower-income parents of color have the greatest difficulties collaborating with and confronting their children's middle-class white teachers in the quest for educational opportunity, thereby exacerbating this racialized demographic difference. The parents I met who filed race discrimination cases at OCR were typically working parents of color, not poor but not upper middle class either. They were teachers' aides, bus drivers, and office workers. The educators they confronted were almost exclusively white. Since most teachers are white and middle class, Warren (2005) argues, "On her own, a low-income parent of color typically lacks the status and education to collaborate as an equal with her child's teacher." Warren calls for "efforts to build trust and to foster meaningful collaboration among principals, teachers, parents, and community members" in order "to confront these power inequalities" (137–38). U.S. educational discourse has long called for "parental involvement" in schools (see Lawrence-Lightfoot 2003; Diamond and Gomez 2004; Lareau 2003; Weiss et al. 2005; Henderson et al. 2007). While research on "parental involvement" or "family/school partnership" suggests pleasant collaboration, research also suggests that parents must confront educators in order to secure key opportunities for their children. With particular urgency, advocates advise parents of color to "advocate" for their children, since the opportunity a parent is able to argue for has been shown to be a deciding factor between that child thriving and failing (Mickelson and Cousins 2008; Lareau 2003). In 2000, one academic at an OCR conference on early elementary education summed up the situation: "In the U.S., parent advocacy has become a requirement for school success." Parents of color in particular had to be "informed" about "how to advocate for their kids"—that is, informed about which opportunities to demand. Bob Moses states explicitly that "the *only* ones who can really demand the kind of education they need and the kind of changes to get it are the students, their parents, and their community" (2001, 151).

4. Many complainants of color combined the expectations of what Simpson (1998) calls the "civil rights" and "post–civil rights" generations. Simpson argues that the "integration" generation of African Americans born between

1959 and 1975 is fundamentally pessimistic about the treatment of black people at the hands of white people, in comparison to the "civil rights generation" born between 1943 and 1958, who believed that equality would eventually be possible. Members of what Simpson calls the "civil rights generation" were "at crucial stages in the development of their political attitudes during the peak years of the civil rights movement and the black power movement"; those in the "post–civil rights generation" "were in the early stages of political socialization after the civil rights movement and during the decline of the black power movement" (17). Building on data from a National Black Politics Study, 1993–94, conducted by Ronald Brown from Wayne State University and Michael Dawson from the University of Chicago, Simpson contends that the younger generation's pessimism has been bred in part through "subtle" harms in integrated spaces: "The post–civil rights generation . . . may not have had the same experiences, but they have come face-to-face with a different kind of racism, one that is more subtle but just as powerful" (22); although they "were [not] made to sit at the back of the bus or experience any other aspect of the segregated South," they retain an acute "mistrust of whites and discomfort among whites" (20). Rather than integration diminishing the importance of race, "this failure of blacks to become an integrated part of larger society has led to a strengthening of group identity and the elevation of black nationalist sentiments" (27). Simpson concludes that "members of the post–civil rights generation are . . . more separatist than members of the civil rights generation" (16). The claim of "separatism" does not describe OCR complainants, but "pessimism" about the likely treatment of children in white-controlled spaces does. As Siddle Walker, Snarey, and their colleagues argue (2004), a core experience of schooling in segregated, black-controlled community institutions that was lost with desegregation was the sense, among black parents and children, that educators would care for students of color as if they were their own. Black parents before *Brown* often funded black-run community schools, even while demanding access to well-resourced, publicly funded white schools (Anderson 1988). After the 1954 *Brown* decision, black parents worried about their children's treatment in white-controlled schools, while celebrating the potential of expanding their children's educational resources and opportunities. See Payne 2004.

5. I discuss this literature in chapter 4. Much qualitative research in education makes this case explicitly. For example, Fine (1997, 57) writes of the "cumulative privileging" white students experience through actions in schools over time; T. Perry (2003) writes of how a "school's day-to-day practices participate in the creation of underachievement" of black students. For a famous exploration of how daily actions in schools accumulate to help reproduce patterns of class inequality, see Willis 1977.

6. See Greenhouse, Yngvesson, and Engel 1994, 12. As legal anthropologists have found, enlisting the formal apparatus of the law in a U.S. community often strikes neighbors as an aggressive intrusion into a world imagined as self-regulating and not needing the intervention of legal or bureaucratic authorities for evaluating fairness. Greenhouse, Yngvesson, and Engel (1994) noted a "recurrent theme" in their fieldwork on "talk about law use" in three

American towns: "the prevailing sense among our informants that communities can be destroyed by people who assert their claims to entitlement in courts of law" (10). When people argue that asserting claims legally is a negative and destructive force in community relationships, they are assuming without question that the existing order serves people just fine. Indeed, to satisfied community members, acting in a "community" manner requires that subgroup members suppress their frustration that it does not work for them. Iris Marion Young contends that in struggles over ideas of "justice," the very "ideal of community" often "suppresses difference among subjects and groups" such that when subgroup members argue that they have been treated unjustly or differently within the community, this argument strikes other community members as "threatening" the community and its identity as harmonious. This impulse to avoid internal conflict over fairness, Young suggests, "often coincides with a desire to preserve identity and in practice excludes others who threaten that sense of identity" (Young 1990, 12).

7. Ewick and Silbey 1998, 15.

8. As Sullivan, Zimmer, and White explain, legally "the plaintiff must prove that the real reason for the challenged action was the prohibited one" rather than the "pretext" offered by the school or district (2002, 65).

9. OCR's sexual harassment policy guidelines indicated that adults in school settings are required to investigate and respond when "given notice" of sexual harassment within an institution. This standard was typically used for racial harassment as well. In one complaint I investigated, the complainant argued that school and district staff had failed to respond to her communications about a petition her children had put together to denounce a white student's verbal and physical harassment of them and other children at the elementary school. More than a dozen other children had signed the petition. Vin, the OCR attorney I was working with on the case, treated the petition as an internal "notice" of harassment that, by law, required a school administrator's response. He indeed asked me to investigate "if they [had] responded yet" to it, and as it turned out, they had not. The district administrators later asserted that they "couldn't deal with [the petition] because it had the [accused perpetrator's] name on it." Still, administrators continued to assert that they had made every effort to meet with dissatisfied parents. One administrator told us, as I wrote in my notes, that he had "said he would meet with any parents—an open invitation—nobody took them up on it."

10. As a legal agency, Ewick and Silbey suggest, it is normal that OCR would determine discrimination separately in each case: "Although law claims to be a distinctive arena of general rationality, it is, like most other work, operating on the basis of variable rules. Legal practice proceeds on a case-by-case basis." OCR work was about applying general "rules" and "criteria" to specific individual cases (1998, 18).

11. Title VI of the Civil Rights Act of 1964, 42 U.S.C.2000d et seq.

12. This point appears both in empirical analyses of conversational interchanges (see Duranti and Goodwin 1992; Erickson 2004) and in the theoretical work of Mikhail Bakhtin (1981).

13. Krieger 1995. OCR is one of the few high-profile educational organizations in the nation that still uses the word "discrimination" to examine educational policy and practice regarding students of color. Many nonprofit advocacy organizations, lawyers, and educators now say they are working for "social justice" and "educational equity" instead.

14. In *San Antonio v. Rodriguez* (1973), the Supreme Court rejected both a framing of "the poor" as a class in need of civil rights protections and the principle that any child has a "fundamental right" to an education under the Constitution. Taylor (1986) discusses the *Rodriguez* case, which challenged inequities in the financing of public schools on the basis of the Fourteenth Amendment but failed by a 5–4 decision: "The claimants argued that strict scrutiny should be applied to school financing because public education was a 'fundamental right' and because most of those who suffered inequity under the Texas finance plan were low-income people. But the majority was clearly troubled by the lack of limiting principles in the plaintiffs' claim. The class of people disadvantaged in the view of the majority was not well-defined by income. And if public education were deemed a fundamental right, could not similar claims be made about such matters as police and fire protection, nutrition, and housing?" (1727–28.) As Schrag's work documents (2003), many finance cases have proceeded at the state level, using the language of entitlement to an "adequate" education that appears in many state constitutions.

15. Martha Minow (1990) provides an excellent analysis of this basic paradox.

16. The argument is prevalent in social theory. Iris Marion Young argues, "The principle of equal treatment originally arose as a formal guarantee of fair inclusive treatment. This mechanical interpretation of fairness, however, also suppresses difference. The politics of difference sometimes implies overriding a principle of equal treatment with the principle that group differences should be acknowledged in public policy and in the policies and procedures of economic institutions, in order to reduce actual or potential oppression. . . . Sometimes recognizing particular rights for groups is the only way to promote their full participation" (1990, 11).

17. In Pollock 2008, sixty-five authors engage the educator's complex reality: addressing racial inequality in education requires both recognizing racial differences in human experience or student outcome and treating students "the same." For another analysis of concrete disputes over achieving fairness by emphasizing or ignoring various forms of student difference, see Abu El-Haj 2006. Some disability complaints demonstrated how school and district people seemed especially confused about whether treating or not treating children as "different" was discriminatory. At OCR, I heard about one large district that was having trouble determining whether to apply districtwide standardized tests to "Special Education" students; a coworker handling the case described to me the district's desire "to give Special Ed sixth graders second-grade tests so they don't come home with scores feeling stupid." I asked myself in my notes the same question the district was wrestling with: "It is it discriminatory to *not* test Special Ed kids, or *to* test them with standardized tests?" Similarly, it was often unclear to educators when even labeling children "dis-

abled" was discriminatory, or a move against discrimination. Different parents wanted different things. On one day at OCR, two disability cases crossed my desk in which one parent alleged that calling her child "disabled" was discriminatory ("Parents not *wanting* this diagnosis," I wrote), while another parent alleged that *not* calling her child "disabled" was discriminatory ("Complainant wanted *more Special Ed* for kid," I wrote). See Morison, White, and Feuer 1996 for a discussion of complex legal battles in which African American parents in the 1970s called the use of IQ tests for Special Education placement discriminatory, and argued in the 1990s that not having IQ tests available to black children was discriminatory.

18. Since only a diagnosis of disability legally entitles children to accommodation, students must be professionally and/or medically labeled "disabled" to get civil rights protection. I regularly encountered parents in disability cases who vehemently insisted to OCR that their children "had deficits." I found their insistence surprising until I understood that schools would not recognize and support children with extra services unless "disability" were diagnosed. While many white, middle-class parents pursue outside medical testing to get their children diagnosed with learning disabilities in order to obtain Special Education services, poor parents often cannot afford to have their children tested, and parents of color often find that their children are stigmatized by disability labels rather than served by them. See Hehir 2005; Losen and Orfield 2002.

19. Balkin and Siegel (2003–4) point out that today many Americans interpret civil rights laws as outlawing *even classifying* people racially, although the laws' intent was to outlaw *subordinating or excluding* people because of their race. Many lower courts have taken the same analytic path, outlawing as suspect even voluntary district plans that take race category membership into account when assigning or admitting students to schools (Ryan 2003).

20. An article in the Cleveland *Plain Dealer* described OCR refusing, on other bureaucratic grounds, a district's request that OCR investigate the district's own practices. The regional OCR office rejected a request from the Parma school district to investigate a local complaint from a black parent who was arguing to the district that her child was discriminated against. The director of the regional OCR office told the paper that only formal complaints filed by citizens could be investigated; the district could, however, register a complaint on itself with the parent's approval. Hagan 2002.

21. Halpern (1995, chapter 6) describes longstanding debates over OCR's jurisdiction in institutions receiving varying amounts of federal funding.

22. By 2007, as I discuss later in this chapter, this part of the manual included explicit advice against using "statistical" information as evidence, now reading, "In order for OCR to proceed, the complainant must provide OCR with sufficient information to support the factual basis for the complainant's belief that discrimination has occurred and when it occurred. Generally, statistical data alone are not sufficient, absent allegations that actions by a recipient, if true, would violate one of the laws that OCR enforces." Section 106: Determine Whether There Is Sufficient Factual Basis to Proceed," http://

www.ed.gov/about/offices/list/ocr/docs/ocrcrm.html#I_6 (accessed June 14, 2007).

23. See Pell 1997. Pell wrote critically, regarding OCR under the Clinton's administration's assistant secretary Norma Cantu, that "an OCR investigation not only intimidates local administrators fearful of bad publicity, but also 'empowers' (to use one of Cantu's favorite expressions) those within a school district who favor OCR's leftist approach to such issues as sexual and racial harassment. By initiating an investigation, the agency shifts the balance of power in a local district. At schools and universities alike, those attempting to expand the boundaries of harassment and discrimination have an eager friend and ally in OCR." A reporter for *Education Week* observed, "In 1994, in another high-profile case, House Republicans complained that the OCR overstepped its mandate by looking for racial bias in Ohio's mandatory high school exit exam" (Hoff 1997).

24. A fellow investigator told me about an elementary Special Education complaint in which the black mother suggested that she had a "sense" of teachers' "low expectation in general" for black children at the school, especially "black boys." The investigator had had to ask the mother how concretely these "low expectations" seemed manifest in actual behavior she had witnessed. As I wrote in my notes at the time, lawyers sometimes usefully "made the analysis of opportunity denial concrete." Still, we also rejected many complaints for insufficient "evidence": As *Education Week* reported in 1997, "In fiscal 1996 alone, the OCR received 4,828 complaints. Sixty percent of those resulted in an investigation; the rest were dismissed after a brief review. Many were rejected because they already were the subject of a lawsuit or a review by a state agency. Others lacked enough evidence to justify a detailed inquiry." Hoff 1997.

25. Freeman (1978) has written of a "perpetrator" perspective in civil rights law that required a finding of the "perpetrator's" intention to harm, a framing that Freeman argues obfuscated much analysis of the "victim's" experience of harm.

26. Krieger 1995, 1168. In the past, most scholars of law contend, the "intention" of actors to deny people opportunities because of race was far more easily proved than today. According to Loewen, "Before about 1960, white Americans were much more forthright regarding racism and sexism since it was perfectly alright to express such sentiments" (1982, 12). Today, this quest to find intent is a dead end largely because unstated bias so often cannot be proved. Banaji (2001) and colleagues (Nosek, Banaji, and Greenwald 2002, 102) use computer test research that shows *unconscious*, "implicit bias"—"prejudice and stereotypes that operate outside conscious awareness or conscious control"—to contest these analytic restrictions. See also Kang and Banaji 2006. Krieger (1995) argues that *implicit* bias, or racially biased decision making that decision makers do not consciously "intend," should count for lawyers as evidence of discrimination.

27. Mickelson (2003, 1052) provides the following definition of racial discrimination in education: "Racial discrimination in education arises from actions of institutions or individual state actors, their attitudes and ideologies, or

processes that systematically treat students from different racial/ethnic groups disparately or inequitably." Educators busy defending their "attitudes and ideologies" often were unwilling to analyze unintentionally harmful "actions" or "processes."

28. In the sociological field of symbolic interaction, scholars such as Blumer (1969) maintain that people are always interpreting one another's actions and responding accordingly. Studying how people interpret one another's ongoing actions has also been central to interpretive anthropology (see Geertz 1973) and close anthropological analysis of interaction (McDermott, Gospodinoff, and Aron 1978).

29. White people who use the phrase "race lens" are often marking racial "difference" between viewers themselves. The phrase itself, as Crenshaw (1997) shows, implies that typical social life is not "racial" and that people of color, who are regarded as the only raced persons in the interaction, make race relevant. Crenshaw observes that "the frequent deployment of the metaphor of 'the race card' . . . presumes a social terrain devoid of race until it is (illegitimately) introduced" (1997, 104). For Crenshaw, such presumptions of race's irrelevance exemplify the practice that Gotanda (1991) calls "non-recognition," in which a "technique of 'noticing but not considering race' implicitly involves recognition of the racial category and a transformation or sublimation of that recognition so that the racial label is not 'considered.' "

30. On such defiant claims of "colorblindness" in school, which I call "color-muteness" because people actually refuse to talk about race's relevance, see Pollock 2004a; Lewis 2003a; Schofield 1995.

31. Another case I saw at OCR vividly demonstrated that even when race labels were not used, everyday interactions could appear highly racialized to participants and observers. In this case, the complainant, who did not describe herself or her son racially on the complaint form, alleged that her son's coaches had sworn at him and his friends, calling them "fucking pussies." The coach was displaying such hostility routinely to the son and his teammates, and the complainant was suggesting this hostility was racial. The coach had punched her son during a game, but the boy had been charged with assault. In a meeting regarding his removal from the football team, the mother wrote, one administrator told her to go get a lawyer, while another laughed and told her to "call Jesse Jackson, if I didn't like it." Colleagues scribbling notes on the circulating case records pointed out that the comment about Jesse Jackson indeed suggested racial hostility. "Is student AA [African American]?" someone jotted. "Why did D [district] tell parent to call Jesse Jackson? Potential Title VI problem."

32. As Krieger argues, a pervasive societal stereotype, such as *Latinos are in gangs*, can "operate beyond the reach of decision-maker self-awareness" and "bias intergroup judgment and decision making" (1995, 1187–88). Krieger's research, along with that of Banaji, Greenwald, and their colleagues exploring the brain's unconscious responses to images (see Nosek, Banaji, and Greenwald 2002, 102), suggests that since the dean might hold *unconscious* stereotypical associations between "Latinos" and "gangs," and take harmful actions based on unconscious animus to perceived group-based characteristics,

such activity should count as "discrimination." Sullivan, Zimmer, and White (2002) make a related argument about implicit bias in gender discrimination.

33. Academics analyzing which acts in a child's life constitute "discrimination" routinely define "discriminatory" acts as those fueled by racial "prejudice," which to many suggests racial animus. For example, in her own discussion of analyzing *which* acts contributing to cumulative *disadvantage* over a child's life in the educational domain are actually *discrimination*, Blank (2005) tellingly uses as an example of a "discriminatory" act teachers whose internal "prejudices" have them "more likely to place young children-of-color in lower reading groups" (101), leading later to unequal participation in higher-track classes.

34. As Steinberg (2001) argues, much scholarship also suggests that the quest is to find racism lodged finally in people's minds and hearts. Typically, scholars describing discrimination's "covert" contemporary forms focus on how racial "attitudes" once expressed overtly now are self-censored and even unconscious, but still present (Bonilla-Silva 1997, 476; Bobo and Tuan 2006; Banaji 2001; Shelton and Richeson 2006). Bonilla-Silva argues relatedly that scholars have psychologized discussion of "racism" by treating racism as internal (and abnormal) prejudice rather than normalized behavior. Still, in his article proposing a more "structural" theory of "racism," Bonilla-Silva himself calls "racism" a "racial ideology" that can be found in interviews even when people deny its existence (1997, 474); this framing still suggests that racism lies ultimately inside hearts and minds.

35. In an interview for the National Education Association, OCR assistant secretary Norma Cantu noted indirectly the sort of resistance we at OCR encountered in our "fault-finding" mission: "Fault-finding is part of our job, but we're not here to label people as racist" (Weiss 1994).

36. The "victim" perspective, Freeman argued, appeared only fleetingly in race discrimination law. For example, in the 1970s some school desegregation cases ordered that remedies (busing students, increasing school resources) should affirmatively assist students to enjoy a full context of equal opportunity, even after remedying the specific, isolated, supposedly aberrational acts deemed discriminatory (i.e., the legally enforced segregation of students' bodies). Freeman 1978, reprinted in Crenshaw et al. 1995.

37. Crenshaw et al. 1995, xiv. Crenshaw paraphrases Freeman's argument in the introduction to an anthology of key works in critical race theory, in a section titled "Intellectual Precursors: Early Critique of Conventional Civil Rights Discourse." "The legal adoption of the perpetrator perspective is part of an ideological process through which forms of racial power that do not register on the perpetrator framework get implicitly represented as 'not racism' and, thus, are pushed beyond the scope of remediation" (1995, 3).

38. Cases involving disability and discipline sometimes raised slightly more complex issues of causation. One complaint I saw, for example, alleged that a student was suspended for swearing that the student himself was unable to avoid "because of" a "defiance disorder." The complainant felt the suspension was unfairly "caused" by the student's disability.

39. Sullivan, Zimmer, and White write that "Indeed, *discrimination* is now a term of art that embraces several different definitions, each with its own distinctive theory and methods of proof" (2002, 3).

40. In technical legal analysis of intentional disparate treatment, lawyers must "give the defendant the opportunity to offer an explanation of why the action was taken" and to articulate some "legitimate, nondiscriminatory reason" for the actions taken against the victim (Sullivan, Zimmer, and White 2002, 63).

41. Lawrence 1987, 319–20. Advocates (such as the National Women's Law Center) calling for using disparate impact analysis to analyze gender discrimination have made similar arguments. See http://www.nwlc.org/pdf/ ReynoldsOppositionLetter.pdf (accessed March 22, 2005).

42. Under "Section 106: Determine Whether There Is Sufficient Factual Basis to Proceed," the text reads, "Generally, statistical data alone are not sufficient, absent allegations that actions by a recipient, if true, would violate one of the laws that OCR enforces." http://www.ed.gov/about/offices/list/ocr/docs/ ocrcrm.html#I_6 (accessed October 18, 2006).

43. Nowak argues that since the late 1980s, courts have actively attempted to constrain efforts to "help racial minorities," specifically by limiting available ways of analyzing how discrimination works. "The Supreme Court seems to have turned against racial minorities, as it has narrowed earlier rulings concerning the Equal Protection Clause and restricted the efforts of legislatures," Nowak contends (1995, 349). This "narrowing" has particularly manifested through courts requiring proof of intent to harm. Civil rights groups challenged *Alexander v. Sandoval*'s restrictions with a bill introduced in Congress titled "FAIRNESS: The Civil Rights Act of 2004" (HR 3809 and S 2088).

44. Losen and Orfield (2002) write, "Although the government and individuals filing complaints with government agencies may still use the Title VI regulations to redress the racially disparate impact of neutral policies, enforcement of disparate impact regulations is more vulnerable to an administration's enforcement policy preferences than ever before" (xxvi–xxv).

45. Lenhardt (2004) argues similarly that "the current legal framework's focus on intent," even *unconsciously* intended harm, "fosters a defensiveness about racial issues" that obstructs analysts' ability to "detect the presence of actual harm rather than motive" (811). The "Panel on Methods for Assessing Discrimination" convened by the Committee on National Statistics in 2001 argued pointedly that "we do not believe that a social science research agenda for measuring discrimination should be limited by . . . legal definitions" (Blank, Dabady, and Citro 2004, 41).

46. See Pollock 2004a, chapters 2 and 6.

47. E.g., Kozol 2005.

48. As a colleague put it, OCR's evidentiary requirements often seemed to demand "some kind of freak parent" who ran around documenting not just his own child's experience but also "everything happening to other people's children." Some parents did gather an overwhelming amount of evidence that offered *too* much detail for readers to be able to handle. One unusually communicative complainant in a disability case (a white woman) sent OCR a huge

stack of the faxes she had sent daily to her son's principal before and after filing her OCR complaint. Each was a detailed description of the school's various failures at communication, written in single-spaced, ten-point type. One of her main complaints was that school personnel did not respond adequately to her complaints. As I wrote in my notes, these parents had collected and demanded so many responses in writing that the school administration had tried to limit communications by imposing little-used rules on them, such as a twenty-minute limit on parent meetings with administrators and a limit to the length of faxes that would be accepted by the school machine. But many more moderate complainants knew that to claim harm successfully, they had to keep careful, detailed records on everyday practice. While a few revealed themselves to be somewhat obsessive record-keepers as they approached OCR, all demonstrated that many people in and around schools are constantly informally measuring the treatment they receive and comparing it with the treatment of other "classes of persons" (Frake 1980). Many parents had long kept detailed written notes on whether meetings on their children were scheduled promptly, how quickly phone calls or faxes were returned, whether medications were administered to children according to prescriptions, whether their children were suspended using the same printed rule as other children, and so on. A few of my assigned complaints also included as data records kept by the children themselves. Laura Cachon's children had made a petition as a way of documenting the slurs one white child was using against them and a number of other students of color. They turned the petition in to the school principal, and Cachon submitted a copy of it to OCR as evidence. It turned out to be a key piece of evidence, as it demonstrated that the school administration had received "notice" of the harassment and prompted analysis of whether they had responded adequately.

49. See Fine et al. 1997 on the often silent normalization of "white" experience in schools.

50. See Orfield and Eaton 1996 for discussion of resegregation's dynamics, and for a discussion of key desegregation rulings cutting off avenues for interdistrict desegregation and releasing districts from desegregation orders.

51. Orfield and Eaton 1996.

52. Singer and Willett (2003) make clear that statistical analysis of cumulative educational experiences requires, by definition, longitudinal data that track individuals over time: "Today we know that it is possible to measure change, and to do it well, *if you have longitudinal data* . . . . To model change, you need longitudinal data that describe how each person in the sample changes over time" (3, 9).

53. See also Solórzano and colleagues (2000, 2002) on how racial "microaggressions" accumulate to become racially hostile climates.

54. See Weiss et al. 2005; Lawrence-Lightfoot 2003. Lawrence-Lightfoot argues in her study of black parents' relationships with white educators that "the collaboration of black families and schools is the only hope for the successful schooling of black children" (1978, 175).

55. Lawrence-Lightfoot 1978, 167. Lawrence-Lightfoot continues, "Parents' and teachers' perceptions of each other as uncaring about children and as de-

valuing the educational process lead to distance and distrust and the need to blame one another. Misperceptions, rarely articulated and confronted, always nurtured by hostile stereotypes, lead to increasing disregard for each other's place in the lives of black children" (167).

56. Loewen has observed that "lawsuits, particularly those involving charges of ill treatment, typically involve a factual dispute as well as a legal argument with parties and witnesses on each side of the courtroom asserting quite different things about the facts and their interpretation" (1982, 3).

57. A few complainants stated explicitly to me that if comparative evidence could be found to disprove their sense of differential treatment, they would gladly "stand corrected." One Latino father who had been arrested when a school-based police officer came to investigate his son's truancy remarked to his principal that if such officers "run warrant checks on other families, I will accept it. If there's a difference in how you've treated my family/my son, it's not acceptable."

58. For examples, see Pollock 2004a, chapter 2; Ward 2008; and Tatum 2008.

59. Many actors in these dramas demanded formal findings of discrimination's summative presence or absence. As I wrote in my notes after discussing a complaint resolution with one district, "Nobody asked us if we made a 'formal finding' of discrimination! Maybe because this is new for them."

60. Pollock 2004a, 2004b, 2008.

61. Both complainants and recipients so quickly assimilated some of OCR's basic habits of argumentation that despite their discomfort with the bureaucratic apparatus of the law, they were clearly familiar with the legalistic requirement of proving harm to be "because of race." One complaint form created by the Longview district to resolve the Stedley case, for example, had a check box to show that copies had been given to both "Complainant" and "Defendant." On the permeation of "legal" ways of thinking into American daily life, see also Ewick and Silbey 1998; Greenhouse, Yngvesson, and Engel 1994; Engel 1991, 1993.

62. Stone, Patton, and Heen (2000) describe resolving such disputes over "facts" as central to the work of the Harvard Negotiation Project.

63. Bonilla-Silva (2003b) suggests that in predominantly white and white-controlled "environs," people of color may actually find "daily discrimination" "more apparent" than in all-of-color spaces "because they have at least secured access to previously inaccessible social space" (274). In criticizing the ways other actors claimed or dismissed claims of harm to children, complainants and recipients articulated larger American tensions about how those who are framed as "different" are expected or assisted to "fit in" to local "communities" and "norms." Greenhouse, Yngvesson, and Engel 1994.

64. Notably, the law does not state that perpetrators and victims must be of different races for harm "on the ground of race" to occur and be called discrimination. According to precedent, members of a group can discriminate against other members of their own group, just as non-members can. But complaints arriving at OCR almost always suggested that people from one group discriminated against people from another group.

65. According to this survey of Asian American community leaders, Asian Americans had many complaints similar to those filed by Latino and African American complainants (particularly about language service and racial harassment) but did not often file them formally.

REBUTTAL TWO
Harms to Children of Color Should Not Be Discussed

1. During the Reagan administration, federal officials argued that even asking districts to report on their compliance was a "burden" and a denial of local "control." The U.S. Department of Education Annual Report on OCR's work in 1982 noted that "In FY 1982 the Department's Office for Civil Rights (OCR) furthered the goals of the Reagan Administration to reduce burdensome reporting requirements imposed on our Nation's schools and to return the control of education to State and local officials while still ensuring the proper enforcement of civil rights" (U.S. Department of Education Annual Report, Fiscal Year 1982, 1). In 1987, one critic wrote classically of OCR work that, "Ignoring the 'back to basics' preferences of most black and Hispanic families, it [OCR] has tried to mandate bilingual instruction, outlaw father-son social events, forbid school dress codes that distinguish between boys and girls, and crack down on standardized tests and on schools that group children by academic ability. It intimidates principals who suspend unruly students. . . . The agency has forced schools to build elaborate systems based on its ultra-egalitarian assumptions" (Uzzell 1997).

2. Informal negotiation with those whose activities are subject to regulation is actually central to all U.S. administrative agencies, not just civil rights ones. K.C. Davis (1978) estimates that "more than ninety percent of all administrative action is informal," involving off-the-record negotiation that vanishes behind official policy documents. According to Davis, "Agencies do not necessarily either adjudicate or make rules when they initiate, investigate, threaten, publicize, conceal, plan, recommend, and supervise. Some informal action of agencies is in the nature of informal adjudication . . . some informal action is neither adjudication nor rulemaking" (13–14). Stewart (1975) notes that policy work in administrative agencies is about "adjusting," often informally, between "the competing claims of various private interests affected by agency policy"; such "adjustments" inherently weaken federal power. Stewart writes that given such informal "adjusting," "the function of agencies can no longer be conceptualized simply as that of putting broad legislative directives into practice" (Stewart 1975, cited in Edwards and Nordin 1980, 40).

3. Derrick Bell (1995a) suggested as early as the 1970s, as white resistance to desegregation plans boiled over, that had lawyers "discussed" harms and remedies with "local school authorities" rather than simply "enforcing" desegregation, they might have moved the civil rights cause forward more effectively. White people in power over children of color either as policymakers or

practitioners, Bell argued, had to be convinced that action providing children with equitable opportunity was necessary and important, and even in their own interest; Bell called this situation "interest convergence." Hinting at persistent dynamics of hostile skepticism in white-controlled school systems, Bell argued circa 2000 that the lawyerly role in education fifty years after *Brown* should still be as counsel and advisor, not enforcer (personal e-mail communication, November 26, 2004). Carmichael and Hamilton (1967) argue in *Black Power* that coalitions between blacks and whites based solely on white "good will," rather than whites' sense of shared "interests" with black people, would inevitably be disadvantageous to black people. Other observers have suggested more broadly that for white people to work in the interests of people of color, they need to become convinced that not providing people of color with equitable opportunity is morally wrong (see Warren 2006), or that opportunities given to people of color are not being taken away from themselves or their children (see Hochschild and Scovronick 2003).

4. Cohen, Raudenbush, and Ball 2003.

5. Legal scholarship demonstrates that one function of courts is to name harm: to publicly voice social and ethical norms through resolving legal disputes. On "norm articulation" by courts, see Cover 1980–81; see also Linde 1972. Over time, courts have increasingly functioned to name fewer harms to students of color, rather than more. This leaves OCR increasingly responsible for naming such harms.

6. Mansbridge (1996) analyzes three ways to get someone who does not want to leave a room to leave it. One way is to pick the person up and carry her out of the room, so she cannot resist. The second is to put a gun to the person's head, so she can at least choose to say "shoot me." This is coercion with force, but not absolute force. The third is to convince the person to leave the room. People follow rules, Mansbridge argues, either because of force or the threat of force, or because they are convinced. In democracies, by definition, convincing people should take precedence over force (1996, n. 2). More often than not in disability complaints, taking the basic, matter-of-factly confrontational stance that punishment would result if disability laws were found to be violated often got educators to provide the specific services requested, even as they grumbled about doing so. However, in many disability cases, districts were already negotiating a remedy with the complainants, following disability law's clear process for assessment and service provision; the OCR complaint simply accelerated that process. One colleague who had analyzed the disability complaints in our region told me that by the time they arrived at OCR, many districts and schools already had scheduled "upcoming IEP meetings offering the opportunity to resolve the case." In other cases, the district simply "didn't know what the problems were. Only around 17 percent of districts knew and were [acting in] bad faith," she concluded. In these cases, sometimes the fact that OCR was a federal agency seeking educational remedies for children rather than a private legal firm seeking monetary damages prompted what one complainant called a "so sue us" attitude. A complainant struggling with such a situation maintained that the school's stance amounted

to "not wanting to acknowledge or accommodate my son's disability. The school is trying to disprove that he is ill."

7. As described in this chapter, this slowdown in federal "enforcement" started early in OCR's history, particularly once Nixon and then Congress blocked the agency's efforts to enforce desegregation by revoking federal funding. See Halpern 1995. In 1977, Carter signed the Eagleton-Biden Amendment to the 1964 Civil Rights Act, which prevented OCR "from using Title VI to require school systems to bus children" (Halpern 1995, 154). By forcing OCR to refer such cases to the Justice Department, the Amendment "eliminated the enforcement mechanism that made Title VI effective: the termination of funds after administrative proceedings" (155). By 1989–90, the department's report to Congress noted that an order terminating federal financial assistance to one school district that refused to grant OCR access to information "was the first fund termination in more than eight years" (U.S. Department of Education 1989–90, 8.

8. Rebell and Block (1985) write, "[OCR] had proved its efficiency in bringing about desegregation in southern school districts. In the first six years of enforcement of Title VI, six hundred administrative proceedings had been undertaken against school districts, and funding was actually terminated in two hundred of them (in all but four of these districts, the federal aid subsequently was restored)" (60–61). As the 1966 HEW annual report to Congress noted, HEW's civil rights wing framed these Title VI enforcement efforts as designed to "assist" segregated districts in "complying" with the new legal requirements: "During May and June 1966, the Equal Educational Opportunities Program directed much of its effort toward school districts accomplishing the least progress in school desegregation, in an effort to assist them in complying with Title VI in order to remain eligible for Federal assistance. Efforts include analysis of progress reports submitted by school districts and on-site staff visits to school districts to determine how progress could be achieved. In addition, staff members participated in regional information meetings with State and local school officials, civil rights organization representatives, and others, to explain policy in relation to the guidelines" (U.S. Department of Health, Education, and Welfare 1966, 133).

9. Halpern 1995, chapter 4. Nixon fired OCR's director, Leon Panetta, in 1970 for strident desegregation efforts. The Nixon administration briefly shifted its attention to Northern desegregation and then moved away from desegregation altogether. See Orfield 1978; Rebell and Block 1985; Rabkin 1989, 154; Panetta and Gall 1971.

10. Orfield (1978) argues that by 1971, "fund cutoffs had been publicly abandoned" by OCR (291).

11. "OCR efforts turned, during this period, to a greater emphasis on negotiation and compliance rather than termination of funds, although funds did continue to be terminated when noncompliance required it. The office made an extra effort to keep channels of communication open, and the effort appeared to pay dividends," 53 (U.S. Department of Health, Education, and Welfare 1969, 53).

12. By 1974, Orfield (1978) argues, OCR was still doing investigations, but it now refused to invoke punitive consequences: "HEW would prove constitutional violations, then continue to pay federal subsidies, hoping someone else might enforce the law" (295).

13. The report also stated, "In some cases such schools [dual systems] continue to exist with OCR's knowledge. The policy of the Nixon administration appears to be chiefly responsible for OCR's inactivity in this area" (Commission on Civil Rights 1975, 52, 131).

14. Bunch and Mindle 1993, 6.

15. See Orfield 2000; Halpern 1995, chapter 6. In the mid-1980s, the Committee on Government Operations concluded bluntly that "OCR has failed to meet its enforcement responsibilities. This is a direct result of cases languishing for years at DOJ [the Department of Justice, where OCR often referred thorny Title VI complaints], and the acceptance of settlements that do not provide the kind of anti-discriminatory relief Congress had intended when it enacted the four major laws enforced by the DOEd. By refusing to fully use its authorized powers of enforcement, OCR effectively sends a message to the recipients of Federal education funds that the U.S. Government is not willing to use its complete enforcement authority when violations of civil rights laws are found." Union Calendar No. 271; Investigation of Civil Rights Enforcement by the Office for Civil Rights at the Department of Education, 1985, 18.

16. In the Department of Education annual report for 1981, Secretary T. H. Bell wrote, "The Department has moved to resolve pending legal cases through a spirit of conciliation rather than confrontation in order to achieve solutions that best serve students and further the goals of education" (U.S. Department of Education 1981, 2).

17. The Department of Education's self-report for 1982 offered pointed examples: "Through good faith negotiation, OCR and the New York City Public Schools reached a new accord dealing with the racial makeup of school faculties" (U.S. Department of Education, 1982, 2). Regarding OCR's efforts in New York City, Rebell and Block (1985) write that OCR was very unlikely to find offenses and unlikely to convince listeners, in its communications, of the investigation's legitimacy: "The strategy for the Big City Reviews may have been politically ingenious in pressing a major civil rights enforcement thrust against the Democratic-controlled urban centers, without raising spectres of forced integration and busing that would rankle the Republican ranks wherever applied. But it also had an inherent flaw which was to plague OCR's efforts throughout the reviews: without a prior finding of intentional segregation of students, both the school district officials being charged with violations and general public opinion had difficulty accepting the legitimacy of OCR's allegations" (68).

18. Weiss 1994, 7. Healy (1999) reported that "many college officials and civil-rights watchers consider her the most aggressive—and fearsome—advocate of minority, disabled, and female students in the last 20 years."

19. Cantu called for OCR to "collaborate" with educators even as she wrote more pugnaciously in her annual reports to Congress that "discrimination against students is an ugly reality" (Office for Civil Rights 1994, 2).

20. Office for Civil Rights 1995, p. 2. As the Clinton administration attempted to engage local communities in egalitarian conversations about race, Cantu's 1993 and 1994 reports to Congress also declared, "OCR will help others to learn to solve their problems of securing equal access to quality education. OCR will focus on systemic education reform that enables communities throughout the nation to understand, commit to and implement strategies that provide opportunities for all to learn." Office for Civil Rights 1993, p. 10, and 1994, p. 12.

21. Organizations opposed to affirmative action admissions know well this power of the "d-word" in the new civil rights era. In the early 2000s, as the NAACP reported, anti–affirmative action groups like the Center for Equal Opportunity were pressuring universities to halt their affirmative action efforts by simply threatening to file OCR complaints of "discrimination" against white students. See NAACP 2005.

22. Authors studying policymaking and "implementation" as a cultural arena, such as Sutton and Levinson (2001) and Shore and Wright (1997), investigate policy less as a set of static mandates than as a process of negotiating over power. The very term "policy," they argue, often disguises such battles over power and politics between those who "make" policy and those who live its "implementation."

23. As Shore and Wright (1997) argue, policymaking always involves power struggles over which ideas and opinions will be explicitly written into final policies, even though at the end of such negotiations, it seems as if "the policy document . . . sets out clearly what inescapably ought to be done . . . and cannot be negotiated or bargained over" (quoted in Brayboy 2005, 18).

24. In another case, the complainant, a teacher, was worried about retaliation, and a manager advised me that it would be "*very* inflammatory" to state in the closure letter that some educators were afraid of "losing their jobs." As I wrote in my notes, such language "might get the district to say 'who said that, we want proof,' etc. Maybe just as good to use the suggestive phrase 'afraid of adverse actions'—it will accomplish the same thing without raising district's defensiveness." In my initial phone conversation with Anne Hardy in Longview, I first noted how language itself could prompt a lengthy battle over evidence and proof. I had matter-of-factly asked Hardy about how the district and school had dealt with the "racially hostile environment" alleged by Stedley. In my mind, my question was not an intentionally forceful accusation but rather a phrase designed to open discussion on how the district's climate was experienced as hostile by Stedley. But Hardy immediately rose to "defend the district" from the phrase "racially hostile environment" by arguing bluntly that "no such environments existed" in Longview. Vin, the lawyer on the case, later told me that I could have avoided some of her defensiveness by simply softening my actual descriptions of Stedley's allegations. The phrase "racially hostile environment" "may have been too government," I jotted down. "Maybe could say the kids '*experienced* racial slurs'?"

25. See Halpern (1995, 208) on the establishment of this tactic of "early complaint resolution" during the Reagan administration.

26. Some complainants to OCR dismissed the entire idea of "diversity training," but they typically requested that such trainings be of high quality. For

example, in one complaint filed at an OCR regional office, several black families, dissatisfied with OCR's ordering of a "diversity training," next filed suit in court for monetary damages that in the end totaled $7.5 million. Still, the plaintiffs demanded that this money be put toward administrative and curriculum changes to encourage racial diversity—in essence, professional development (Orarke and Heckman 2002).

27.  Policy scholar Frederick Hess argued at the June 2005 Achievement Gap Initiative conference at Harvard University that "nice" policies conducted in the spirit of collaboration may simply support and await good-faith efforts from educators, while "mean" relations of punitive accountability may be necessary to move complacent educators to actually serve children well or to goad meek administrators to make the hard decisions that might anger colleagues.

28.  Similarly, in a complaint regarding the overrepresentation of black and Hispanic children in one large district's Special Education program, a *New York Times* reporter quoted an advocate who "said he was hopeful that the Federal intervention would spur improvement. He suggested that 'Everyone knew this wasn't right. . . . But they almost needed an outside force, an authority, to say, 'You've got to do it differently' " (J. Steinberg 1997).

29.  Miller 2001, 541.

30.  MINSPED cases (Minorities in Special Ed) at OCR were typically cases about the unwarranted overrepresentation of students of color in Special Education. In many districts, IQ tests are one method of assessment involved in placement.

31.  Uzzell 1987, 39.

32.  In 2000, a *Boston Globe* article reported a classic description of OCR's "voluntary resolution" dynamics when reporting an agreement made between OCR and the Boston school district to resolve a case in which a light-skinned Cape Verdean teacher had physically and verbally abused dark-skinned Cape Verdean children in her elementary school class. The school agreed to have a "corrective crash course in sensitivity training, which will be closely monitored by federal authorities." The article quoted a Boston school district spokeswoman: "We're pleased that this agreement will bring resolution to the complaint. We are always looking for ways to improve upon our processes to make sure that any instances of harassment or discrimination do not occur." The OCR national spokesperson, Rodger Murphey, predictably downplayed OCR's enforcement power: "Our role is not to point fingers but to make sure all students get equal access to a quality education and that a district is abiding by the civil rights statutes required by law." The article noted that "while the OCR could have taken away $7.8 million in federal funding from the Boston school district, the Boston school officials were very cooperative and voluntarily hosted training sessions on sensitivity for school officials, faculty, and staff as a means to prevent a similar case from happening again" (Kahn 2000).

33.  In a draft letter of findings on a "big city review" of New York City in the 1970s, according to Rebell and Block (1985), OCR found that "minority" students received less funding, and had worse classroom conditions, fewer guidance counselors, and less experienced teachers than did white students. They were suspended so often that student suspensions were a "pervasive

practice of punishing students on the basis of race and ethnicity." They languished in segregated classrooms and were tracked into lower-performing classrooms in which little effort was made to "remediate academic deficiencies" (115). This letter was withdrawn for political reasons when the New York chancellor accused the head of OCR of "headline hunting" and was then revised (116). The rewording of the charges failed to mention the denial of equal educational resources for "minorities." "The revised letter did not accuse the board of overall discriminatory design. It expressed varying degrees of concern or suspicion that violations may have occurred, but it withheld judgment pending receipt of further information" (118). The assistant director of OCR, Martin Gerry, wrote another letter denouncing this situation, arguing that "the letter of agreement . . . represents little more than a promise by the school system to comply with the law and a tacit acceptance by OCR of both the continued segregation of hundreds of thousands of minority children in low level ability groups and the continued disparate treatment of minority children under the student discipline system" (129). Gerry argued that "it was unprecedented for OCR to accept a plan that neither compensates for widespread past discrimination nor establishes meaningful procedures to prevent future discrimination" (129).

34. Littlejohn (1998) argued that "under the mantle of defending the civil rights of English language learners, OCR staff are in and out of classrooms, looking over teachers' shoulders, second-guessing teachers and administrators, judging the quality of instructional programs and materials, and generally being educationally intrusive in ways never contemplated by the drafters of the civil rights statutes" (1). Littlejohn even suggested falsely that OCR mandated bilingual education: "Under OCR's perverse standards (i.e., other-language instruction for LEP students before English instruction), the agency is unable to find a 'successful' program and routinely places substantial and highly burdensome requirements on school systems to evaluate their programs and report the results. What is the justification for this bureaucratic excess? OCR bases its judgments on assumptions of questionable legitimacy, then forces districts to produce mountains of paperwork whose only value may be perpetuating federal employment" (36).

35. Pell 1997. Pell argued that "Cantu understands and exploits the fact that in many cases civil rights enforcement is most intrusive when it is kept so low-profile as to be out of sight," and added ominously that "officials' increasing reliance on bureaucratic anonymity and subterfuge suggests they know that the public is tired of the civil rights bureaucracy. Further efforts at disguising what these agencies are doing may only hasten the day that the public does away with them altogether."

36. This controversy is documented in Schnaiberg 1998.

37. State-level initiatives to enforce English-only instruction for the children of immigrants has constricted OCR employees' efforts to help districts provide ELLs with their civil rights to language services: these laws have made OCR higher-ups so worried about external critics that they sometimes refuse to call for language assistance at all. One OCR employee told me that in her region, a state proposition banning any form of native-language instruction for English-

language learners had "created a climate" in which districts felt they had severely limited options for providing academic services to ELL students as federal law requires.

38. Ewick and Silbey (1998) call the very paper of legal documents "a realm of strategic power": "Paper, after all, occupies space. It concretizes and makes both visible and intransigent otherwise fleeting and temporal interventions" (7). The very act of producing paper documents was paramount at OCR; Weber (1947) observed as much of bureaucracies in general.

39. Fiss (1984) also argues against overreliance on "settlement" in law, arguing that "alternative dispute resolution" relies too heavily on social relations that have already broken down, and functions as "a truce more than a true reconciliation" (1075). He also argues that in settlement, "Consent is often coerced . . . and although dockets are trimmed, justice may not be done" (1075).

40. As Gloria Ladson-Billings put it in our Early Learning conference (described in chapter 3), "often kids . . . have disciplinary problems . . . because of some perception of unfairness that they're not equipped to deal with constructively."

41. A pattern of ejecting students from classrooms or school as punishment is common nationwide in the disciplinary treatment of students of color (Noguera 2008).

42. My notes indicated that according to the school handbook, the piercing incident should technically have been treated as a dress code violation, as with a white student who showed up wearing inappropriate shoes: "should've been 'go home and change,' " I wrote. Granley educators indicated that they made many "judgment calls" (as one support room monitor put it) about the need to discipline José with heightened severity. Regarding another suspension, I wrote, the school handbook's list of infractions and consequences suggested that teachers "should have just restricted [José's] recess, not *suspended* him." I noted after an interview with school and district staff that the vice principal and superintendent were not clear when a next offense would lead to a suspension, a "visit to the support room," or a "warning."

43. For discussion of schools successfully debating and retooling unsuccessful discipline practices, see Noguera 2008.

44. Similarly, when the Quail district agreed in its VRP to conduct a "diversity" workshop to remedy its racially hostile climate, I found in a follow-up phone call that the workshop they booked was actually on generic "character development" rather than addressing racial harassment or hostility in particular. As advocates have observed, written statements of compliance often leave open the question of the success of the actual activity undertaken. A report from the Commission on Civil Rights argued as early as 1975 that OCR's "reliance on statistical data and other written information to determine the compliance status of school districts was by nature superficial" (1975, 104).

45. According to the U.S. Commission on Civil Rights, for example, despite its 1996 recommendation that the agency (under Clinton) provide explicit written "guidance or other materials to schools seeking to ensure that their ability grouping practices complied with Title VI," in 2004 OCR had yet to produce final documents on this issue for the public (2004, 18).

46. Pollock 2004a.

47. Mehan (1996) notes that this creation of texts describing "disabilities" and disability services is key in even producing a "disability" and a "disabled" child, though Mehan is concerned about such texts' negative effects on children and parents who do not want such diagnoses.

48. Pollock 2004a, 108.

49. An article titled "How to Respond to a Complaint from OCR" in *The Special Educator* (January 30, 1998, vol. 13, no. 12) cited attorney Jose Martin, who viewed OCR as a problem solver rather than a troublemaker: " 'OCR is more interested—in modern times—in solving problems than in the past,' said Jose Martin, a school attorney with Richards, Lindsay & Martin in Austin, Texas. That said, solving the problem quickly should be your goal as an administrator, said Martin, who spoke at several workshops at the recent Texas Association of Section 504 and Hearing Officers' conference." In advising school administrators on ways to handle an OCR complaint, Martin urged, "I mean, you will devote the next three days to this issue. Forget the rest of life." Martin offered the following communication advice for administrators: "Let the investigator know you're looking into the matter and will get back to him in a few days. Then do so! Stay cool and composed. . . . Let them know you're on the ball. It creates a cooperative atmosphere. . . . Get out your calendar, because when OCR conducts an on-site investigation, you're going to be busy. The investigator will park himself in an office in your building, request loads of documents and interview your staff. They're going to take a lot of your time. . . . Plus, you don't know what else they'll find. Suddenly, the issues have multiplied."

## Rebuttal Three
### Harms to Children of Color Cannot Be Remedied

Bob Moses is a civil rights leader who works to expand opportunity in education. He explains, "The 'we' refers to a complex configuration of individuals; educational institutions of various kinds; local, regional, and national associations and organizations (both governmental and nongovernmental); actual state governments as well as the national political parties; and the executive, legislative, and judicial branches of the national government. The 'it'—the goal of educating all our children well—rests on a complex conceptual consensus that is woven into the cultural fabric of this country: the idea that young people who grow up in the United States are entitled to free public education, from kindergarten through twelfth grade" (2001, 92).

1. In 1965, the Department of Health, Education, and Welfare (HEW) began its short term of pressuring defiantly segregated districts in the South, and in 1967, the Office for Civil Rights was created within HEW to do this work. In 1980, years after OCR had stopped vigorously enforcing desegregation, OCR was moved into the new U.S. Department of Education. On the agency's active first year, see U.S. Department of Health, Education, and Welfare 1967.

2. *Grutter v. Bollinger*, 539 U.S. 306 (2003).

3. Ryan 2003; these cases were *Parents Involved in Community Schools v. Seattle School District No. 1; Meredith v. Jefferson County Board of Education.*

4. In 2005, the NAACP Legal Defense and Education Fund argued that under Bush, the OCR booklet was playing a key role in misleading both universities and school districts into thinking that race-based activity was inherently illegal and must be curtailed. Its report argued that OCR higher-ups were actively counseling universities to avoid race-conscious strategies for admission and retention (NAACP 2005). An admissions officer at a large state university suggested to me in 2005 that the "race-neutral" booklet was having a chilling effect among many university admissions officers across the country, who feared that any consideration of students' race in their admissions procedures would invite OCR complaint or court challenge.

5. See *Parents Involved in Community Schools v. Seattle School District No. 1*, Slip Op. at XX (Kennedy, J., concurring).

6. For discussion of this logic in contemporary education cases, see Ryan 2003. Siegel (2004) explains this shift in logic as having occurred in U.S. courts over the past half century since *Brown*: courts responding to white resistance to desegregation orders reframed (and misinterpreted) *Brown*'s logic as suggesting that it was unconstitutional to classify people by race even to equalize opportunity. See also Crenshaw et al. 1995.

7. Standard scholarly wisdom suggests that in invoking law, people increase the law's power. Ewick and Silbey argue that "repeated invocation of the law sustains its capacity to comprise social relations" (45). I show here that people can also reduce the law's perceived power by invoking its presumed inapplicability. OCR employees imagined a limited potential for our own legal tools' reach and in doing so limited the potential of those tools to improve education for children of color. Halpern (1995, 130) demonstrates how OCR employees have long struggled, in "embattled" paranoia, to implement Title VI despite external critics. I demonstrate here how circa 2000, this paranoia had us limiting our own internal efforts.

8. On "rhetorics of intransigence," or the argument that change will not be secured, see Hirschman 1991, 168.

9. Many researchers have demonstrated that children of color often lack essential opportunities to learn and thrive in their states, districts, schools, and classrooms. See, e.g., Orfield and Eaton 1996; Darling-Hammond 1997; Hochschild and Scovronick 2003. Such research also measures racial inequities in opportunities to learn and thrive as existing not just between schools but also within them in ordinary classrooms. See Oakes et al. 1990; Darity, et al. 2001; Mickelson 2005; Lewis 2003a. Students of color are more likely to be placed without warrant in segregated Special Education settings and in lower-track classes in "integrated" schools (Losen and Orfield 2002; Oakes et al. 1990). They are also more likely to be disciplined harshly (Noguera 2008). While some researchers locate the primary causes of such inequalities outside schools, in economic disparities in health, housing, and employment, they note that such inequalities are exacerbated in schools, often in children's early years. See Rothstein 2004; Noguera 2003; Fryer and Leavitt 2004.

10. Hirschman (1991) would probably call the arguments I explore in this chapter examples of a key "rhetoric of reaction": the "jeopardy" thesis, which suggests that the proposed moves will jeopardize past accomplishments. My colleagues and I often framed our self-constraining as an attempt to save the agency's basic tools for assisting students of color—a hallmark of "jeopardy" rhetoric. Open discussion of active efforts to assist such students, we reasoned, could result in hostile enemy targeting of these very tools. As Hirschman argues, the "jeopardy" argument is often made by "conservatives" resisting change, but "progressives" sometimes use it to derail their own work; in the hands of both conservatives and progressives, such rhetorics become "rhetorics of intransigence" (168). Less obviously, our arguments about the likely failures of the Early Learning Project were an example of the "futility" thesis, which suggests that the changes demanded really will not work; but this thesis better fits the arguments I describe in chapter 4, which suggest that OCR remedies were too "small" to "make a dent" (Hirschman 1991, 45) in racial inequality.

11. Foucault (1979) provides a historical analysis of such self-regulation in institutions; Wieder (1974) provides an ethnographic analysis of it.

12. Anthropologists generally recommend learning from "apprenticeship" to a community of practice; on learning as apprenticeship, see Lave and Wenger 1991.

13. Through the twentieth century, however, states were still removing statutes excluding various racially defined groups from the public schools. See Wollenberg 1976 on Chinese exclusion amendments to the California state constitution.

14. Examples are the Campaign for Fiscal Equity, which sued the state of New York, and the *Abbott* lawsuit against the state of New Jersey.

15. The nation's public education system was based originally on an eighteenth-century ideological premise that expanding public schooling to all young, white residents of U.S. states was desirable and necessary. A pervasive ideology stressing the government's "duty" to educate the nation's white youth as future democratic citizens spawned a related discourse on the child's right to go to school (David Tyack, personal conversation with the author, 2004). Public schooling was expanded to non-white citizens in part to acculturate and assimilate a workforce. See Anderson 1988.

16. Chinese American children, even American citizens born in the United States, were intermittently refused publicly funded schools in late nineteenth-century San Francisco, for example, forcing Chinese parents to fund their own private schools. When offered publicly funded schools, the "Chinese" were segregated (Wollenberg 1976).

17. By 1930, "eighty-five percent of Mexican children in the Southwest were attending either separate classrooms or entirely separate schools" (Donato 1997, 13).

18. As Weinberg (1977) documents, Native American children were often forced into residential schools and punished for practicing their cultural traditions, including speaking their native languages.

19. For an early such account, see Woodson 1919.

20. See Donato 1997; Weinberg 1977. As Valencia (2005) notes, Mexican American parents tried for some time to fight segregation by arguing that their children were "white."

21. On Mexican American struggles for equal educational opportunity, see Valencia 2005; on Chinese struggles, see Wollenberg 1976. See Espiritu 1992 on early twentieth-century national origin divisions before the pan-national "Asian" and "Latino" movements of the 1960s. These divisions, Espiritu suggests, were often acts of purposeful "ethnic disidentification" to avoid shared stigma.

22. Although Mexican Americans had argued against segregation through some district court battles before *Brown*, framing segregation as a violation of the Fourteenth Amendment's equal protection logic, federal desegregation logic was codified explicitly around black students. Mexican Americans continued to challenge the treatment of Hispanics via more local court cases as well (Donato 1997, Valencia 2005).

23. Crawford 1995.

24. OCR's analysis of discrimination against ELLs demonstrates how today, OCR's basic definitions of discrimination against students rest on federal legislation, Supreme Court rulings, federal regulations, and policy memos written by various administrations to interpret all these laws and regulations—and each administration's perspective regarding their interpretation and implementation. For example, OCR's basic definitions of discrimination against language-minority students today stem from Title VI's basic prohibition against national origin discrimination; the 1968 Bilingual Education Act, another piece of federal legislation ordering that language-minority students be given specific assistance as students who do not yet know English; the Supreme Court ruling in *Lau v. Nichols* of 1974 (and a key lower court decision *Castaneda v. Pickard*, which ordered that schools both provide English-language learners programmatic assistance and evaluate whether such assistance was working); and the famous May 25, 1970, OCR memorandum interpreting Title VI as arguing that academic services had to be provided for language minorities. OCR's actual work to protect or not protect language-minority children is also guided by current political trends supporting or critiquing bilingual education and political responses to various local English-only movements. See Crawford 1995.

25. "Despite an initial lack of direction, a body of agency law does evolve over time, as the 'expert' agencies define problems, make policy and apply standards to particular cases" (Edwards and Nordin 1980, 39). Edwards and Nordin note that "Congress is empowered to delegate the legislative power necessary for administrative agencies to implement its policies and programs," and they argue that "Congress should limit the discretion it vests in those agencies by precise legislative formulation of its directives to them. . . . Where the legislature specifies in detail the policies to be followed by administrators, agencies will be properly limited to 'filling in the details' of congressional directives." See also Edley 1990.

26. As Halpern (1995, 285) writes, "Depending upon how OCR officials chose to use their discretion, they could either maximize the impact of Title VI or neutralize the provision."

27. According to Bunch and Mindle (1993), "on more than one occasion Congress enacted legislation to express its displeasure with OCR's behavior, restricting OCR's capacity to mandate school busing for purposes of racial desegregation . . . forbidding deferral of federal funding for new programs to school districts suspected of racial discrimination, [and] reassigning half of OCR's enforcement personnel to the investigation of Northern discrimination."

28. See Orfield 1978. From the mid-1960s through the early 1970s, especially after the Supreme Court cases *Green* (1968) and *Swann* (1971) ordered the nation's school districts to dismantle their segregated systems, OCR played an active role in desegregating Southern school districts by launching investigations into enrollment practices and threatening to cut off federal funding. Southern districts fumed at the imposition of federal control and particularly resisted busing. "In numerous instances, the threat of Congressional opposition was sufficient to prompt OCR to back down" (Bunch and Mindle 1993). Rebell and Block (1985) note that in the early years of the Nixon administration, OCR purposefully turned its attention to Northern rather than Southern desegregation, before discontinuing its desegregation work altogether.

29. Orfield 1978; Panetta 1971. Congress, under Carter, would later stop OCR from enforcing busing as a desegregation remedy, by forcing OCR to refer such cases to the Justice Department (which did not enforce either) (Halpern 1995, 154).

30. 356 F. Supp. 92 (D.D.C. 1973).

31. Bartolomeo 2004.

32. Halpern (1995) argues that over several decades, the *Adams* litigation ironically focused OCR's efforts on managerial efficiency rather than thorough enforcement.

33. Orfield 1978; Rebell and Block 1985. Orfield (2000) argues that Nixon also pushed the office toward investigating English services for language minorities in the de facto segregated North primarily to take the office's focus away from Southern desegregation.

34. Rebell and Block 1985, 68.

35. Ibid. See also Orfield 1978.

36. Halpern 1995. Rabkin (1989) argues that after *Adams*, OCR was "Forced . . . to devote the bulk of its resources to processing complaints. By the late 1970s, the agency's offices expended from 70 to 80 percent of their manpower on the processing of individual complaints, and this proportion rose still higher in the 1980s" (168).

37. Bunch and Mindle 1993, 5.

38. Ibid.

39. Bunch and Mindle 1993, 6.

40. Rabkin 1989, 169. One regional director told a group in our office that the biggest issue numerically in their complaints was FAPE, the "free and appropriate public education" that federal regulations have deemed a civil right of students labeled "disabled," even though informally their own "biggest

concern" regionally was ongoing civil rights violations against "ELL kids (LEP kids)." Our own regional office director estimated that our office received just four complaints a year on behalf of English-language learners, while a "huge percentage of OCR complaints are disability."

41. Bunch and Mindle 1993. Rabkin (1989) notes similarly, "The fact remains that OCR's preoccupation with complaint investigation shifted the great bulk of its efforts to just those constituencies which were already most sophisticated about their rights and already best situated to assert their claims without direct enforcement assistance from OCR" (169).

42. As Orfield remarks, civil rights laws are only as effective as those wielding them choose to make them: "The Civil Rights Act makes serious civil rights enforcement possible in American education, but it only works effectively when the executive branch is committed to full implementation and when this standard is supported by the courts. Unfortunately, since 1986 the enforcement process has been under severe political attack and during twenty of those years the White House has been occupied by some of the attackers" (2000, 128).

43. As an *Education Week* article on OCR assistant secretary appointments noted in September 2001, politics have long seemed paramount in selecting an assistant secretary: "Since the creation of the Education Department in 1980, the two Democratic presidents to serve in that time have appointed lawyers with long experience in civil rights litigation or enforcement to fill the important position of assistant secretary for civil rights. The three Republican presidents, meanwhile, have tended to nominate lawyers with solid conservative political credentials, including a young Clarence Thomas, but without extensive experience in civil rights law" (Walsh 2001). In 2001, Bill Taylor, vice chairman of the Leadership Conference on Civil Rights, critiqued George W. Bush's choice of Gerry Reynolds more explicitly: "We now have some evidence that the Department of Education is a parking place or a dumping ground for ideological right-wingers" (Schemo 2001).

44. Walsh (2001) wrote summatively that "Counting Mr. [Gerry] Reynolds, all five OCR chiefs nominated by Republican presidents have been African-Americans without substantial ties to traditional civil rights groups" (30).

45. In an interview with the National Education Association, Norma Cantu, the assistant secretary in the Clinton administration, explicitly critiqued her "predecessor under the Bush administration" for "imagining that race-targeted scholarships were a major civil rights problem for white students" (Weiss 1994).

46. Orfield 2000, 113, 126.

47. Norma Cantu, interview by the author, Cambridge, MA, March 24, 2005.

48. Weiss 1994.

49. Pell 1997.

50. The remainder filed were complaints of age discrimination (2 percent), complaints where people alleged multiple forms of discrimination (nearly 15 percent), and complaints filed on issues over which OCR did not have jurisdiction.

51. Majority Staff of the Committee on Education and Labor 1988, 4.

52. See http://www.onpointradio.org/shows/2004/12/20041214_a_main.asp. This general distaste for disparate impact analysis was widespread. In the *Sandoval* case, the Supreme Court made such analysis under Title VI impossible as a legal strategy. As Ryan (2003) argues, OCR became the *only* place where such analysis was and still is technically allowed in education, despite higher-ups' discouragement of its use.

53. Greenberger 2004. Lawyers from advocacy groups such as the NAACP, MALDEF, the NWLC, the ACLU, disability advocacy groups, and, more recently, advocacy groups opposed to affirmative action, such as the Center for Equal Opportunity, still file complaints at OCR and make clear in their public comments that they know the definitions of academic discrimination employed by the agency shift in the political winds. The NAACP widely criticized OCR's "race-neutral approaches" document, pointing out that the document fundamentally misled districts on the Supreme Court's actual approval of race-conscious, non-quota-based affirmative action policies serving to create diversity in student enrollment. Conversely, as *Education Week* reported, observers who opposed race-conscious approaches described the "Race-Neutral Approaches" document as simply an "empirical" document finally defining racial discrimination correctly (Davis 2004).

54. http://www.ed.gov/about/offices/list/ocr/docs/ocrcrm.html#I_6 (accessed October 18, 2006).

55. Cavanagh 2004.

56. As a report from the U.S. Commission on Civil Rights (2004) noted with concern, the Bush administration actively left vacant, during Bush's first term, the assistant secretary position and two other key positions within OCR, apparently in an effort to shift agency policy without risking controversial confirmation hearings.

57. NAACP 2005, 10.

58. Davis 2004.

59. See http://www.ed.gov/policy/rights/guid/ocr/boyscouts.html (accessed August 8, 2004). The Web site provided links for readers to file complaints with OCR regarding the new Boy Scouts of America Equal Access Act, which contends that schools receiving federal funds must allow the Boy Scouts and other patriotic groups to meet on their premises. Discrimination against "patriotic" groups was defined largely as exclusion from public school meeting space, which has been some school administrators' response to the fact that the Boy Scouts themselves exclude gay youth. Since January 2002, OCR has been mandated to enforce this act, since it was lodged in Bush's No Child Left Behind (NCLB) education bill of 2001. (The link to the full text of the Boy Scouts act is http://www.ed.gov/policy/elsec/leg/esea02/pg112.html#sec9525.) The OCR Web site pointed to additional, less often discussed administration priorities lodged in NCLB. For example, NCLB prohibited districts or schools receiving the act's funding from offering contraceptives (SEC. 9526) and mandated that secondary schools receiving funding allow military recruiters to access students' names, addresses, and telephone listings (SEC. 9528).

60. Goring 2000.

61. U.S. Commission on Civil Rights 2004, 23. See http://www.ed.gov/offices/OCR/archives/pdf/TestingResource.pdf (accessed August 9, 2004).

62. For the "Topics A to Z" list, see http://www.ed.gov/about/offices/list/ocr/topics.html?src=rt.

63. On similar examples nationwide, see Tyson 2008; Mickelson and Cousins 2008; Rubin 2008.

64. For a similar argument, see Cohen, Raudenbush, and Ball 2003.

65. See Fryer and Leavitt 2004; Farkas 2003. Farkas suggests that analysis of tracking's causation is central to analyses of racial discrimination in education, although he uses a rather reductive definition of "discrimination" in education (i.e., teacher prejudice). The *Abbott v. Burke* case in New Jersey directly tackled inequity in preschool access by ensuring universal preschool in the state's predominantly low-income, of-color districts.

66. In a report after the symposium, I noted that research "demonstrates that students tracked into low 'ability' groups rarely make it back to desired levels of achievement; low 'ability' tracking in the early elementary grades usually begins a pattern of skills and content denial that accumulates for children's schooling careers."

67. OCR's high school tracking investigations had themselves been a response to complaints filed in the mid-1990s that critiqued university affirmative action as a form of race-based preference. Investigating high school tracking was one way for OCR to examine whether opportunities to prepare for college application were inequitably distributed along racial lines. Under Cantu, OCR had launched some "compliance review" investigations in school districts to examine the tracking of what it called "underrepresented minority students" at the high school level. These reviews had shown that critiquing unequal tracking demographics at the high school level was too little, too late. Preventing racially biased patterns in high school class placement seemed to require attention to equal opportunities in the early elementary years, when students' academic trajectories are formed.

68. See also Ryan 2006.

69. Colleagues often brought up the work of David Armor, a key research consultant whom defendants employed in court cases to provide evidence that disparities were socioeconomically based rather than racial.

70. Office for Civil Rights 1996, pp. 5–6.

71. NCLB prescribed so much testing and such stringent requirements for improvement in test scores as to greatly influence the lives of local teachers and students.

72. Beyond narrowing academic opportunity provision to test preparation, NCLB's standardized testing requirements, as Losen (2004) and McNeil (2005) have each argued, often have led states and districts to exclude students from the ranks of those tested (leading them to drop out), or simply to lower the state standard so that all groups pass.

73. *Education Week* reported on the controversy over this inconsistency: "As President Bush debated Sen. John Kerry of Massachusetts, his Democratic opponent for the White House, in their final campaign face-off last week, he told

the audience, 'Reading is the new civil right.' " But a draft report posted on the Web site of the U.S. Commission on Civil Rights compiles a laundry list of concerns about the administration's civil rights record on education. The controversial draft calls the No Child Left Behind Act flawed in its ability to close the achievement gap and says it will "inhibit equal education opportunity" (M. Davis 2004).

74. Losen 2004.

75. See OCR's main Web site at http://www.ed.gov/about/offices/list/ocr/index.html.

76. This administrator explained to me contradictorily that while he believed that new ideas should be pushed forward to become OCR policy "before the new administration comes in," it was more pragmatic to be silent about new framings of harm, since there was "a danger that a new administration would take all the immediately controversial stuff and trash it." As one supervisor put it to me bluntly in the summer of 2000, "the message" about the "transition federally" was to act "under the radar—this is not a time to be controversial."

77. Moses 2001; Oakes and Rogers 2006.

78. Loewen (1982) argues, "Once a right has been declared, someone deprived of that right does not have to prove, through some kind of social science reasoning, that the deprivation caused measurable injury" (8).

REBUTTAL FOUR
Harms to Children of Color Are Too "Small" to Fix

1. Payne 1984, 38.

2. Bonilla-Silva 2003b, 272. See also Feagin, Vera, and Batur 2001.

3. See, e.g., Kozol 2005.

4. Essed (2002) and Young (1990) offer, respectively, empirical and philosophical analyses of the "everyday" production of "structural" inequality by "well-meaning people." Essed frames "everyday racism" as the re-creation of "structures of racial and ethnic inequality through situated practices" normalized in everyday life (18). Young writes that today, the concept of "oppression" can "[designate] the disadvantage and injustice some people suffer not because a tyrannical power coerces them, but because of the everyday practices of a well-intentioned liberal society . . . in short, the normal processes of everyday life" (41). Given this, Young adds, "We cannot eliminate this structural oppression by getting rid of the rulers or making some new laws" (41). See also Feagin 2000, chapter 5.

5. On the dismissal of everyday harms they call "microaggressions," see also Solórzano and Carroll 2002; Solórzano, Ceja, and Yosso, 2000.

6. Historian and educational theorist Carter Woodson argued in 1933 that daily educational interactions in environments controlled by white educators, particularly the choice and discussion of curriculum, excluded "Negro" stu-

dents from full knowledge of their past and potential contributions (1972 [1933]). As the NAACP pressed for integration, in 1935, W.E.B. Du Bois suggested that what happened inside schools was paramount: "The Negro needs neither segregated schools nor mixed schools. What he needs is an education" (1935, 335).

7. See powell 2002 for discussion.

8. Bell 1995b, 10. By pushing changes in student placement "without regard to the educational effect of such assignments" on students' daily lives, Bell argues, "court orders mandating racial balance may be (depending on the circumstances) educationally advantageous, irrelevant, or even *disadvantageous*" (1995b, 8). This argument was made repeatedly about *Brown* during its fiftieth anniversary year. While some contended that desegregation was given too little time to work, others argued that racism followed black children to schools staffed by white educators and that black educators were essentially pushed out of the role of educating and socializing black students. Evidence of academic and disciplinary disparities inside desegregated schools has borne out Bell's predictions, even while research shows that desegregation has often succeeded in distributing educational opportunity far more equitably to students of color than segregated schools now do. Many schools have also resegregated along suburban/urban lines, and within districts released from desegregation orders (Orfield and Eaton 1996). "Statement of American Social Scientists of Research on School Desegregation," a brief prepared by the Civil Rights Project at Harvard University in 2006 and designed to be used in that year's Supreme Court challenges to voluntary K–12 desegregation programs, amassed hundreds of research examples showing desegregation's basic successes at distributing resources, learning opportunities, and social networking opportunities more equally to students of color while dismantling concentrations of student poverty. I signed the brief as a supportive researcher.

9. Powell 2002; Mickelson 2005; Perry 2002. See also the essays in Pollock 2008.

10. Cohen, Raudenbush, and Ball 2003.

11. See Farkas 2003 for this critique of discrimination analysis in education more generally.

12. One former OCR official put it this way to a reporter for *Education Week*: "It's one of the most difficult jobs because everybody hates you. You're not doing enough, or you're doing too much" (Hoff 1997).

13. Bunch and Mindle 1993, 9. Halpern (1995) also critiques OCR's focus on "insignificant complaints" rather than compliance reviews (285).

14. For discussion of flaws in this process as applied, see Losen and Orfield 2002; Hehir 2005. Section 504 regulations provide the concept of the "free appropriate public education" (FAPE) as the "handicapped" student's legal right, defining a FAPE as a no-charge education that is "appropriate" in its individualized plans to meet a particular student's academic needs. The Section 504 regulations read that "the provision of an appropriate education is the provision of regular or special education and related aids and services" that are specifically "designed to meet individual educational needs of handicapped per-

sons as adequately as the needs of nonhandicapped persons are met" (104.33 34 CFR Ch. 1, 7–1-98 edition, 344).

15. As Hirschman (1991, 45) suggests more generally, analytic pessimism produces diminished will: "As long as the social world moves at all in response to human action for change, even if in the wrong direction, hope remains that it can somehow be steered correctly. But the demonstration or discovery that such action is incapable of 'making a dent' at all leaves the promoters of change humiliated, demoralized, in doubt about the meaning and true motive of their endeavors."

16. In this sense, OCR would be considered classically bureaucratic. For a foundational framing of bureaucracy's mania for detail, see Weber 1947.

17. Pell 1997.

18. As one spokesperson for a school district told a reporter for *Education Week* regarding serving English-language learners, "We have a pretty fundamental disagreement [with the OCR] about who ought to be served and whether teachers and principals can use their professional judgment" (Walsh 1998).

19. One complainant, for example, alleged that disabled students in his son's district were discriminated against by a bus schedule that got them to school minutes later than other students and by the superintendent's failure to attend graduation at the district's school for the "disabled" while attending those at other schools. Accordingly, my task to assess equal opportunity was to count the minutes of instruction nondisabled students received and the number of times the superintendent had attended other graduations. OCR was the only place that would count many everyday interactions. As a colleague put it to me about this case, "Usually, school suits come here because there are no damages to be awarded, so private lawyers would never take it . . . for education, we are 'the freebie'—and who else would take on issues of whether a superintendent went to the disabled kid's graduation like the other graduations? There's no money in that!"

20. Office for Civil Rights 1991, p. 7. In many courts today, similarly, most "discrimination claims . . . are individual disparate treatment cases" (Sullivan, Zimmer, and White 2002, 61). See also Halpern 1995 for discussion of how OCR has been critiqued for decades for addressing discrimination complaint by complaint instead of through compliance reviews.

21. Office for Civil Rights 1993, p. 10. See also Office for Civil Rights 1994, p. 12, and http://www.ed.gov/about/offices/list/ocr/strategic2000.html.

22. Orfield (1978) critiques OCR for dropping the large-scale project of desegregating the nation's schools beginning in the 1970s.

23. See Rebell and Block 1985, chapter 6. By 1980, the Department of Education's annual report to Congress similarly focused on "within-school segregation": "OCR has increasingly encountered situations in which overall school integration masks discriminatory student assignments on the basis of race, national origin, handicap, and/or sex. Involved are not only discriminatory assignments to classrooms, but also courses of study, special education programs, classes for the educable mentally retarded, and extracurricular activities" (73). "There are strong indications that within-school segregation is

a national problem. Both Hispanics and blacks, for example, are disproportionately educated in schools which use 'ability grouping', and both groups are vastly overrepresented in the 'low ability' groups at these schools. One of every three Hispanic children in schools using ability grouping is in these groups, compared to one of seven similarly situated Anglo children" (U.S. Department of Education 1980, 73).

24. Orfield 1978, 315.

25. Rebell and Block 1985, 67.

26. Bell has suggested that similarly, pursuing desegregation in lieu of everyday opportunity equalization failed "to encompass the complexity of achieving equal educational opportunity for children to whom it so long has been denied" (1995b, 7). Bell paraphrased colleague LeRoy Clark, who argued in 1975 that civil rights lawyers had simply become falsely confident through cases "in which the conflict involved easily identifiable adversaries, a limited number of variables, and issues that courts could resolve in a manageable way" (1995b, 18). Clark, J., *Calhoun v. Cook*, 522 F. 2d 717, 718 (5th Cir. 1975), cited in Bell 1995b, 18.

27. Many disability cases were resolved early, thus resulting in no "finding" of discrimination, but Bunch and Mindle's analysis would apply to complaints going to full investigation and resolution, as well.

> Today, roughly eighty percent of OCR's resources are devoted to complaint investigations, resulting in a finding of "no violation" more than 57% of the time, an utterly inefficient allocation of agency resources. At the behest of the judiciary, OCR became a small claims court for civil rights, an agency whose primary activity (complaint investigations) is of no consequence more than half the time; and even when it is, the scope of most complaints is so limited that fewer Americans now benefit from the violations it corrects. (1993, 9)

28. Office for Civil Rights 1992 (published 1993), p. ii.

29. See also Guinier 2004; Lenhardt 2004; Lawrence 1987; Freeman 1978; Crenshaw 1997, 1988; Bell 1995b; Krieger 1995.

30. Higher-ups have also narrowed the "scope" of investigations more indirectly. As a congressional panel found in the 1980s, when Reagan "narrowed" the time OCR was allowed to take to investigate a case from 195 days to 105, this policy move narrowed the scope of potential issues that could or would be uncovered. "As a consequence . . . OCR regional office staff indicated that the scope of issues for investigation is being narrowed" (Majority Staff of the Committee on Education and Labor 1988, 4).

31. Pell (1997), a former OCR employee in the Reagan administration, labels any efforts at going beyond "particular instances of harassment" to improve the environment of an educational institution "activism." He mocks some Title VI efforts through which OCR offered technical assistance to schools and districts attempting to change their hostile climates as fostering the "trickle-clown [*sic*] of higher education's diversity industry into the lower schools."

32. Taylor 1986.

33. Cowan 2005. Cowan quoted a longtime teacher-administrator as saying, "The focus of the administration changed . . . from asking the question, 'What's

best for the child?' to asking, 'What is our minimal requirement under the law?'"

34. Taylor (1986) argues that legal habits actively minimize remedies for racial discrimination in particular: "Such axioms may indeed furnish useful guidance in cases involving individual victims and perpetrators, discrete violations and easily identifiable consequences of the violations. But how does one match remedy to the scope of a violation consisting of the creation of a state-enforced caste system, where the wrong subjected a whole class of people to conditions of isolation and deprivation for more than three centuries?" (1717). Eaton, Feldman, and Kirby (1996) argue that remedies that gave state-sponsored compensatory funding to segregated school districts rather than desegregate them after the Milliken II decision in 1977 essentially violated the legal axiom of righting the wrong: "It appears that the primary function of the remedies is not 'to restore victims of discriminatory conduct to the position they would have occupied in the absence of such conduct,' but, rather, to serve as a way for school districts and states to sustain a temporary and superficial punishment for discrimination" (145).

35. An OCR lawyer at the Early Learning conference put up on the overhead projector a Venn diagram demonstrating the intersection of the concepts "equal," "effective," and "equitable" and summed up, "OCR is on the strongest ground with equal—but giving all kids exactly the same thing isn't necessarily equitable or effective." In classrooms, of course, providing identical resources or minutes of attention for each child does not necessarily provide resources enabling all students equally to succeed, since children (as group members and as individuals) sometimes need different resources or attention in order to succeed similarly (Abu El-Haj 2006). As a colleague standing in a paper-filled office in the Education Department's D.C. research wing commented, "equitable could mean equally mediocre." The Early Learning Project made clear, however, that even identical academic treatment for young students of color would be a huge advance past current opportunity denials.

36. Halpern 1995.

37. Observers of legal efforts often point out the slow pace of legally oriented change. Bell (1995b) argues that in the aftermath of *Brown*, lawyers were learning that "in most cases, that goal [obtaining compliance with *Brown* as soon as possible] would not be realized before the named plaintiffs had graduated or left the school system" (7).

38. Daniel Losen, Harvard Civil Rights Project, personal conversation with the author, fall 2004. For a similar argument, see Halpern 1995, e.g., p. 321.

39. Others have noted that through various forms of such "processing," bureaucracies can end up slowing rather than facilitating civil rights efforts. Valencia (2005, 412) argues that after various lower court decisions to desegregate Texas school districts serving Mexican Americans in the 1940s and 1950s, refusals to comply were in part abetted by "a complex bureaucratic system of grievances and redress."

40. Karabel (2005) writes that even some of the civil rights changes now most seen as fundamental—the implementation of affirmative action in higher

education, for example—were mollifying handouts designed by government to avoid the deep revolutions of the 1960s. My colleague Reba described such government actions as "designed to let the government display it is doing *something*" and called them tantamount to "lifting the lid to let a little steam out of a boiling pot." Winant (2004) argues that "the state" is "incapable of more than palliative antiracist action" (23).

41. Many of the arguments about OCR's misguided, "small" efforts explored in this chapter are perfect examples of what Hirschman (1991) calls the "futility" thesis: the argument that "in one way or another any alleged change is, was, or will be largely surface, façade, cosmetic, hence illusory, as the 'deep' structures of society remain wholly untouched" (43). "Futility" arguments, Hirschman notes, can be "self-fulfilling," as the changes derided often get "outright abandon[ed]." At other times, they can prompt "more determined, and better informed efforts at achieving real change" (78). In the arguments explored here, people typically risked abandoning the changes they derided.

42. Dolby 2003, 268. Dolby, arguing that scholars should recognize the potentially transformative power of youths' creation and employment of popular culture, suggests that "radical democratic theories, in contrast to . . . liberal theories . . . explode the idea that electoral politics is the only site of agency and power within society. Instead, many sites become potential loci of change and transformation, including people's small, often discounted, everyday acts" (268).

43. I have heard this argument personally from legal scholars (Lani Guinier, personal conversation, Cambridge, MA, 2006), sociologists (Bonilla-Silva and Embrick, in Pollock 2008), economists, and others.

44. Rebecca Blank's work on "cumulative discrimination" (2005) demonstrates, crucially, that unequal educational opportunity for students of color aggregates *across generations* and *across social domains* like housing, health, and education, as well as *within single domains* like education (and within "single institutions," like schools). Still, the authors (including Blank herself) of an amicus brief submitted to the Supreme Court in favor of desegregation policies (*Parents Involved in Community Schools v. Seattle District No. 1*, and *Meredith v. Jefferson County Board of Education*) imply dismissively that actual analysis of the accretion of disadvantage within a specific "institution," like a school, is misguided: "We cannot adequately understand the process, or the production of durable racial inequality, more generally, only by examining singular discriminatory episodes or by looking at the practices or procedures of a single institution" (13) ("Brief of the Caucus for Structural Equity as *Amicus Curiae* Supporting Respondents," http://kirwaninstitute.org/publications/ki_pub _docs/Caucus_for_Structural_Equity_Brief.pdf [accessed April 30, 2007]). While I agree that neither "singular discriminatory episodes" nor "practices" inside schools should ever be held to be the singlehanded cause of "durable racial inequality" or educational disadvantage for young people of color in the United States, I contend that *without* analyzing the concrete, actual "practices or procedures of a single institution" like a school or district (*alongside* analyzing the practices or procedures of other institutions, *and* analyzing the accumu-

lation of disadvantage across generations and domains), educators will easily see themselves playing no role at all in the "production" of "racial inequality."

45. The "macro/micro" debate in social science is rife with arguments that daily events and common interactions should not be analyzed as if they matter much to social structure. Cicourel (1981) points out that scholars who study what they call "macro" social structures (such as national patterns of racial inequality) often critique studies of everyday interactions as overly local examples that fail to successfully analyze or link up to larger systems. To Collins, "micro" studies attempt to analyze empirically how real people negotiate "ordinary reality" (1981, 85). Winant (2004, pp. 188–204) calls explicitly for linking "micro" and "macro" analysis of racial inequality.

46. Hirschman (1991) argues that "radical" commentators, like "conservative" ones, "deride attempts at change" and employ the "futility thesis" when denouncing attempts to change anything other than "structures." "Radical reasoning" "has often taken progressives or reformers to task for ignoring basic 'structures' of the social system and for nourishing and propagating illusions about the possibility of introducing, without prior 'fundamental' changes in those structures, this or that 'partial' improvement" (79).

47. In their foundational analyses of racism in *Black Power*, Stokely Carmichael and Charles Hamilton (1967) denounced the reductionism of analyzing interactions between individuals and urged attention to the role of institutional racism in the reproduction of racist systems. Sociologist Stephen Steinberg (2001) contends that too few social scientists since then have followed their advice: "Instead of focusing on the historical and structural processes that reproduce racial inequalities from one generation to the next, discrimination is reduced to the level of discrete acts by discrete individuals." Steinberg notes in passing that a central problem Carmichael and Hamilton had with analyses of individual racism was that those analyses seemed to always rely on a reductive notion of intentionally racist acts. Institutional racism, in contrast, "did not depend on intentional acts of racial animus, but was embedded in established and respected institutions of society." Steinberg continues: "Here was a truly revelatory way of looking at racism, one that avoided the reductionist tendencies within sociology, and that treated racism as a systemic problem that required systemic change. Despite these theoretical advances, the insurgent sociology of the 60s never developed a full-fledged alternative paradigm." Feagin (2000) explicitly merges "individual" and "systemic" analysis to argue that "systemic racism is about everyday experience" (4).

48. Guinier (2004) critiques this focus on intent (and laws' refusal to analyze "structure") when arguing that the legal tools of *Brown* were a "minimalist" approach to measuring and remedying the nation's deep and foundational racism (96). *Brown* falsely "positioned the . . . American race 'problem' as a psychological and interpersonal challenge rather than a structural problem rooted in our economic and political system" (100). Guinier argues that this "minimalist" logic failed at outlining "the massive tasks that still await us: to extirpate a complex system of relationships that have tortured this country from its earliest beginnings and then to refashion a new social and economic order in

its place" (98). Payne (2004) argues similarly that "by mid-century, national discourse about race" codified in the *Brown* opinion "reduced" the definition of discrimination to encompass only intentionally hostile acts against black people by individual racist white people, rather than seeing racial discrimination fully as a "system" of organized unequal treatment and oppression (84). Payne also argues that the *Brown* strategy analytically "reduced" the phenomenon of racism in society (and in education) to mean segregation itself (the "separate"), rather than encompassing the resources systematically given to whites over blacks (the un-"equal") and the deeply ingrained ideological system of white supremacy.

49. For a similar critique of statements that fail to envision possibilities for "everyday" "antiracist" activity, see also Winant 2004, Feagin 2000.

50. "The Shame of the Nation," Monday, October 24, 2005, First Parish Church, Cambridge, MA.

51. In his book, Kozol (2005) crucially describes gross disparities within and between districts, where students of color attend crumbling buildings with exorbitant dropout rates and white students attend schools with gleaming new facilities geared toward college.

52. In their draft contributions to a book I edited on "everyday antiracist" strategies for educators (Pollock 2008), a few contributors first argued that pursuing equality through reorganizing the everyday interactions of schooling was an inherently useless strategy in comparison to social revolution.

53. Solórzano et al. (Solórzano and Carroll 2002; Solórzano, Ceja, and Yosso, 2000) make clear that many observers dismiss the claim that "microaggressions" in educational settings, particularly for middle-class students who have reached higher education, can truly have "devastating" "cumulative effects" on student performance and educational experience as well as on campus climate (72). The authors contend that "even at high levels of accomplishment [i.e., at elite undergraduate universities], where educational conditions might on the surface appear to be equal, inequality and discrimination still exist—albeit in more subtle and hidden forms" (71). Of course, calling harm or inequality of opportunity "subtle and hidden" also contributes to the very dismissals the authors critique.

54. Cicourel (1981) suggests that sociologists should study people's everyday processes of aggregating individual events they experience into claims about larger patterns in their social world. He contends that sociologists themselves often make "macro" claims about social structures while only indirectly referencing the importance of "micro-events" (the interactions of everyday life). Or, conversely, they make claims about "micro-events" while only indirectly referencing the "macro-structures" that are the larger contexts for these events.

55. Cohen 2008 summarizes much research on *subjective inequality* in the following way: "Negatively stereotyped students, such as African Americans and Latinos, are more likely than other students to perceive that they are being treated unfairly. This perception, which can occur regardless of the actual level of bias that exists in the classroom, reinforces disparities in performance between different racial-ethnic groups. My colleagues and I call this subjective

inequality. Group members' perceptions that they are being treated unequally can reinforce objective inequalities between those groups."

56. Edwards and Nordin 1980, 19.

57. Moses 2001, 112. Miller (2001) notes relatedly that "recipients of disrespectful treatment" often seek "to educate the perpetrator about the more general unacceptability of his or her behavior, not merely its unacceptability vis-à-vis the victim" (541).

58. Ewick and Silbey 1998, 192.

59. Psychological research shows that people desire intently to be treated with respect, just as they desire additional resources (Miller 2001, 530–31). Lenhardt (2004), following, in part, Loury (2002), writes of measuring racial harm as equaling stigmatizing and exclusionary treatment that implies the stigmatized person's lesser worth. Political theorist Iris Marion Young (1990) writes, "Rights are not fruitfully conceived as possessions. Rights are relationships, not things; they are institutionally defined rules specifying what people can do in relation to one another. Rights refer to doing more than having, to social relationships that enable or constrain action" (25). Young notes that most political theorists evaluate the fairness only of the distribution of social goods at some end state, rather than evaluating the "processes" along the way that "produce distributive patterns" (28). She argues that while some "static or end-state" evaluations of outcomes of resource distribution are essential ("some distributions must come into question no matter how they came about"), they too rarely are taken as a starting point for evaluating processes of distribution.

60. According to Dewey, who also wrote in chapter 2 of *Democracy and Education* (1916) that "the office of the school environment is to balance the various elements in the social environment and to see to it that each individual gets an opportunity to escape from the limitations of the social group in which he was born," "the immediate and direct concern of an educator is . . . with the situations in which interaction takes place. The individual, who enters as a factor into it is what he is at a given time. It is the other factor, that of objective conditions, which lies to some extent within the possibility of regulation by the educator. . . . [The notion of] 'objective conditions' covers a wide range. It includes what is done by the educator and the way in which it is done, not only in the words spoken but the tone of voice in which they are spoken. It includes equipment, books, apparatus, toys, games played. It includes the materials with which an individual interacts and, most important of all, the total *social* set-up of the situations in which a person is engaged." See Dewey 1963 (1938), 43, 45. I am grateful to Fred Erickson for this reference. Much work within the anthropology and sociology of education has zoomed in as well on the crucial importance of everyday interaction. See Varenne and McDermott 1998; Erickson 2004; Mehan 1996; Thorne 1993; and Fine 1991 for particularly useful examples.

61. Henderson et al. 2007; Lawrence-Lightfoot 2003; Lareau 2003; Diamond and Gomez 2004.

62. On resource use, see Cohen, Raudenbush, and Ball 2003.

63. On policies' impact on instruction, see, e.g., Elmore, Peterson, and McCarthy 1996.

64. On caring relationships, see Siddle Walker and Snarey 2004; Ladson-Billings 1997. Iris Marion Young (1990) argues similarly that "education is primarily a process taking place in a complex context of social relations," rather than a simple system of distributing things (26). Even when material resources or dollars are equivalently distributed to various groups of children, everyday opportunity to succeed may not actually be: "In the cultural context of the United States, male children and female children, working-class children and middle-class children, Black children and white children often do not have equally enabling educational opportunities even when an equivalent amount of resources has been devoted to their education. This does not show that distribution is irrelevant to educational opportunity, only that opportunity has a wider scope than distribution" (26). Young acknowledges that traditional theories of justice do at times imagine distributing "nonmaterial social goods" (16) other than typical goods and services, such as self-esteem, "rights," and opportunities more broadly. Yet, Young argues, such theories of justice still imagine "justice" too narrowly as some equitable distribution of "things" and "material goods," rather than also "the justice of decisionmaking power and procedures" (19–20). Miller (2001) argues similarly from psychological research that people experience injustice in the form of unequal processes (such as not being heard fairly) as well as unequal goods distribution.

65. Young 1990, 26.

66. As Foucault demonstrates in *Discipline and Punish* (1979), the more rules are specified, the more rule-breaking can be identified. Similarly, the more harms to children are specified, the more people can avoid harming them. McClung (1981), a lawyer who was both an attorney for students and a legal consultant to state education agencies, argues that too often, educators know little about the law's specific prohibitions and entitlements: "Education policy in many states and districts continues to be designed and implemented without sufficient sensitivity to the legal rights of students and other affected parties. This in turn generates litigation, more judicially-determined education policy, and further legalization of education. At times education litigation appears to outpace educators' ability to cope—and the result is confusion, frustration and even hostility towards the law" (37). McClung argues that "public education is a field where legal knowledge and preventive practice is especially important because so many of its activities affect the civil rights of students" (42).

67. Labeling and diagnosis were central to Section 504, which outlines federal protections for any "qualified handicapped person" in education, defined by the law as any person with a "physical or mental impairment which substantially limits one or more major life activities," as well as someone with a "record of such an impairment" or even someone "regarded as having such an impairment." Such labels, of course, imply inherent disadvantage; in Title VI cases, we were arguing over whether students of color were being "disadvantaged" because of their race in any given action or situation.

68. Research demonstrates that students of color are disproportionately placed in Special Education classrooms, often mistakenly and in restrictive educational placements, but white parents disproportionately utilize the disabil-

ity services bureaucracy to secure specific academic services for their children, who are more likely to remain "mainstreamed" in "regular" classrooms and receive targeted assistance (Losen and Orfield 2002).

69. Some casework I saw had OCR people investigating where educators placed "ELL" students, such as one example uncovered by a colleague in which a school's "lowest-level ESL kids" and "lowest-performing African American kids" were left to flounder together in low-level reading groups, an academically chaotic situation that harmed both populations. In many other districts, colleagues found numerous illegal academic travesties, such as English-language learners "thrown into mainstream classes without assessments"; many districts admitted that tests designed to gauge students' subject matter knowledge were typically available only in English, making it very difficult to understand what English-language learners really knew about academic subjects such as math or science. In countless cases, my colleagues found that in violation of federal law, no teacher or administrator in a school was identifying whether "LEP" students had English proficiency needs at all. See also Olsen 1995.

70. Of course, Republicans also have daughters. But unlike disability cases, which did not seem collectively controversial at any point while I was around OCR, our office's Title IX gender equity cases, particularly athletics, were often under fire as too proactive in calling for opportunities for girls and women, suggesting that disability work held a special status as uncontroversial in comparison to work on either gender or racial equality of opportunity.

71. Pt. 104, App. A., 34 CFR Ch. 1, 7–1-98 edition, 354. Section 504 regulations clarify that "equally effective" aids, benefits, and services "are not required to produce the identical result or level of achievement for handicapped and nonhandicapped persons," but "must afford handicapped persons equal opportunity to obtain the same results, to gain the same benefit, or to reach the same level of achievement, in the most integrated setting appropriate to the person's needs" (104.4 34 CFR Ch. 1, 7–1-98 edition, 338). The Section 504 regulations decree specifically that "different or separate" benefits and services must not be provided to "handicapped persons" "unless such action is necessary to provide qualified handicapped persons with aid, benefits, or services that are as effective as those provided to others" (104.4, 34 CFR Ch. 1, 7–1-98 edition, 337).

72. In 1996, the U.S. Commission on Civil Rights had found that the public seemed to understand the federal regulations for implementing Section 504 in education, but "OCR staff and officials" themselves had noted "that the general public has little understanding of Title VI in comparison with Section 504" (U.S. Commission on Civil Rights 2004, 16).

73. See 106.41, 34 CFR Ch. 1, 7–1-98 edition, 386.

74. Title IX regulations weigh in on how to measure the "comparability" of services and facilities offered to the sexes, decreeing, for example, that sex-segregated housing provided on campuses must be "proportionate in quantity" as well as "comparable in quality" (106.32, 34 CFR Ch. 1, 7–1-98 edition, 383).

75. These regulations state, for example, that funding formulas will be "presumed unlawfully discriminatory" if they give vocational institutions with greater proportions of minority students than the statewide average a level of per-pupil funding lower than the statewide average. The vocational education appendices also prohibit counselors from promoting or perpetuating stereotypes regarding various vocational programs or from directing students to particular career paths in vocational programs "based upon the student's race, color, national origin, sex, or handicap" (Pt. 100, App. B, CFR Ch. 1, 7–1-98 edition, 322). They argue that the basic fact of "minority or nonminority" student overrepresentation in a vocational program can appear unlawful (Pt. 100, App. B, CFR Ch. 1, 7–1-98 edition, 318).

76. Lareau 2003; Rothstein 2004; Blank 2005.

77. While most of the academics at the early learning symposium critiqued my requested checklist of necessary K–3 opportunities as an activity that inherently prompted reductive or "small" analysis of the full range of opportunities necessary for children, they themselves argued that it was necessary for educators to have a clear and precise list of equal opportunity "standards" toward which to reach.

78. The arguments I discuss in the next section have come not just from my work at OCR but also from talks I have attended by activists attempting to demand resources from their district and state, educators who have tried to detrack their high schools, and students and adults doing "participatory action research" to document racial inequalities in opportunities to learn at their schools.

79. Hochschild and Herk (1990) argue that "to the degree that survey data accurately depict people's views, . . . to whites, racial discrimination has declined almost to the vanishing point; the future of racial equality is promising; and black suffering results as much from individual failings as from external impediments" (319). Hochschild (2004) also points out that black survey respondents downplay harm to Latinos or Asian Americans (11).

80. Guinier 2004.

81. On statistical analysis of learning experiences over time, see Singer and Willett 2003. Tautologically, in her important discussion of "cumulative disadvantage," Blank (2005) reserves the term "cumulative *discrimination*" for the subset of "discriminatory" acts *causing* the cumulative disadvantage. This definition implies that many acts of disadvantaging (implicitly, those not caused by measurable "prejudice"; p. 101) should not be termed "discrimination." Still, Blank urges that rather than simply trying to "causally separate discrimination as one component of disadvantage" (which would require determining which acts inside schools "counted" as "discrimination" and which did not, the very dead-end analysis that stymied us at OCR), analysts instead study *cumulative disadvantage itself* and collect "more and more detailed longitudinal data" on the many interactions occurring in people's lives over "many years" (Blank 2005, 102).

82. Losen and Orfield (2002) argue that "all analysts who attempt to sort out the causes of inequality in U.S. institutions of course face the dilemma that

some of the differences in subtracted control variables are themselves products of other forms of racial discrimination. . . . For example, if a researcher determined that 40 percent of the association between race and shorter life expectancy could be explained by poverty, we have to understand that the poverty in question may be influenced by employment discrimination or be due in part to a second-generational effect of segregated schooling. . . . What happens in school is only a subset of the far more pervasive impact of racial discrimination that affects minority families and their children" (2002, xxii–xxiii; see also Blank 2005).

83. *Parents Involved in Community Schools v. Seattle School District No. 1; Meredith v. Jefferson County Board of Education.*

84. Blank 2005.

85. Dovidio and Gaertner (2005) describe laboratory situations "in which white participants witnessed a staged emergency involving a black or white victim." White "aversive racists," who "do not act in overtly bigoted ways," failed far more often to help black victims than white victims when the participants thought someone else would take care of the emergency. Bobo, Kluegel, and Smith (1997) argue that "laissez-faire" racists "condone" racial inequality.

86. One colleague relayed a classic example in which multiple parents in one district went to the school board to complain about the lack of English-language services for their children and "were ignored" by the board; they then contacted a lawyer and came to OCR. Throughout OCR's attempts to resolve most cases, complainants argued that school and district people were ignoring their attempts to set up meetings, not returning phone calls, or ignoring faxes or letters of complaint sent internally. In the Quail district, the vice principal had responded to the complainant's charge of racial harassment rampant on campus by arguing that diversity training "wouldn't work and would just waste time." Contemporary work at OCR often involved looking at whether educators had received notice of harm to children (especially harassment) and if so, whether (and how, and how quickly) they had responded. At the Early Learning symposium, one OCR lawyer suggested more generally that if those assigned to provide opportunity to children knew that the opportunities provided were inadequate yet did nothing to remedy this, they could possibly be charged with "deliberate indifference." As Krieger (personal conversation with the author, 2004) argues, doing nothing about harmful patterns and practices might indeed be analyzed as discriminatory in legal terms. Loewen argues of previous decades' discrimination laws, "Usually, if an official board has never acted to undo an overly discriminatory past practice, it can still be found to be perpetuating discrimination today" (1982, 12).

87. Philosopher Iris Marion Young argues that "evaluating [endpoint] patterns of [resource] distribution is often an important starting point for questioning about justice. For many issues of social justice, however, what is important is not the particular pattern of distribution at a particular moment, but rather the reproduction of a regular distributive pattern over time" (1990, 29). Yet in urging the analysis of inequality "over time," Young herself distinguishes "isolated acts of isolated individuals" from the "processes" and "flow

of everyday life" (28). The analytic difficulty her statement reveals is considering how acts aggregate into "processes" and "patterns."

88. One district I encountered at OCR convinced me irrevocably of the number of actors involved in opportunity provision. This district had earmarked many thousands of dollars to buy its students computers, yet due to district administrators' failure to actually transfer the computers to schools, the computers had remained unopened in the district warehouse for several years. As I saw as a teacher, student access to computers inside school buildings relies on administrators or librarians deciding to keep computer labs open during lunchtime, or classroom teachers or aides knowing how to turn on computers, log in, and start a word processing program.

89. Ward 2008; Lareau 2003; O'Connor 1997.

90. A panel of academics convened by the National Academy of Sciences (Blank, Dabady, and Citro 2004) on "measuring discrimination" outlined numerous problematic causality arguments that arose in attempts to prove "discrimination" in a complex world of multiple actors. Even audit tests, in which identically qualified people who differ only in face, voice, or name are sent out to see if they will receive obviously different treatment in hunts for jobs or apartments, could be critiqued for overlooking other potential causal factors of the negative treatment. The panel recommended that analysts study both the aggregation of harmful acts over time and "ordinary decision-making processes," rather than only isolated moments of explicit "prejudice," but it admitted that such analysis fell outside the purview of most legal thinking. Still, harm seems clear to the naked eye. In a "Secret Apartheid" campaign, New York City ACORN (Association of Community Organizations for Reform Now) sent black and white testers to New York City schools to request information on programs. White parents were invited to view classes, offered information on "gifted" classes, and told that spaces were available in programs at a much higher rate than were black parents. See http://www.acorn.org/index.php?id=549.

91. See Farkas 2003. Farkas, who defines discrimination in education as some subset of personally "prejudiced" acts on an educator's part, demonstrates the difficulties of knowing conclusively whether such educator acts have 1) occurred or 2) partially caused or even contributed to disparities in discipline or achievement. For an overview of such arguments in educational research triggered by the concept of "discrimination," see Mickelson 2003. Other related disputes over analyzing discrimination in complex systems include the problem of analyzing practices that seem neutral but have unfair effects, and the problem of determining whether disproportionate patterns can serve as evidence of potentially unfair treatment (see, e.g., Oppenheimer 1993; Perry 1991; Lawrence 1987). Employment (hiring, promotions, and firings) provides a similarly complex system for analyzing discrimination. See Sullivan, Zimmer, and White 2002; Krieger 1995. Rebell and Block (1985) indicate that OCR has long been snarled in even more basic disputes over whether, in complex systems, the agency can demand equality of outcome or solely equality of input. Crenshaw (1988), writing on antidiscrimination law more broadly,

critiques legal logic as typically constrained to analyze only racially unequal inputs, which she calls a "restrictive" view of equality. More rare and far preferable, Crenshaw argues, is the kind of legal logic that allows concern over racially equal outcomes (like disparities in achievement) as well, which she calls an "expansive" view. In education, analyzing unequal outcomes is particularly vexed, however, in large part because analyses of causation are so rarely analyses of partial contribution (Pollock 2001).

92. Lucas 2008 also notes the danger of educators having such aggregated statistics in their minds when approaching individual children, as teachers can mentally slot children themselves into the preexisting pattern.

93. Mickelson and Cousins 2008; Hehir 2005; McNeil 2005; Fine 1991. Ethnographic investigations of inequality are typically less interested in quick statements of causation or endpoints than in uncovering the various everyday interactions gradually producing inequality patterns. For a foundational example, see Willis 1977. For other detailed ethnographic analyses of social reproduction, see Varenne and McDermott 1998; Mehan 1996; Moll and Diaz 1993; Thorne 1993; Fine 1991; Page 1991. Still, anthropologists of education also often simply denounce unequal endpoints. Cicourel (1981) suggests that this habit of describing patterns without explaining those patterns' production characterizes much "macro" research in social science; Collins (1981) calls this habit providing "glosses on the underlying reality" (85).

94. Essed 2002, 180.

95. Payne 1984, 9.

96. Ibid., 38, 40.

97. Rothstein (2004) argues that to provide equal educational opportunity, schools must give low-income students access to the physical and social benefits and advantages middle-class students get both inside and outside schools. On working parents and poverty, see Yoshikawa, Weisner, and Lowe 2006.

98. Fryer and Leavitt 2004; Brooks-Gunn and Markman 2005.

99. Of all social scientists, anthropologists of education particularly caution accordingly against reductive explanatory and causal analysis that fails to look at people's ongoing experiences in schools. Some have zoomed in to an exceptional level of detail, with slowed video footage, to show the interactive complexity of the moment-to-moment production of an educational outcome (see Varenne and McDermott 1998; Mehan 1993). Other analysts may try to speed up the tape, yet still examine interactional processes in children's lives.

100. Valenzuela 1999; Heath 1983.

101. Cooper et al. 2004.

102. Valdes 1996.

103. Garcia 2008.

104. Noguera 2008; Ferguson 2000.

105. August and Hakuta 1998.

106. Ferguson 2008; see also Kenschaft 2005.

107. Lareau 2003.

108. Losen and Orfield 2002.

109. Darling-Hammond 1999.

110. Noguera 2008.

111. Moll and Diaz 1993.

112. Analysis of distributed causation not only lowers defenses of the conversation partners (as Stone, Patton, and Heen [2000] assert); it also helps pinpoint how different everyday moves could help undo the pattern. I have found in other research that stressing the reality of distributed responsibility for racial disparities is not just more empirically accurate but also most convincing to those who must make everyday efforts to serve children equitably. Reductive causal accusations tend more often to provoke the "accused" to resist acknowledging playing any part in the production of disparities and to blame other actors exclusively (Pollock 2001).

113. The NAS panel (Blank, Dabady, and Citro 2004) found that controlled experiments, typically conducted using psychological methods, were the only studies successfully isolating specific mechanisms causing discrimination "because of race" in legal terms. If a subject viewed specific photographs of blacks and whites that led directly to an increase in their agreements with stereotyping statements regarding blacks or whites, for example, this increase could be attributed without much worry to the experience with the photographs.

114. Payne 1984, 13. Work at OCR demonstrated that if analysis focuses solely on figuring out which acts singlehandedly cause harm, or on figuring out which actors singlehandedly produce unequal outcomes, taking each in isolation, rather than on pinpointing the full range of acts that together cause harm to children of color, solutions get stalled behind causal analysis.

115. Rowe 1974 uses this image in discussing gender inequality. In law and federal policy guidance on sexual harassment, lawyers talk literally of using the standards of a "reasonable woman" to evaluate whether incidents that occurred to a woman were truly harmful to her. Schultz (2001) argues that framings of sexual harassment in workplaces as equaling only explicitly "sexual conduct" has "deflect[ed] our attention away from arguably more common, non-sexual forms of gender-based hostility" and exclusion: that is, all the behaviors that function in workplaces "to exclude the women or to communicate the message that they are different or inferior." She includes, among such actions, "everyday micro-aggressions—such as excluding the women from social interactions and training, or picking on them constantly."

116. Some academic critics of racism may unintentionally promote this minimizing framing of contemporary discrimination: when Solórzano and colleagues scrutinize "microaggressions" as consequential yet "subtle and hidden" harms, such words suggest "small" harms that are hard to see. See Solórzano, Allen, and Carroll 2002, 71; Solórzano, Ceja, and Yosso 2000. Loewen (1982, 1) notes that in comparison to the first civil rights era, "today . . . the factual situation is subtler." Eduardo Bonilla-Silva (2003b), like Joe Feagin (with McKinney 2003), argues that the "new racism" of today differs from Jim Crow–era racism because "racist" and "discriminatory" acts are now "covert," a framing that also suggests acts are difficult to find.

117. As one colleague noted to me, the relative absence of OCR Title VI complaints against administrators of color could mean that complainants of color

felt less warranted or comfortable filing such complaints, rather than that white administrators were the only ones "discriminating."

## CONCLUSION
Arguing toward Everyday Justice in the New Civil Rights Era

1. Hochschild (2004), for example, sums up "whites' simultaneous endorsement of the norm of [racial] equality *and* rejection of steps that could promote it." To researchers, white people in the post–civil rights era report anxieties and resentments about opportunities they feel have been or will be stolen from them by people of color by means of "civil rights" remedies. Increasing numbers file lawsuits against desegregation plans and affirmative action admissions; others quietly support these suits. On cases challenging voluntary K–12 desegregation plans, see Ryan 2003. See also Civil Rights Project 2006. While not all white people object to equality measures for non-white people, many white Americans say they believe that Americans of color now receive opportunities equal or even superior to their own; they resist, in researchers' presence, analyzing whether advantages still accrue to them as "whites." See Doane and Bonilla-Silva 2003 and Myers 1997 for a sampling of essays analyzing such racial dynamics in what Myers calls the "post Reagan-Bush era." On white Americans' resentment of Americans of color, see also Sears, Sidanius, and Bobo 2000; Lamont 2000a; Bobo and Tuan 2006; Lewis 2003b; McKinney and Feagin 2003; Ditomaso, Parks-Yancy, and Post 2003. Bobo (1988) argues that "whites" in particular tend to disapprove particularly of "specific policies aimed at improving the social and economic position of blacks" (cited in Wells and Crain 1997, 9), yet he also points out (2000) that much research on public opinion has promoted a "distorted view" that whites *monolithically* oppose racialized equalization policies (138). Steeh and Krysan (1996) suggest that (white) Americans would actually support more equal opportunity measures on surveys if those measures were worded more precisely.

2. See Hochschild 2004. Reacting to white perceptions in the post–civil rights era, some public intellectuals and politicians of color oppose civil rights–oriented strategies for ensuring equal opportunity for their own groups in part because, they contend, credit for their achievements may be assigned to such policies rather than to their own efforts and abilities. See Chavez 1996; McWhorter 2000.

3. Scholars assert that among Americans of color, pessimism about attaining equality by legal and bureaucratic means is coupled with a more general despair about the possibility of achieving real equality in collaboration with white Americans. According to Simpson's analysis of African Americans' survey responses, for example, "a fourth of the post–civil rights generation feel that blacks will never achieve racial equality, compared with only a fifth of the civil rights generation" (1998, 20). Using national survey data, Hochschild and

Herk (1990) find similarly that "blacks have become increasingly pessimistic during the past three decades about ending racial prejudice and discrimination, and blacks see much more persistent white racism than whites do" (308); "In the mid-1960s, 55 to 75 percent of blacks anticipated integration and full racial equality sometime in the future. Since the late 1970s, that proportion has dropped to 30 to 45 percent" (317).

4. Ryan 2003.

5. Crenshaw et al. 1995, xvii. See also Siegel 2004 and Balkin and Siegel 2003–4 on "anticlassification" arguments since *Brown* (that is, the argument that the Constitution forbids classifying people racially, even when equalizing opportunities for subordinated minorities). Siegel argues that this argument was not in fact *Brown's* argument but was constructed after *Brown* in response to white resistance to desegregation.

6. In *Grutter v. Bollinger* (02–241) 539 U.S. 306 (2003), Justice Sandra Day O'Connor argued famously that she supported affirmative action policies as a means to diversify school enrollments racially, but she anticipated that such policies would only be necessary (and, implicitly, allowed) for twenty-five years. In his opinion on *Parents Involved in Community Schools v. Seattle School District No. 1* and *Meredith v. Jefferson County Board of Education*, Justice Kennedy similarly suggested a limited support for narrowly tailored "race-conscious" desegregation. Crenshaw et al. (1995) suggest that both policymaking "authorities" and "the American people" have had enough of "civil rights" strategies to equalize opportunity: "The 1990s marks a rejection of the always fragile civil rights consensus and the renunciation . . . by federal, state and city authorities (indeed, the American people themselves) that government not only can but must play an active role in identifying and eradicating racial injustice" (xxxii). Crenshaw et al. observe that a "breakdown of the national consensus for the use of law as an instrument for racial redistribution" began as early as the late 1960s (xvii). Given this resistance, Crenshaw et al. suggest the final decades of the twentieth century might also be called the "Age of Repudiation" (xx). Arguing more generally that African Americans have enjoyed only "shades of freedom" since slavery, Leo Higginbotham wrote in 1996 that "progress toward racial equality has been halting, at best. Instead, the nation often seems to be retreating from the values of a time in which there existed substantial consensus on the need for racial pluralism in positions of power and for the opportunity of upward mobility." Higginbotham agreed with a comment in Justice Blackmun's dissenting opinion in a 1989 civil rights case (*Wards Cove Packing Co. v. Antonio*, 490 U.S. 642, 662): "sadly, . . . one wonders whether the majority [of the Supreme Court justices] still believe that . . . race discrimination against nonwhites is a problem in our society, or even remembers that it ever was' " (vii).

7. See Guinier 2004; Crenshaw et al. 1995; Krieger 1995.

8. Alan Schoenfeld, a civil rights lawyer and one generous reader of this manuscript, warned of this risk of suggesting "precise" analysis of particular necessary opportunities. Schoenfeld cited a "canon of statutory construction" "commonly used in interpreting federal law": the expression *expressio unius est exlusio alterius*, or "the express inclusion of one thing implies the purposeful

exclusion of another." Alan Schoenfeld, personal conversation with the author, May 28, 2007.

9. One regional director of the National Council of Christians and Jews told me of the organization's evolution, in its provision of antiracist trainings, away from the "stand up and own your shit" model, in which the point was for white people to confess their inner racism, preferably while crying and while people of color clapped. The organization had decided over time that this tactic seemed simply to raise the defensiveness of white participants in trainings and did not seem to lead to changes in practice after the trainings, since participants had catharses but still left with no ideas about what to do differently in daily life. Dovidio and Gaertner (2005) argue further that "aversive racists" "will commonly deny any intentional wrongdoing when confronted with evidence of their bias. Indeed, they do not discriminate intentionally." They also argue that "because of its pervasiveness, subtlety, and complexity, the traditional techniques for eliminating bias that have emphasized the immorality of prejudice and illegality of discrimination are not effective for combating aversive racism. Aversive racists recognize prejudice is bad, but they do not recognize that they are prejudiced." Thus, they argue, "abstaining from wrongdoing that is immediately obvious to us is not enough. . . . In order to address contemporary racism, even and especially among well-intentioned people, it is necessary to establish new, positive norms for action that replace our current norms for avoidance of responsibility."

10. Lenhardt (2004) argues similarly that lawyers and courts could take a "harm-based approach," since "formulating the problem in terms of good or bad motives means that people, quite naturally, become preoccupied with demonstrating that they are not inherently racist instead of trying to understand how their behavior might have contributed to racial stigma" (which she defines as acts contributing to social exclusion) (811).

11. Ladson-Billings 1999.

12. Cohen 2008. Cohen calls this "subjective inequality." He demonstrates that students perceiving bias from teachers can underperform. See also Solórzano, Ceja, and Yosso 2000, who argue that since the *experience* of "microaggressions" can depress student performance, "the campus racial climate must continue to be viewed through the lenses of African American and other students of color" (71). Some legal scholars assert that harm is found in part in the victim's experience of exclusion; see Lenhardt 2004.

13. Dovidio and Gaertner (2005) build upon years of psychological experiments to argue that today, white people are *"inconsistently"* "biased" against people of color, leading to a deep "climate of suspicion and distrust" among people of color: "Whereas the subtle nature of contemporary bias leads whites to underestimate the impact of racial prejudice, it leads blacks to be particularly attuned to these inconsistent and unpredictable racist behaviors. This inconsistency erodes blacks' confidence in a person and leads to a spiral of distrust." Dovidio and Gaertner argue that accordingly, a key aspect of antiracist work is diminishing distrust (see also Cohen 2008; Aronson 2008; Tatum 2008). White people can do so, they urge, by "listening deeply" and seriously to claims of racial harm: "So what can we each do about racism when we don't

know what we don't know yet? Here are some simple (but not easy) suggestions for action. When a person of color brings up race as an issue in an interpersonal or organizational setting—listen! If the person indicates he or she is offended, don't be defensive. Instead try to understand the other person's perspective on the issue. Remember your perceptions can be very different from the everyday experience of others. As the data indicate, whites tend to underestimate the impact of discrimination. Do not begin talking quickly, explain why they are misinterpreting the situation, or begin crying. These are some of the most infuriating responses people of color encounter when they challenge a situation that feels wrong. Take time, if you need it, to think about the situation after listening fully to the other person's perspective. If you hear problems third-hand, don't get angry because you were not approached directly. You probably need to talk through the situation at some point, but remember it is almost never completely safe for a person of color to challenge a dominant perception. Listen deeply."

14. Miller 2001, 531.

15. Ibid., 537. Miller suggests the utility of apologies, but adds that "of course, only if the apologies are perceived as sincere will they have the effects just described. When victims perceive apologies to be insincere and designed simply to 'cool them out,' they often react with more rather than less indignation" (538).

16. Ibid., 543.

17. Hochschild and Herk 1990, 316. The authors note that the particularly vast array of caveats white Americans offer when asked their opinions on concrete policies for equal opportunity (though Americans of color sometimes offer such caveats when asked to provide opportunities to "racial" groups other than their own; Hochschild 2004, 2) demonstrate the difficulties of getting them to agree on equality-minded public policy at all: "Even if each person added only a very small number of 'but . . . s' to their global 'yes' to racial equality, the total number and array of 'but . . . s' is formidable indeed" (316).

18. Tyson 2008.

19. Cited in Guinier 2004, 117, emphasis added. Guinier notes that discrimination is not just "differential" treatment in comparison to whites but "demeaning treatment within a racialized hierarchy" (109). Darder and Torres (2003) suggest, as does Guiner, that racial comparisons of harm can sometimes obscure necessary human rights alliances (or class-based ones).

20. Some related yet incomplete arguments have been made by legal scholars. Yoshino (2006) contends that "civil rights must rise into a new, more inclusive register"; "we must shift away from claims that demand equality for particular groups toward claims that demand liberty for us all." The courts are increasingly resistant to claims of rights for particular groups, and "in an increasingly diverse society, the courts must look to what draws us together as citizens rather than to what drives us apart," Yoshino contends. Today, he argues, the courts should protect all individuals' rights as human rights, rather than protect group rights as if they were separate rights for special people. Siegel (2004) argues convincingly that whites resisted *Brown* because it seemed to favor the well-being of blacks over that of whites; Guinier (2004) also argues that the public framing of *Brown* masked the common interests of poor black and white Americans. I suggest retaining analysis of group experience—spe-

cifically, of the experiences of "historically oppressed" and "historically excluded" racial groups (Siegel 2004, 1473) in contemporary schools—but supporting it with analysis of ideal treatment for children generally. Yoshino contends that replacing "civil rights" logic with "human rights" logic is not only legally palatable but also logically sound. Both "Martin Luther King Jr. and Malcolm X [came] to argue for the transition from civil rights to human rights at the ends of their lives. It is time for American law to follow suit." Yoshino describes some movement in this direction, citing recent cases in which the Supreme Court upheld the rights of intimate partners of the same sex and of physically disabled persons not on the basis of group rights to equal treatment but rather on the basis of liberties all Americans share. "In these cases," Yoshino concludes, "the court implicitly acknowledged the national exhaustion with group-based identity politics. . . . By emphasizing the interest all individuals have in our own liberty, the court focused on what unites us rather than on what divides us" (Yoshino 2006, adapted from his book *Covering: The Hidden Assault on Our Civil Rights* [New York: Random House, 2006]).

21. Pollock 2008.

22. Abu El Haj 2006; Pollock 2004a; Pollock 2008.

23. McClung (1981) suggests that "policymakers and their legal counsel" designing new "education policy" ask specific, "preventive" questions about potential "injury" to "any person or persons" and about potential aggregated "injury" to members of groups, such as, "Will the policy cause disproportionate effects among any racial, linguistic, ethnic or other protected minority group?" (39). McClung adds, "Racially disproportionate effects provide the classic trigger for judicial analysis. Such disproportionate effects by themselves usually do not constitute illegal action, but raise the legal issues that need to be evaluated" (39). McClung argues that in school districts, "avoidable conflict" often ends up in legalistic battles over fault and harm: "By the time problems are litigated, . . . the positions have usually polarized and all parties have lost considerable control over the resolution of their differences" (38). Doing "preventive" self-analysis of what acts might harm children and groups can avoid both the social drama of complaints and grievances and their expense. McClung argues that preventive analysis can avoid unnecessary effort as well, since "the time and expense of this kind of preventive legal review is minimal compared to that involved in litigation" (40). Yet as McClung himself notes, such "preventive law assumes a good faith intent, sometimes absent, to design and implement policy consistent with legal requirements" (41).

24. Loewen (1982) writes, "We Americans believe the law is not only an instrument of power wielded disproportionately on behalf of those who already have wealth and prestige but also a route of redress for persons who, owing to their race, sex, poverty, age, or other characteristic, have not been treated fairly" (1). Critical race theorists, while some of the loudest critics of civil rights tools' restrictive nature and use, have also argued that a "rights discourse" has had a "social and transformative value" in the United States and has been central in particular to "African Americans re-imagining themselves as full, rights-bearing citizens within the American political imagination." Critical Race Theory scholars view civil rights law and its remedies as useful even while compromised. Crenshaw et al. "wanted to acknowledge the centrality of rights discourse even as we recognized that the use of rights language was

not without risks" (1995, xxiv). For example, "Critical Race Theory supports affirmative action as a limited approach which has achieved a meaningful, if modest measure of racial justice" (xxx). I came to the same conclusion about civil rights tools after two years at OCR.

25. Despite our disputes about what if anything to do about concrete experiences of inequality, we live in an era when basic ideas about the righteousness of equality of opportunity are shared. Bob Moses, a civil rights activist and the founder of the Algebra Project, suggests optimistically that "in recent years, a real national consensus, on the political left and on the political right, has been emerging that holds that all children can learn, and that all children deserve the best education they can get. And that such an education is absolutely necessary. This is actually a new consensus; it did not exist fifty years ago. . . . Of course, . . . this commitment to making the effort to provide them the opportunity is an ideal that's often given lip service more than real action. . . . But it is a widespread public viewpoint." Moses suggests that this new emerging "consensus" is "something more specific and powerful" than even the basic notion "that young people who grow up in the United States are entitled to free public education, from kindergarten through twelfth grade" (2001, 92–93).

26. Blank 2005, 101. Blank also suggests provocatively that rather than get caught up solely in the task of proving which acts "causing" racially unequal outcomes are "discriminatory," analysts can focus on analyzing, in detail, *processes* of cumulative racial disadvantage by collecting "more and more detailed longitudinal data, following the same individuals . . . for many years" (102). "Expanding the literature on cumulative disadvantage may be necessary before trying to causally separate discrimination as one component of disadvantage," Blank writes (102). Singer and Willett (2003) make clear that longitudinal data (data tracking the same individuals over time) is essential for studying students' educational experiences over time. Often, districts examining test score growth over several years of school reform, for example, fail to actually track the same group of students across those years.

27. While much research has argued that white Americans in particular are unable to see "systemic" or "structural" racial inequality of opportunity today, I suggest that Americans (and particularly those of us who are white) also fail to see or successfully describe how everyday acts by ordinary, well-meaning people play a role in producing inequality patterns locally. Sociologists examining racism in particular have made this argument that white people cannot see "systemic" and "structural" racial inequality (Bonilla-Silva 2003a, 2003b; Feagin, Vera, and Batur 2001; Doane and Bonilla-Silva 2003). Lewis (2003b) argues that white people typically see inequality in terms of "individual" failures, not "structural" inequality of opportunity.

28. Blank 2005.

29. At our Early Learning conference, one academic argued that while OCR should tackle, at the "policy" level, the unequal distribution of credentialed teachers in and between districts as a core aspect of the "uneven distribution of opportunities to learn," "redistributing teachers between schools without addressing conditions within schools won't work."

30. As much contemporary historiography reminds us (e.g., Savage 2000), the roots of the 1950s and 1960s civil rights movement go much deeper into history. Similar struggles for political, legal, and social rights took place in earlier historical periods, such as in the North before the abolition of slavery and in the Reconstruction-era South.

31. Valencia (2005) points out that Americans of Mexican descent have long pushed for equal educational opportunities through five channels: the work of individual activists, advocacy organizations, political demonstrations, legislation, and litigation. See Kluger 1975, Taylor 2004, and Ogletree 2004 on direct struggles over law, and Moses 2001, and Beals 1995 on broader everyday demands for civil rights.

32. On the concept of "everyday activism," particularly "everyday feminists" who put women's movement principles into practice on a daily, informal basis and whose activism is rarely celebrated, see Mansbridge and Flaster 2007.

# Bibliography

Abu El-Haj, Thea Renda. 2006. *Elusive Justice: Wrestling with difference and educational equity in everyday practice.* New York: Routledge.

Almaguer, Tomas. 1994. *Racial Fault Lines: The historical origins of white supremacy in California.* Berkeley: University of California Press.

American Anthropological Association. 1998. AAA statement on "race." *Anthropology Newsletter* (May 17): 1.

Anderson, James. 1988. *The Education of Blacks in the South, 1860–1935.* Chapel Hill: University of North Carolina Press.

Aronson, Joshua. 2008. Knowing students as individuals. In *Everyday Antiracism*, ed. Pollock.

August, Diane, and Kenji Hakuta, eds. 1998. *Educating Language-Minority Children.* Washington, DC: National Academy Press.

Bakhtin, Mikhail. 1981. *The Dialogic Imagination.* Austin: University of Texas Press.

Balkin, Jack M., and Reva B. Siegel. 2003–4. The American civil rights tradition: Anticlassification or antisubordination? *University of Miami Law Review* 58(9): 9–34.

Banaji, Mahzarin. 2001. "Ordinary prejudice": Science briefs. *Psychological Science Agenda* (January–February): 9–11.

Bartolomeo, Christina. 2004. Separate but unequal in higher education. *American Federation of Teachers* (May–June 2004).

Beals, Melba. 1995. *Warriors Don't Cry: A searing memoir of the battle to integrate Little Rock's Central High.* New York: Washington Square Press.

Bell, Derrick A., Jr. 1995a. *Brown v. Board of Education* and the interest convergence dilemma. In *Critical Race Theory*, ed. Crenshaw et al., 20–29.

———. 1995b. Serving two masters: Integration ideals and client interests in school desegregation litigation. In *Critical Race Theory*, ed. Crenshaw et al., 5–19.

———. 1992. *Faces at the Bottom of the Well: The permanence of racism.* New York: Basic Books.

Blank, Rebecca M. 2005. Tracing the economic impact of cumulative discrimination. *American Economic Review* 95(2): 99–103.

Blank, Rebecca M., Marilyn Dabady, and Constance F. Citro, eds. 2004. *National Research Council panel on methods for assessing discrimination.* Washington, DC: National Academies Press.

Blumer, Herbert. 1969. *Symbolic Interactionism: Perspective and method.* Upper Saddle River, NJ: Prentice-Hall.

Bobo, Lawrence. 2000. Race and beliefs about affirmative action: Assessing the effects of interests, group threat, ideology, and racism. In *Racialized Politics: The debate about racism in America*, ed. David O. Sears, Jim Sidanius, and Lawrence Bobo. Chicago: University of Chicago Press.

Bobo, Lawrence. 1997. Race, public opinion, and the social sphere. *Public Opinion Quarterly* 61(1): 1–15.

Bobo, Lawrence. 1988. Group conflict, prejudice, and the paradox of contemporary racial attitudes. In *Eliminating Racism: Profiles in Controversy*, ed. Phyllis A. Katz and Dalmas A. Taylor. New York: Plenum.

Bobo, Lawrence, and Mia Tuan. 2006. *Prejudice in Politics: Group position, public opinion, and the Wisconsin treaty rights dispute*. Cambridge, MA: Harvard University Press.

Bobo, Lawrence, James Kluegel, and Ryan Smith. 1997. Laissez-faire racism: The crystallization of a kinder, gentler, antiblack approach. In *Racial Attitudes in the 1990s: Continuity and change*, ed. Stephen Tuch and Jack K. Martin. Westport, CT: Praeger.

Bonilla-Silva, Eduardo. 2003a. *Racism without Racists: Color-blind racism and the persistence of racial inequality in the United States*. Lanham, MD: Rowman and Littlefield.

———. 2003b. "New racism," color-blind racism, and the future of whiteness in America. In *White Out*, ed. Doane and Bonilla-Silva, 271–84.

———. 1997. Rethinking racism: Toward a structural interpretation. *American Sociological Review* 62(3): 465–80.

Bonilla-Silva, Eduardo, and David G. Embrick. 2008. Recognizing the likelihood of reproducing racism. In *Everyday Antiracism*, ed. Pollock.

Brayboy, Bryan McKinley Jones. 2005. A policy and legal examination of a legal challenge to a federally funded American Indian teacher training program. Paper presented at the annual meeting of the American Anthropological Association, Washington, DC, December 1.

Brooks-Gunn, Jeanne, and Lisa B. Markman. 2005. The contribution of parenting to ethnic and racial gaps in school readiness. *The Future of Children* 15(1): 139–68.

Bunch, Kenyon D., and Grant B. Mindle. 1993. Judicial activism and the administration of civil rights policy. *BYU Education and Law Journal* (Spring). http://www.law2.byu.edu/jel/index.php?page=archives_1993&subof=archives (accessed fall 2004).

Carmichael, Stokely, and Charles V. Hamilton. 1967. *Black Power*. New York: Vintage Books.

Cashin, Sheryll. 2004. *The Failures of Integration: How race and class are undermining the American dream*. New York: Public Affairs Books.

Cavanagh, Sean. 2004. Title of federal civil rights official questioned. *Education Week* (April 21).

Chavez, Linda. 1996. Promoting racial harmony. In *The Affirmative Action Debate*, ed. George E. Curry. Reading, MA: Addison-Wesley.

Cicourel, Aaron V. 1981. Notes on the integration of micro and macro levels of analysis. In *Advances in Social Theory and Methodology: Toward an integration of micro- and macro-sociologies*, ed. Karin Knorr-Cetina and Aaron V. Cicourel, 51–80. Boston: Routledge and Kegan Paul.

Civil Rights Project, Harvard University. 2006. Statement of American social scientists of research on school desegregation. http://www.civilrightsproject.harvard.edu/news/pressreleases/amicus_brief-10–10–06 .php (accessed November 2006).

Cohen, Geoffrey L. 2008. Providing supportive feedback. In *Everyday Antiracism*, ed. Pollock.

Cohen, David K., Stephen W. Raudenbush, and Deborah Loewenberg Ball. 2003. Resources, instruction, and research. *Educational Evaluation and Policy Analysis* 25(2): 119–42.

Collier, Jane, and Bill Maurer, eds. 1995. *Sanctioned Identities*. Special issue of *Identities: Global studies in culture and power* 2(1–2).

Collins, Randall. 1981. Micro-translation as a theory-building strategy. In *Advances in Social Theory and Methodology: Toward an integration of micro- and macro-sociologies*, ed. Karin Knorr-Cetina and Aaron V. Cicourel, 81–107. Boston: Routledge and Kegan Paul.

Commission on Civil Rights. 1975. *The Federal Civil Rights Enforcement Effort, 1974*. vol. 3, *To Ensure Equal Educational Opportunity: A Report of the Commission on Civil Rights*. January 1975.

Cooper, Catherine R., Jane Brown, Margarita Azmitia, and Gabriela Chavira. 2004. Including Latino immigrant families, schools, and community programs as research partners on the good path of life (*el buen camino de la vida*). In *Discovering Successful Pathways in Children's Development*, ed. Weisner, 359–85.

Cose, Ellis. 1997. *Colorblind: Seeing beyond race in a race-obsessed world*. New York: HarperCollins.

Cover, Robert M. 1980–81. The uses of jurisdictional redundancy: Interest, ideology, and innovation. *William and Mary Law Review* 22:639–82.

Cowan, Alison Leigh. 2005. Amid affluence, a struggle over special education. *New York Times*, April 24.

Crawford, James. 2007. A diminished vision of civil rights: No Child Left Behind and the growing divide in how educational equity is understood. *Education Week* 26(39): 40.

———. 1995. *Bilingual Education: History, politics, theory, and practice*. 3rd ed. Los Angeles: Bilingual Educational Services, Inc.

Crenshaw, Kimberle Williams. 1997. Color-blind dreams and racial nightmares: Reconfiguring racism in the post–civil rights era. In *Birth of a Nation'hood: Gaze, script, and spectacle in the O.J. Simpson Case*, ed. Toni Morrison and Claudia Brodsky Lacour, 97–168. New York: Pantheon Books.

———. 1988. Race, reform, and retrenchment: Transformation and legitimation in antidiscrimination law. *Harvard Law Review* 101:1331–87.

Crenshaw, Kimberle Williams, Neil Gotanda, Gary Peller, and Kendall Thomas, eds. 1995. *Critical Race Theory: The key writings that formed the movement*. New York: New Press.

Darder, Antonia, and Rodolfo D. Torres. 2003. Shattering the "race" lens: Toward a critical theory of racism. In *The Critical Pedagogy Reader*, ed. Antonia Darder, Marta Baltodano, and Rodolfo D. Torres, 245–61. London: RoutledgeFalmer.

Darity, William, Domini Castellino, Karolyn Tyson, Carolyn Cobb, and Brad McMillen. 2001. Increasing opportunity to learn via access to rigorous courses and programs: One strategy for closing the achievement gap for at-risk and minority students. Report prepared for the North Carolina Department of Public Instruction, Evaluation Section, Raleigh, N.C. http://www.ncpublicschools.org/docs/racg/resources/increasingopportunities.pdf (accessed October 17, 2007).

Darling-Hammond, Linda. 1999. Race, education, and equal opportunity. In *The African American Predicament*, ed. Christopher H. Foreman, 71–81. Washington, DC: Brookings Institution Press.

———. 1997. *The Right to Learn: A blueprint for creating schools that work.* San Francisco: Jossey-Bass.

Davis, K. C. 1978. *Administrative Law Treatise.* 2nd ed. Vol. 1. San Diego: K. C. Davis Publishing.

Davis, Michelle R. 2004. Bush has own view of promoting civil rights. *Education Week* 24 (8):1,32.

Delgado, Richard, and Jean Stefancic. 2000. *Critical Race Theory: The cutting edge.* Philadelphia: Temple University Press.

Delpit, Lisa. 1995. *Other People's Children: Cultural conflict in the classroom.* New York: New Press.

Dewey, John. 1963 (1938). *Experience and Education.* London: Collier.

Diamond, John B., and Kimberley Gomez. 2004. African American parents' orientations toward schools: The implications of social class and parents' perceptions of schools. *Education and Urban Society* 36(4): 383–427.

Ditomaso, Nancy, Rochelle Parks-Yancy, and Corinne Post. 2003. White views of civil rights: Color blindness and equal opportunity. In *White Out*, ed. Doane and Bonilla-Silva, 189–98.

Doane, Ashley W., and Eduardo Bonilla-Silva, eds. 2003. *White Out: The continuing significance of racism.* New York: Routledge.

Dolby, Nadine. 2003. Popular culture and democratic practice. *Harvard Educational Review* 73(3): 258–84.

Donato, Ruben. 1997. *The Other Struggle for Equal Schools: Mexican Americans during the civil rights era.* Albany: State University of New York Press.

Dovidio, John F., and Samuel L. Gaertner. 2005. Color blind or just plain blind? The pernicious nature of contemporary racism. *Nonprofit Quarterly* 12(4). http://www.nonprofitquarterly.org/section/788.html (accessed May 2006).

Du Bois, W.E.B. 1935. Does the Negro need separate schools? *Journal of Negro Education* 4(3): 328–35.

Duranti, Alessandro, and Charles Goodwin, eds. 1992. *Rethinking Context: Language as an interactive phenomenon.* Cambridge: Cambridge University Press.

Eaton, Susan, Joseph Feldman, and Edward Kirby. 1996. Still separate, still unequal: The limits of Milliken II's monetary compensation to segregated schools. In *Dismantling Desegregation*, ed. Orfield and Eaton, 143–78.

Edley, Christopher. 1990. *Administrative Law: Rethinking judicial control of bureaucracy.* New Haven: Yale University Press.

Edwards, Harry T., and Virginia Davis Nordin. 1980. *An Introduction to the American Legal System: A supplement to Higher Education and the Law.* Cambridge, MA: Harvard University Institute for Educational Management.

Elmore, Richard F., Penelope L. Peterson, and Sarah J. McCarthey. 1996. *Restructuring in the Classroom: Teaching, learning, and school organization.* San Francisco: Jossey-Bass.

Engel, David M. 1994. The ovenbird's song: Insiders, outsiders, and personal injuries in an American community. In *Law and Community in Three American Towns*, ed. Carol J. Greenhouse, Barbara Yngvesson, and David M. Engel, 27–53. Ithaca, NY: Cornell University Press.

———. 1993. Origin myths: Narratives of authority, resistance, disability and law. *Law and Society Review* 27:785–826.

———. 1991. Law, culture, and children with disabilities: Educational rights and the construction of difference. *Duke Law Journal* 40:166–205.

Erickson, Frederick. 2004. *Talk and Social Theory: Ecologies of speaking and listening in everyday life*. Cambridge: Polity Press.

Espiritu, Yen Le. 1992. *Asian-American Panethnicity: Bridging institutions and identities*. Philadelphia: Temple University Press.

Essed, Philomena. 2002. Everyday racism: A new approach to the study of racism. In *Race Critical Theories: Text and Context*, ed. Philomena Essed and David Theo Goldberg, 176–94. Malden, MA: Blackwell.

———. 1990. *Everyday Racism: Reports from women of two cultures*. Claremont, CA: Hunter House.

Ewick, Patricia, and Susan S. Silbey. 1998. *The Common Place of Law: Stories from everyday life*. Chicago: University of Chicago Press.

Falk Moore, Sally, ed. 2004. *Law and Anthropology: A reader*. Malden, MA: Blackwell.

Farkas, George. 2003. Racial disparities and discrimination in education: What do we know, how do we know it, and what do we need to know? *Teachers College Record* 105(6): 1119–46.

Feagin, Joe R. 2000. *Racist America: Roots, current realities, and future reparations*. New York and London: Routledge.

Feagin, Joe R. 1997. Fighting white racism: The future of equal rights in the United States. In *Civil Rights and Race Relations in the Post Reagan-Bush Era*, ed. Myers, 29–46.

Feagin, Joe, Hernán Vera, and Pinar Batur. 2001. *White Racism: The basics*. 2nd ed. New York: Routledge.

Felstiner, William L. F., Richard L. Abel, and Austin Sarat. 1980–81. The emergence and transformation of disputes: Naming, blaming, claiming. *Law and Society Review* 15(3/4): 631–54.

Ferguson, Ann Arnett. 2000. *Bad Boys: Public schools in the making of black masculinity*. Ann Arbor: University of Michigan Press.

Ferguson, Ronald F. 2008. Helping students of color meet high standards. In *Everyday Antiracism*, ed. Pollock.

Fine, Michelle. 1997. Witnessing whiteness. In *Off-White*, ed. Fine, Weis, Powell, and Wong, 57–65.

———. 1991. *Framing Dropouts: Notes on the politics of an urban public high school*. Albany: State University of New York Press.

Fine, Michelle, Lois Weis, Linda C. Powell, and L. Mun Wong, eds. 1997. *Off-White: Readings on race, power, and society*. New York: Routledge.

Fiss, Owen. 1984. Against settlement. *Yale Law Journal* 93:1073–90.

Fleischer, Doris Zames, and Frieda Zames. 2001. *The Disability Rights Movement: From charity to confrontation*. Philadelphia: Temple University Press.

Foucault, Michel. 1979. *Discipline and Punish: The birth of the prison*. Trans. Alan Sheridan. New York: Vintage Books.

Frake, Charles. 1980. *Language and Cultural Description*. Stanford, CA: Stanford University Press.

Freeman, Alan David. 1978. Legitimizing racial discrimination through anti-discrimination law: A critical review of Supreme Court doctrine. *Minnesota Law Review* 62:1049–119. Reprinted in *Critical Race Theory*, ed. Crenshaw et al., 29–46.

Fryer, Roland G., and Steven D. Leavitt. 2004. The black-white test score gap through third grade. September 2004. http://post.economics.harvard.edu/faculty/fryer/papers/fryer_levitt_ecls2.pdf (accessed October 2006).

Garcia, Eugene E. 2008. Valuing students' home worlds. In *Everyday Antiracism*, ed. Pollock.

Geertz, Clifford. 1973. *The Interpretation of Cultures*. New York: Basic Books.

Goffman, Erving. 1963. *Stigma: Notes on the management of spoiled identity*. Englewood Cliffs, NJ: Prentice-Hall.

Goring, Darlene C. 2000. Private problem, public solution: Affirmative action in the 21st century. *Akron Law Review* 33:209.

Gotanda, Neil. 1991. A critique of "Our Constitution is colorblind." *Stanford Law Review* 44(1): 1–68.

Greenberger, Marcia D. 2004. Action needed to remove barriers to advancement of women and people of color in math, science and engineering faculties. National Women's Law Center, January 15, 2004. http://www.nwlc.org/details.cfm?id=1753&section=newsroom (accessed July 10, 2007).

Greenhouse, Carol J. 1986. *Praying for Justice: Faith, order, and community in an American town*. Ithaca: Cornell University Press.

Greenhouse, Carol J., Barbara Yngvesson, and David M. Engel. 1994. Introduction: Ethnographic issues. In *Law and Community in Three American Towns*. Ithaca, NY: Cornell University Press.

Grofman, Bernard, ed. 2000. *Legacies of the 1964 Civil Rights Act*. Charlottesville: University Press of Virginia.

Guinier, Lani. 2004. From racial liberalism to racial literacy: *Brown versus Board of Education* and the interest-divergence dilemma. *Journal of American History* 91(1): 82–118.

Guinier, Lani, and Gerald Torres. 2002. *The Miner's Canary: Enlisting race, resisting power, transforming democracy*. Cambridge, MA: Harvard University Press.

Gupta, Akhil, and James Ferguson, eds. 1997. *Anthropological Locations: Boundaries and grounds of a field science*. Berkeley: University of California Press.

Hagan, John F. 2002. Feds balk at review of Parma incidents. *Plain Dealer* (Cleveland), December 6, B2.

Halpern, Stephen C. 1995. *On the Limits of the Law: The ironic legacy of Title VI of the 1964 Civil Rights Act*. Baltimore: Johns Hopkins University Press.

Haney Lopez, Ian. 1996. *White by Law*. New York: New York University Press.

Healy, Patrick. 1999. A lightning rod on civil rights. *Chronicle of Higher Education*, September 17, 46 (4).

Heath, Shirley Brice. 1983. *Ways with Words: Language, life and work in communities and classrooms*. Cambridge: Cambridge University Press.

Hehir, Thomas. 2005. *New Directions in Special Education: Eliminating ableism in policy and practice*. Cambridge, MA: Harvard Education Publishing Group.

Henderson, Anne T., Vivian Johnson, Karen L. Mapp, and Don Davies. 2007. *Beyond the Bake Sale: The essential guide to family/school partnerships*. New York: The New Press.

Henry, Jules. 1963. *Culture against Man*. New York: Vintage Books.

Higginbotham, A. Leo Jr. 1996. *Shades of Freedom: Racial politics and presumptions of the American legal process*. New York: Oxford University Press.

Hirschman, Albert O. 1991. *The Rhetoric of Reaction: Perversity, futility, jeopardy*. Cambridge, MA: Harvard University Press.

Hochschild, Jennifer. 2004. Ambivalence about equality in the United States, or, how did Tocqueville get it wrong and why should we care? Interrupting Oppression and Sustaining Justice Conference, Teachers College, Columbia University, New York, February 27–28.

Hochschild, Jennifer, and Nathan Scovronick. 2003. *The American Dream and the Public Schools*. New York: Oxford University Press.

Hochschild, Jennifer, and Monica Herk. 1990. "Yes, but . . .": Principles and caveats in American racial attitudes. In *Majorities and Minorities*, Nomos 31 (Yearbook of the American Society for Political and Legal Philosophy), ed. John W. Chapman and Alan Wertheimer, 308–35. New York: New York University Press.

Hoff, David J. 1997. In the line of fire. *Education Week*, December 3, (17) (15).

Hollins, Etta, and Maria Torres Guzman. 2005. Research on preparing teachers for diverse populations. In *Studying Teacher Education: The report of the AERA panel on research and teacher education*, ed. Marilyn Cochran-Smith and Kenneth M. Zeichner, 477–528. Mahway, N.J.: Lawrence Erlbaum Associates.

Honig, Meredith, ed. 2006. *New Directions in Educational Policy Implementation*. Albany: State University of New York Press.

Hu-DeHart, Evelyn. 1997. Race, civil rights, and the new immigrants: Nativism and the new world order. In *Civil Rights and Race Relations in the Post Reagan-Bush Era*, ed. Myers, 11–27.

Jamieson, Kathleen Hall. 1996. *Packaging the Presidency: A history and criticism of presidential campaign advertising*. 3rd ed. Oxford: Oxford University Press.

Johnson, Deborah J. 2004. The ecology of children's racial coping: Family, school, and community influences. In *Discovering Successful Pathways in Children's Development*, ed. Weisner, 87–110.

Johnson, Susan Moore. 2004. *Finders and Keepers: Helping new teachers survive and thrive in our schools*. San Francisco: Jossey-Bass.

Kahn, Rick. 2000. Two probes say teacher hit children. *Boston Globe*, November 5, Sunday, third edition, p. 11.

Kang, Jerry, and Mahzarin Banaji. 2006. Fair measures: A behavioral realist revision of "affirmative action." *California Law Review* 94:1063–1118.

Karabel, Jerome. 2005. *The Chosen: The hidden history of admission and exclusion at Harvard, Yale, and Princeton*. Boston: Houghton Mifflin.

Kenschaft, Patricia Clark. 2005. Racial equity requires teaching elementary school teachers more mathematics. *Notices of the AMS* 52(2): 208–12.

Kluger, Richard. 1975. *Simple Justice*. New York: Vintage Books.

Kozol, Jonathan. 2005. *The Shame of the Nation: The restoration of apartheid schooling in America*. New York: Crown Books.

———. 1991. *Savage Inequalities*. New York: Harper.

Krieger, Linda Hamilton. 1995. The content of our categories: A cognitive bias approach to discrimination and equal employment opportunity. *Stanford Law Review* 47(6): 1161–1248.

Ladd, Helen F., Rosemary Chalk, and Janet S. Hansen, eds. 1999. *Equity and Adequacy in Education Finance: Issues and perspectives*. Washington, DC: National Academy Press.

Ladson-Billings, Gloria. 1999. Preparing teachers for diversity: Historical perspectives, current trends, and future directions. In *Teaching as the Learning Profession: Handbook of policy and practice*, ed. L. D. Hammond and G. Sykes. San Francisco: Jossey-Bass.

———. 1997. *The Dreamkeepers: Successful teachers of African American children*. San Francisco: Jossey-Bass.

Lakoff, George. 2004. *Don't Think of an Elephant: Know your values and frame the debate*. White River Junction, VT: Chelsea Green Publishing.

Lamont, Michèle. 2000a. *The Dignity of Working Men: Morality and the boundaries of race, class, and immigration*. New York: Russell Sage Foundation; Cambridge, MA: Harvard University Press.

———. 2000b. The rhetoric of racism and anti-racism in France and the United States. In *Rethinking Comparative Cultural Sociology: Repertoires of evaluation in France and the United States*, ed. Michèle Lamont and Laurent Thévenot, 25–55. London: Cambridge University Press; Paris: Presses de la Maison des sciences de l'homme.

Lareau, Annette. 2003. *Unequal Childhoods: Class, race, and family life*. Berkeley: University of California Press.

Lave, Jean, and Etienne Wenger. 1991. *Situated Learning: Legitimate peripheral participation*. Cambridge: Cambridge University Press.

Lawrence, Charles R. III. 1987. The id, the ego, and equal protection: Reckoning with unconscious racism. *Stanford Law Review* 39:317–88.

Lawrence-Lightfoot, Sara. 2003. *The Essential Conversation: What parents and teachers can learn from each other*. New York: Random House.

———. 1978. *Worlds Apart: Relationships between families and schools*. New York: Basic Books.

Leadership Conference on Civil Rights Education Fund. Why is it now easier for publicly funded service programs to discriminate? Fact Sheet, February 9, 2004. http://www.civilrights.org/issues/enforcement/CRA_public services.pdf (accessed August 9, 2004).

Lenhardt, Robin A. 2004. Understanding the mark: Race, stigma, and equality in context. *NYU Law Review* 78:803.

Levinson, Bradley A. U. 1996. Social difference and schooled identity at a Mexican secundaria. In *The Cultural Production of the Educated Person: Critical ethnographies of schooling and local practice*, ed. Bradley A. Levinson, Douglas B.

Foley, and Dorothy C. Holland, 211–38. Albany: State University of New York Press.

Levinson, Bradley A. U., Margaret Sutton, and Teresa Winstead. 2005. Policy as a practice of power: Theorizing cultural critique and democratic praxis in the anthropology of education policy. Paper presented to the American Anthropological Association, Washington, DC, December 3.

Lewis, Amanda. 2003a. *Race in the Schoolyard: Negotiating the color line in classrooms and communities.* New Brunswick, NJ: Rutgers University Press.

———. 2003b. Some are more equal than others: Lessons on whiteness from school. In *White Out*, ed. Doane and Bonilla-Silva, 159–72.

Linde, Hans A. 1972. Judges, critics, and the realist tradition. *Yale Law Journal* 82:227, 238.

Littlejohn, Jim. 1998. *Federal Control out of Control: The Office for Civil Rights' hidden policies on bilingual education.* Washington, DC: Center for Equal Opportunity.

Loewen, James W. 1982. *Social Science in the Courtroom: Statistical techniques and research methods for winning class-action suits.* Lexington, MA: Lexington Books.

Losen, Daniel J. 2004. Challenging racial disparities: The promise and pitfalls of the No Child Left Behind Act's race-conscious accountability. *Howard Law Journal* 47(2): 243–98.

———. 1999. Silent segregation in our nation's schools. *Harvard Civil Rights and Civil Liberties Law Review* 34:517–45.

Losen, Daniel J., and Gary Orfield, eds. 2002. Introduction to *Racial Inequity in Special Education.* Cambridge, MA: Harvard Education Publishing Group.

Loury, Glenn. 2002. *The Anatomy of Racial Inequality.* Cambridge, MA: Harvard University Press.

———. 1996. Performing without a net. In *The Affirmative Action Debate*, ed. George E. Curry, 49–54. Reading, MA: Addison-Wesley.

Lucas, Samuel R. 2008. Constructing colorblind classrooms. In *Everyday Antiracism*, ed. Pollock.

Mack, Kenneth W. 2005. Rethinking civil rights lawyering and politics in the era before *Brown. Yale Law Journal* 115:256–354.

Majority Staff of the Committee on Education and Labor, U.S House of Representatives. 1988. *A Report on the Investigation of the Civil Rights Enforcement Activities of the Office for Civil Rights, U.S Department of Education.* 100th Cong., 2d Sess. December 1988. 100-FF.

Mansbridge, Jane. 1996. Using power/fighting power: The polity. In *Democracy and Difference: Contesting the boundaries of the political*, ed. Seyla Benhabib, 46–66. Princeton: Princeton University Press.

Mansbridge, Jane, and Katherine Flaster. 2007. The cultural politics of everyday discourse: The case of "male chauvinist." *Critical Sociology* 33(2–3): 627–60.

Markowitz, Joy, Shernaz B. Garcia, and Joy Eichelberger. 1997. Addressing the disproportionate representation of students from racial and ethnic minority groups in special education: A resource document. Office of Special Education Programs, U.S. Department of Education, March 14.

McClung, Merle Steven. 1981. Preventive law and public education: A proposal. *Journal of Law and Education* 10(1): 37–42.

McDermott, R. P., Kenneth Gospodinoff, and Jeffrey Aron. 1978. Criteria for an ethnographically adequate description of concerted activities and their contexts. *Semiotica* 24 (3/4): 245–75.

McKinney, Karyn D., and Joe R. Feagin. 2003. Diverse perspectives on doing antiracism: The younger generation. In *White Out*, ed. Doane and Bonilla-Silva, 233–52.

McNeil, Linda M. 2005. Faking equity: High stakes testing and the education of Latino youth. In *Leaving Children Behind: How "Texas-style" accountability fails Latino youth*, ed. Angela Valenzuela, 57–111. Albany: State University of New York Press.

McWhorter, John. 2000. *Losing the Race: Self-sabotage in black America*. New York: The Free Press.

Meertens, Roel W., and Thomas F. Pettigrew. 1997. Is subtle prejudice really prejudice? *Public Opinion Quarterly* 61:54–71.

Mehan, Hugh. 1996. Beneath the skin and between the ears: A case study in the politics of representation. In *Understanding Practice: Perspectives on activity and context*, ed. Jean Lave and Seth Chaiklin, 241–68. Cambridge: Cambridge University Press.

———. 1993. Why I like to look: On the use of videotape as an instrument in educational research. In *Qualitative Voices in Eduational Research*, ed. Michael Schratz. London: Falmer Press.

Merry, Sally Engle. 1990. *Getting Justice and Getting Even: Legal consciousness among working-class Americans*. Chicago: University of Chicago Press.

Mickelson, Roslyn. 2005. Address at "Meeting the Challenge of" *Grutter*: Affirmative action in twenty-five years." Ohio State University Moritz College of Law, February 24–25.

———. 2003. When are racial disparities in education the result of racial discrimination? A social science perspective. *Teachers College Record* 105(6): 1052–86.

Mickelson, Roslyn Arlin, and Linwood H. Cousins. 2008. Informing parents about available opportunities. In *Everyday Antiracism*, ed. Pollock.

Miller, D. T. 2001. Disrespect and the experience of injustice. *Annual Review of Psychology* 52:527–53.

Minow, Martha. 1990. *Making All the Difference: Inclusion, exclusion, and American law*. Ithaca, NY: Cornell University Press.

Mishler, Elliot G. 1986. *Research Interviewing: Context and narrative*. Cambridge, MA: Harvard University Press.

Moll, Luis C., and Stephen Diaz. 1993. Change as the goal of educational research. In *Minority Education: Anthropological perspectives*, ed. Evelyn Jacob and Cathie Jordan, 67–79. Westport, CT: Ablex Publishing.

Moll, Luis C., Cathy Amanti, Deborah Neff, and Norma Gonzalez. 1992. Funds of knowledge for teaching: Using a qualitative approach to connect homes and classrooms. *Theory into Practice* 31(2): 132–41.

Moran, Peter William. 2005. Too little, too late: The illusive goal of school desegregation in Kansas City, Missouri, and the role of the federal government. *Teachers College Record* 107:1933–55.

Morison, Patricia, Sheldon H. White, and Michael J. Feuer, eds. 1996. Board bulletin: The use of IQ tests in special education decision making and planning. Board on Testing and Assessment, Commission on Behavioral and Social Sciences and Education, National Research Council. Washington, DC: National Academy Press.

Moses, Robert, with Charles E. Cobb, Jr. 2001. *Radical Equations: Civil rights from Mississippi to the Algebra Project*. Boston: Beacon Press.

Myers, Samuel L., Jr., ed. 1997. *Civil Rights and Race Relations in the Post Reagan-Bush Era*. Westport, CT: Praeger.

NAACP Legal Defense and Educational Fund, Inc. 2005. Closing the gap: Moving from rhetoric to reality in opening doors to higher education for African-American students. June 23. http://www.naacpldf.org/content/pdf/gap/Closing_the_Gap_-_Moving_from_Rhetoric_to_Reality.pdf (accessed October 17, 2007).

Nader, Laura. 2002. *The Life of the Law: Anthropological projects*. Berkeley: University of California Press.

———, ed. 1980. *No Access to Law: Alternatives to the American judicial system*. New York: Academic Press.

Noguera, Pedro A. 2008. What discipline is for: Connecting students to the benefits of learning. In *Everyday Antiracism*, ed. Pollock.

———. 2003. *City Schools and the American Dream: Reclaiming the promise of public education*. New York: Teachers College Press.

Nosek, Brian A., Mahzarin R. Banaji, and Anthony G. Greenwald. 2002. Harvesting implicit group attitudes and beliefs from a demonstration web site. *Group Dynamics: Theory, Research, and Practice* 6(1): 101–15.

Nowak, John E. 1995. *Brown v. Board of Education* after forty years: The rise and fall of Supreme Court concern for racial minorities. *William and Mary Law Review* 36:345.

Oakes, Jeannie, and John Rogers. 2006. *Learning Power: Organizing for education and justice*. New York: Teachers College Press.

Oakes, Jeannie, Kevin Welner, and Susan Yonezawa. 1998. Mandating equity: A case study of court-ordered detracking in the San Jose schools. California Policy Research Center, California Policy Seminar Brief Series, March.

Oakes, Jeannie, Tor Ormseth, Robert Bell, and Patricia Camp. 1990. *Multiplying Inequalities: The effects of race, social class, and tracking on opportunities to learn mathematics and science*. Santa Monica, CA: Rand Corporation.

O'Connor, Carla. 1997. Dispositions toward (collective) struggle and educational resilience in the inner city: A case analysis of six African-American high school students. *American Educational Research Journal* 34(4): 593–629.

Office for Civil Rights. 1996. *Annual Report to Congress, Fiscal Year 1996, Office for Civil Rights (ED)*. Washington, DC. Published 1997.

———. 1995. *Annual Report to Congress, Fiscal Year 1995, Office for Civil Rights (ED)*. Washington, DC. Published 1996.

Office for Civil Rights. 1994. *Annual Report to Congress, Fiscal Year 1994, Office for Civil Rights (ED)*. Washington, DC. Published 1995.

―――. 1993. *Annual Report to Congress, Fiscal Year 1993, Office for Civil Rights (ED)*, Washington, DC. Published 1994.

―――. 1992. *Annual Report to Congress, Fiscal Year 1992, Office for Civil Rights (ED)*, Washington, DC. Published 1993.

―――. 1991. *Annual Report to Congress, Fiscal Year 1991, Office for Civil Rights (ED)*. Washington, DC.

Ogletree, Charles J. 2004. *All Deliberate Speed: Reflections on the first half century of* Brown v. Board of Education. New York: W. W. Norton.

Olsen, Laurie. 1995. School restructuring and the needs of immigrant students. In *California's Immigrant Children: Theory, research, and implications for educational policy,* ed. Ruben G. Rumbaut and Wayne A. Cornelius, 209–33. San Diego: Center for U.S.-Mexican Studies, University of California San Diego.

Omi, Michael, and Howard Winant. 1994. *Racial Formation in the United States: From the 1960s to the 1990s.* 2nd ed. New York: Routledge.

Oppenheimer, David Benjamin. 1993. Negligent discrimination. *University of Pennsylvania Review* 141:899.

Orarke, Mike, and Candace Heckman. 2002. Civil rights suit settled in Puyallup schools. *Seattle Post-Intelligencer Reporters*, Sept. 18.

Orfield, Gary. 2000. The 1964 Civil Rights Act and American education. In *Legacies of the 1964 Civil Rights Act*, ed. Bernard Grofman, 89–128. Charlottesville: University Press of Virginia.

―――. 1978. *Must We Bus? Segregated schools and national policy.* Washington, DC: Brookings Institution.

Orfield, Gary, and Susan Eaton. 1996. *Dismantling Desegregation: The Quiet Reversal of* Brown v. Board of Education. New York: The New Press.

Orfield, Gary, Daniel Losen, Johanna Wald, and Christopher B. Swanson. 2004. Losing our future: How minority youth are being left behind by the graduation rate crisis. Harvard University Civil Rights Project, February 25.

Page, Reba Neukom. 1991. *Lower Track Classrooms: A curricular and cultural perspective.* New York: Teachers College Press.

Panetta, Leon, and Peter Gall. 1971. *Bring Us Together: The Nixon team and the civil rights retreat.* Philadelphia: Lippincott.

Payne, Charles M. 2004. "The whole United States is Southern!!" *Brown v. Board* and the mystification of race. *Journal of American History* 91(1): 83–91.

―――. 1984. *Getting What We Ask For.* Westport, CT: Greenwood Press.

Pell, Terence J. 1997. A more subtle activism at the Office of Civil Rights. *Academic Questions* (Summer), 10 (3). http://cir=usa.org/articles/65.html.

Perry, Pamela. 2002. *Shades of White: White kids and racial identities in high school.* Durham, NC: Duke University Press.

Perry, Pamela. 1991. Two faces of disparate impact discrimination. *Fordham Law Review* 59: 523.

Perry, Theresa. 2003. Freedom for literacy and literacy for freedom: The African-American philosophy of education. In *Young, Gifted, and Black,* by Theresa Perry, Claude Steele, and Asa Hilliard III, 11–51.

Perry, Theresa, Claude Steele, and Asa Hilliard III. 2003. *Young, Gifted, and Black: Promoting high achievement among African-American students.* Boston: Beacon Press.

Pollock, Mica, ed. 2008. *Everyday Antiracism: Getting real about race in school.* New York: The New Press.

———. 2006. Toward everyday justice: On demanding equal educational opportunity in the new civil rights era. *Ohio State Law Review* 67(1): 245–76.

———. 2004a. *Colormute: Race talk dilemmas in an American school.* Princeton: Princeton University Press.

———. 2004b. Race wrestling: Struggling strategically with race in educational practice and research. *American Journal of Education* 111(1): 25–67.

———. 2001. How the question we ask most about race in education is the very question we most suppress. *Educational Researcher* 30(9): 2–12.

Post, Robert C. 2003. Foreward: Fashioning the legal constitution: Culture, courts, and law. *Harvard Law Review* 117:4–112.

powell, john a. 2002. An integrated theory of integrated education. Paper presented at Center for Civil Rights, University of North Carolina, August.

powell, john a., Gavin Kearney, and Vina Kay, eds. 2001. *In Pursuit of a Dream Deferred: Linking housing and education policy.* New York: Peter Lang.

Rabkin, Jeremy. 1989. *Judicial Compulsions.* New York: Basic Books.

Rebell, Michael A., and Arthur R. Block. 1985. *Equality and Education: Federal civil rights enforcement in the New York City school system.* Princeton: Princeton University Press.

Rivkin, Dean Hill. 2002. Lawyering admidst inequality. Paper presented to Harvard Law School Faculty Workshop.

Rothstein, Richard. 2004. *Class and Schools: Using social, economic, and educational reform to close the black-white achievement gap.* Washington, DC: Economic Policy Institute; New York: Teachers College, Columbia University.

Rowe, Mary P. 1974. Saturn's rings. *Graduate and Professional Education of Women.* American Association of University Women. Pp. 1–9.

Rubin, Beth C. 2008. Grouping in detracked classrooms. In *Everyday Antiracism,* ed. Pollock.

Ryan, James E. 2006. A constitutional right to preschool? *California Law Review* 94(1): 49–100.

———. 2003. Race discrimination in education: A legal perspective. *Teachers College Record* 105(6): 1087–1118.

Sarat, Austin, Bryant Garth, and Robert A. Kagan, eds. 2002. *Looking Back at Law's Century.* Ithaca, NY: Cornell University Press.

Savage, Barbara. 2000. Biblical and historical imperatives: Toward a history of ideas about the political role of black churches. In *African Americans and the Bible: Sacred Texts and Social Textures,* ed. Vincent Wimbush. New York: Continuum Press.

Schemo, Diana Jean. 2001. Affirmative action foe picked for rights post. *New York Times,* June 27, A20.

Schnaiberg, Lynn. 1998. Report: Agency pushes use of bilingual ed. *Education Week,* December 2, 18(14): 25.

Schofield, Janet Ward. 1995. The colorblind perspective in school: Causes and consequences. In *Handbook of Research on Multicultural Education*, ed. James Banks and Cherry A. McGee Banks, 265–88. New York: Macmillan.

Schrag, Peter. 2003. *Final Test: The battle for adequacy in America's schools*. New York: New Press.

Schultz, Vicki. 2001. Symposium: Panel VI: Talking about harassment. *Journal of Law and Policy* 9:417.

Sears, David O., Jim Sidanius, and Lawrence Bobo, eds. 2000. *Racialized Politics: The debate about racism in America*. Chicago: University of Chicago Press.

Setty, Sudha. 1999. Leveling the playing field: Reforming the Office for Civil Rights to achieve better Title IX enforcement. *Columbia Journal of Law and Social Problems* 32:331.

Shelsby, Ted. 2004. Harford County schools target of bias complaints; blacks are punished more severely, group says. *Baltimore Sun*, June 3, 6B.

Shelton, J. N., and J. A. Richeson. 2006. Interracial interactions: A relational approach. *Advances in Experimental Social Psychology* 38: 121–81.

Shore, Cris, and Susan Wright, eds. 1997. *Anthropology of Policy: Critical perspectives on governance and power*. New York: Routledge.

Siddle Walker, Vanessa, and John Snarey, eds. 2004. *Race-ing Moral Formation: African American perspectives on care and justice*. New York: Teachers College Press.

Siegel, Reva B. 2004. Equality talk: Antisubordination and anticlassification values in constitutional struggles over *Brown*. *Harvard Law Review* 117: 1470–1547.

Siegelman, Peter, and John J. Donohue III. 1990. Studying the iceberg from its tip: A comparison of published and unpublished employment discrimination cases. *Law and Society Review* 24:1133–70.

Simpson, Andrea. 1998. *The Tie That Binds: Identity and political attitudes in the post–civil rights generation*. New York: New York University Press.

Singer, Judith D., and John B. Willett. 2003. *Applied Longitudinal Data Analysis: Modeling change and event occurrence*. Oxford: Oxford University Press.

Skrentny, John David. 2002. *The Minority Rights Revolution*. Cambridge, MA: Belknap Press of Harvard University Press.

———. 1996. *The Ironies of Affirmative Action: Politics, culture, and justice in America*. Chicago: University of Chicago Press.

Solórzano, Daniel, W. Allen, and G. Carroll. 2002. A case study of racial microaggressions and campus racial climate at the University of California, Berkeley. UCLA *Chicano/Latino Law Review* 23:15–111.

Solórzano, Daniel, Miguel Ceja, and Tara Yosso. 2000. Critical race theory, racial microaggressions, and campus racial climate: The experiences of African American college students. *Journal of Negro Education* 69:60–73.

Steeh, Charlotte, and Maria Krysan. 1996. The polls—trends: Affirmative action and the public, 1970–1995. *Public Opinion Quarterly* 60:128–58.

Steinberg, Jacques. 1997. Special education practices in New York faulted by U.S. *New York Times*, May 31, Saturday, late edition-final, sect. 1, p. 1, col. 1.

Steinberg, Stephen. 2001. "Race relations": The problem with the wrong name. *New Politics*, n.s., 8(2) no. 30. http://www.wpunj.edu/newpol/issue30/steinb30.htm (accessed October 18, 2006).

Steinberger, Ruth. 2002. Rosebud Sioux file complaint saying schools target tribal youth. *Native American Times* (Tulsa, OK) April 1, 2002, 8(7): A5.

Stewart, Richard B. 1975. The reformation of American administrative law. *Harvard Law Review* 88:1669, 1671–76.

Stone, Douglas, Bruce Patton, and Sheila Heen. 2000. *Difficult Conversations: How to discuss what matters most*. New York: Penguin Books.

Sullivan, Charles A., Michael J. Zimmer, and Rebecca Hanner White. 2002. *Employment Discrimination: Law and practice*. 3rd ed. Vol. 1. New York: Aspen Publishers.

Sutton, Margaret, and Bradley A. U. Levinson, eds. 2001 *Policy as Practice: Toward a comparative sociocultural analysis of educational policy*. Westport, CT: Ablex Publishing.

Tatum, Beverly Daniel. 2008. Cultivating the trust of black parents. In *Everyday Antiracism*, ed. Pollock.

Taylor, William L. 2004. *The Passion of My Times: An advocate's fifty-year journey in the civil rights movement*. New York: Carroll and Graf.

———. 1986. *Brown*, Equal protection, and the isolation of the poor. *Yale Law Journal* 95(8): 1700–1735.

Thorne, Barrie. 1993. *Gender Play: Girls and boys in school*. New Brunswick, NJ: Rutgers University Press.

Tushnet, Mark V. 1994. *Making Civil Rights Law: Thurgood Marshall and the Supreme Court, 1956–1961*. New York: Oxford University Press.

Tyson, Karolyn. 2008. Providing equal access to "gifted" education. In *Everyday Antiracism*, ed. Pollock.

U.S. Commission on Civil Rights, Office of Civil Rights Evaluation. 2004. Ten-year check-up: Have federal agencies responded to civil rights recommendations? Draft report for Commissioners' review, May 27, 2004. http://www.usccr.gov/pubs/10yr04/10yr04.pdf (accessed August 8, 2004).

U.S. Department of Education. 1989–90. *U.S. Department of Education Annual Report, Fiscal Year 1989–90*. Readex ED 1:989–90 Aug. 93–18178. U.S. Govt. Publications.

———. 1982. *U.S. Department of Education Annual Report, Fiscal Year 1982*. Published 1983–01–20. Secretary T. H. Bell.

———. 1981. *U.S. Department of Education Annual Report, Fiscal Year 1981*. Published 1982. Secretary T. H. Bell.

———. 1980. *U.S. Department of Education Annual Report, Fiscal Year 1980*. Secretary Shirley Hufstedler.

U.S. Department of Health, Education, and Welfare. 1969. *Annual Report 1969*. Obtained via U.S. Government Publications (Depository). Published July 1970. No. 10195. Readex microprint. New York. Secretary Robert H. Finch. Commissioner of Education James E. Allen, Jr.

———. 1967. *Annual Report 1967*. U.S. Government Publications (Depository). Published September 1968, Readex microprint 12871. New York.

U.S. Department of Health, Education, and Welfare. 1966. *Annual Report 1966*. Obtained via U.S. Government Publications (Depository). Published May 1967. No. 8190. Readex microprint. New York. Secretary John W. Gardner. Commissioner of Education Harold Howe II.

Uzzell, Lawrence. 1987. Running the rights scam at DOE. *National Review* March 13, 39(4): 39.

Valdes, Guadalupe. 1996. *Con Respeto. Bridging the Distances between Culturally Diverse Families and Schools: An ethnographic portrait*. New York: Teachers College Press.

Valencia, Richard R. 2005. The Mexican American struggle for equal educational opportunity in *Mendez v. Westminster*: Helping to pave the way for *Brown v. Board of Education. Teachers College Record* 107(3): 389–423.

———. 1991. The plight of Chicano students: An overview of schooling conditions and outcomes. In *Chicano School Failure and Success: Research and policy agendas for the 1990s*, ed. Richard Valencia, 3–51. London: Routledge/Falmer Press.

Valenzuela, Angela. 1999. *Subtractive Schooling: U.S.-Mexican youth and the politics of caring*. Albany: State University of New York Press.

Varenne, Herve, and Raymond McDermott. 1998. *Successful Failure: The school America builds*. Boulder, CO: Westview Press.

Walsh, Mark. 2001. OCR choice renews debate on credentials needed for job. *Education Week*, September 12, 21(2): 26, 3p.

———. 1998. Federal officials take Denver to task over bilingual ed. Program. *Education Week*, September 3, 17(1).

Ward, Janie Victoria. 2008. Helping parents fight stereotypes about their children. In *Everyday Antiracism*, ed. Pollock.

Warren, Mark. 2006. White activists and racial justice in education. Paper presented to the annual meeting of the American Educational Research Association, San Francisco, April.

———. 2005. Communities and schools: A new view of urban education reform. *Harvard Educational Review* 75(2): 133–73.

Weber, Max. 1947. *The Theory of Social and Economic Organization*. Trans. A. M. Henderson and Talcott Parsons. Glencoe, IL: The Free Press.

Weinberg, Meyer. 1977. *A Chance to Learn: A history of race and education in the United States*. Cambridge: Cambridge University Press.

Weisner, Thomas S., ed. 2005. *Discovering Successful Pathways in Children's Development: Mixed methods in the study of childhood and family life*. Chicago: University of Chicago Press.

Weiss, Heather B., and Harvard Family Research Project. 2005. *Preparing Educators to Involve Families: From theory to practice*. Thousand Oaks, CA: Sage Publications.

Weiss, Stefanie. 1994. She's the enforcer. *NEA Today*, December, 13(5): 7.

Wells, Amy Stuart, and Robert L. Crain. 1997. *Stepping over the Color Line: African-American students in white suburban schools*. New Haven: Yale University Press.

White, Eugene E. 1992. *The Context of Human Discourse: A configurational criticism of rhetoric*. Columbia: University of South Carolina Press.

Wieder, D. L. 1974. *Language and Social Reality: The case of telling the convict code.* Paris: Mouton.

Willis, Paul. 1977. *Learning to Labor: How working-class kids get working-class jobs.* New York: Columbia University Press.

Winant, Howard. 2004. *The New Politics of Race: Globalism, difference, justice.* Minneapolis: University of Minnesota Press.

Wollenberg, Charles M. 1976. *All Deliberate Speed: Segregation and exclusion in California schools, 1855–1975.* Berkeley: University of California Press.

Woodson, Carter Godwin. 1972 (1933). *The Mis-Education of the Negro.* New York: AMS Press.

———. 1919. *The Education of the Negro.* Brooklyn, NY: A & B Books Publishers.

Wright, Susan. 2005. Framing an anthropology of education policy: Present and future. Paper presented to the American Anthropological Association, Washington, DC, December 3.

Wyman, Leisy, and Grant Kashatok. 2008. Getting to know students' communities. In *Everyday Antiracism,* ed. Pollock.

Yngvesson, Barbara. 1988. Making law at the doorway: The clerk, the court, and the construction of community in a New England town. *Law and Society Review* 22:409.

Yoshikawa, Hirokazu, Thomas S. Weisner, and Edward D. Lowe, eds. 2006. *Making It Work: Low-wage employment, family life, and child development.* New York: Russell Sage Foundation.

Yoshino, Kenji. 2006. The pressure to cover. *New York Times Magazine,* January 15.

Young, Iris Marion. 1990. *Justice and the Politics of Difference.* Princeton: Princeton University Press.

Yudof, Mark G., David L Kirp, and Betsy Levin, eds. 1992. *Educational Policy and the Law.* 3rd ed. St. Paul, MN: West Publishing Company.

# Index

achievement gaps, 9, 118–34, 137
*Adams v. Richardson*, 109, 110, 151
administrators, school. *See* educators
Advanced Placement classes, 8, 15, 166
affirmative action, 12, 101, 111, 114
African Americans: physical abuse
  against, 28; racial slurs against, 27, 28,
  31, 32, 35, 36, 43, 58, 77; and segregated
  education, 106, 107; in Special Education, 7, 24, 113, 118, 129, 156. *See also*
  racial discrimination
*Alexander v. Sandoval*, 52–53
arbitration, 65. *See also* collaboration vs.
  punitive action
Asian Americans: as English-language
  learners, 61, 72; racial slurs against, 58;
  and segregated education, 106, 107
attention deficit disorder (ADD), 17

Bell, Derrick, 139, 181
bilingual education, 72, 84
blame, avoidance of, 76–77
Blank, Rebecca, 136, 184
Bonilla-Silva, Eduardo, 136
Boy Scouts, 115
Bunch, Kenyon D., 149
Bush, George H. W., 111
Bush, George W., 113–16, 131
busing, 109, 139

Campaign for Fiscal Equity, 117
Cantu, Norma, 52, 67, 75, 111–12, 113,
  116, 129, 131, 149
*Case Resolution and Investigation
  Manual*, 52
Center for Equal Opportunity, 114
Chavez, Linda, 84
civil rights: and education, 104–5, 116–35,
  145, 181, 183; new civil rights era, 11–
  15, 175–85
Civil Rights Act, Title VI. *See* Title VI
class and race, 123, 167–68
*Code of Federal Regulations*, 3
collaboration vs. punitive action, 66–
  75, 86
colormuteness, 98

Commission on Civil Rights, 66
communication: collaboration vs.
  punitive action, 66–75, 86; consequences of OCR's communication
  policy, 98–100; between educators and
  complainants, 25, 29–30, 60–61, 87, 179;
  language of "concerns," 74–82, 95–97,
  182–83; resolution documents, 82–87,
  145–47, 150–53
comparative harm, 30–31, 32–33, 39, 41,
  48, 53–58, 93, 179–81
compensatory education, 81–82, 142–43
complainants: communication with educators, 25, 29–30, 60–61, 87, 179; desire
  to educate the educators, 78; listening
  to, 179; opinion of OCR, 62; perceived
  by educators, 25, 29–30, 32, 37; race of,
  61–62; remedies demanded by, 6–8
complaints: growing number for disability discrimination, 16–17, 110; for individual students, 7–8, 142, 148, 149;
  statistics, 112
concerns, language of, 74–82, 95–97
Crenshaw, Kimberle Williams, 49,
  106, 149
critical race theory, 49
cumulative nature of harm, 5, 155–56,
  165–74

defiance, discipline against, 51, 55, 88, 92,
  93–97, 157, 170
desegregation: and everyday justice, 148;
  vs. integration, 139; and Office for Civil
  Rights, 66–67, 101, 109, 148; resistance
  to, 2, 12, 109, 165; and Title VI, 1–2, 66–
  67, 101
detailing of harm, 13–16, 97–98, 176–
  77, 185
Dewey, John, 158
disabilities, children with: advocacy for,
  17; attention deficit disorder (ADD), 17;
  Individual Education Plans (IEPs), 80–
  82; Latino, 80–81
disability discrimination: early resolution,
  71; everyday justice, 142, 158, 159, 160;